T0339870

The Behavioral Economics of Climate Change

The Behavioral Economics of Climate Change

Adaptation Behaviors, Global Public Goods, Breakthrough Technologies, and Policy-Making

S. Niggol Seo

**Muaebak Institute of Global Warming Studies
Seoul, Korea
Chulalongkorn University, Bangkok, Thailand**

ACADEMIC PRESS

An imprint of Elsevier

Academic Press is an imprint of Elsevier
125 London Wall, London EC2Y 5AS, United Kingdom
525 B Street, Suite 1800, San Diego, CA 92101-4495, United States
50 Hampshire Street, 5th Floor, Cambridge, MA 02139, United States
The Boulevard, Langford Lane, Kidlington, Oxford OX5 1GB, United Kingdom

Notices
Knowledge and best practice in this field are constantly changing. As new research and experience
broaden our understanding, changes in research methods, professional practices, or medical treatment
may become necessary.

Practitioners and researchers must always rely on their own experience and knowledge in evaluating and
using any information, methods, compounds, or experiments described herein. In using such information
or methods they should be mindful of their own safety and the safety of others, including parties for
whom they have a professional responsibility.

To the fullest extent of the law, neither the Publisher nor the authors, contributors, or editors, assume
any liability for any injury and/or damage to persons or property as a matter of products liability,
negligence or otherwise, or from any use or operation of any methods, products, instructions, or ideas
contained in the material herein.

Library of Congress Cataloging-in-Publication Data
A catalog record for this book is available from the Library of Congress

British Library Cataloguing-in-Publication Data
A catalogue record for this book is available from the British Library

ISBN: 978-0-12-811874-0

For information on all Academic Press publications visit our website at
https://www.elsevier.com/books-and-journals

Working together
to grow libraries in
developing countries

www.elsevier.com • www.bookaid.org

Publisher: Candice Janco
Acquisition Editor: J. Scott Bentley
Editorial Project Manager: Susan Ikeda
Production Project Manager: Julie-Ann Stansfield
Designer: Victoria Pearson Esser

Typeset by TNQ Books and Journals

Contents

Author Profile

Prof. S. Niggol Seo is a natural resource economist who specializes in the study of global warming. He was born in a rural village in South Korea in 1972; he studied at Seoul National University and the University of California at Berkeley and received a PhD degree in Environmental and Natural Resource Economics from Yale University in May 2006 with a dissertation on microbehavioral models of global warming. While at Yale University, he learned from Robert Mendelsohn and William Nordhaus. Since 2003, he has worked with the World Bank on various climate change projects in Africa, Latin America, and Asia. He held professor positions in the United Kingdom, Spain, and Australia from 2006 to 2015. Since September 2015, he is Professor of Environmental and Natural Resource Economics at the Muaebak Institute of Global Warming Studies in Seoul, Korea. He is a visiting Professor at Chulalongkorn University in Bangkok, Thailand. Prof. Seo has published four books and over 50 international journal articles on the economics of global warming. He frequently serves as a journal referee for more than 30 international journals and has been on the editorial boards of the two journals *Food Policy* and *Applied Economic Perspectives and Policy*. He received an Outstanding Applied Economic Perspectives and Policy Article Award from the Agricultural and Applied Economics Association in Pittsburgh in June 2011.

Preface

This book is written as a comprehensive treatise on the economics of climate change from the perspectives of the adaptation paradigm of global warming policy responses. The book encompasses all major topics of global warming economics and policy making. It deals thoroughly with the economic theories of global warming and empirical models of global warming economics. These features of the book make it a suitable textbook for a graduate course on climate change economics or environmental economics.

In addition, the book is written to present an alternative policy framework rooted on behavioral decisions of individuals. The author provides a comprehensive review of an array of policy instruments, experiences with various policies, and an alternative policy framework. The book is thorough on policy negotiations at the United Nations Framework Convention on Climate Change level, and many of the important policy efforts in the United States and the European Union are highlighted throughout the book. These aspects of the book will make it a worthy reading for policy makers, practitioners, and anyone who is interested in keeping pace with policy negotiations.

In this book, the author provides a full account of the adaptation paradigm for global warming policy making as an alternative conceptual policy framework. In the adaptation paradigm, an economic agent makes decisions simultaneously on both adaptive responses to the changes brought about by global warming and the consequences of her/his actions on greenhouse gas emissions and global warming. The conceptual foundation of the adaptation paradigm is critically analyzed in comparisons with other policy approaches such as carbon price, cap and trade, temperature/emissions ceilings, and technological solutions. The author highlights, based on the empirical adaptation research literature, an array of adaptation portfolios pertinent to economic sectors and climate actors tailored to certain contexts and time periods through the 21st century.

Wish you a pleasantly memorable journey through the forests, oceans, atmosphere, and cities in the book, which awakens new strength in your life and for the Earth!

S. Niggol Seo
From Dabo Hall at the Muaebak Institute of Global Warming Studies, Seoul, Korea

Companion Website

Additional materials and information are available from the book's companion website
https://www.elsevier.com/books-and-journals/book-companion/9780128139387.

An Introduction to the Behavioral Economics of Climate Change for Provision of Global Public Goods

1

Chapter Outline

1. Global Public Goods in the Modern World

Planet Earth has been increasingly transformed into one community at an ever faster rate especially since the Industrial Revolution and the communication revolution (Smith, 1776). At this particular moment in human history, information is shared from one person to another on any place on the Earth at the speed of light with the quality of virtual reality. People wirelessly communicate more than ever before and travel more than ever before to remote places across the globe. A travel from one location to another anywhere on the planet can be completed within a day's time. Humanity is in a vigorous search for living beings on another planet and a planet where humans can get to and settle.

The innovations in productions, transportations, and communication technologies have made the national economies in the 21st century bigger, vastly more connected, and interdependent than ever before. At the same time, global-scale policy issues have increased in numbers and have emerged to the forefront of international policy dialogues. Salient examples are, inter alia, nuclear proliferation, free trade, a global financial system and crisis, meteoroids and asteroids, worldwide information sharing and risk, modifications of human genetic codes, advances in artificial intelligence, large hadron collider experiments, robots and war robots, terrorism and antiterrorism efforts, and global warming (Nordhaus, 1994; Sandler, 1997; Kaul et al., 2003; Posner, 2004).

In a globalized today's world, multinational companies manufacture their products in the countries where the costs and barriers are low, sell them to the countries where the demands are high, and sell them through online outlets to international buyers (Ricardo, 1817; Ohlin, 1933). Purchased goods are delivered by a global courier delivery service to any place on the globe within a few days.

Countries are increasingly aware of the benefits and damages of trading freely with other countries by signing a free trade agreement with a group of countries or bilaterally (Stiglitz, 2006; White House, 2017). Within a free trade bloc, traditional territorial boundaries are less meaningful in that people and businesses can cross the boundaries with little hassle while money can flow from one country to another with few restrictions. In the eurozone where member countries discarded their own currencies and adopted a single currency, the Euro, there is no need to exchange moneys whenever one crosses a national border.

For businesses and transactions across national borders, corporations rely on international financial organizations, such as banks, investment banks, insurance, resources companies, mortgages, equity markets, bond markets, and exchange markets, to finance their operations (Fabozzi et al., 2009). As such, returns of different assets in different countries as well as regulations regarding them have also become more correlated, increasing the power of as well as the systemic risk in the financial sector.

A financial crisis in one country can quickly spread to the rest of the world, jeopardizing the economy of an entire region or even of the world (Shiller, 2005, 2009; Akerlof and Shiller, 2009). Examples are the burst of the US real estate bubble in 2008, which quickly spread and caused a great recession in many countries of the world; the Asian Financial Crisis in 1997, which spread quickly from Thailand to other countries across the Asian region; and the European Union sovereign debt crisis in the 2010s, in which many countries were not able to pay the government debts and had to be rescued by international monetary organizations.

Advances of the Internet, personal computer, and wireless cellular communication technologies have made people around the world wirelessly connected in the worldwide web of communication channels and hotspots (Nordhaus, 2007b). A person in Monte Video in Uruguay can talk to a person in Seoul through a video chatting program such as the SKYPE without charge. A large group of scientists can gather at a video conference without the need to convene at one geographical spot paying a large amount of money for travel and accommodation expenses. This implies that, besides the goods and services, the information and knowledge gained in one country can flow freely to the other countries without limitations, barring any controls of cross-border communications and information sharing by a certain government.

The communication revolution during the past century has contributed, to a large degree, to a remarkable growth of productivity in the global economy (Nordhaus, 2007b). At the same time, the communication revolution has greatly increased the global risk of information leakage and manipulations. It unraveled the risk of being hacked and manipulated by an unidentified source from an unknown country of private information, classified government documents, secret business information, and scientific communications (Akerlof and Shiller, 2015).

Amid the rapid growth of the global economy in the past century, human population has increased remarkably since the dawn of the 20th century. Global population stood at 2 billion people at the dawn of the century, which at the end of year 2015 stands at 7 billion people. The world population is projected to continue to grow throughout the 21st century, but at a reduced rate of growth (IIASA, 2007; Lutz et al., 2014).

One of the main causes of population growth is advances in medical sciences. Many infectious diseases that had been fatal are now treatable with vaccines. Examples include malaria, cholera, tuberculosis, polio, small pox, and measles (WHO, 2016a). Advances in genetic sciences in coding the entire human (and some animal) genomes as well as advances in stem cell research hold great promise in treating diseases previously incurable (US DOE, 2008; Aksoy et al., 2014). The average life expectancy of most developed countries has increased noticeably during the past century (WHO, 2016b).

With an ever faster increase in human population and increased consumption to support it, human footprints on planet Earth's environment started to surface clearly in the latter half of the 20th century (US EPA, 1990, 2010). A large increase in the emissions of various pollutants from industrial activities has resulted in the environmental problems of, inter alia, smog, acid rain, ozone depletion, water contamination, and particulate matter pollution, which in turn have affected the health and livelihoods of people and ecosystems (US EPA, 2014). Extensive applications of pesticides, insecticides, and fertilizers have resulted in infiltrations of toxic chemicals into human and natural systems, which are harmed gravely by these chemicals (Carson, 1962). As human footprint on the planet has become ever bigger, unmanaged natural systems such as wilderness and wildlife have shrunken (Leopold, 1949).

Anthropogenic influences on the environmental qualities and natural resources have become ever more evident to humanity through global footprints. An increase in the emissions of carbon dioxide, a primary by-product of industrialization, was reported to affect the global climate system, which has been stable for thousands of years (IPCC, 1990; Hansen et al., 2006). An increase in CO_2 concentration in the global atmosphere has been observed from 320 ppm in the 1950s to 400 ppm in 2015, which caused the global atmosphere to warm (Keeling et al., 2005). By the end of the 21st century, the Earth's climate is predicted to warm significantly from the long-term stabilized climate, that is, the 20th century average climate (Le Treut et al., 2007; IPCC, 2014a).

Of the many global policy issues, the most salient feature of the global warming phenomenon is that it is a truly global-scale policy issue. It is not a single country that causes the planet to warm, neither is it a single country that can stop the globally warming trend. The policy experiments in the past decades indicate that not even the entire continent of Europe, the European Union more precisely, was able to contain the increase in carbon dioxide concentration in the global atmosphere or the increase in global temperature through the coordinated efforts under the Kyoto Protocol (UNFCCC, 1998, 2009). The Paris Agreement at the end of 2015, the culmination of the Durban Platform for Enhanced Action, embodies the primary lesson of the past global negotiations, that is, the trend of global warming cannot be reversed unless all the nations join the efforts to cut greenhouse gases (GHGs) (UNFCCC, 2011a, 2015).

At the same time humanity is faced with global warming challenges, ceaseless inventions and innovations have made it possible for humanity to go beyond the environment of planet Earth. Humans are sending spacecraft to the Moon, exploring Mars by sending multiple rovers for possible future human settlements thereof, sending an exploratory spacecraft to Jupiter, and sending a planetary voyager past the Solar System and the Pluto. With Hubble, Kepler, and other telescopes, scientists have been searching successfully for an exoplanet where humans can habituate (NASA, 2016a). Private companies are also actively engaged in making a paid round trip to Mars come true in the very near future for any individual who can pay for the trip.

The challenges and innovations that have taken place over the past century bring humanity to the time in history in which human communities around the globe are ever more interdependent and connected; the human race is powerful enough to alter the natural systems of the Earth, even perhaps uncontrollably; the Earth can be viewed from far outside the Earth as a single entity as small as a baseball; and the human race can as a whole look out for the places and life forms outside the Earth. At this particular juncture in human history, scientific and policy endeavors on the problems and creative solutions for a truly global policy issue such as global warming can never be more pertinent.

2.   Global Warming as a Global Public Good

In the economics literature, global warming is a special type of goods, called a global public good (Nordhaus, 1994). The goal of this book is to address the great challenges posed by global warming, and the theory of public goods and their efficient provisions will take a central place throughout the book (Samuelson, 1954, 1955). Unlike private goods, a public good is a special type of goods and services that is shared by all the members of a community, e.g., a nation. It is a jointly (collectively) consumed good by all consumers once it has been provided (Samuelson, 1954).

In olden times when each nation lived and ran the national economy by and large independently of other nations, there was the commons. The commons in a village is the area that all community members can rely on and make use of for free. It is not possible to exclude a member in the village from appropriating the commons because no one owns it. The commons will be overutilized as community members compete for the resources the commons provide (Hardin, 1968). As the size of the population grows in the village, competition will intensify and an informal agreement may emerge among the village members with regards to the protocol of appropriating the commons (Ostrom, 1990, 2009). Or a local government may divide the commons and assign private property rights among the members of the village.

In the sovereign countries, a national defense and security system is a national commons, i.e., a national public good (Samuelson, 1954). The national defense system is freely available to anyone in the country, once it is provided, in other words, as long as the country exists. It is not possible to exclude a citizen in the country from enjoying the services of the national defense system. A citizen's relishing of the national defense/security system does not diminish the other citizens' enjoyment of it. It is bulk provided for every citizen. The public goods have these two defining characteristics: nonexcludable and nonrivalrous (Buchanan, 1965, 1968; Mas-Colell et al., 1995).

If a good or service has these two characteristics, the market does not provide it efficiently (Samuelson, 1954). A private security company cannot provide the national defense because it will not be able to exclude a citizen from enjoying the service once it is provided. Even though the citizen does not pay for the cost, he/she still can enjoy the national defense. One by one, citizens of the country will opt to free ride and let others pay for the cost of providing the national defense and security (Buchanan, 1968). There is no way by the private company to prevent the free-riding behaviors of the citizens. The national defense provision must be regulated by the government law and the tax system (Samuelson and Nordhaus, 2009).

Clean air in a megacity such as New York is a local public good. Polluting the clean air through the emissions of a variety of pollutants by coal-fired power plants is a local public bad (Mendelsohn, 1980; Smith and Huang, 1995; Smith, 2008). The pollutants such as SO_2, NO_x, ozone, and particulate matters emitted into the atmosphere will harm people, ecosystems, and economy (Viscusi and Aldy, 2003; Muller and Mendelsohn, 2009; US EPA, 2014). Once the air is polluted by, e.g., SO_2 emissions, it is not possible, or very costly at the least, to exclude a New Yorker from the polluted air. Neither does the harm received by a citizen reduce the harm that is received by others. It has the two characteristics of a public good.

The local clean air of New York will be overappropriated in that every citizen will pollute the clean air as long as polluting behaviors bring a higher profit to him/her. Without any regard to the other citizens and the city, a New Yorker will be tempted by a higher profit to pollute the clean air of the city. He/she does not care for the externality (external effects) of his/her behaviors on the others (Pigou, 1920). Producers will rush to abuse the clean air, i.e., pump out pollutants into the air to manufacture goods and services and sell them for profits, as long as there is no cost charged for the pollution behaviors. Without any intervention by the governments, the local public good, that is, the clean atmosphere in New York, will be overly abused (Baumol and Oates, 1988).

As in the village commons described earlier, an informal agreement among the New Yorkers may arise to address the harmful consequences of air or water pollution. But it is hard to imagine that such a voluntary agreement would be realized in New York because there are a large number of polluters as well as a large number of pollution victims in New York, i.e., over 20 million people. In other words, the transaction cost for such a bargaining is too large for a mutual bargaining to clean up the SO_2 or NO_x pollution to be successful (Coase, 1960).

However, as in the case of the village commons, it is possible to assign a type of property rights to the clean atmosphere in the form of penalty for pollution. A ton of pollution of, e.g., SO_2, can be charged a certain level of penalty based on a cost—benefit analysis of the pollution (Baumol and Oates, 1988; Hartwick and Olewiler, 1997; Mendelsohn and Olmstead, 2009). Such a price (penalty) system for SO_2 emissions can be enforced only through a mandate from the citizens of New York through, e.g., a referendum or an election. The local government would lead the efforts to set the price of pollution, collect the penalty from violators, and monitor implementations of firms and individuals.

Besides the price (charge) approach, an alternative way of charging SO_2 or NO_x pollution through a marketable permit system is also widely adopted. A permit system for SO_2 emissions can be designed in which the local government determines the total number of permits. Polluters would purchase the number of permits they need. Polluters are allowed to trade permits among them, through which transactions the market price of permits is determined (Montgomery, 1972; Tietenberg, 1980; Stavins, 1998).

For the entire planet Earth, it is hard for one to imagine that there would be a commons shared by all members of the planet like the village commons. It dawned on William Nordhaus that such a commons exits in an aptly titled paper "How fast should we graze the global commons" published in the journal *American Economic Review* (Nordhaus, 1982). The pioneer and leading economist on the economic aspects of global warming saw it as a new world and provided a grand economic analysis with a proposal of a set of policy instruments for dealing with this unprecedented anthropogenic challenge in the highly acclaimed book entitled *Managing the Global Commons* (Nordhaus, 1991, 1994).

In Nordhaus' works, the global commons is the global atmosphere and/or the global climate system. A traditional thinking was definitely that the sky belongs to the country underneath it. Each country, therefore, owns its portion of the global atmosphere. If one country pollutes the atmosphere by emitting SO_2, it is the citizens of the country that are harmed. Therefore the country should take care of its own sky, say, the atmosphere.

This traditional thinking of the sky breaks down when it comes to carbon dioxide (CO_2). This molecule is called a greenhouse gas (GHG) because it forms a greenhouse-like blanket in the atmosphere, which reflects back to the Earth the outgoing long-wave infrared solar radiation. Because the reflected long-wave solar radiation is trapped under the greenhouse-like blanket, the consequence is to warm the atmosphere underneath it (Arrhenius, 1896; UNFCCC, 1992).

The processes of CO_2 accumulation and the greenhouse effect led to the creation of the global commons. The CO_2 molecule once released into the atmosphere quickly mixes in a way that equalizes the CO_2 concentration across the globe and stays there, on average, for more than a century. There is little difference in the CO_2 concentration level across the Earth. The greenhouse effect warms planet Earth, which alters ecosystems and harms (or benefits) human activities in all the countries and individuals on the Earth (Le Treut et al., 2007).

When it comes to carbon dioxide and the greenhouse effect, the global atmosphere is shared by all countries on Earth. More precisely, a stable global climate regime is shared by all the citizens of the Earth. A stable global climate system provides the elements and amenities needed for humans and natural beings to survive on this planet. The global climate system absorbs and reflects a proper amount of the solar radiation. It provides sufficient amount water on Earth. It helps provide sufficient amounts of carbon dioxide, nitrogen, and oxygen needed for plants and animals to grow on this planet (Schlesinger, 1997).

Unknowingly at first and then knowingly, however, countries started to "overgraze" the global greenhouse commons because no single country owns or controls it. Industrial countries have become rich by putting up a large amount of carbon dioxide to the degree that it disrupted the Earth's climate system and developing countries are in a rush to spew out carbon dioxide to obtain energy needed for the economic development and well-being of their citizens (Keeling et al., 2005; IPCC, 1990).

The carbon dioxide and the greenhouse effect is a global public good. Once carbon dioxide is emitted into the atmosphere, it is not possible to exclude a country from the greenhouse effect. Furthermore, the effect of increased carbon dioxide on a single country does not diminish the effect on the other countries. It has the characteristics of nonexcludability and nonrivalry at a global scale. It is a jointly "consumed" good by the citizens of the world.

We may call carbon dioxide and the greenhouse effect is a global public bad. Alternatively, we may call a stable global climate system a global public good. Or removal and reduction of carbon dioxide may be called a global public good. The effect of the removal and reduction of CO_2 is felt by all countries without exception. The effect of the removal and reduction of CO_2 on one country does not diminish the effect on the other countries.

3. The Science of Global Warming

Being a global-scale problem, it has taken many decades, if not a century, for humanity to establish the science of global warming. The warming effect of carbon dioxide in the atmosphere was first calculated by a Swedish physicist Svante Arrhenius, from which he explained the occurrences of Ice Ages on the Earth (Arrhenius, 1896).

Scientists have endeavored for more than a century to be able to measure the global average temperature precisely (NOAA, 2016). There are at present two instrumental methods for measuring the global average temperature: on-the-ground weather station observations and satellite observations. Based on a number of continuous observations from these methods during the past century, climate scientists conclude that the Earth has been warming during the past century (Mann et al., 1999; Hansen et al., 2006; Le Treut et al., 2007). There are sometimes, nonetheless, disagreements on the degree of global temperature increase between weather station—based models and satellite-based models.

In Fig. 1.1, temperature records from 1960 to 2015 from the two models are put together. The NASA temperature anomaly data are based on weather station observations of weather variables and are available from 1880 (NASA, 2016b). The satellite data are from the University of Alabama at Huntsville satellite program, which is also funded by the federal government in the United States (UAH, 2016). The base period for the satellite data is 1981—2010. Satellite data are broken down into globe, land, and ocean data. Both instrumental records show a similar warming trend.

A closer examination of the two instrumental records is made in Fig. 1.2 by recalibrating the base period of the NASA data to 1981—2010, the same base period of the satellite data. More often than not, the two records are in agreement. However, there are conspicuous disagreements. The years 1998 and 2015 are said to be the two strongest El Niño years in the historical data. In the 2 years, the two instrumental records deviate by as far as 0.3°C. One of the reasons for the disagreements is that the satellite data record temperatures in the low troposphere, whereas the weather station data record temperatures on the grounds.

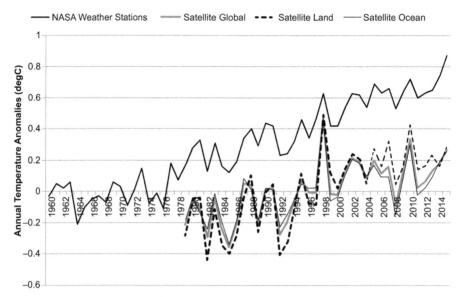

Figure 1.1 Annual temperature anomalies (1960−2015): weather stations versus satellite. (1) NASA data are anomalies from the base period of 20th century. (2) Satellite data are from the University of Huntsville and the base period is 1981−2010.

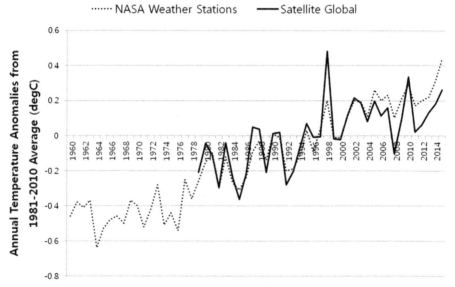

Figure 1.2 Annual temperature anomalies (1960−2015) from the base period of 1981−2010.

The level of carbon dioxide in the atmosphere has been measured without interruptions since the early 1950s under the supervision of Charles David Keeling (Keeling et al., 2005; GCP, 2014). A linear increase in the concentration of CO_2 has been recorded at the Mauna Loa observatory in Hawaii. The concentration of CO_2 is now measured at a number of places across the globe, including the South Pole. From the preindustrial level of 280 ppm (parts per million), it passed 400 ppm by the end of 2015.

Climate scientists have painstakingly built a precise climate change prediction model, called an Atmospheric Oceanic General Circulation Model (AOGCM), which can predict the climate conditions on the Earth far into the future (Revelle and Suess, 1957; Hansen et al., 1981). In the Climate Model Intercomparison Project Phase 5, there are more than a score of AOGCM models examined by the Project (Taylor et al., 2012). The AOGCM models can provide an answer to the critical policy question: how much and how fast will the Earth warm in the future or will the Earth's climate system change?

A prediction of future global temperature cannot be done, however, without assuming how human society will behave in the future. Climate scientists have taken a scenario (storyline) approach to represent a range of possibilities in future economies and societies (Nakicenovic et al., 2000). The representative families of scenarios constructed by the Intergovernmental Panel on Climate Change (IPCC) are A1, A2, B1, and B2. Climate scientists cannot tell which of these scenarios is more or less likely, which means that they cannot assign probabilities to climate prediction outcomes. One report, however, moves away from economic and social scenarios, which are ignored in the Representative Concentration Pathway scenarios (IPCC, 2014a).

Across the array of climate models and future scenarios, climate scientists can only provide a range of predictions on future temperature changes. By the end of the 21st century, climate scientists predict a temperature increase that ranges from 1.2 to 4.5°C (IPCC, 2014a). The range is quite large. When all climate models and scenarios that are considered to be extremely unlikely by the IPCC are taken into account, the range of outcomes is much wider than this range. An extremely unlikely climate prediction outcome can be as large as above 10°C increase in temperature. The best guess estimate of equilibrium climate sensitivity is 3°C increase in temperature in response to carbon dioxide doubling in the atmosphere.

Why are the world citizens concerned about global warming and climate changes? This is certainly because global warming will lead to a host of changes that are harmful to the Earth and individuals (IPCC, 2014b). Global warming may lead to melting and breaking apart of particularly vulnerable glaciers and ice sheets around the world in ways that could threaten livelihoods and regional economies (Oppenheimer and Alley, 2005). The sea level may rise unexpectedly, threatening coastal cities (Nicholls and Cazenave, 2010). Global warming and climatic changes may lead to decreases in yields of various staple grains, grasslands, animals, and trees through, inter alia, changes in insects and pests (Ainsworth and Long, 2005; Denman et al., 2007; Hahn et al., 2009). Changes in atmospheric and ocean temperatures may lead to generations of more intense hurricanes and may be associated with extreme weather and climate events (Emanuel, 2008; Titley et al., 2016). A large degree of warming may lead to changes in the Earth's thermohaline circulation in the oceans (Broecker, 1997).

Continuation of the buildup of carbon dioxide may lead to an abrupt shift in regional or global climate regimes (NRC, 2013b).

What is the economic value of all these changes that are expected to be incurred by global climatic changes (Mendelsohn and Neumann, 1999)? Studies of revealed preferences, i.e., observed economic activities, by affected individuals in low-latitude developing regions using household-level economic surveys indicate that individuals in agricultural and natural resource—intensive industries have adapted to changes in the climate system historically (Seo and Mendelsohn, 2008; Seo, 2010b, 2014a). The total economic damage from global warming estimated and reported by various groups of researchers is varied from one study to another (Tol, 2009). The wide range of damage estimate is by and large accounted for by how well these studies take into account adaptation possibilities and constraints (Seo, 2015a, 2016a,b). The mean value of the range of total damage estimates reported by global warming studies may lie at about 2.5% loss of annual income with a warming by 3°C and may be smaller with exclusion of no adaptation models (Mendelsohn and Williams, 2007; Tol, 2009; Seo, 2016d).

4. Economics of an Optimal Provision of Global Warming

Having established the fact that the phenomenon of global warming will continue to unravel far into the future and harm the economies and ecosystems on the Earth, how should the world provide the global public good of a climate stabilization or removal of CO_2 and other GHGs? This is the essential policy question on global warming that has not yet been answered successfully. This book will provide a comprehensive review of the academic and policy endeavors to conceptualize and provide a policy remedy to the problem of global warming as a global public good.

In contrast to the other books on climate change economics that are current in the market (Nordhaus, 2008, 2013; Stern, 2009; Tol, 2014; Wagner and Weitzman, 2015), this book is centered on behavioral aspects of global warming and policy instruments. The behavioral aspects of global warming are multifaceted, which will be painstakingly elucidated by the author throughout the book. Stated in its simplest terms, the heart of the behavioral economics of climate change is that changes in behaviors by individuals, businesses, and public sectors are conditioned by global warming and climatic changes but also affect global warming and climatic changes, as such can be relied upon as a primary policy instrument for addressing the unprecedented challenges of global warming (Seo, 2015a, 2016d). The behavioral economics of climate change described in this book will present a novel policy platform where a multitude of policy and market responses to deal with global warming are integrated (Seo, 2013a, 2015b, 2016c).

The classical theory of an optimal provision of a global public good is built upon the Samuelson's pure theory of public expenditure (Samuelson, 1954). It was Paul Samuelson who first coined the term "public good" and "a collectively consumed good" (Samuelson, 1955). In a jointly consumed good, he showed that an optimal provision of the public good can be achieved only through public taxation and expenditure because the market fails to provide it efficiently due to the jointly consumed characteristic.

An efficient provision of a global public good—and ultimately global warming—can be thought of in the same conceptual way as the Samuelson's pure theory of public expenditure (Nordhaus, 1994). In the world in which the global atmosphere is freely available, no country is willing to provide the global public good, that is, the removal of Earth-heating gases from the atmosphere, voluntarily. Even if one country is determined to cut all the GHGs the country emits, the country's efforts would not make a small dent at all in the global atmospheric concentration of CO_2 or the trend of global atmospheric temperature. As countries rather have a strong incentive to free ride, the needed provision of climate stabilization would not take place at all in the *laissez-faire* global economy (Buchanan, 1968). Therefore a policy solution to the problem of global warming must be provided by the intervention of the "global government."

Assuming that global governance is established, William Nordhaus proposed a policy instrument called carbon tax or price, which, by way of correcting for market incentives, purports to provide a globally optimal amount of the removal of GHGs (Nordhaus, 1991, 1992). By weighing the benefits against the costs of the removal (or reduction) of each ton of carbon dioxide, an optimal carbon tax is determined and harmonized across the globe.

Once the carbon tax is in place and with legal force, each country should decide on how much carbon emissions the country should reduce to maximize the country's economic welfare. By increasing the level of carbon price over time in tandem with the rise of global temperature and resulting severer economic damages, the world will be able to contain the rise of carbon dioxide and global temperature over a century timescale (Nordhaus, 2008).

This policy remedy, which I call the Samuelson—Nordhaus framework in this book, has been the classical and standard policy instrument offered in the economics of global warming. By and large, economists' works on global warming or climate change have attempted to address one of the many aspects in the Samuelson—Nordhaus framework of carbon tax, e.g., discount rate, uncertainties, climate damages, induced technologies, catastrophes, reallocation of carbon revenues (Arrow et al., 1996; Kolstad, 1996; Mendelsohn and Neumann, 1999; MacCracken et al., 1999; Pizer, 1999; Goulder and Mathai, 2000; Newell and Pizer, 2001; Popp, 2004; Carraro et al., 2006; Seo, 2007, 2012a; Stavins, 2007; Stern, 2009; Weitzman, 2009; Barrett, 2010; Tol, 2009; Metcalf, 2009 Tietenberg, 2013; Wagner and Weitzman, 2015).

As far as policy experiences are concerned, the carbon tax approach has never been adopted at a global scale, but was nevertheless adopted at a subnational level, e.g., by the province of British Colombia in Canada, as a way to cut the level of carbon dioxide emissions (Goulder, 2007; Tietenberg, 2013). There were also attempts to introduce carbon tax at the national level in the United States (US House of Representatives, 2009). The Samuelson—Nordhaus framework has played a critical role in the only international climate policy treaty that was ever implemented, the Kyoto Protocol (UNFCCC, 1998). The European Union's Emissions Trading Scheme (ETS) implemented during the first phase of the Kyoto Protocol from 2008 to 2012 was the central policy instrument by the Annex B countries to meet the Kyoto commitments (Ellerman and Buchner, 2007). An evaluation of the EU ETS in terms of a variety of economic and climate indicators is only possible with reference to the globally harmonized carbon price (penalty) approach (Nordhaus, 2007a; Stavins, 2007; Stern, 2009).

Major countries such as the United States, China, and India committed to no emission reduction responsibilities under the first phase of the Kyoto Protocol. Furthermore, countries such as Japan, Canada, Russia, and Australia withdrew from the Protocol at the end of the first phase of the Kyoto Protocol. The efforts to negotiate the second phase of the Kyoto Protocol in Bali and Copenhagen ended in shambles at the end of 2009 (UNFCCC, 2007; 2009).

What has eluded an international agreement on global warming policy actions (Seo, 2012a)? This book offers a behavioral perspective on global warming policy negotiations by way of a noncooperative game theory. The carbon tax approach proposed by the Samuelson—Nordhaus framework is implicitly assuming that there would emerge cooperation among the participating nations with regard to a global warming policy protocol. This book elucidates why there would be divergent incentives among the world nations with regard to a global carbon tax policy or a global emissions trading system that would eventually fail an international agreement, even with complementary policy measures and alterations of incentives through monetary transfers (Carraro et al., 2006; Barrett, 2010; Nordhaus, 2015).

Countries are faced with heterogeneous realities, among other things, on the degree of climate change, national benefits of abatement, comparative advantages, a portfolio of polluters and victims, natural resource endowments, economic developments, and national culture and history. The consequence is that there may be no Nash equilibrium in the game of climate negotiations (Nash, 1950, 1951). In the game in which each country is interested in maximizing the benefits to the country from an internationally agreed protocol, there is no stable equilibrium in the climate game, that is, global negotiations on a climate change policy (Seo, 2012a).

International negotiations on global warming have faltered and been largely unsuccessful. The first international Protocol on climate change—the Kyoto Protocol—excluded developing nations such as China, India, Russia, Brazil, and South Africa (UNFCCC, 1998). It was rejected in the US Congress because of the omissions of the above-mentioned developing countries and the United States did not ratify the Protocol. The first phase of the Kyoto Protocol was implemented in the European Union only, which ended with no success in containing CO_2 concentration in the global atmosphere (Nordhaus, 2008, 2011, 2010). The international efforts to renew the Kyoto Protocol for the second phase of the Protocol failed in Copenhagen (UNFCCC, 2009). Subsequently, Japan, Canada, Russia, and Australia walked out from the Kyoto Protocol, leaving it a dormant international treaty. The Paris Agreement arrived at an agreement, although not a protocol, in which all the parties of the United Nations Framework Convention on Climate Change (UNFCCC) are included. But it fails to assign any legal responsibilities to any country (UNFCCC, 2015).

The international policy experiences before and after the Kyoto Protocol shed much light on the true difficulty of providing optimally the global public good of a stable climate system. This difficulty can be reinterpreted from an economic analysis of production technologies. Unlike many other global issues to be discussed shortly, an optimal response to global warming entails an additive production technology (Hirshleifer, 1983; Nordhaus, 2006).

Let us first take a look at the global problem of protection of the Earth from an asteroid or meteoroid collision (Chapman and Morrison, 1994; Guardian, 2016). A particularly large asteroid can strike the Earth, without any intervention, and disturb the cyclical rotations of the Earth around the Sun. Smaller asteroids may disturb the natural systems of the Earth, affecting all the citizens of the globe, besides destroying those who are directly hit. Provision of global protection against such a disaster would certainly benefit the entire world and be considered as a global public good.

The asteroid example brings up for our discussions the characteristic of a production technology that is needed for production of a global public good. In the case of global warming, what matters in global warming policy responses is the aggregate of individual countries' contributions of GHG reductions. By contrast, an efficient provision of asteroid protection can be accomplished by a single country (NASA, 2007). That is, the success in protecting the Earth from an asteroid collision hinges on whether there is a single country that succeeds in shooting down and killing a fast-approaching asteroid. The best shot determines the outcome of the efforts for providing a global public good, for which reason this type of production technology is called a best-shot technology (Hirshleifer, 1983).

By contrast, the global public good of preventing dangerous global warming or stabilizing the climate system is provided via an additive production technology (Nordhaus, 2006). That is, for a successful outcome, individual nations' abatements and absorptions of carbon dioxide must add up to the total abatement and absorption that must be sufficient to achieve the global goal of containing global warming optimally for the world.

The third type of production technology is called a weakest-link technology. A classic example of this is the construction of a dike or a seawall across a coastal line to prevent seawater inundation. The success of a dike in preventing a flooding from the sea depends on whether the weakest point of the dike can withstand the sea waves and surges, regardless of how strong and formidable the dike is at all other spots of the dike.

The weakest-link production technology is pertinent to provision of nuclear nonproliferation or elimination of an infectious disease such as malaria or smallpox. The success of providing each of these goods is determined by what happens in the weakest point, i.e., the largest nuclear nation or the most susceptible country to malaria in sub-Saharan Africa (Barrett, 2008).

With regard to the economics of public goods, some authors noted that some public goods may be voluntarily provided by individuals or countries voluntarily cooperate on a global warming policy (Kotchen and Moore, 2007; Kotchen, 2009; Barrett, 2010). For various reasons, individuals and communities may voluntarily contribute to provision of a public good. For example, many individuals choose voluntarily not to drive a car personally, or purchase only organic foods, or purchase a cleaner low-carbon car, or purchase energy from the utilities of renewable sources, e.g., wind and solar.

Voluntary actions with regard to provision of a public good are most often meaningful only in a limited local context. The larger the spatial scale of a public good in concern is, the harder do voluntary behaviors make a difference in providing a public good. In a large spatial scale problem, voluntary behaviors are easily dominated by the economic behaviors driven by monetary incentives. In the case of global warming, voluntary reductions of carbon dioxide by enthusiast nations may not add up to the aggregate amount that is sufficient for a stabilization of the global climate system and may have many leakages elsewhere not covered by the regulations by the enthusiast nations (Nordhaus, 2010, 2011).

5. Technological Innovations: Breakthroughs and Incremental Advances

Given the conceptual challenges and experiences of failures in international negotiations on global warming policy making, possibilities for technological breakthroughs have come to the fore of the discussions on how the world should manage global climatic changes. Is there or will there be a technological breakthrough that can shoot down the problem of global warming in a similar way as a fast-approaching asteroid is shot down? The answer to this question was "yes" even in the early years of global warming debates and has become ever more convincing over the course of time (Nordhaus, 1977, 1991).

By the time of this writing, the list of breakthrough technologies that are reported to have the capabilities to contain inexorable global warming with relatively low cost includes nuclear fusion energy (LLNL, 2015;ITER, 2015), nuclear fission energy with an enhanced safety and storage capacity (US DOE, 2015), solar energy (IPCC, 2011; MIT, 2015), electric vehicles (NRC, 2013a; McConnell, 2013), and new lighting methods such as the light-emitting diode bulbs (Akasaki et al., 2014). These technologies are often referred to as a backstop technology in economics, a technology or an alternative fuel that can provide energy permanently at a fixed cost, thereby replacing fossil fuels (Nordhaus, 1973; Heal, 2010).

The list of breakthrough technologies also includes another set of technologies that instead targets engineering of the Earth's climate directly, commonly called geoengineering or climate engineering: a carbon-capture-storage technology (Lackner et al., 2012; IPCC, 2005a; IEA, 2013), geoengineering of the climate system (Barrett, 2008), ocean iron fertilization (Martin et al., 1994), and reflecting solar radiation from the outside the Earth (NRC, 2015).

The author will provide a detailed review in Chapter 5 of these technologies that can make a breakthrough in global warming policy responses. The review in Chapter 5 also includes another set of technologies that the author calls a microtechnology. In contrast to the breakthrough technologies mentioned earlier, a microtechnology is a novel technological advance that enables an individual or an enterprise to better cope with changing climates. Furthermore, a microtechnology is more often than not an incremental technological advance rather than a path-breaking discovery.

One of such micro and incremental technologies is a methane reduction and capture technology from ruminant animals such as cattle, sheep, and goats, which are the major sources of methane emissions, a potent GHG that is 20 times more powerful than carbon dioxide per unit emission in a century timescale (US EPA, 2014; Schaefer et al., 2016; Seo, 2015b, 2016c). A methane reduction technology may become realized through changes in animal diets or feed additives (US EPA, 2006; Soussana et al., 2010).

In addition to the methane capture and reduction technology, the list of such microtechnologies includes, inter alia, developments of heat-tolerant species of grains or animals (Evenson and Gollin, 2003), developments of cures for infectious diseases on humans and animals (Aksoy et al., 2014), a smart energy grid (Joskow, 2012), and developments of alternatives to conventional coolants in refrigerators and air conditioners, such as hydrofluorocarbons (HFCs) and hydrochlorofluorocarbons (HCFCs) (IPCC, 2005b; EC, 2016).

The long list of the breakthrough and incremental microtechnologies entails that the cost of policy responses to address global warming as well as an optimal level of mitigation efforts is dependent on how fast these technologies could become developed and practical for widespread adoptions by various climate actors. Large uncertainties with regard to times of introductions and practical applications of many of the breakthrough technologies would affect future expectations and changes of behaviors by individuals and policy makers (Kolstad, 1996; Nordhaus, 2008).

From another angle, it should be heeded that a policy instrument that can induce technological innovations should be preferred to one that cannot induce such technological innovations. With the former type policy instrument, the unit cost of abating carbon will fall at a faster rate over time, leading to a higher level of abatement over the course of time, than under the latter type policy instrument (Goulder and Mathai, 2000; Popp, 2004).

Policy-induced technological innovations can occur through many channels (Nordhaus, 2002; Gillingham et al., 2008). The most prevalent method relied upon by governments is an increase in the size of research and development investment to accelerate technological changes by way of numerous governmental subsidies, e.g., ethanol subsidies, electric vehicle subsidies, wind energy subsidies, and solar startup subsidies in the United States and elsewhere (White House, 2013).

However, it should be made clear that any of these energy subsidies does not guarantee either an efficient or a cost-effective policy response to global warming problems by the government. That is, a large subsidy given to solar or ethanol companies is certain to be a costlier option for the present time for the goal of achieving the target level of emissions reductions. In other words, there are many other cheaper alternatives to accomplish the required mitigation target for now.

Put differently, a technological option is just one component of the full portfolio of policy options for dealing and coping with global warming, not the panacea for the problem. As many technologies are to be developed in the decades to come, those novel technologies should be incorporated into individual and policy responses to address the challenges of global warming and climatic changes. It is people, businesses, and public sectors that should adopt these technologies in ways to cope with climatic changes and reduce emissions of GHGs (Graziano and Gillingham, 2015; Seo, 2015a, 2016d). How societies can encourage or induce adoptions of novel and powerful technologies is an important area of climate research.

6. An Adaptation Paradigm of Global Warming Policy

An adoption behavior of a new technology by an individual or a community is one form of behavioral adaptations to climate change. More formally, a behavioral adaptation is changes in an individual's behaviors in response to or in anticipation of global warming to either make the best use of a changed climate or take the least-cost actions to cut GHGs (Mendelsohn, 2000; Seo, 2015b, 2016c). A private actor will make a decision considering the benefits and costs of available strategies, and also risks, values, and extreme consequences that may result from changes in the prevalent climate regime (Nash, 1950; Neumann and Morgenstern, 1953; Kahneman and Tversky, 1979; Shiller, 2005; Thaler, 2015; Seo, 2016a,b).

For the past 2 decades, climate researchers have conducted substantial research on adaptation behaviors to climatic changes (Seo, 2006, 2010b; Seo and Mendelsohn, 2008; Kurukulasuriya et al., 2011; Olmstead and Rhode, 2011; Kala, 2015). These researches reveal a large array of adaptation measures and strategies that have been utilized by individuals and businesses in response to changes in climatic conditions (Seo, 2015a, 2016d). In addition, adaptation researches quantified the economic value of adapting by choosing one system of enterprise over another (Seo, 2016a,b). That is, adapting sensibly in an efficient way reduces the cost of climate change and global warming significantly that is experienced by an affected individual.

Empirical studies of revealed and observed adaptation behaviors have concentrated on agricultural and natural resource enterprises in low-latitude developing countries such as sub-Saharan Africa, South America, and South Asia. In sub-Saharan Africa, farmers are found to change agricultural systems from a crops-only system to a mixed crops–livestock system and a livestock-only system to adapt to a higher temperature (Seo, 2010a). Furthermore, in hotter temperatures farmers switch from large ruminant animals such as cattle to small ruminant animals such as sheep and goats (Seo and Mendelsohn, 2008). When climate becomes more volatile and risky through larger variability in yearly rainfall, sub-Saharan farmers are found to switch from specialized systems such as a crops-only or a livestock-only system to an integrated crops–livestock system (Seo, 2012c). When climate becomes hotter and wetter, farmers are found to increase the adoption of forest systems of natural resource managements such as a crops–forest system (Seo, 2010c, 2014a,b). Furthermore, farmers are found to adapt to a hotter and wetter climate by adopting goats and chickens more often and cattle and sheep less often (Seo and Mendelsohn, 2008).

Adaptation strategies that have been adopted by sub-Saharan farmers hold much importance to designing future climate change policy responses. Adapting efficiently to changes in climate is critical first because agricultural and natural resource managers will suffer greatly without such adjustments of current practices. A study in the US agriculture is illuminating (Schlenker and Roberts, 2009). If US farmers were to continue to grow corns (maize), one of the two major grains in the United States along with wheat, in the future with a high degree of warming scenario unfolding, US corn farmers are predicted to lose as much as 80% of the current yields of corns by the end of this century.

A forecast of severe damages on agriculture that results from global warming was one of the signature climate change studies in the early literature of global warming, which continues to hold sways on policy discussions (IPCC, 1990; Adams et al., 1990; Rosenzweig and Parry, 1994; Schlenker et al., 2005; Schlenker and Roberts, 2009; Lobell et al., 2011). What these early studies were not capable of capturing is that agricultural and natural resource managers can respond to changes in climate by substituting inputs of production and changing systems of agriculture (Mendelsohn et al., 1994; Seo, 2013b, 2014b).

The economic significance and value of sensible adaptation actions on an individual who undertakes the actions is large and evident. A series of studies on Latin American agriculture shows that an increase in temperature will lead to an increased adoption of the mixed system of agriculture and a livestock-only agriculture, which replaces a crops-only agriculture (Seo, 2010b). A hotter and wetter climate will increase adoptions of forests-based activities such as a crops–forests enterprise or a forests-only enterprise (Seo, 2012b). When Latin American farmers can adjust their current enterprises in response to climatic changes, the impact of climate change on Latin American agriculture will be about a couple percent loss of land value by the middle of the 21st century in a range of climate scenarios, whereas it can be an order of magnitude larger without efficient adaptive adjustments (Seo, 2016a,b).

A more profound aspect of adapting to climatic changes is that these behavioral changes have consequences on the amount of emissions of GHGs by an individual farmer and enterprise (Seo, 2015b). An increase in forests and forest-based activities because of global warming means that adaptation activities will also lead to increased absorptions of carbon dioxide by forests (Seo, 2012b). An increase in grasslands and grassland-based activities, such as animal husbandry, because of global warming means that carbon dioxide absorptions can increase by increasing managed grasslands, decreasing managed croplands, and decreasing a conversion of forests to croplands (Seo, 2014a). A hotter climate would make people to move to local areas with good forest covers. Property developers and local governments will increase ecosystem managements in ways that increase forest covers (Seo, 2016c).

There is no doubt that adaptation behaviors do not always lead to abating and absorptions of carbon dioxide and other GHGs. For example, an increase in livestock systems will lead to increased emissions of methane (CH_4) from ruminant animals such as cattle, sheep, and goats (US EPA, 2006, Schaefer et al., 2016). However, animal emissions of methane can be reduced with a much lower cost than, e.g., sucking carbon dioxide directly out of the atmosphere. As noted earlier, dietary changes and feed additives of livestock can reduce methane emissions from ruminant animals while other more effective methods are being developed (Soussana et al., 2010).

This is one of the areas where marginal technological innovations can play a breakthrough role in a different sense (Seo, 2016c). A small innovation such as animal feed additives can make a big contribution to reducing emissions of GHGs by way of influencing decisions of individuals to adapt to changing climates. It does not always have to be a grand technology such as nuclear fusion or solar reflector to be a meaningful strategy for the humanity's responses to global warming.

In Chapter 5 of this book, the author will elaborate an adaptation paradigm of global warming policy making. A full list of adaptation measures and strategies that have been studied by climate researchers and found to be effective in the fields will be explained in the chapter. The list will also include adaptation behaviors beyond agricultural and natural resource sectors. As an example, a historical study of US population statistics shows that the introduction of air conditioner in the 20th century reduced US mortality rate due to high temperature by more than 50% (Barreca et al., 2016). This is another example of a technological innovation that has made a big difference to global warming responses, more precisely, weather responses.

Again, a further spread of air conditioning as a response to a warmer world will have consequences on individuals' GHG emissions. The widely used refrigerants of air conditioners and refrigerators, HFCs and HCFCs, are major sources of greenhouse warming (IPCC, 2005b; UNEP, 2016). The agreement between the United States and China to phase out the HFCs means that the emissions of these gases can be eliminated by forcing climate-friendly replacements such as hydrocarbons (White House, 2013; EC, 2016). Air conditioning is another example of adaptation to global warming that can simultaneously reduce the amount of GHG emissions when an adaptation strategy is coupled with technological options.

Another salient finding in adaptation research is that behavioral adaptations are highly effective strategies to mitigate the disasters from catastrophic and extreme events associated with global warming (Emanuel, 2008). Empirical evidence is found in adaptation responses to hurricanes. As hurricane intensity increases, the number of fatalities increases nonlinearly. At the same time, adaptation strategies such as early warning systems, evacuations, education and training, and hurricane path projections reduce the number of fatalities due to hurricanes nonlinearly. A range of hurricane simulations by the end of the 21st century reveals that the increase in the number of fatalities due to a potential increase in hurricane intensity that is caused by global warming will be by and large offset by the decrease in the number of fatalities due to an increase in income by way of increased adoptions of the above-mentioned adaptation strategies (Seo, 2015d; Seo and Bakkensen, 2016).

The list of adaptation behaviors, measures, and strategies mentioned earlier make it clear that adaptation to climate change and global warming is induced by private incentives of an individual and achieves two goals simultaneously: first, reduction of vulnerability and damages to climatic changes and, second, reduction of GHG emissions. Furthermore, adaptation behaviors and strategies actively engage with and make the best use of technological innovations in tandem with new technologies becoming practical options over the course of the concerned policy timeline.

A fundamental question with regard to the adaptation paradigm of global warming policy responses is whether it will do the job of providing efficiently the global public good, in this case a stabilization of the global climate system (Seo, 2016c). In Chapter 6 of this book, the author will present an adaptation paradigm composed of an array of adaptation behaviors and measures that will be in the portfolio of behavioral and policy actions for accomplishing the task of putting a stop to an inexorable global warming.

The success of the adaptation paradigm in providing the global public good of climate stabilization is predicated on a number of factors. First, the phenomenon of global warming does not unfold abruptly, i.e., it does not rise sharply unexpectedly to individuals and scientists (NRC, 2013b). It is a gradual warming process over several decades and centuries to come. As such, individuals and capital investments can adjust in an optimal way to a series of gradual changes in the climate regime.

Second, a large array of adaptation strategies and measures is and will be adopted and put into practice in response to and in anticipation of a gradual unfolding of climatic changes (Mendelsohn, 2000; Hanemann, 2000). Individuals, businesses, and public sectors can take climatic changes into consideration in relevant long-term activities and projects. A changing climate will create an incentive for individuals, businesses, and public sectors to engage known and future adaptation options.

Third, the full set of technological options available now and in the future that could help societies and individuals deal with global warming are extensive. Both mighty breakthrough technologies and microincremental technologies will be available in large numbers over the course of the 21st century. In an adaptation paradigm of global warming policy responses, an individual and a business will have incentives to adopt the needed technologies in a gradual way in tandem with the phenomenon of global warming unfolding ever more severely.

Fourth, public sectors are given a mandate and therefore motivated to manage natural resources and protect the citizens "optimally" in the changing external conditions through climatic shifts. Therefore vital roles by the public sectors to be played at various levels of the government are guaranteed. A local government is concerned with managing efficiently natural resources that they own because it does not want its natural resources to become uncompetitive or deserted due to global warming. It does want to make the municipality a people's choice of destination for living and tourism under even a warmer-climate world. A local government can make important contributions to global warming adaptations of the municipality by reinforcing existing housing, roads, energy, and transportation regulations and infrastructure.

Fifth, existing international organizations devoted to climate change matters have important resources and incentives to make global warming responses worldwide meaningful for the planet as a whole. The organizations such as the United Nations, the World Bank, and the International Monetary Fund should be a place for international dialogues, coordination, and monitoring of global warming responses of the worldwide communities. The IPCC and the UNFCCC may continue to play a critical role on climate research and global negotiations. In Chapter 7 of this book, the author will outline future roles of the existing international organizations in facilitating adaptations of numerous climate actors and directions of future negotiations.

7. International Negotiations for a Global Public Good

From the perspectives of the adaptation paradigm of global warming policy responses, international negotiations during the past 3 decades for limiting the increase in the emissions of carbon dioxide, which have often faltered, can be reinterpreted and refocused. The Kyoto Protocol and the efforts to extend the Kyoto Protocol into the second phase have failed repeatedly (UNFCCC, 1998, 2007, 2009). The current status of the international negotiation processes is encapsulated in the Paris Agreement, which was signed at the end of year 2015 (UNFCCC, 2015). In Chapter 7 of this book, the author will provide a detailed review of the history of global negotiations thus far and international organizations such as the UNFCCC and the IPCC.

The process to arrive at the Paris Agreements was launched by climate negotiators in 2011 by the agreement of the Durban Platform for Enhanced Action signed in Durban, South Africa (UNFCCC, 2011a). Countries agreed in the city of Durban to initiate a negotiation process for an international climate protocol in which all parties of the convention should share legal responsibilities and to have such a protocol signed at the latest by the end of 2015 at the meeting then planned in Paris, France.

Negotiators came to an agreement in Paris entitled the Paris Agreement, which was widely lauded as a landmark global agreement or a turning point in global negotiations. The two crucial shortcomings of the Paris Agreements are also widely recognized. First, the agreement is based on voluntary commitments by participant countries called the Intended Nationally Determined Contributions (INDCs) proposals (UNFCCC, 2015). Considering all national circumstances, participating countries were asked to express their target levels of emission reductions to the UNFCCC. Whether these INDCs sum up to become a globally meaningful endeavor remains to be answered. The author will provide a comprehensive review of individual countries' INDC submissions and point out strategic natures of these countries' proposals.

The second critical shortcoming of the Paris Agreement recognized by the negotiators is that there is no legal obligation agreed to carry out any of countries' proposed INDCs (UNFCCC, 2015). There is no penalty for falling short of the INDC targets. Furthermore, monitoring of progresses in accomplishing the reduction commitments lies entirely in the hands of individual countries. Therefore there is no international monitoring or record keeping.

On another front of international negotiations led by the UNFCCC, negotiators and Conferences of Parties have increasingly embraced the critical roles of adaptation measures and strategies. At the back stage of the Copenhagen Conference in the city of Copenhagen in 2009, the Green Climate Fund (GCF) was announced as a monetary mechanism to help poor developing countries to cope with the devastating consequences climatic changes. It was agreed that the GCF will be funded by rich countries with the size of the fund over US$100 billion annually (UNFCCC, 2009). The GCF was formally established in Cancun, Mexico, the following year (UNFCCC, 2010). The GCF secretariat was formed and the city of Songdo in South Korea was selected among many competitors as the site of the headquarters of the GCF secretariat (UNFCCC, 2011b, 2012).

The GCF mechanism intends to establish the fund of US$100 billion by the year 2020 and thenceforth collect $100 billion annually from donors of rich countries. The amount of pledged contributions as of June 2016 falls far short of the ambition (GCF, 2016). The UNFCCC has announced that it will spend a half of US$100 billion on various adaptation programs and another half on mitigation programs in poor countries.

Because of the large size of the fund promised by the rich countries, the GCF has become the focal point of contention in the international negotiations since it was announced in Copenhagen in 2009. Parties of the convention from developing countries demanded a future GCF allocation of a fraction of the fund to their countries as a precondition for joining an international agreement. In fact, the INDC proposals from developing countries in many cases state their commitments of emissions reduction with and without the future allocations of the GCF fund to their countries (UNFCCC, 2015).

A more grave concern going forward with regard to the GCF policy scheme is that there are no guidelines and rules for allocating the large-size fund annually to a large number of countries and relevant programs (Seo, 2015c). There are no guidelines on which counties, which projects, and which sectors should receive the fund and by how much. It is not at all a handy task either to establish the principles and priorities in the allocations of the fund. At the worst case scenario, a GCF funding scheme can even discourage efficient adaptations by individuals or even encourage maladaptations by various actors, which will be one of the important topics to be dealt with in Chapter 7 (Seo, 2015c).

Taking into consideration the current status of international agreements and various policy instruments developed up to now, what should be future directions of international negotiations and ideal roles of international organizations? In the final chapter, the author puts forth a number of ideas on this regard with an emphasis on accomplishing humanity's efficient adaptations to global warming.

8. Road Map of the Book

The book is structured with the following chapters. In Chapter 1, the author provides an introduction to the behavioral economics of climate change, encompassing all the major topics analyzed throughout the book, including global public goods, global warming policy challenges, carbon price, technological innovations, an adaptation paradigm of global warming policy responses, and the UNFCCC policy negotiations.

Chapters 2 and 3 are devoted to theoretical and conceptual aspects of global public goods and global warming. The author provides in Chapter 2 a comprehensive review of the economics literature on public goods and their efficient provisions. Discussed in the chapter are classical theories of public goods and club goods, salient examples of public goods especially in the fields of environmental pollution, market failures, various standard policy instruments for correcting inefficient provisions of public goods, bargaining solution and other nonstandard policy instruments, and global public goods.

Chapter 3 is concerned with policy challenges of global warming. The chapter begins with distinct characteristics of global warming and contrasts with other major global public goods. The range of policy challenges covered in the chapter includes heterogeneity in damages, heterogeneity in economic status of countries, heterogeneity in abatement costs, a club provision, a compensation and transfer scheme, uncertainty and extremes, time preferences, and governance. These challenges and proposed remedies to standard policy instruments to overcome these challenges are discussed in the Samuelson—Nordhaus framework of global warming policy making.

From Chapters 4 to 7, the author deals with analytical and empirical aspects of global warming policy responses. Chapter 4 provides an analysis of the carbon price (tax) approach, the standard policy instrument for global warming policy responses, using a variety of Integrated Assessment Models (IAMs) of global warming (Nordhaus, 1991; Manne et al., 1995). A full description of the DIC/RICE [Dynamically (Regionally) Integrated model of Climate and Economy] model, the most well-established IAM of all, is given (Nordhaus, 1992, 1994, 2008, 2013). Using a modified DICE model, the author provides an analysis of behavioral consequences of a global carbon tax policy. The analyses in the chapter highlight that there is no Nash equilibrium in climate negotiations in which the parties of the convention act in a noncooperative manner (Nash, 1950, 1951; Seo, 2012a).

In Chapter 5, switching the tone of the book temporarily from economics of climate change to engineering, the author provides a broad review of technological options that are predicted to hold promises in addressing the challenges of global warming. The range of technologies includes both breakthrough technologies and microincremental technologies. Examples of the former are nuclear fusion, carbon-capture-storage, climate engineering, solar energy, ocean fertilization, and new lighting methods, among other things. The author also makes a point that microincremental technologies can play a crucial role in individuals' adaptation responses to global warming.

In the chapter, the author emphasizes that a technological solution is neither a panacea nor a cost-effective means for achieving an economic and social goal. The economic questions that must be answered with regard to a technological approach are elaborated: how to induce technological innovations and how to motivate individuals and businesses to adopt these technologies.

Chapter 6 is devoted to establishing an adaptation paradigm of global warming policy responses in which both adapting behaviors to changes in climate regimes and abatement behaviors of GHGs are integrated. The conceptual framework of the adaptation paradigm is provided, along with a sample of adaptation measures and strategies, drawing from existing research, which are projected to be unfolded gradually over time in the near term, medium term, and long term. The author presents a trajectory of carbon emissions control rate through the 21st century as well as a trajectory of global temperature increase under the adaptation paradigm.

The final chapter, Chapter 7, provides a critical review of historical challenges, achievements, and failures of global warming negotiations for the past 3 decades at the level of the UNFCCC. Major outcomes and agreements from the Kyoto Protocol, Copenhagen Accord, Durban Platform, and Paris Agreements are put together within historical contexts, with an emphasis on the Paris Agreements, which is the current international policy framework. Developments in the establishment of the GCF and future challenges are surveyed. Two non-UNFCCC agreements pertinent to global climate change responses are included in the chapter: the amended Montreal Protocol and the Carbon Offsetting and Reduction Scheme for International Aviation (UNEP, 2016; ICAO, 2016). The final chapter is concluded with the author's predictions and suggestions of future directions in global policy negotiations in the framework of behavioral economics of adaptation to climate change developed throughout the book.

Acknowledgments and Recommendations

This book is written as a comprehensive treatise on the economics of climate change from the perspectives of the adaptation paradigm of global warming policy responses. The book encompasses all major topics of global warming economics and policy making. It is written thoroughly on the economic theories of global warming and empirical models of global warming economics. These features of the book make it a suitable textbook for a graduate course on climate change economics or environmental economics.

In addition, the book is written to present an alternative policy framework rooted on behavioral decisions of individuals. The author provides a comprehensive review of an array of policy instruments, experiences with various policies, and an alternative policy framework. The book is thorough on policy negotiations at the UNFCCC level while many of the important policy efforts in the United States and the European Union are highlighted throughout the book. These aspects of the book will make it a worthy reading for policy makers, practitioners, and anyone who is interested in keeping pace with policy negotiations.

The author has had the honor of personally learning from preeminent scholars on climate change economics. Among them are William Nordhaus and Robert Mendelsohn both of whom occupy an indispensable place in the literature on climate change economics as well as in the theories presented in this book. I owe them much gratitude. The author also would like to acknowledge numerous important scholarly exchanges on the topics addressed in this book with Robert Evenson, Daniel Esty, Kerry Emanuel, and Laura Bakkensen.

Finally, the author would like to express deep appreciation to the Elsevier editorial team who has done an outstanding work on making this book a reality. I owe special thanks to Scott Bentley and anonymous reviewers who provided valuable comments during the preparation of the prospectus of the book.

References

Adams, R., Rosenzweig, C., Peart, R.M., Ritchie, J.T., McCarl, B.A., Glyer, J.D., Curry, R.B., Jones, J.W., Boote, K.J., Allen, L.H., 1990. Global climate change and US agriculture. Nature 345, 219–224.

Aksoy, S., Attardo, G., et al., 2014. Genome sequence of the Tsetse fly (*Glossina morsitans*): vector of African Trypanosomiasis. Science 344 (6182), 380–386.

Ainsworth, E.A., Long, S.P., 2005. What have we learned from 15 years of free-air CO_2 enrichment (FACE)? A meta-analysis of the responses of photosynthesis, canopy properties and plant production to rising CO_2. New Phytologist 165, 351–372.

Akasaki, I., Amano, H., Nakamura, S., 2014. Blue LEDs — Filling the World with New Light. Nobel Prize Lecture. The Nobel Foundation, Stockholm. Available at: http://www. nobelprize.org/nobel_prizes/physics/laureates/2014/popular-physicsprize2014.pdf.

Akerlof, G.A., Shiller, R.J., 2009. Animal Spirits: How Human Psychology Drives the Economy, and Why it Matters for Global Capitalism. Princeton University Press, New Jersey.

Akerlof, G.A., Shiller, R.J., 2015. Phishing for Phools: The Economics of Manipulation and Deception. Princeton University Press, New Jersey.

Arrow, K.J., Cline, W.R., Maler, K.G., Munasinghe, M., Squitieri, R., Stiglitz, J., 1996. Intertemporal equity, discounting, and economic efficiency. In: Bruce, J.P., Lee, H., Haites, E.F. (Eds.), Climate Change 1995: Economic and Social Dimensions of Climate Change. Cambridge University Press, Cambridge.

Arrhenius, S.A., 1896. On the influence of carbonic acid in the air upon the temperature of the ground. Philosophical Magazine 41, 237−276.

Barreca, A., Clay, K., Deschenes, O., Greenstone, M., Shapiro, J.S., 2016. Adapting to climate change: the remarkable decline in the US temperature-mortality relationship over the twentieth century. Journal of Political Economy 124, 105−159.

Barrett, S., 2008. The incredible economics of geoengineering. Environmental and Resource Economics 39, 45−54.

Barrett, S., 2010. Why Cooperate?: The Incentive to Supply Global Public Goods. Oxford University Press, Oxford.

Baumol, W.J., Oates, O.A., 1988. The Theory of Environmental Policy, second ed. Cambridge University Press, Cambridge.

Broecker, W.S., 1997. Thermohaline circulation, the Achilles Heel of our climate system: will man-made CO_2 upset the current balance? Science 278, 1582−1588.

Buchanan, J.M., 1965. An economic theory of clubs. Economica 32, 1−24.

Buchanan, J.M., 1968. The Demand and Supply of Public Goods. Rand McNally & Co., Chicago.

Carraro, C., Eyckmans, J., Finus, N., 2006. Optimal transfers and participation decisions in international environmental agreements. Review of International Organizations 1, 379−396.

Carson, R., 1962. Silent Spring. Houghton Mifflin, Boston.

Chapman, C.R., Morrison, D., 1994. Impacts on the earth by asteroids and comets: assessing the hazard. Nature 367, 33−40.

Coase, R., 1960. The problem of social costs. Journal of Law and Economics 3, 1−44.

Denman, K.L., Brasseur, G., Chidthaisong, A., Ciais, P., Cox, P.M., Dickinson, R.E., Hauglustaine, D., Heinze, C., Holland, E., Jacob, D., Lohmann, U., Ramachandran, S., da Silva Dias, P.L., Wofsy, S.C., Zhang, X., 2007. Couplings between changes in the climate system and biogeochemistry. In: Solomon, S., Qin, D., Manning, M., Chen, Z., Marquis, M., Averyt, K.B., Tignor, M., Miller, H.L. (Eds.), Climate Change 2007: The Physical Science Basis. The Fourth Assessment Report of the Intergovernmental Panel on Climate Change. Cambridge University Press, Cambridge.

European Commission (EC), 2016. Climate-Friendly Alternatives to HFCs and HCFCs. EC, Brussels, Belgium. Available at: http://ec.europa.eu/clima/policies/f-gas/alternatives/index_en.htm.

Ellerman, A.D., Buchner, B.K., 2007. The European Union Emissions Trading Scheme: origins, allocations, and early results. Review of Environmental Economics and Policy 1, 66−87.

Emanuel, K., 2008. The hurricane-climate connection. Bulletin of the American Meteorological Society 89, ES10−ES20.

Evenson, R., Gollin, D., 2003. Assessing the impact of the green revolution 1960−2000. Science 300, 758−762.

Fabozzi, F.J., Modigliani, F.G., Jones, F.J., 2009. Foundations of Financial Markets and Institutions, fourth ed. Prentice Hall, New York.

Gillingham, K., Newell, R.G., Pizer, W.A., 2008. Modeling endogenous technological change for climate policy analysis. Energy Economics 30, 2734−2753.

Global Carbon Project (GCP), 2014. Global Carbon Budget 2014. Available at: http://cdiac.ornl. gov/GCP/.

Goulder, L., 2007. California's bold new climate policy. Economist Voice 4. Article 5.

Goulder, L., Mathai, K., 2000. Optimal CO_2 abatement in the presence of induced technological change. Journal of Environmental Economics and Management 39, 1−38.

Graziano, M., Gillingham, K., 2015. Spatial patterns of solar photovoltaic system adoption: the influence of neighbors and the built environment. Journal of Economic Geography 15, 815−839.

Green Climate Fund (GCF), 2016. Status of Pledges and Contributions Made to the Green Climate Fund. Status Date: 23 July 2015. GCF, Songdo City, South Korea.

Guardian, 2016. Earth Woefully Unprepared for Surprise Comet or Asteroid, NASA Scientist Warns, 13 December 2016. Available at: https://www.theguardian.com/science/2016/dec/13/space-asteroid-comet-nasa-rocket.

Hahn, G.L., Gaughan, J.B., Mader, T.L., Eigenberg, R.A., 2009. Chapter 5: Thermal indices and their applications for livestock environments. In: DeShazer, J.A. (Ed.), Livestock Energetics and Thermal Environmental Management. American Society of Agricultural and Biological Engineers, St. Joseph, Michigan, pp. 113−130.

Hanemann, W.M., 2000. Adaptation and its management. Climatic Change 45, 511−581.

Hansen, J., Johnson, D., Lacis, A., Lebedeff, S., Lee, P., Rind, D., Russell, G., 1981. Climate impact of increasing atmospheric carbon dioxide. Science 213, 957−966.

Hansen, J., Sato, M., Reudy, R., Lo, K., Lea, D.W., Medina-Elizade, M., 2006. Global temperature change. Proceedings of the National Academies of Sciences USA 103, 14288−14293.

Hardin, G., 1968. The tragedy of the commons. Science 162, 1243−1248.

Hartwick, J.M., Olewiler, N.D., 1997. The Economics of Natural Resource Use, second ed. Pearson, New York.

Heal, G., 2010. Reflections: the economics of renewable energy in the United States. Review of Environmental Economics and Policy 4, 139−154.

Hirshleifer, J., 1983. From weakest-link to best-shot: the voluntary provision of public goods. Public Choice 41, 371−386.

International Civil Aviation Organization (ICAO), 2016. Carbon Offsetting and Reduction Scheme for International Aviation (CORSIA). ICAO, Montreal, Canada.

IIASA (International Institute of Applied Systems Analysis) World Population Program, 2007. Probabilistic Projections by 13 World Regions, Forecast Period 2000−2100, 2001 revision. IIASA, Vienna, Austria. Available online at: http://www.iiasa.ac.at/Research/POP/proj01/.

International Energy Agency (IEA), 2013. Technology Roadmap: Carbon Capture and Storage. IEA, France.

Intergovernmental Panel on Climate Change (IPCC), 1990. Climate Change: The IPCC Scientific Assessment. Cambridge University Press, Cambridge.

Intergovernmental Panel on Climate Change (IPCC), 2005a. Special Report on Carbon Dioxide Capture and Storage. Cambridge University Press, Cambridge.

Intergovernmental Panel on Climate Change (IPCC), 2005b. Special Report on Safeguarding the Ozone Layer and the Global Climate System: Issues Related to Hydrofluorocarbons and Perfluorocarbons. Cambridge University Press, Cambridge.

Intergovernmental Panel on Climate Change (IPCC), 2011. Special Report on Renewable Energy Sources and Climate Change Mitigation. Cambridge University Press, Cambridge.

Intergovernmental Panel on Climate Change (IPCC), 2014a. Climate Change 2014: The Physical Science Basis, The Fifth Assessment Report of the IPCC. Cambridge University Press, Cambridge.

Intergovernmental Panel on Climate Change (IPCC), 2014b. Climate Change 2014: Impacts, Adaptation, Vulnerabilities, The Fifth Assessment Report of the IPCC. Cambridge University Press, Cambridge.

International Thermonuclear Experimental Reactor (ITER), 2015. ITER: The World's Largest Tokamak. Available at: https://www.iter.org/mach.

Joskow, P.L., 2012. Creating a smarter U.S. electricity grid. Journal of Economic Perspectives 26, 29–48.

Kahneman, D., Tversky, A., 1979. Prospect theory: an analysis of decision under risk. Econometrica 47, 263–291.

Kala, N., 2015. Ambiguity Aversion and Learning in a Changing World: The Potential Effects of Climate Change from Indian Agriculture (Ph.D. dissertation). Yale University, New Haven, CT.

Kaul, I., Conceicao, P., Goulven, K.L., Mendoza, R.U. (Eds.), 2003. Providing Global Public Goods: Managing Globalization. Oxford University Press, Oxford.

Keeling, C.D., Piper, S.C., Bacastow, R.B., Wahlen, M., Whorf, T.P., Heimann, M., Meijer, H.A., 2005. Atmospheric CO_2 and $^{13}CO_2$ exchange with the terrestrial biosphere and oceans from 1978 to 2000: observations and carbon cycle implications. In: Ehleringer, J.R., Cerling, T.E., Dearing, M.D. (Eds.), A History of Atmospheric CO_2 and Its Effects on Plants, Animals, and Ecosystems. SpringerVerlag, New York, pp. 83–113.

Kolstad, C.D., 1996. Learning and stock effects in environmental pollution: the case of greenhouse gas emissions. Journal of Environmental Economics and Management 31, 1–18.

Kotchen, M., Moore, M.R., 2007. Private provision of environmental public goods: household participation in green-electricity programs. Journal of Environmental Economics and Management 53, 1–16.

Kotchen, M.J., 2009. Voluntary provision of public goods for bads: a theory of environmental offsets. Economic Journal 119, 883–899.

Kurukulasuriya, P., Kala, N., Mendelsohn, R., 2011. Adaptation and climate change impacts: a structural Ricardian model of irrigation and farm income in Africa. Climate Change Economics 2, 149–174.

Lackner, K.S., Brennana, S., Matter, J.M., Park, A.A., Wright, A., Zwaan, B.V., 2012. The urgency of the development of CO_2 capture from ambient air. Proceedings of the National Academy of Sciences USA 109 (33), 13156–13162.

Lawrence Livermore National Laboratory (LLNL), 2015. How NIF Works. Available at: https://lasers.llnl.gov/about/how-nif-works.

Leopold, A., 1949. A Sand County Almanac: And Sketches Here and There. Oxford University Press, New York.

Le Treut, H., Somerville, R., Cubasch, U., Ding, Y., Mauritzen, C., Mokssit, A., Peterson, T., Prather, M., 2007. Historical overview of climate change. In: Solomon, S., Qin, D., Manning, M., Chen, Z., Marquis, M., Averyt, K.B., Tignor, M., Miller, H.L. (Eds.), Climate Change 2007: The Physical Science Basis. The Fourth Assessment Report of the Intergovernmental Panel on Climate Change. Cambridge University Press, Cambridge.

Lobell, D., Schlenker, W., Costa-Roberts, J., 2011. Climate trends and global crop production since 1980. Science 333, 616–620.

Lutz, W., Butz, W., KC, S. (Eds.), 2014. World Population and Global Human Capital in the 21st Century. Oxford University Press, Oxford.

MacCracken,, C.N., Edmonds, J.A., Kim, S.H., Sands, R.D., 1999. The economics of the Kyoto Protocol. The Energy Journal 20, 25–71 (special issue).

Mann, M.E., Bradley, R.S., Hughes, M.K., 1999. Northern hemisphere temperatures during the past millennium: inferences, uncertainties, and limitations. Geophysical Research Letters 26, 759–762.

Manne, A.S., Mendelsohn, R., Richels, R.G., 1995. MERGE: a model for evaluating regional and global effects of GHG reduction policies. Energy Policy 23, 17–34.

Martin, J.H., Coale, K.H., Johnson, K.S., Fitzwater, S.E., et al., 1994. Testing the iron hypothesis in ecosystems of the equatorial Pacific Ocean. Nature 371, 123–129.

Mas-Colell, A., Whinston, M.D., Green, J.R., 1995. Microeconomic Theory. Oxford University Press, Oxford.

Massachusetts Institute of Technology (MIT), 2015. The Future of Solar Energy: An Interdisciplinary MIT Study. MIT, MA.

McConnell, V., 2013. The New CAFÉ Standards: Are They Enough on Their Own? Resources for the Future Discussion Paper 13-14. Washington, DC.

Mendelsohn, R., 1980. An economic analysis of air pollution from coal-fired power plants. Journal of Environmental Economics and Management 7, 30–43.

Mendelsohn, R., 2000. Efficient adaptation to climate change. Climatic Change 45, 583–600.

Mendelsohn, R., Neumann, J., 1999. The Impact of Climate Change on the United States Economy. Cambridge University Press, Cambridge.

Mendelsohn, R., Nordhaus, W., Shaw, D., 1994. The impact of global warming on agriculture: a Ricardian analysis. American Economic Review 84, 753–771.

Mendelsohn, R., Williams, L., 2007. Dynamic forecasts of the sectoral impacts of climate change. In: Schlesinger, M.E., Kheshgi, H.S., Smith, J., Chesnaye, F.C., Reilly, J.M., Wilson, T., Kolstad, C. (Eds.), Human-Induced Climate Change: An Interdisciplinary Approach. Cambridge University Press, Cambridge.

Mendelsohn, R., Olmstead, S., 2009. The economic valuation of environmental amenities and disamenities: methods and applications. Annual Review of Resources 34, 325–347.

Metcalf, G., 2009. Designing a carbon tax to reduce US greenhouse gas emissions. Review of Environmental Economics and Policy 3, 63–83.

Montgomery, W.D., 1972. Markets in licenses and efficient pollution control programs. Journal of Economic Theory 5, 395–418.

Muller, N.Z., Mendelsohn, R., 2009. Efficient pollution regulation: getting the prices right. American Economic Review 99, 1714–1739.

Nakicenovic, N., Davidson, O., Davis, G., Grübler, A., Kram, T., La Rovere, E.L., Metz, B., Morita, T., Pepper, W., Pitcher, H., Sankovski, A., Shukla, P., Swart, R., Watson, R., Dadi, Z., 2000. Emissions Scenarios. A special report of working group III of the Intergovernmental Panel on Climate Change, Geneva, Switzerland.

National Aeronautics and Space Administration (NASA), 2007. Near-Earth Object Survey and Deflection: Analysis of Alternatives. Report to Congress. NASA, Washington, DC. http://www.nasa.gov/pdf/171331main_NEO_report_march07.pdf.

NASA, 2016a. Current Missions. Jet Propulsion Laboratory, NASA. NASA, Washington, DC. Available at: http://www.jpl.nasa.gov/missions/?type=current.

NASA, 2016b. Vital Signs of the Planet. NASA, Washington, DC. Available at: http://climate.nasa.gov/.

Nash, J., 1950. Equilibrium points in n-person games. Proceedings of the National Academy of Sciences USA 36, 48–49.

Nash, J., 1951. Non-cooperative games. The Annals of Mathematics 54 (2), 286–295.

Neumann, Jv, Morgenstern, O., 1953. Theory of Games and Economic Behavior. Princeton University Press, Princeton, NJ.

Newell, R., Pizer, W., 2001. Discounting the Benefits of Climate Change Mitigation: How Much Do Uncertain Rates Increase Valuations? Pew Center, Washington, DC.

Nicholls, R.J., Cazenave, A., 2010. Sea-level rise and its impact on coastal zones. Science 328, 1517–1520.

NOAA National Centers for Environmental Information (NCEI), 2016. State of the Climate: National Overview for Annual 2015 published online January 2016, retrieved on September 9, 2016 from. http://www.ncdc.noaa.gov/sotc/national/201513.

Nordhaus, W., 1973. The allocation of energy resources. Brookings Papers on Economic Activities 1973, 529–576.

Nordhaus, W., 1977. The economic growth and climate: the carbon dioxide problem. American Economic Review 67, 341–346.

Nordhaus, W., 1982. How fast should we graze the global commons? American Economic Review 72, 242–246.

Nordhaus, W., 1991. To slow or not to slow: the economics of the greenhouse effects. The Economic Journal 101, 920–937.

Nordhaus, W., 1992. An optimal transition path for controlling greenhouse gases. Science 258, 1315–1319.

Nordhaus, W., 1994. Managing the Global Commons. MIT Press, Massachusetts.

Nordhaus, W., 2002. Modeling induced innovation in climate change policy. In: Grubler, A., Nakicenovic, N., Nordhaus, W. (Eds.), Technological Change and the Environment. Resources For the Future Press, Washington, DC.

Nordhaus, W.D., 2006. Paul Samuelson and global public goods. In: Szenberg, M., Ramrattan, L., Gottesman, A.A. (Eds.), Samuelsonian Economics and the Twenty-First Century. Oxford Scholarship Online.

Nordhaus, W., 2007a. To tax or not to tax: alternative approaches to slowing global warming. Review of Environmental Economics and Policy 1 (1), 26–44.

Nordhaus, W.D., 2007b. Two centuries of productivity growth in computing. Journal of Economic History 67 (1), 128–159.

Nordhaus, W.D., 2008. A Question of Balance—Weighing the Options on Global Warming Policies. Yale University Press, New Haven.

Nordhaus, W., 2010. Economic aspects of global warming in a post-Copenhagen environment. Proceedings of the National Academy of Sciences USA 107 (26), 11721–11726.

Nordhaus, W., 2011. The architecture of climate economics: designing a global agreement on global warming. Bulletin of Atomic Scientists 67 (1), 9–18.

Nordhaus, W., 2013. The Climate Casino: Risk, Uncertainty, and Economics for a Warming World. Yale University Press, New Haven.

Nordhaus, W., 2015. Climate clubs: overcoming free-riding in international climate policy, 105 (4), 1339–1370.

National Research Council (NRC), 2013a. Transitions to Alternative Vehicles and Fuels. The National Academies Press, Washington, DC.

National Research Council (NRC), 2013b. Abrupt Impacts of Climate Change: Anticipating Surprises. Committee on Understanding and Monitoring Abrupt Climate Change and Its Impacts. The National Academies Press, Washington, DC.

National Research Council (NRC), 2015. Climate Intervention: Reflecting Sunlight to Cool Earth. Committee on Geoengineering Climate: Technical Evaluation and Discussion of Impacts. The National Academies Press, Washington, DC.

Ohlin, B., 1933. Interregional and International Trade. Harvard University Press, Cambridge, MA.

Olmstead, A.L., Rhode, P.W., 2011. Adapting North American wheat production to climatic changes, 1839–2009. Proceedings of the National Academy of Sciences USA 108, 480–485.

Oppenheimer, M., Alley, R.B., 2005. Ice sheets, global warming, and Article 2 of the UNFCCC. Climatic Change 68, 257–267.

Ostrom, E., 1990. Governing the Commons: The Evolution of Institutions for Collective Action. Cambridge University Press, Cambridge.

Ostrom, E., 2009. Beyond Markets and States: Polycentric Governance of Complex Economic Systems. Nobel Lecture. The Royal Swedish Academy of the Sciences, Sweden.

Pigou, A.C., 1920. Economics of Welfare. Macmillan and Co., London.

Pizer, W., 1999. Optimal choice of climate change policy in the presence of uncertainty. Resource and Energy Economics 21, 255−287.

Popp, D., 2004. ENTICE: endogenous technological change in the DICE model of global warming. Journal of Environmental Economics and Management 48, 742−768.

Posner, R.A., 2004. Catastrophe: Risk and Response. Oxford University Press, New York.

Revelle, R., Suess, H.E., 1957. Carbon dioxide exchange between atmosphere and ocean and the question of an increase of atmospheric CO_2 during the past decades. Tellus 9, 18−27.

Ricardo, D., 1817. On the Principles of Political Economy and Taxation. John Murray, London.

Rosenzweig, C., Parry, M., 1994. Potential impact of climate change on world food supply. Nature 367, 133−138.

Samuelson, P., 1954. The pure theory of public expenditure. The Review of Economics and Statistics 36, 387−389.

Samuelson, P., 1955. Diagrammatic exposition of a theory of public expenditure. Review of Economics and Statistics 37, 350−356.

Samuelson, P., Nordhaus, W., 2009. Economics, nineteenth ed. McGraw-Hill Education, New York.

Sandler, T., 1997. Global Challenges: An Approach to Environmental, Political, and Economic Problems. Cambridge University Press, Cambridge.

Schaefer, H., Fletcher, S.E.M., Veidt, C., et al., 2016. A 21st century shift from fossil-fuel to biogenic methane emissions indicated by $^{13}CH_4$. Science 352, 80−84.

Schlenker, W., Hanemann, M., Fisher, A., 2005. Will US agriculture really benefit from global warming? Accounting for irrigation in the hedonic approach. American Economic Review 95, 395−406.

Schlenker, W., Roberts, M., 2009. Nonlinear temperature effects indicate severe damages to crop yields under climate change. Proceedings of the National Academy of Sciences USA 106 (37), 15594−15598.

Schlesinger, W.H., 1997. Biogeochemistry: An Analysis of Global Change, second ed. Academic Press, San Diego.

Seo, S.N., 2006. Modeling Farmer Responses to Climate Change: Climate Change Impacts and Adaptations in Livestock Management in Africa (Ph.D. dissertation). Yale University, New Haven.

Seo, S.N., 2007. Is Stern review on climate change alarmist? Energy and Environment 18, 521−532.

Seo, S.N., 2010a. Is an integrated farm more resilient against climate change? A microeconometric analysis of portfolio diversification in African agriculture. Food Policy 35, 32−40.

Seo, S.N., 2010b. A microeconometric analysis of adapting portfolios to climate change: adoption of agricultural systems in Latin America. Applied Economic Perspectives and Policy 32, 489−514.

Seo, S.N., 2010c. Managing forests, livestock, and crops under global warming: a microeconometric analysis of land use in Africa. Australian Journal of Agricultural and Resource Economics 54, 239−258.

Seo, S.N., 2012a. What eludes global agreements on climate change? Economic Affairs 32, 73–79.

Seo, S.N., 2012b. Adapting natural resource enterprises under global warming in South America: a mixed logit analysis. Economia: Journal of the Latin American and Caribbean Economic Association 12, 111–135.

Seo, S.N., 2012c. Decision making under climate risks: an analysis of sub-Saharan farmers' adaptation behaviors. Weather, Climate, and Society 4, 285–299.

Seo, S.N., 2013a. Economics of global warming as a global public good: private incentives and smart adaptations. Regional Science Policy and Practice 5, 83–95.

Seo, S.N., 2013b. An essay on the impact of climate change on US agriculture: weather fluctuations, climatic shifts, and adaptation strategies. Climate Change 121, 115–124.

Seo, S.N., 2014a. Evaluation of agro-ecological zone methods for the study of climate change with micro farming decisions in sub-Saharan Africa. European Journal of Agronomy 52, 157–165.

Seo, S.N., 2014b. Adapting sensibly when global warming turns the field brown or blue: a comment on the 2014 IPCC Report. Economic Affairs 34, 399–401.

Seo, S.N., 2015a. Micro-Behavioral Economics of Global Warming: Modeling Adaptation Strategies in Agricultural and Natural Resource Enterprises. Springer, Cham, Switzerland.

Seo, S.N., 2015b. Adaptation to global warming as an optimal transition process to a greenhouse world. Economic Affairs 35, 272–284.

Seo, S.N., 2015c. Helping low-latitude poor countries with climate change. Regulation. Winter 2015–2016, 6–8.

Seo, S.N., 2015d. Fatalities of neglect: adapt to more intense hurricanes? International Journal of Climatology 35, 3505–3514.

Seo, S.N., 2016a. Modeling farmer adaptations to climate change in South America: a micro-behavioral economic perspective. Environmental and Ecological Statistics 23, 1–21.

Seo, S.N., 2016b. The micro-behavioral framework for estimating total damage of global warming on natural resource enterprises with full adaptations. Journal of Agricultural, Biological, and Environmental Statistics 21, 328–347.

Seo, S.N., 2016c. A theory of global public goods and their provisions. Journal of Public Affairs. http://dx.doi.org/10.1002/pa.1601.

Seo, S.N., 2016d. Microbehavioral Econometric Methods: Theories, Models, and Applications for the Study of Environmental and Natural Resources. Academic Press (Elsevier, Amsterdam.

Seo, S.N., Mendelsohn, R., 2008. Measuring impacts and adaptations to climate change: a structural Ricardian model of African livestock management. Agricultural Economics 38, 151–165.

Seo, S.N., Bakkensen, L.A., 2016. Did adaptation strategies work? High fatalities from tropical cyclones in the North Indian Ocean and future vulnerability under global warming. Natural Hazards 82, 1341–1355.

Shiller, R.J., 2005. Irrational Exuberance, second ed. Princeton University Press, NJ.

Shiller, R., 2009. Subprime Solution: How Today's Global Financial Crisis Happened and What to Do About it. Princeton University Press, New Jersey.

Smith, A., 1776. An Inquiry Into the Nature and Causes of the Wealth of Nations. W. Strahan and T. Cadell, London.

Smith, V.K., 2008. Reflections on the literature. Review of Environmental Economics and Policy 2 (2), 292–308.

Smith, V.K., Huang, J.-C., 1995. Can markets value air quality? A meta-analysis of hedonic property value models. Journal of Political Economy 103, 209–227.

Soussana, J.F., Tallec, Blanfort, V., 2010. Mitigating the greenhouse gas balance of ruminant production systems through carbon sequestration in grasslands. Animal: An International Journal of Animal Bioscience 4, 334−350.

Stavins, R., 1998. What can we learn from the grand policy experiment? Lessons from SO_2 allowance trading. Journal of Economic Perspectives 12, 69−88.

Stavins, R., 2007. A US Cap-and-Trade System to Address Global Climate Change. Hamilton Project Discussion Paper 2007-13. The Brookings Institution, Washington, DC.

Stern, N., 2009. The Economics of Climate Change: The Stern Review. Cambridge University Press, Cambridge.

Stiglitz, J.E., 2006. Making Globalization Work. W.W. Norton & Company, New York.

Taylor, K.E., Stouffer, R.J., Meehl, G.A., 2012. An overview of CMIP5 and the experiment design. Bulletin of the American Meteorological Society 93, 485−498.

Thaler, R.H., 2015. Misbehaving: The Making of Behavioral Economics. W.W. Norton Company, New York.

Tietenberg, T., 1980. Transferable discharge permits and the control of stationary source air pollution: a survey and synthesis. Land Economics 56, 391−416.

Tietenberg, T., 2013. Reflections − carbon pricing in practice. Review of Environmental Economics and Policy 7, 313−329.

Titley, D.W., Hegerl, G., Jacobs, K.L., Mote, P.W., Paciorek, C.J., Shepherd, J.M., Shepherd, T.G., Sobel, A.H., Walsh, J., Zwiers, F.W., Thomas, K., Everett, L., Purcell, A., Gaskins, R., Markovich, E., 2016. Attribution of Extreme Weather Events in the Context of Climate Change. The National Academies of Sciences, Engineering, and Medicine. The National Academies Press, Washington, DC.

Tol, R.S.J., 2009. The economic effects of climate change. Journal of Economic Perspectives 23, 29−51.

Tol, R.S.J., 2014. Climate Economics: Economic Analysis of Climate, Climate Change and Climate Policy. Edward Elgar, London.

University of Alabama at Huntsville (UAH), 2016. Global Temperature Record. Available at: http://nsstc.uah.edu/climate/.

United Nations Environmental Programme (UNEP), 2016. Handbook for the Montreal Protocol on Substances that Deplete the Ozone Layer. UNEP, Nairobi.

United Nations Framework Convention on Climate Change (UNFCCC), 1992. United Nations Framework Convention on Climate Change. New York.

United Nations Framework Convention on Climate Change (UNFCCC), 1998. Kyoto Protocol to the United Nations Framework Convention on Climate Change. UNFCCC, New York.

United Nations Framework Convention on Climate Change (UNFCCC), 2007. Report of the Conference of the Parties on Its Thirteenth Session, Held in Bali from 3 to 15 December 2007. UNFCCC, New York.

United Nations Framework Convention on Climate Change (UNFCCC), 2009. Copenhagen Accord. UNFCCC, New York.

United Nations Framework Convention on Climate Change (UNFCCC), 2010. Cancun Agreements. UNFCCC, New York.

United Nations Framework Convention on Climate Change (UNFCCC), 2011a. The Durban Platform for Enhanced Action. UNFCCC, New York.

United Nations Framework Convention on Climate Change (UNFCCC), 2011b. Report of the Transitional Committee for the Design of Green Climate Fund. UNFCCC, New York.

United Nations Framework Convention on Climate Change (UNFCCC), 2012. Decisions Adopted by the Conference of the Parties on Its Eighteenth Session, Held in Doha from 26 November to 8 December 2012. UNFCCC, New York.

United Nations Framework Convention on Climate Change (UNFCCC), 2015. The Paris Agreement. Conference of the Parties (COP) 21. UNFCCC, New York.

United States Department of Energy (US DOE), 2008. Genomics and Its Impact on Science and Society: The Human Genome Project and Beyond. Human Genome Program. US DOE, Washington, DC.

United States Department of Energy (US DOE), 2015. Waste Isolation Pilot Project (WIPP). US DOE, Washington, DC. Available at: http://www.wipp.energy.gov/.

United States Environmental Protection Agency (US EPA), 1990. The Clean Air Act Amendments. US EPA, Washington, DC.

United States Environmental Protection Agency (US EPA), 2006. Global mitigation of non-CO_2 greenhouse gases. US EPA, Washington, DC.

United States Environmental Protection Agency (US EPA), 2010. The 40th Anniversary of the Clean Air Act. US EPA, Washington, DC. Available at: http://www.epa.gov/airprogm/oar/caa/40th.html.

United States Environmental Protection Agency (US EPA), 2014. National Emissions Inventory (NEI) 2014. US EPA, Washington, DC.

United States House of Representatives, 2009. H.R.2454-American Clean Energy and Security Act of 2009. US House of Representatives, Washington, DC.

Viscusi, W.K., Aldy, J.E., 2003. The value of a statistical life: a critical review of market estimates throughout the world. Journal of Risk and Uncertainty 5, 5−76.

Wagner, G., Weitzman, M.L., 2015. Climate Shock: The Economic Consequences of a Hotter Planet. Princeton University Press, New Jersey.

Weitzman, M.L., 2009. On modeling and interpreting the economics of catastrophic climate change. Review of Economics and Statistics 91, 1−19.

White House, 2013. The President's Climate Action Plan. Executive Office of the President. The White House, Washington, DC.

White House, 2017. Presidential Memorandum Regarding Withdrawal of the United States from the Trans-Pacific Partnership Negotiations and Agreement. The White House, Washington, DC.

World Health Organization (WHO), 2016a. Global Atlas of Infectious Diseases. WHO, Italy. Available at: http://apps.who.int/globalatlas/.

World Health Organization (WHO), 2016b. Global Health Observatory Data Repository: Life Expectancy. WHO, Italy. Available at: http://apps.who.int/gho/data/view.main. SDG2016LEXv?lang=en.

Further Reading

Houghton, R.A., 2008. Carbon flux to the atmosphere from land-use changes: 1850−2005. In: Trends: A Compendium of Data on Global Change. Carbon Dioxide Information Analysis Center, Oak Ridge National Laboratory, U.S. Department of Energy, Oak Ridge, TN.

Muller, N.Z., Mendelsohn, R., Nordhaus, W., 2011. Environmental accounting for pollution in the United States. American Economic Review 101, 1649−1675.

United Nations Framework Convention on Climate Change (UNFCCC), 2013. Further Advancing the Durban Platform. UNFCCC, New York.

United States Environmental Protection Agency (US EPA), 1999. The Benefits and Costs of the Clean Air Act: 1990−2010. EPA Report to Congress. EPA 410-R-99-001. US EPA, Washington, DC.

The Theory of Public Goods and Their Efficient Provisions

2

Chapter Outline

1. Introduction to the Theory of Public Goods

A large number of goods and services are produced, sold, purchased, and traded in the free market economy. Most of these goods and services can be produced, sold, purchased, and traded as a single unit to a single economic agent. A smartphone can be produced, sold, purchased, and traded as a single unit to a single consumer. A buyer of the smartphone pays the price for it to a seller at an agreed predetermined level. These goods are called a privately consumed good or a private consumption good (Samuelson, 1954, 1955). In short, it can be called a private good.

A free market economy is unmatched in allocating resources to private goods (Smith 1776; Walras, 1954). In the economics terminology, it achieves a Pareto efficiency in allocating resources. In simple terms, it means that the free market finds the best ways to produce private goods at market-determined prices. In the free-market world, resources are optimally managed and used (Pareto, 1906).

A conspicuous trouble in this perfect world is that there are many goods in the free market economy that cannot be produced only for a single individual. For this distinct type of goods, if they are ever produced, they are produced as a community good that is shared by the members of the community. The community is most often a country, but can be a village, a tribe, or a group of countries. This type of good is called a public consumption good, or a public good in short (Samuelson, 1955; Buchanan, 1965).

Because of many factors such as advances in transportation, communication, increasing trades among communities, industrial pollution, and migration, individual communities have become ever more interdependent and more intertwined in economic and social activities. These changes in the economy tend to increase the type of goods that have the characteristic of a public good, also called a collectively consumed good.

The discussions of public goods always boil down to how concerned communities can provide a public good (Samuelson, 1954). In other words, an efficient provision of a public good is not a handy task by invisible hands in a free market economy, but rather stumbles upon many unusual obstacles that often scupper the effort by invisible hand (Smith 1776). A free-rider is one such obstacle, one who awaits others to provide the public good and enjoys the good once it is provided (Buchanan, 1968; Hirshleifer, 1980).

The theories on public goods have engaged with the role of the public sector in the provision of a variety of public goods (Samuelson and Nordhaus, 2009). The public sector can be engaged at varied levels. For example, the public entity can be a federal government, a state government, a county government, or a city government. The most appropriate public entity that may be called upon depends upon the public good concerned. That is, the size of the community in which the public good is shared will determine the level of the most efficient public intervention.

The role of the public sector in a free market economy is, no doubt, not limited to provision of public goods (Samuelson and Nordhaus, 2009; Mankiw, 2014). For example, the public sector is, among other things, responsible for reducing economic inequality among the citizens and maintaining the rule of law and fairness. Furthermore, the engagement of the public sector does not occur exclusive of private sector participations. Therefore, the theory of public goods will be led to the intersection of the public and private institutions (Coase, 1960).

A global public good is a public good concerned at the level of the entire globe called the global commons (Nordhaus, 1982, 1994). That is, the geographical scale of the problem of a global public good is as large as the entire globe. Hence, the appropriate political entity to be engaged in the provision of and intervention with a global public good should also be as large as the global commons. Of course, such a global government does not exist.

The most prominent example of a global public good is the problem of global warming and climate change. As the world has experienced during the past three decades with various policy approaches and endeavors on global warming, a policy solution to the problem of a global public good is more difficult than that of a national public good. A large number of stakeholders in the provision of a global public good makes it extremely challenging to have an agreement on a policy proposal by all parties involved (Nordhaus, 2001, 2010; Seo, 2012). Furthermore, nonexistence of a global government means that any agreement reached after hard-fought negotiations may not be enforceable.

In this chapter, the present author will provide a comprehensive review of the theory of public goods, global public goods, and their efficient provisions. Being intended as a textbook for upper undergraduate and graduate courses on economics, this chapter will also provide mathematical formulations of the problems and solution mechanisms with regard to public goods and global public goods wherever possible (Baumol and Oates, 1988; Mas-Colell et al., 1995). The chapter will focus on a variety of environmental problems, e.g., air, water, mobile pollution problems, and policy experiences with them in the past many decades in the contexts of public goods and global public goods (Tietenberg and Lewis, 2014).

2. Defining Characteristics of a Public Good

A public good is an abbreviated terminology for a public consumption good. A public consumption good is defined in contrast to a private consumption good, which is called in short a private good (Samuelson, 1954). A public good has a feature of "publicness" in its consumption. Before Samuelson, authors referred to the term "social goods" (Bowen, 1943; Musgrave, 1959).

A public good is defined by two prominent features in its consumption: nonrivalrous and nonexcludable. A public good has the property of nonrivalry in that consumption of a public good by an individual does not decrease the supply available for other individuals. As Paul Samuelson first described it, goods "which all enjoy in common in the sense that each individual's consumption of such a good leads to no subtractions from any other individual's consumption of that good..." are goods with nonrivalry (Samuelson, 1954).

A privately consumed good, by contrast, is rivalrous in that consumption of the private good by one individual reduces the supply of the good available to other individuals. More strictly stated, for each additional unit that is appropriated by individual i, there is one unit less available for consumption by individuals $j \neq i$.

With X the amount of the public good supplied and x_i the amount of consumption by individual i, nonrivalry of a public good is expressed as follows:

$$x_1 = x_2 = ... = x_n = X. \tag{2.1}$$

The characteristic of nonrivalry, also called nondepletability, of a public good is easier to comprehend in the example of a public knowledge. Let this be a certain public health announcement from the federal government, e.g., information on Zika virus. The appropriation of this knowledge by one person does not decrease the supply of the knowledge to the others.

A partial rivalry or nonrivalry can exist in some types of goods known as a club good (Buchanan, 1965). In the club goods, crowding and congestion effects make the benefits of the club diminished to some degree as an additional member is added to the club (Brown, 1973). A relevant example is a public highway. The benefits of the public highway get diminished as the number of users of the highway at a point of time increases. Crowding and congestion make the public highway less effective and enjoyable.

In the club goods, consumption of one unit of a good by an individual diminishes the consumption of the other individuals of the good to some degree, although not by one unit. With the same notations used earlier and k being the congestion effect parameter, which is assumed to be ≤ 1, the congestion effect of a club good is expressed as follows (Mas-Colell et al., 1995):

$$x_1 = x_2 = \ldots = x_n = k \cdot X. \tag{2.2}$$

The smaller the k, the larger the congestion/crowding effect. When k equals 1, the good is a purely public good. The club goods exist in the "Samuelson gap between the purely private good and the purely public good" (Buchanan, 1965).

Another defining characteristic of a public good is nonexcludability. Nonexcludability means that once a good is supplied, it is not possible to exclude someone from consuming the good. That is, it is supplied to the public at large. A private good is, by definition, exclusively consumed by an individual. It has the characteristic of excludability. A public good is nonexcludable in the sense that it is not possible to exclude someone from consumption once the good is provided. Or, it is said to be nonexcludable because, even if it is feasible to exclude, it is very costly to exclude someone from the benefits provided by the public good.

Examples of a public good, among other things, are national defense and air quality. National defense is a publicly consumed good. Once it is supplied to the public, it is very costly to exclude someone from the benefits of national defense. Air quality in an urban area is a publicly consumed good. Although it is possible to exclude someone from the benefits of air quality, it is very costly to do so.

In some cases, excludability of a public good can be achieved at a limited level, albeit not at a full scale. A certain set of knowledge and technology, for example, can be provided for an exclusive use of a holder through a patent system or a subscription system. Others without a patent are disallowed by law to appropriate the set of knowledge. In this case, the patented knowledge becomes rather a private good than a public good.

The club goods, explained earlier, are excludable goods. Only those who are a member of the club are given access to the good and its service. For example, satellite television (TV) is available only to those with a subscription. To the club members, the satellite TV is nonrivalrous as long as there is no congestion and/or crowding in the use of the good.

Another distinction to make with regard to public goods is that a public good does not always mean a good thing or a desirable commodity. Smog in a metropolitan city such as Beijing is a public good, even though it affects all residents of Beijing in a harmful manner. In this case, a public good is a public bad. A public bad is conceptually the same as a public good. In addition, a public good is always existent as the mirror image of a public bad. For example, removal of smog in Beijing through a variety of policy or technological interventions is considered a public good, whereas smog itself is a public bad.

3.   A Spatial Dimension of Public Goods

Public goods are inseparably defined by the spatial dimension within which the public goods are shared. Depending on the size of the community to which provision of a public good is made, the good is defined to be a local public good, a state public good, or a national public good (Samuelson and Nordhaus, 2009).

In most contexts, a public good means a national public good. In the national public goods, the concepts of nonrivalry and nonexcludability are pertinent to the spatial dimension of a national boundary. The size of the community with which provision of a national public good is concerned is a sovereign nation. National public goods are often at a center of heated national policy debates.

An example of a national public good is national defense. Provision of national defense is done for the nation as a whole. The boundary of the nation is protected. Anyone who is a citizen of the country is protected by the national defense system. National defense can be provided at a local level, but very costly to do so and not Pareto optimal for the country to do so.

A state public good is a public good at the level of a state if in the United States, or a province if in other parts of the world, i.e., a second administrative division of a large country. A public education system is managed at the state level in the United States. Each state has a public education system that includes a large number of academic institutions, such as universities, public schools, and public health systems. In many countries whose land size is relatively small, e.g., Denmark or South Korea, a public education system is a national public good.

A primary reason that a public education system is a state public good in the United States, while it is a national public good in South Korea, is the cost of provision. That is, the same benefit from a public education system can be reaped with the least cost in a state-level public education system in the United States. The size of a state is sufficiently large to achieve the same benefit that a national public education provides, but is small enough to significantly minimize the cost of provision due to coordination, transportations, communications, and transactions. One of the reasons for the high transaction cost in providing a national education system in the United States is unique cultural and historical backgrounds across the states.

A local public good is a public good provided at a local level. An example of a local public good is the department of public works in a city. The department provides various public works, such as waste collections, snow removal, street tree maintenance, and road maintenance. A city-level engagement is the least cost way to provide this public good.

In many developing countries, property rights are not well defined for many local commons, i.e., common space for a locality (Ostrom, 1990, 2009). A local commons is shared by the members of the community. The community is often a village whose members are tightly knit by blood or cultural heritage.

A local commons is an example in which crowding/congestion effect is significant (Brown, 1973). The larger the number of members of the community, the smaller the size of the benefit from the local public good is to an individual member of the community, especially when the point of congestion/crowding is reached.

Nonexcludability of a local commons is not stringent. A local commons is most often managed by an informal arrangement among the community members or by a cultural heritage (Ostrom, 1990). In a certain culture with a spiritual or an informal leader, anyone who is reported to abuse the commons can be forced to be excluded from the use of the commons.

4. Pareto Optimality in Provision of a Public Good

What does the optimal provision of a public good look like? To answer this question, we need to first define optimality. Pareto optimality or efficiency, after the 19th century Italian economist Vilfredo Pareto, is the most widely used definition of optimality and efficiency in economics (Pareto, 1906). Nash equilibrium is another essential concept in economics for explaining resources' allocations (Nash, 1950, 1951; Fudenberg and Tirole, 1991). The two concepts will also play an integral role throughout this book for the analysis of global warming policy options. The author will explain Pareto optimality here and come back to Nash equilibrium in Chapter 4 for explanations of noncooperative behaviors.

At the scale of a national macroeconomy, a Pareto optimality or efficiency is defined as a state in resource allocations in which it is impossible to make one individual better off without making at least one individual worse off (Mas-Colell et al., 1995). Given an initial allocation of resources among individuals, a reallocation that makes at least one individual better off without making any other individual worse off is called a Pareto improvement. An allocation is defined to be Pareto optimal or efficient when no further Pareto improvements can be made.

Let us consider the following economy with one public good, L traded private goods, and I consumers. Let x denote the quantity of the public good and $\mu_i(x)$ the utility of individual i from the consumption of the public good. The cost of supplying q units of the public good is defined as $c(q)$.

A Pareto optimal allocation must maximize the aggregate welfare, which occurs at the level of the public good, which solves the following optimization problem:

$$\underset{q}{\mathrm{Max}} \sum_{i=1}^{I} \mu_i(x) - c(q). \tag{2.3}$$

There are several things to note from the model in Eq. (2.3). First, note that there are no subscripts for x, q because there is only one public good in the model. Second, the model takes a partial equilibrium form in that the quantity of the public good has no effects on the prices of the private goods. Third, each consumer's utility function is quasilinear with respect to the traded private goods, set as the numeraire in the model.

The functional forms of the utility function and the cost function in Eq. (2.3) can be reasonably bounded by assumptions on preferences and production costs that are widely applied (Mas-Colell et al., 1995). First, we assume that the utility function is twice differentiable, with $\mu_i''(x) < 0$ at all $x \geq 0$. Second, the cost function is also assumed to be twice differentiable, with $c''(q) > 0$ at all $q \geq 0$. Third, in the case of a desirable public good whose production is costly, we take $\mu_i'(x) > 0$ at all $i \geq 0$ and $c'(q) > 0$. This formulation can be equally applied to the case of a public bad whose reduction is costly with $\mu_i'(x) < 0$ at all $i \geq 0$ and $c'(q) < 0$.

Under this setting, the necessary and sufficient first-order condition for optimality for the above-mentioned problem is as follows (Samuelson, 1954, 1955):

$$\sum_{i=1}^{I} \mu_i'(q^*) \leq c'(q^*), \quad \text{with equality if } q^* > 0. \tag{2.4}$$

At an interior solution, i.e., $q^* > 0$, the equality in the aforementioned equation should hold. The interior solution is interpreted as follows: at the optimal level of the public good, the sum of individuals' marginal benefits from consumption of the publicly consumed good is equal to the marginal cost of providing the public good.

This optimality condition for the public good can be contrasted with the Pareto optimality condition for the private good. In the private good, the optimality condition holds that each individual's marginal benefit from consumption of the privately consumed good is equal to the marginal cost of providing the private good.

The Pareto optimality of the solution depicted in Eq. (2.4) is guaranteed only if there are no other (environmental) externalities in the economy (Goulder et al., 1997). In the presence of other externalities than the externality concerned in the policy decision, the solution is understood to be the second best policy.

5. Market Provision of a Public Good

Can the market provide the public good at the optimal level as defined in Eq. (2.4)? Let us imagine that there is a market for the public good and each individual decides how much of the public good ($x_i \geq 0$) to buy, taking the market price of the public good (p) as given. On the supply side, let us imagine that there is a single profit-maximizing firm with the cost function $c(\cdot)$. The firm makes a supply decision taking the market price as given. Alternatively, the supply behavior of this firm can be understood as the industry supply behavior composed of many individual firms that are price-takers and whose aggregate cost function is $c(\cdot)$.

At a competitive equilibrium with price p^M, an individual consumer purchases x_i^M amount of the public good to maximize his/her utility by solving the following optimization problem:

$$\max_{x_i \geq 0} \mu_i\left(x_i + \sum_{k \neq i} x_k^M\right) - p^M x_i. \tag{2.5}$$

What is behind the formulation of Eq. (2.5) is that, in determining the individual's optimal purchases, the consumer takes as given the amount of the private good purchased by other consumers, the second argument inside the utility function. The necessary and sufficient first-order condition for optimality for the purchase of the consumer's public good is (Dixit, 1990)

$$\mu_i'\left(x_i^M + \sum_{k \neq i} x_k^M\right) \leq p^M, \quad \text{with equality if } x_i^M > 0. \tag{2.6}$$

Note that $x^M = x_i^M + \sum\limits_{k \neq i} x_k^M$. This is the equilibrium level of the public good. Substituting this yields that for each consumer,

$$\mu_i'(x^M) \leq p^M, \quad \text{with equality if } x_i^M > 0. \tag{2.7}$$

The firm's problem is to supply q^M that solves the following optimization problem:

$$\underset{q \geq 0}{\text{Max}} \left(p^M q - c(q) \right). \tag{2.8}$$

The necessary and sufficient first-order condition for optimality is (Dixit, 1990)

$$p^M \leq c'(q^M), \quad \text{with equality if } q^M > 0. \tag{2.9}$$

At a competitive equilibrium, $q^M = x^M$. The conditions in Eqs. (2.7) and (2.9) can be combined into a single equation using an indicator function Λ_i:

$$\sum_i \Lambda_i \left[\mu_i'(q^M) - c'(q^M) \right] = 0, \tag{2.10}$$

where

$$\Lambda_i = 1 \quad \text{if } x_i > 0 \text{ and } \Lambda_i = 0 \quad \text{if } x_i = 0. \tag{2.11}$$

Recalling that $\mu_i'(\cdot) > 0$ and $c'(\cdot) > 0$, Eq. (2.10) implies that whenever there is more than one individual consumer and the optimal level of the public good is greater than zero, we have

$$\sum_{i=1}^{I} \mu_i'(q^M) > c'(q^M). \tag{2.12}$$

Comparing Eq. (2.4) with Eq. (2.12), we see that whenever $q^* > 0$ and $I > 1$, the level of the public good provided is too low; that is, $q^M < q^*$.

An insufficient provision of a public good in the market is depicted in Fig. 2.1. An optimal provision of the public good is determined by the intersection between the marginal cost curve and the aggregate marginal utility (benefit) curve. A market provision of the public good is determined by the intersection of the marginal cost curve and an individual marginal utility (benefit) curve. The q^M is much smaller than q^*.

The optimal price of the public good is determined as the corresponding price to q^* in either the aggregate marginal benefit function or the marginal cost function. This means that the optimal price equals the aggregate of marginal benefits of the society with regard to the provision of the public good. At the same time, the optimal price equals the marginal cost of provision of the public good.

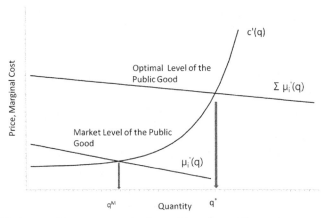

Figure 2.1 Market provision versus optimal provision of a public good.

Note that the aggregate marginal benefit curve $\sum_{i=1}^{I} \mu_i'(q)$ is constructed by a vertical summation of the individual marginal cost curves given the level of the public good. This can be contrasted with aggregate demand curve of a private good, which is constructed by summing horizontally the individual demand curves given the level of price of a private good (Samuelson, 1955; Field and Field, 2016).

Note that the aggregate marginal benefit is much larger than the marginal cost of provision of the public good at the market equilibrium provision of the public good. That is to say, the society would benefit from increasing marginally the level of the public good from the market level of provision. In other words, there is room for Pareto improvements. There is welfare loss occurring in the market provision of the public good.

The inefficiency in the market provision of the public good can be explained from the standpoints of a free-rider problem. Once the good that is a public good is provided by an individual, it benefits not only the individual but also other individuals. An individual has an incentive to wait for others to provide the public good and, once provided, enjoy the public good without paying for the cost of provision. For the individual, "optimal results can be attained by allowing others to supply the public good to the maximum extent while he enjoys a 'free ride'; that is, secures the benefits without contributing to the costs. Even if an individual should enter into such a cost-sharing agreement, he will have a strong incentive to break his own contract, to chisel on the agreed terms" (Buchanan, 1968).

The free-rider problem takes a stark form if individual marginal benefit curves have certain characteristics. Let us suppose that individuals can be ordered according to their marginal benefits as follows: $\mu_1'(x) < \mu_2'(x) < \ldots < \mu_I'(x)$ for all $x \geq 0$. Under this situation, it can happen that only individual I provides the public good. That is, only the individual who derives the largest benefit from the public good will provide it and all others will have no incentive to provide the public good at all. In this case, the private provision of q^M in Fig. 2.1 will be determined by the marginal benefit curve, $\mu_I'(q)$.

6. Environmental Disamenities as a Public Good

Treatments of environmental and natural resource-related problems such as environmental disamenities by economists have been by and large anchored by the concept of externality (Baumol and Oates, 1988). Externality is said to exist when an individual incurs the cost or benefit to another person, but is not obligated to pay for the cost to the victim(s) or receive the payment from the beneficiaries (Pigou, 1920). The former case is called negative externality, whereas the latter is called positive externality.

In interpreting market externalities in a novel manner, Ronald Coase showed that a bargaining solution should arise between the victims and environmental polluters in many of the environmental externality problems (Coase, 1960). The bargaining takes place by the mutual interests of both parties. In the simplest example, if an individual dumps wastes in front of the house of his/her neighbor, the neighbor will force him/her to remove the wastes or pay for the removal.

A more realistic and relevant environmental problem that can be placed in the Coase's bargaining context is when an upriver factory dumps waste materials into a river and a downstream village is harmed by the water pollution. Because of the legal framework that protects the life and properties of an individual, a negotiation can take place between the factory and the village community members. A mutually agreed bargaining solution can arise from the negotiation, which would approximate the Pareto optimal allocations.

A breakdown of the Coase's bargaining solution is unavoidable if the number of parties involved in an environmental problem increases exponentially. In the water-polluting upstream factory example, if the number of villages downstream are very large and diverse in terms of economic status and livelihoods, the possibility of a deal diminishes rapidly. Furthermore, if the number of water-polluting upstream factories increases to more than several factories, a bargaining solution among a large number of parties is even more unlikely.

As such, Coase did not solve the problem of environmental externality but rather reframed it as a problem of transaction cost. When the transaction cost is negligible, the externality problem becomes negotiable among the involved parties. By contrast, when the transaction cost becomes large, the externality problem has little chance of being bargained away through a mutually agreed deal.

Most environmental disamenities problems, however, pertain to the situation in which the transaction cost is too large for a bargaining solution to take place. Major environmental problems such as acid rain, smog, particulate matters, ozone depletion, mobile source pollution, and non—point source pollution all involve a large number of victims as well as a large number of polluters, making the transaction cost for a bargaining among them extremely high (Mendelsohn and Olmstead, 2009).

Let us first consider the acid rain problem. Sulfur dioxide (SO_2) and nitrogen oxides (NO_x) are the principal pollutants that cause acid precipitation (Likens and Bormann, 1974). Sulfur dioxide and nitrogen oxide emissions released into the atmosphere react with water vapor and other pollutants to form acids that eventually fall back on Earth via rainfall or snowfall.

Power plants that generated electricity by burning fossil fuels, such as coal, natural gas, and oil, are responsible for over two-thirds of the annual SO_2 emissions in the

United States. The rest is emitted from various industrial processes and transportation. More than half of the annual NO_x emissions results from various forms of transportation, e.g., passenger cars, buses, trucks, and trains. About a third of the annual NO_x emissions are from electricity-generating power plants. The rest is emitted from various industrial and chemical processes (US EPA, 2014).

Acid rain, wet deposition of acids that have been accumulated in the atmosphere, can increase temporarily the acidity in lakes and other water bodies. The high acidity thereof, which may last for several days or even many weeks, causes damage to fish and other aquatic life forms (Likens and Bormann, 1974).

The air pollutants that cause acid rain do more than damage the ecosystems and environment—they can damage human health (Mendelsohn, 1980). High levels of SO_2 in the air aggravate various lung problems in people with asthma and can cause breathing difficulties in children and the elderly. In some instances, breathing high levels of SO_2 can even damage lung tissue and cause premature death (Smith and Huang, 1995; Muller and Mendelsohn, 2009).

In the acid rain problem, the number of victims is very large and perhaps even difficult to count. Also, the number of power plants is large. The US Clean Air Act was established to deal with the problems such as acid rain because, inter alia, the possibility of a market solution is near nonexistent (US EPA, 1990, 2010). A government intervention was needed and the Clean Air Act amendment led to the establishment of the marketable permit system for sulfur dioxide emissions (Baumol and Oates, 1988; Stavins, 1998; Burtraw and Szambelan, 2009).

Another major environmental externality problem is smog. The primary component of smog is ground-level ozone. The two types of chemicals that are the main ingredients in forming ground-level ozone are volatile organic compounds (VOCs) and NO_x. VOCs are released by cars burning gasoline, petroleum refineries, chemical manufacturing plants, and other consumer and business products contain VOCs. NO_x are produced when cars and other sources such as power plants and industrial boilers burn fuels such as gasoline, coal, or oil (Mauzerall et al., 2005; US EPA, 2010).

Ground-level ozone can cause various human health problems, affect forests, and reduce yields of agricultural crops (Bell et al., 2004; Felzer et al., 2007; Wang et al., 2016). Repeated exposures to ozone can make people more susceptible to respiratory infections and lung inflammation. These also can aggravate preexisting respiratory diseases, such as asthma (Muller and Mendelsohn, 2009).

Again the number of victims in smog pollution is too large for coordination of a bargaining with the polluters to take place successfully. Furthermore, the number of polluters is very large, which makes it nearly impossible to negotiate a deal between the victims and the polluters. Again, the transaction cost is too high to make an effort for such a deal. It necessitates a policy intervention by the government in a form of regulation either through penalty or quantity limits on certain thresholds (Baumol and Oates, 1988; Tietenberg, 2006; Burtraw and Szambelan, 2009).

The third example of environmental externality is pollution of air particles. Particle pollution, also known as particulate matter (PM2.5, PM10), includes the very fine dust, soot, smoke, and droplets that are formed from chemical reactions, and produced when fuels, such as coal, wood, or oil, are burned. Sulfur dioxide and nitrogen oxide gases from motor vehicles, electric power generation, and industrial facilities react with sunlight and water vapor to form particles. Particles may also come from fireplaces, wood stoves, unpaved roads, and crushing and grinding operations, and may be blown into the air by the wind (US EPA, 2010).

Fine particulate matters are distinguished by the size of the particle. PM10 is the particulate matter whose diameter is smaller than 10 μm. One micron is one-millionth of 1 m or one-thousandth of 1 mm. PM2.5 is the particulate matter whose diameter is smaller than 2.5 μm.

Experts are concerned about particle pollution because very small or fine particles such as PM2.5 can get deep into the lungs and these particles can escape various control measures such as scrubbers and travel farther with winds (Pope et al., 2002; Woodruff et al., 2006). These fine particles, by themselves or in association with other air pollutants, can cause increased emergency room visits and hospital admissions for respiratory illnesses, and tens of thousands of deaths each year (Cropper and Oates, 1992). They can aggravate asthma, cause acute respiratory symptoms such as coughing, reduce lung function resulting in shortness of breath, and cause chronic bronchitis. The elderly, children, and asthmatics are particularly susceptible to health problems caused by breathing fine particles. Individuals with preexisting heart or lung diseases are also at an increased risk of health problems because of particle pollution (Muller and Mendelsohn, 2009).

In addition to human health effects, fine particles also cause haze, reducing visibility in places such as national parks and wilderness areas that are known for their scenic vistas. Fine particles also make buildings, statues, and other outdoor structures dirty. Fine particles can remain suspended in the air and travel long distances with the wind. For example, over 20% of the particles that form haze in the Rocky Mountains National Park have been estimated to come from hundreds of miles away (Muller and Mendelsohn, 2009; US EPA, 2010).

In the particle pollution, the Coase bargaining solution is infeasible because the number of victims is too large and the number of polluters is also too large. The transaction cost is too large. Let alone the large number of parties involved, quantifying the magnitude of health-related damages is a long and arduous process (Mendelsohn and Olmstead, 2009; Freeman et al., 2014). There is a need for government intervention to deal with the problem. In fact, the US Environmental Protection Agency put a limit on the amount of large particles and fine particles (US EPA, 1990, 2010).

In the environmental pollution problems described in this section, the characteristics of a public good are prominent. The acid rain problem, for example, is nonrivalrous. That is, that one individual suffers from the acid rain problem does not diminish the suffering of other individuals in the affected areas. Furthermore, it is very costly to exclude someone from the damaging effects of acid rains.

7. Policy Instruments for an Optimal Provision of the Public Good

The discussions up to now give a rationale for the government to intervene to improve the Pareto efficiency or reduce the inefficiency in the market in the provision of a public good. Broadly, the government can intervene through either a quantity-based policy, which employs a set of standards, or a price-based policy, which employs a set of charges (Baumol and Oates, 1971, 1988; Hartwick and Olewiler, 1997). In the former, the government sets the amount of the public good at the socially optimal level or at any other level that is deemed rational by the government. In the latter, the government determines the market price at the socially optimal level of the public good through fees, taxes, or subsidies to induce the optimal level of the public good by affecting demand and production behaviors. A third policy option is a blended policy in which a quantity-based policy instrument is mixed with a price-based policy instrument.

In the price-based approach, a charge in the form of a tax, a subsidy, or a fee is created to internalize the market externality, often called a Pigouvian tax (Pigou, 1920; Samuelson, 1954). In the following, the author adopts the notations primarily from Baumol and Oates (1988) and Mas-Colell et al. (1995) to describe the price-based policy instrument and the other policy approaches.

Let us suppose that there are two consumers with benefit functions $\mu_1(x_1 + x_2)$ and $\mu_2(x_1 + x_2)$, where x_i is the amount of the public good purchased by consumer i and $q^* > 0$ the optimal amount of the public good. Let us suppose that a subsidy to each consumer i per unit purchased is imposed by $s_i = \mu'_{-i}(q^*)$. Equivalently, the government may impose a tax per unit that the consumer's purchases of the public good fall below some specified level by $t_i = -\mu'_{-i}(q^*)$.

If $(\widetilde{x}_1, \widetilde{x}_2)$ are the competitive equilibrium levels of the public good purchased by the two consumers given these subsidies, and if $\widetilde{p}$ is the equilibrium price, then consumer i's purchases of the public good, $\widetilde{x}_i$, must solve the following optimization problem:

$$\underset{x_1 \geq 0}{\text{Max}}\, \mu_1(x_1 + \widetilde{x}_2) + s_1 x_1 - \widetilde{p}x_1. \tag{2.13}$$

The necessary and sufficient first-order condition for the solution of the aforementioned problem is (Dixit, 1990):

$$\mu'_1(\widetilde{x}_1 + \widetilde{x}_2) + s_1 \leq \widetilde{p}, \ \text{with equality if}\ \widetilde{x}_1 > 0. \tag{2.14}$$

Substituting for s_1 and using Eq. (2.9) and the market clearing condition that $\widetilde{x}_1 + \widetilde{x}_2 = \widetilde{q}$, we conclude that $\widetilde{q}$ is the total amount of the public good in the competitive equilibrium given these subsidies if and only if:

$$\mu'_1(\widetilde{q}) + \mu'_{-1}(q^*) \leq c'(\widetilde{q}), \ \text{with equality for some if}\ \widetilde{q} > 0. \tag{2.15}$$

In these notations for tax and subsidy, the subsidy, $s_i = \mu'_{-i}(q^*)$, is set to the positive externality of consumer i's action on the rest of the economy $(-i)$ and the tax, $t_i = -\mu'_{-i}(q^*)$, is set to the negative externality of consumer i's action on the rest of the economy, which is measured at the level of the optimal public good provision.

The level of tax or subsidy determined and implemented thus ensures that the solution to Eq. (2.15), $\tilde{q}$, is equal to the solution to Eq. (2.4), q^* (Baumol and Oates, 1988). This is of course conditional on that there are no other externalities or distortions in the market economy (Goulder et al., 1997).

The second policy instrument to provide the public good, a quantity-based approach or a set of standards approach, is for the government to put a limit (standard) on the amount of the public good q^*. If a concerned public good should be provided by the aggregate efforts by the individual firms, the government will set the optimal quantity (standard) for the economy and enforce the economy-wide limit (standard) by requiring firms to provide a fraction of the total amount of the public good. The quantity-based approach is also called a command-and-control approach (Field and Field, 2016).

The command-and-control approach was in fact the foundation of the first set of environmental regulations introduced in the United States and other developed economies. To be more specific, the Clean Air Act of 1970 determined six criteria pollutants and set national ambient air quality standards of these pollutants (US EPA, 1990; Tietenberg and Lewis, 2014). In the 1970 Clean Air Act, the six criteria pollutants were ground-level ozone, particulate matter, carbon monoxide, lead, sulfur dioxide, and nitrogen dioxide. Notably, greenhouse gases, including carbon dioxide, were not included in the six criteria pollutants at the time.

Another policy example of the command-and-control–type policy instrument in the context of global public goods is the Kyoto Protocol (UNFCCC, 1998). The Kyoto Protocol, the first international treaty on global warming, set the target global carbon dioxide emissions at 5% below the 1990 level of emissions, which must be achieved by the global community as a whole (Manne and Richels, 1999; Nordhaus and Boyer, 1999).

Regarding the command-and-control approach, the quantity limit is set, more often than not, at an arbitrary level or, perhaps more precisely, at a level that is not optimal for the economy. The above-mentioned national air quality standards in 1970 were determined "arbitrarily," that is, without any rigorous benefit–cost analysis of the chosen standards (Hahn and Dudley, 2007; US EPA, 1999). The standards (limits) were set, by and large, at the threshold values beyond which harmful effects of the pollutants were understood to start rising sharply.

Another drawback of the standards-based policy is that there is no consensus rule for dividing and allocating the economy-wide target amount of emissions into individual firms (polluters). An obvious option is to allocate the target emissions equally into individual firms. This, however, does not guarantee the cost-effective policy to achieve the target amount of emissions and abatement. Indeed, without reliance on the optimal price for externality and varying costs of abatement across the firms, it is not possible to achieve the cost-effective policy (Field and Field, 2016).

The third policy option is a hybrid system that blends a price-based approach with a command-and-control approach. This policy option has been called by various names such as an allowance trading program, an emissions trading system, and a cap-and-trade system (Montgomery, 1972; Stavins, 2007; Tietenberg, 2006; McKibbin and Wilcoxen, 2002).

At the level of the optimal quantity of the public good, q^*, the total number of permits (or allowances) is issued by the government. In other words, the total quantity of emissions is capped by the government. Each permit or allowance allows the holder to have the right for, say, 1 ton of sulfur emissions. The total number of permits is allocated to individual polluters of sulfur dioxide according to a certain rule.

An individual polluter is allowed to trade the allocated permits at a negotiated price with another polluter. A firm that is capable of abating the emissions at a lower cost would sell the permits to another firm that is capable of abating it only at higher cost. That is, it is profitable for the low-cost firm to sell the permit to the high-cost firm at a negotiated price, which would lie between the abatement cost of the low-cost firm and that of the high-cost firm. This transaction is Pareto improving, i.e., benefits both parties.

Where will the permit price settle? That is to say, what is the equilibrium price of the permit for 1 ton of sulfur dioxide emissions? Let p_p be the unit price of the permit, given the maximum amount of permit, q^*. The equilibrium price of the public good (bad) per unit is p^* as before with the same aggregate benefit function and the maximum amount of permit allocated. Let us suppose that there are two firms in the market: one is a low-marginal-cost firm with c'_l and another is a high-marginal-cost firm with c'_h.

A high-cost firm is willing to purchase a permit as long as the permit price is below the marginal abatement cost of the firm. At the same time, a low-cost firm is willing to sell a permit as long as the permit price is above the marginal abatement cost of the firm. Transactions between the two polluter firms will continue as long as

$$c'_l < p_p < c'_h. \tag{2.16}$$

The transaction will cease at the equilibrium price of the permit, p^*_p, in which marginal abatement costs of the two firms are equal:

$$c'_l = p^*_p = c'_h. \tag{2.17}$$

This condition and the fact that the optimal amount of the public good is q^* ensures that the permit equilibrium price equals the optimal price of the public good:

$$p^*_p = p^*. \tag{2.18}$$

The mathematical proof of the optimality condition for the permit trading in Eqs. (2.17) and (2.18) is provided by a no-arbitrage condition. That is, at a point that deviates from Eqs. (2.17) and (2.18), two firms (polluters) still have the incentive to make transactions for mutual benefits.

The no-arbitrage solution for the cap-and-trade system is depicted in Fig. 2.2. There are four relationships in the figure: aggregate marginal damage (MD), marginal abatement cost for a low-cost firm (MAC_low), marginal abatement cost for a high-cost firm (MAC_high), and marginal abatement cost for the economy (MAC).

At the intersection of the MD and the MAC, the optimal quantity and price of the public good is determined, that is, $(q^*, p^*) = (12, 4)$. Let us assume that the policy maker issues 12 tons of emissions permits for the economy and distributes them

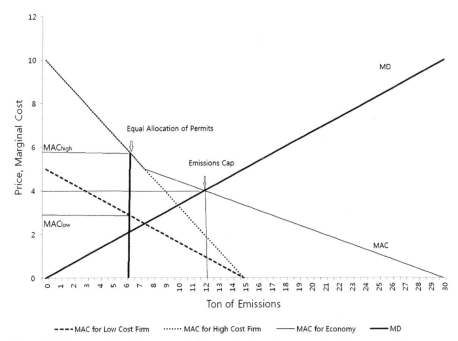

Figure 2.2 A cap-and-trade system. *MAC*, marginal abatement cost; *MD*, marginal damage.

equally into two polluter firms. The equal allocation of permits is marked by the thick black line at $q = 6$.

The figure shows that there is the difference between the marginal abatement cost for the high-cost firm, denoted MAC_high, and that for the low-cost firm, denoted MAC_low at $q = 6$. The high-abatement-cost firm is willing to purchase one unit of emissions permit, instead of cutting that unit of emissions at the cost of MAC_high, at the price range between MAC_high and MAC_low. Such a transaction is beneficial for the firm. At the same time, the low-abatement-cost firm is willing to sell one unit of emissions permit, by cutting that unit of emissions at the cost of MAC_low, at the price range between MAC_high and MAC_low. The transaction is beneficial for the firm.

At equal allocation of the economy-wide permits, the two firms have an incentive to arbitrage for mutual benefits. The no-arbitrage state will be reached when Eq. (2.18) is achieved. That is, when the permit price equals the optimal price, i.e., $p_p^* = p^* = 4$, both firms will no longer have the incentive to make permit transactions. At $p_p^* = p^* = 4$, each firm arrives at an efficient decision on how much to abate and how many permits to purchase.

8.   Moral Suasion, Private Provision, and Lindahl Equilibrium

Other than the three policy instruments described in the previous section, other types of interventions and solutions have been suggested. The author reviews the following three approaches, which all have an emphasis on market and individually motivated solutions: moral suasion, a private voluntary provision, and Lindahl equilibrium.

The first of such alternative approaches is moral suasion and voluntary compliance (Oates and Baumol, 1975). In this approach, the government relies on appeals to people's conscience and their voluntary compliance with the program. Many, including economists, are skeptical of the efficacy of a long-term environmental program that appeals solely to conscience and moral calling because it asks individuals to take costly actions but does not offer any compensation in return.

The role of moral suasion and voluntary programs is understood in the context of unexpected emergencies in which appropriate actions must be taken in a very short period of time and should yield almost immediate effects. In such situations, the time cost of employing one of the three policy instruments described in the previous section is too high.

Private provision of a public good is another alternative solution mechanism that is related to the moral approach but dissimilar in many aspects. A voluntary private provision of a public good is examined in the context of a certain environmental market such as a green electricity market in the United States or a voluntary purchase market of hybrid or electric vehicles (Kotchen and Moore, 2007). Voluntary provision may take the form of a donation to a particular cause or a tariff tied to the consumption of a good.

Green electricity is the electricity generated by renewable energy sources, such as solar, wind, and geothermal. Against the electricity generated from fossil fuels, green electricity results in lower emissions of carbon dioxide, thereby providing the public good. Hybrid or electric vehicles burn less gasoline per mile of driving, providing the public good of reducing the release of carbon dioxide.

Examining the US households' participation in the US green electricity programs statistically with household survey data, the researchers report that households' participation into the voluntary programs increases with household income, environmental concern, and altruistic attitudes, whereas it decreases with the number of people living in the household and a male name on the energy bill.

Like the moral suasion approach, effectiveness of the voluntary provision of a public good in the long term is questionable because it is costly to take part in a voluntary provision of a public good but there is no compensation or benefit in return. Furthermore, stability of the voluntary provision mechanism is most likely weak because such factors as environmental concern and altruistic attitudes can change quickly as households' economies are fluctuated by numerous factors, just as the household's income is swayed by many factors.

With the most sophistication of the three approaches, Erik Lindahl proposed that there is a market institution that can achieve optimality in the provision of a public good, therefore there is no need for government intervention (Lindahl, 1919). Following the notations from Mas-Colell et al. (1995), let us suppose that, for each consumer i, there is a market for the public good as experienced by consumer i. That is, we think of each consumer's consumption of the public good as a distinct commodity with its own market. Let the price of this personalized good be p_i. The p_i may differ across consumers. Suppose also that, given the equilibrium price p_i^{**}, each consumer sees oneself deciding on the total amount of the public good he/she will consume, x_i, so as to solve,

$$\underset{x_i \geq 0}{\text{Max}}\, \mu_i(x_i) - p_i^{**} x_i. \tag{2.19}$$

The equilibrium consumption level must therefore satisfy the necessary and sufficient first-order condition:

$$\mu_i'(x_i^{**}) \leq p_i^{**}, \quad \text{with equality if } x_i^{**} > 0. \tag{2.20}$$

The firm (producer of the good) is now viewed as producing a bundle of I goods with a fixed-proportions (Leontief production) technology, i.e., the level of production of each personalized good is necessarily the same. Thus the firm solves,

$$\underset{q \geq 0}{\text{Max}} \left(\sum_{i=1}^{I} p_i^{**} q \right) - c(q). \tag{2.21}$$

The firm's equilibrium level of output q^{**} therefore satisfies the necessary and sufficient first-order condition:

$$\sum_{i=1}^{I} p_i^{**} \leq c'(q^{**}), \quad \text{with equality if } q^{**} > 0. \tag{2.22}$$

Eqs. (2.20) and (2.22) and the market clearing condition that $x_i^{**} = q^{**}$ for all i imply that

$$\sum_{i=1}^{I} \mu_i'(q^{**}) \leq c'(q^{**}), \quad \text{with equality if } q^{**} > 0. \tag{2.23}$$

Comparing Eq. (2.23) with Eq. (2.4), we see that the equilibrium level of the public good consumed by each consumer is exactly the efficient level: $q^{**} = q^*$.

This type of equilibrium is known as a Lindahl equilibrium after Erik Lindahl who first developed the solution through personalized markets for the public good (Lindahl, 1919). In the personalized markets, each consumer takes the market price as given and fully determines one's own level of consumption of the public good, as in Eq. (2.19). The producer then determines the supply level of the public good, assuming that the consumer will pay the market price for a unit of the public good.

Each consumer is willing to pay the cost of provision of the public good commensurate with one's level of consumption, $p_i^{**} x_i$ in Eq. (2.19). In other words, each consumer of the public good is willing to pay for the externality he/she incurred in accordance with the size of the externalities. In personalized markets of Lindahl, externalities are eliminated from the problem itself.

Although the Lindahl equilibrium offers a fresh perspective, the realism of it is questionable (Mas-Colell et al., 1995). For this equilibrium to make sense, it should be possible to exclude a consumer from the use of the public good provided by others. Otherwise, there would be no reason for the consumer to believe that he/she would end up consuming none of the public good if he/she would not purchase any of it.

Second, in the personalized markets of the public good, there is only one consumer on the demand side for the personalized good provided in the market. It is not reasonable to assume that the consumer will act as a price-taker in the personal market.

The Lindahl equilibrium can be further reinterpreted as a feature of an optimal provision of the public good in personalized markets. Let us go back to the MD function in Fig. 2.2. In the optimal solution for nonpersonalized markets, all polluters are required to pay the cost (equal to MD) for each additional unit of pollution. The aggregated MD curve is the sum of individual MD curves:

$$\text{MD}(q) = \sum_{i}^{I} \text{MD}_i(q). \tag{2.24}$$

In the personalized markets, each polluter is required to pay for the damage equivalent to one's MD quantity, $\text{MD}_i(q^*)$. In the personalized markets in which there is no externality, each individual is asked to pay for one's own damage, which would add up to accomplish the optimal provision of the public good at the society level.

9. Valuation Methods and a Benefit–Cost Analysis

Having comprehended that neither the Coase's bargaining solution nor the Lindahl's personalized market solution can be effective in providing a truly public good, policy makers must resort to one of the three policy instruments: a command-and-control approach, a price-based approach, and a cap-and-trade system (Baumol and Oates, 1988).

Note that for the implementations of the three approaches, we assumed up to this point that the government has the full knowledge of the benefits derived by consumers from the provision of the public good or the damages incurred by the provision of the public bad. To be more specific, the policy maker must know the aggregate marginal benefit function or the aggregate MD function to determine the optimal price for the price-based approach or the optimal quantity of the public good (bad) for the standards approach or the tradable permit system.

In reality, the government does not have the complete knowledge on the marginal benefit function of provision of a public good concerned. This necessitates the research efforts of quantifying the marginal benefit function of a concerned public good. In the literature of environmental public goods such as clean air, clean water, and endangered species protection, valuation of benefits and damages of environmental amenities has taken a center stage of environmental studies (Mendelsohn, 1980; Cropper and Oates, 1992; Maler and Vincent, 2005; Greenstone and Gallagher, 2008; Smith, 2008; Freeman et al., 2014).

Economists have developed many useful methods for quantifying the benefits of provision of the public goods that have been recognized to be important in the policy area of environmental protection (Mendelsohn and Olmstead, 2009). Through these methods, economists aim to learn the marginal willingness to pay for a marginal improvement in a certain environmental quality variable such as a reduction in the level of SO_2 emissions.

Broadly, there are two families of valuation methods: stated preference (attitudinal) methods and revealed preference (behavioral) methods (Cropper and Oates, 1992; Mendelsohn and Olmstead, 2009). A revealed preference method examines revealed and observed behaviors of individuals in the markets to learn the marginal willingness to pay of individuals for an improvement in a specific environmental quality indicator. Widely used in this family of evaluation methods are an averting behavior method, a hedonic property method, a hedonic wage method, and a travel cost method.

In the averting behavior method, a researcher examines behavioral changes of individuals in attempts to mitigate the effects of pollution. For example, individuals in areas with water pollution may increase purchases of bottled water or water purifier to avert the harmful effect of water pollution (Smith and Desvousges, 1986). Individuals in highly polluted outdoor air may increase purchases of air conditioner to filter outdoor pollutants (Dickie and Gerking, 1991). A researcher can establish the relationship between the water pollution level and the payment level for purchases of these devices, from which the marginal willingness to pay for a water quality improvement is derived.

Another revealed preference method is the hedonic property method (Ridker and Henning, 1967; Greenstone and Gallagher, 2008). Researchers examine the variation of property values across the range of locations with varied environmental qualities. The environmental quality of concern, such as the level of smog in the location, is interpreted to be one characteristic of the property and an owner of the property paid for the characteristic as one component of the property price at the time of purchase (Rosen, 1974; Freeman, 1974). Hence, the willingness to pay for a higher environmental quality is measured by the value placed on the component of the property value.

The hedonic wage method applies the same theory as the hedonic property method to the wages individuals receive given varied environmental characteristics of a job offered (Thaler and Rosen, 1976; Viscusi, 1979). An individual faces a trade-off in a wage negotiation between a higher wage and a lower environmental risk. The higher the risk of the job, the higher the wage one is offered. The lower the risk of the job, the lower the wage offered. A certain environmental risk, e.g., risk of death while performing the job, is interpreted to be one characteristic of the job and an individual gets paid for that characteristic as one component of the wage offered to the individual.

An application of the hedonic wage method gives rise to the concept of value of risk, which is expressed as the willingness to accept of an individual to undertake the task which involves a certain probability of death while conducting the job. The value of risk eventually culminates in the critical concept of value of statistical life (VSL). A meta-analysis of hedonic wage studies shows that the median VSL of US workers is $7 million and the income elasticity of the VSL is about 0.5−0.6, meaning that lower-income countries have lower VSLs (Viscusi and Aldy, 2003).

The concept and quantitative estimate of the VSL plays a critical role in assessments of environmental benefits, environmental accounting, and environmental policy (Weitzman, 2009; Muller et al., 2011). It should be reminded that the VSL is not the same as the value of life itself. It is the willingness to pay of an individual for a marginal reduction in the risk of death. The VSL is a meaningful measure because environmental regulations purport to achieve exactly that, i.e., a marginal reduction in the risk of death or a marginal improvement in the quality of environment.

The travel cost method, the fourth revealed preference method in this review, exploits the cost that an individual pays for a travel to an important nature area such as a national park (Clawson, 1959; Knetsch, 1963). A traveler pays for many items needed for a journey, including transportation costs, entrance fees, accommodation expenditure, and meal costs, to enjoy the amenity of the national park. A researcher examines the variation in the travel costs to a site, i.e., an implicit price that an individual pays for a visit to the site, across the individuals that result when individuals from different origins travel to the site. An empirical relationship between the travel cost and visitation rates is estimated, based upon which a demand function for the site is estimated.

Another family of valuation methods is stated preference methods or attitudinal methods, which includes a contingent valuation method (Hanemann, 1994). Stated preference methods attempt to learn people's willingness to pay by directly asking them how much they value a certain environmental goods or services through carefully designed surveys. The surveys are designed to create a hypothetical market in which respondents make decisions on the concerned environmental goods. These decisions are evaluated by a modeler as if actual decisions have taken place in the market.

The stated preference methods are susceptible to not a few well-defined biases. In responding to the survey, a respondent does not face real trade-offs in the market when he/she gives an answer to a specific question; therefore, the answer given in a hypothetical situation may not reflect the true willingness to pay of her/him for the environmental amenity. Furthermore, what answers a respondent gives depend on how the questions are framed in the questionnaire. Third, the answers given can be swayed by various strategic reasons (Diamond and Hausman, 1994; Cropper and Oates, 1992).

Nonetheless, many researchers acknowledge that some types of values of natural assets or environmental amenities cannot be measured by one of the revealed preference methods, i.e., behaviorally based methods. For such values, there are no market behaviors that can be observed. An example is existence value. An individual may know that he/she will never make use of a certain environmental good or a natural asset or visit a certain place during one's lifetime, e.g., polar bears in the Arctic, but nevertheless he/she may express high value attached to it. It is said that the individual simply puts a value on the existence of such a good or place.

The existence value is nonuse value. Nonuse values can sometimes explain a large fraction of the total value attached to a certain policy context such as policies for protection of endangered species or wilderness preservation. To the extent that there are no observed market (transaction) behaviors, it is not possible to estimate the existence value through one of the revealed preference methods. To that extent, researchers have continued to rely on attitudinal methods, despite the well-defined biases pointed out earlier. Economists also debate whether such values should be included in economic analyses or attitudinal methods should be used for policy decisions (Diamond and Hausman, 1994; Hanemann, 1994). For the same environmental regulation, the estimates of benefits measured by the attitudinal methods are often much larger than the estimates of benefits measured by one of the revealed preference methods.

Critics of valuation argue that the range of valuation methods described earlier do not yield the about-the-same value estimate with regard to a certain environmental amenity or natural asset. In fact, the estimates may vary by an order of magnitude or more, whereas some values cannot be measured. Critics of the benefit—cost analysis argue that huge variation in the value estimates across the variety of valuation methods make the benefit—cost analytical framework less pertinent.

However, the benefit—cost analysis has turned out to be an essential tool, perhaps inevitable, for policy assessments of many important policy decisions (Arrow et al., 1996a). Even though the range of valuation methods gives out a wide range of value estimates, it provides an important input into policy decision models (Nordhaus, 1994; Manne et al., 1995). Furthermore, valuation studies have often complemented each other through the course of debates on a certain environmental regulation and the range of estimates has often narrowed over time as additional studies have been conducted on the same issue. In the United States, it is legally required that any environmental policy proposal should be accompanied by a benefit—cost analysis (US EPA, 1999; Mendelsohn and Olmstead, 2009).

10.   Uncertainty: Price Versus Quantity

A degree of uncertainty in the benefit function of an environmental public good is seen unavoidable, even if it can be narrowed down significantly through continued research and experiences. Furthermore, up to now, we assumed that the marginal abatement cost function of the environmental public good is known to the policy maker. That is, it is assumed that there is no uncertainty with regard to the marginal cost functions of individual firms. In reality, the policy maker does not know the marginal abatement cost functions of individual firms.

One of the reasons that there is uncertainty in marginal benefit functions and marginal abatement cost functions is that there is hidden, privately held information on the parts of consumers as well as producers of the public good. Let us say that there is privately held, hidden to others, information in each consumer of the public good and there is privately held, hidden to others, information in each producer of the environmental public good. Either of these hidden information leads to the uncertainty in the marginal benefit functions or the marginal cost functions. Incorporating the uncertainty, let us write the consumer's utility function as $\mu(\cdot,\eta)$ with η denoting the type of the consumer. Similarly, incorporating the uncertainty, the firm's profit function can be written as $\pi(\cdot,\theta)$ with θ denoting the type of the firm (Mas-Colell et al., 1995).

In the presence of privately held (hidden and asymmetrically held) information by both consumers and producers of the public good, a voluntary Coasean bargaining solution between the party of firms and the party of consumers is even more difficult to be achieved than in the absence of such privately held hidden information. However, in a localized externality problem that involves a small number of victims and polluters, the Coase bargaining is a more efficient policy mechanism because two parties will engage in revealing true information held by the other party. In most environmental problems, a large number of victims and polluters are involving, making again the Coase bargaining solution ineffective in the presence of uncertainty.

An important theoretical outcome is that when there is privately held information that the policy maker does not have knowledge, a quantity-based policy instrument and a price-based policy instrument are not perfect substitutes of each other anymore. Which of the two instruments is superior in terms of welfare loss depends on the shapes of the marginal utility function of consumers and the marginal profit function of firms (Weitzman, 1974).

Let us suppose that the policy maker does not have full knowledge on the shapes of the marginal abatement cost functions of individual firms. If the MD function is such that the optimal amount of the public good (bad) does not vary with the type of the firm (θ), then the quantity-based approach is superior because the policy maker can set a strict limit on the quantity of the good.

This situation occurs when the MD function is so steep that it increases abruptly with the increase of the public bad and may become infinite beyond the threshold level of the public bad. Regardless of the shape of the marginal abatement cost function, the situation dictates that an optimal policy is to enforce the limit (threshold).

Let us suppose again that the policy maker does not know the shapes of the marginal abatement cost functions of individual firms. If the MD function were to be independent of the level of the public bad, then the price-based instrument would be superior. This case would occur if the MD from the unit of the public bad does not vary much with the increase of the public bad. Regardless of the marginal abatement cost function, by setting the price of the public bad at the fixed level that equals the MD, a price-based instrument can achieve the optimal levels of the public bad. Given the price chosen by the policy maker, individual firms will make optimizing decisions on the units of abatement of the public bad, i.e., the units of the quantity of the public good. That is, there is no need for the government to know the individual marginal abatement cost functions.

Once the two extreme cases are comprehended, it is easier to express intermediate cases. In the intermediate cases, advantage of one approach over the other would be determined by the elasticity of MD function relative to the elasticity of the marginal abatement cost function (Weitzman, 1974; Pizer, 1997). If the elasticity of the MD function is larger than the elasticity of the marginal abatement cost function at around the optimal level of the public bad, a quantity-based approach is superior to a price-based approach with regard to expected social welfare from a chosen policy.

If, on the other hand, the elasticity of the MD function is smaller than the elasticity of the marginal abatement cost function at around the optimal level of the public bad, a price-based approach outperforms a quantity-based approach in terms of expected social welfare from a chosen policy. The reason is that a misjudgment on the marginal abatement cost function leads to a smaller welfare loss under a price-based approach than under a quantity-based approach.

The analysis of uncertainty in this section is pertinent to an analysis of global warming policies that deal with a stock pollutant (Newell and Pizer, 2003). A stock pollutant is the pollutant that, once released, remains in the atmosphere for a long time, i.e., as long as a century, and is accumulated in the atmosphere (Le Treut et al., 2007). An analyst must measure the damage of 1 ton of carbon dioxide emissions today that would occur in 100 years (Tol, 2002; Seo, 2016a,b).

11.   Environmental Justice: Price Versus a Cap-and-Trade

A price approach and a cap-and-trade system would achieve the Pareto optimal solution if price is set optimally for the former and the number of permits is issued at the optimal level of emissions for the latter. The two policy instruments, however, achieve very different income redistributions. The choice of one policy instrument over the other determines the distribution of income from one group of stakeholders to another. Therefore, it has important environmental justice implications.

In the United States, the American Clean Energy and Security Act of 2009, known as the Waxman and Markey bill, attempted, without success, to introduce a cap-and-trade system to the United States (US House of Representatives, 2009). A major criticism leveled against the bill was that a cap-and-trade system would reallocate wealth from the public sector to carbon emitting businesses. By contrast, a carbon price approach would reallocate the wealth from carbon emitting businesses to the government and the public sector.

In the price approach, carbon penalty (tax) is collected by the government from the polluting firms for each ton of unabated emissions. The wealth then moves from the polluting businesses to the public sector. The tax revenue in turn can be used by the government for various public welfare improvement projects. It may be used to support low-income families in an effort to alleviate income inequality, for example.

By contrast, a cap-and-trade system allows polluter firms to trade emissions permits to reduce the cost of complying with the regulation, given the number of permits allocated to them initially. Given the permit price in the market, a firm abates the emissions as long as the marginal abatement cost of the firm remains below the permit price in the market. For the remaining emissions for which the marginal abatement cost is higher than the permit price in the market, the firm decides to buy the permit and continues to emit these units of emissions.

Consequently, in the cap-and-trade system, there is no transfer of wealth from polluting firms to the government and the public sector. The wealth remains within the polluting firms. It is just reallocated across the polluting businesses.

From the firms' standpoint, a permit trading system is preferable to an environmental tax if one of the two must be adopted for environmental policy. This is one of the reasons that polluter firms have resisted the latter more strongly than the former, while a cap-and-trade system, i.e., an SO_2 allowance trading program, has been implemented in the United States (Burtraw and Szambelan, 2009). From the general public's standpoints, they are worse off under the permit trading program than under an environmental tax program.

To address the wealth reallocation problem, a cap-and-trade system can be coupled with an initial allocation plan that forces polluting businesses to purchase every unit of permit from the beginning of the program. That is, there is neither free permit allocated to firms nor partially auctioned-off permits. However, it has turned out to be politically too onerous to implement such a strict initial allocation strategy.

All countries that introduced a permit trading system, albeit limited in numbers, opted for a free initial allocation of permits (Tietenberg, 2013). In phases 1 and 2 of the European Union's Emissions Trading System from 2005 to 2012, most allowances were given out to participants for free (EC, 2016). In the first phase of South Korea's emissions trading scheme, which began in 2015, all permits are allocated without charge to selected participants of the program (Korea Exchange, 2016).

12. Extending Discussions to Global Public Goods

The central question of this book is how a global public good, i.e., stabilization of the global climate, can be provided efficiently for the entire globe. A global public good is a public good at a global scale. On first glimpses, an efficient provision of a global public good should not be much different from that of a national public good: it should be thought of as an application of the solution mechanisms, at a global scale, for provision of a national public good (Nordhaus, 1994; Sandler, 1997; Kaul et al., 2003).

However, as will be made clear through many sections of this book, many unique characteristics of a global public good, especially in the case of global warming, make it quite difficult to conceptualize their optimal provisions as a straightforward extension of the theory and policy instruments for national public goods (Seo, 2013, 2016c).

In the description of the public goods, a geopolitical scale of a concerned public good is considered as an integral characteristic that distinguishes a wide variety of public goods. In Section 3 of this chapter, the author introduced the classification of the public goods into a local public good, a state public good, and a national public good. A global public good can be considered to be another category in the above-mentioned classification of the public goods in which the "publicness" of a global public good has the reach over the entire globe.

To describe the distinct characteristics of global public goods, let us imagine that a large asteroid, which is capable of altering the cyclical route of the Earth around the Sun or even destroying the Earth on collision, is rapidly approaching the Earth (Chapman and Morrison, 1994; Posner, 2004; Guardian, 2016). The Earth going off the route permanently is certain to pose a great risk and even a catastrophic risk. Let us assume for the moment that no single country or coalition of countries can protect the Earth on its own. Guarding the Earth from a possible collision against the asteroid through a globally cooperative action must be called for. The action should be taken swiftly because there is only a few years' time between detecting such an asteroid and making a contact with it.

The cooperative protection would benefit all the communities and nations on the Earth. It is not possible to exclude selected nations from the benefit of the protection.

It is nonexcludable at the level of individual nations or states. In addition, the benefit of protection has the characteristic of nonrivalry. The consumption (enjoyment) of the good by one nation does not diminish the enjoyment of the good available to other nations. As in the asteroid example, the first defining characteristic of global public goods is a global geopolitical scale in their provision and consumption. The characteristics of nonexcludability and nonrivalry of public goods would manifest beyond national boundaries and within the global sphere.

The second defining characteristic is a major departure from the characteristic of national public goods: it appears uniquely in the problem of a global public good. That is, there is no governance that can deal with and enforce a policy or coordinate the member nations with the same legal force found in a sovereign nation (Seo, 2015, 2016c). There is no political and legal framework that can enforce any law or Protocol across all countries on the Earth. This feature of global public goods is called the Westphalian dilemma in the environmental literature, which will be further elaborated in the next chapter (Nordhaus, 2006).

This characteristic has critical implications on a policy of global public goods. In the provision of national public goods, a national government's intervention through taxation, standards, or a hybrid system is inevitable. Violators are punished by steep penalties from the government. Absence of such a powerful political entity at a global scale alludes that a straightforward application of the policy instruments for national public goods may not turn out to be effective for a global public good provision.

The third distinguishing feature of global public goods from national public goods may be even more confounding. Adding to the challenge that the provision of a global public good has to be made over the entire region of the Earth, the benefits and costs of provision of a global public good across individual nations and states are varied by a wide range (Seo, 2012). This characteristic is especially salient in the phenomenon of global warming.

That the benefits and costs of an optimal provision of a global public good are disparate across the nations means that any agreement among the nations, which number more than 200, has only a slim chance to occur. It would become even more confounding when individual countries' benefit—cost calculations are entangled with existing geopolitical divisions across the Earth.

The fourth defining feature of a global public good is a long time horizon that is entailed in addressing the problems of a global public good (bad). In many global public good problems, the list of which the author will present in the next section, an efficient provision takes place over a long time horizon. But it takes a longer time horizon in some global public good problems than others. In the case of stopping global warming, an appropriate policy time horizon has been understood to be at least a century (IPCC, 1990; UNFCCC, 1992, 2015).

With a long time horizon in which many generations of people on the Earth are involved, e.g., in the case of global warming, the task of providing a global public good optimally is loaded with challenges that are often unprecedented in other problems. The benefit of, for example, taking a costly action of cutting carbon dioxide emissions today may not materialize for many decades. Put differently, the damage that results from not cutting carbon dioxide emissions today may not be felt for many decades.

With many generations of people who would receive and give benefits and damages of actions over the course of time, it becomes vital for a researcher to conceptualize how different generations should be compared and what values should be placed on the time elapsed (Fisher, 1930; Arrow et al., 1996b).

13. Plans for the Next Chapters

This chapter provided a thorough review of the economic literature on public goods, global public goods, and their efficient provisions. The author has avoided delving into one particular theory or study too long and focused on essential economic theories, methodologies, policy experiences with major lessons, and critiques wherever appropriate.

The author moved gradually from fundamental concepts of public goods and externalities to the problem of global public goods and global warming at the end of this chapter. Major topics presented are public goods, club goods, local public goods, externalities, market versus optimal provisions, bargaining solution, standards versus prices versus cap-and-trade, moral suasion, private provision, Lindahl solution, valuation methods, benefit—cost analysis, uncertainty, and environmental justice. All concepts and theories addressed in this chapter will be utilized and referred to throughout the book.

This chapter ends with the description of distinct characteristics of global public goods and challenges to provide them, which sets the stage well for the ensuing chapters of this book. In the next chapter, the author presents, after surveying a range of global public good issues, a full description of major issues and challenges in designing global warming policies.

Chapter 4 will then provide a complete presentation of the integrated assessment models (IAMs) of global warming. The IAMs put together all aspects of global warming sciences and policy variables into a single integrated optimization decision framework for the global community. Using one of the IAMs, the author will have a chance to provide an analysis of behavioral aspects of a global warming policy decision making in an empirical way.

References

Arrow, K.J., Cropper, M.L., Eads, G.C., Hahn, R.W., Lave, L.B., Noll, R.G., Portney, P.R., Russell, M., Schmalensee, R., Smith, V.K., Stavins, R., 1996a. Is there a role for benefit-cost analysis in environmental, health, and safety regulation? Science 272, 221—222.

Arrow, K.J., Cline, W., Maler, K.G., Munasinghe, M., Squitieri, R., Stiglitz, J., 1996b. Intertemporal equity, discounting, and economic efficiency. In: Bruce, J.P., Lee, H., Haites, E.F. (Eds.), Climate Change 1995: Economic and Social Dimensions of Climate Change, Intergovernmental Panel on Climate Change. Cambridge University Press, New York.

Baumol, W.J., Oates, W.E., 1971. The use of standards and prices for protection of the environment. The Swedish Journal of Economics 73, 42—54.

Baumol, W.J., Oates, O.A., 1988. The Theory of Environmental Policy, second ed. Cambridge University Press, Cambridge.

Bell, M.L., McDermott, A., Zeger, S.L., Samet, J.M., Domenici, F., 2004. Ozone and short-term mortality in 95 US urban communities, 1987−2000. Journal of the American Medical Association 292, 2372−2378.

Bowen, H.R., 1943. The interpretation of voting in the allocation of economic resources. The Quarterly Journal of Economics 58 (1), 27−48.

Brown, K.M., 1973. Welfare implications of congestion in public goods. Review of Social Economy 31, 89−92.

Buchanan, J.M., 1965. An economy theory of clubs. Economica 32, 1−24.

Buchanan, J.M., 1968. The Demand and Supply of Public Goods. Rand McNally & Co., Chicago.

Burtraw, D., Szambelan, S.J., 2009. U.S. Emissions Trading Markets for SO_2 and NO_x. Resources for the Future Discussion Paper 09−40. Resources for the Future, Washington, DC.

Chapman, C.R., Morrison, D., 1994. Impacts on the earth by asteroids and comets: assessing the hazard. Nature 367, 33−40.

Clawson, M., 1959. Methods of Measuring the Demand and Value of Outdoor Recreation. Resources For the Future, Washington, DC. Reprint.

Coase, R., 1960. The problem of social costs. Journal of Law and Economics 3, 1−44.

Cropper, M.L., Oates, W.E., 1992. Environmental economics: a survey. Journal of Economic Literature 30, 675−740.

Diamond, P.A., Hausman, J.A., 1994. Contingent valuation: is some number better than no number? Journal of Economic Perspectives 8, 45−64.

Dickie, M., Gerking, S., 1991. Willingness to pay for ozone control: inferences from the demand for medical care. Journal of Environmental Economics and Management 21, 1−16.

Dixit, A.K., 1990. Optimization in Economic Theory, second ed. Oxford University Press, Oxford.

European Commission, 2016. EU ETS Handbook. European Commission, Brussels.

Felzer, B.S., Cronin, T., Reilly, J.M., Melillo, J.M., Wang, X., 2007. Impacts of ozone on trees and crops. Comptes Rendus Geoscience 339, 784−798.

Field, B.C., Field, M.K., 2016. Environmental Economics: An Introduction, sixth ed. The McGraw-Hill, New York.

Fisher, I., 1930. The Theory of Interest. Macmillan, New York.

Freeman III, A.M., 1974. On estimating air pollution control benefits from land value studies. Journal of Environmental Economics and Management 1, 74−83.

Freeman III, A.M., Herriges, J.A., Cling, C.L., 2014. The Measurements of Environmental and Resource Values: Theory and Practice. RFF Press, New York.

Fudenberg, D., Tirole, J., 1991. Games in strategic form and Nash equilibrium. In: Fudenberg, D., Tirole, J. (Eds.), Game Theory. MIT Press, Cambridge, MA.

Goulder, L.H., Parry, I.W.H., Burtraw, D., 1997. Revenue raising versus other approaches to environmental protection: the critical significance of pre-existing tax distortion. Rand Journal of Economics 28, 708−731.

Greenstone, M., Gallagher, J., 2008. Does hazardous waste matter? Evidence from the housing market and the superfund program. The Quarterly Journal of Economics 123, 951−1003.

Guardian, December, 13 2016. Earth Woefully Unprepared for Surprise Comet or Asteroid, NASA Scientist Warns. Available at: https://www.theguardian.com/science/2016/dec/13/space-asteroid-comet-nasa-rocket.

Hahn, R.W., Dudley, P.M., 2007. How well does the U.S. government do benefit-cost analysis? Review of Environmental Economics and Policy 1, 192−211.

Hanemann, W.M., 1994. Valuing the environment through contingent valuation. Journal of Economic Perspectives 8, 19−43.

Hartwick, J.M., Olewiler, N.D., 1997. The Economics of Natural Resource Use, second ed. Pearson, New York.

Hirshleifer, J., 1980. Price Theory and Applications, second ed. Prentice Hall, Englewood Cliffs, NJ.

Intergovernmental Panel on Climate Change (IPCC), 1990. Climate Change: The IPCC Scientific Assessment. Cambridge University Press, Cambridge.

Kaul, I., Conceicao, P., Goulven, K.L., Mendoza, R.U. (Eds.), 2003. Providing Global Public Goods: Managing Globalization. Oxford University Press, Oxford.

Knetsch, J.L., 1963. Outdoor recreation demands and benefits. Land Economics 39, 387−396.

Korea Exchange, 2016. Introduction to Emissions Trading Scheme. http://open.krx.co.kr/contents/OPN/01/01050401/OPN01050401.jsp.

Kotchen, M., Moore, M.R., 2007. Private provision of environmental public goods: household participation in green-electricity programs. Journal of Environmental Economics and Management 53, 1−16.

Le Treut, H., Somerville, R., Cubasch, U., Ding, Y., Mauritzen, C., Mokssit, A., Peterson, T., Prather, M., 2007. Historical overview of climate change. In: Solomon, S., Qin, D., Manning, M., Chen, Z., Marquis, M., Averyt, K.B., Tignor, M., Miller, H.L. (Eds.), Climate Change 2007: The Physical Science Basis. Contribution of Working Group I to the Fourth Assessment Report of the Intergovernmental Panel on Climate Change. Cambridge University Press, Cambridge.

Likens, G.E., Bormann, F.H., 1974. Acid rain: a serious regional environmental problem. Science 184, 1176−1179.

Lindahl, E., 1919. Just taxation—a positive solution (Translated from German). In: Musgrave, R.A., Peacock A.T. (Ed.), 1958. Classics in the Theory of Public Finance. Macmillan, London.

Mankiw, N.G., 2014. Principles of Economics, seventh ed. Cengage Learning, Stamford, CT.

Manne, A.S., Richels, R.G., 1999. The Kyoto Protocol: a cost-effective strategy for meeting environmental objectives? The Energy Journal 20 (Special Issue), 1−23.

Manne, A.S., Mendelsohn, R., Richels, R.G., 1995. MERGE: a model for evaluating regional and global effects of GHG reduction policies. Energy Policy 23, 17−34.

Maler, K.-G., Vincent, J.R., 2005. The Handbook of Environmental Economics (Vol. 2): Valuing Environmental Changes. North-Holland, Amsterdam.

Mas-Colell, A., Whinston, M.D., Green, J.R., 1995. Microeconomic Theory. Oxford University Press, Oxford.

Mauzerall, D., Sultan, B., Kim, N., Bradford, D.F., 2005. NO_x emissions from large point sources: variability in ozone production, resulting health damages and economic costs. Atmospheric Environment 39, 2851−2866.

Mendelsohn, R., 1980. An economic analysis of air pollution from coal-fired power plants. Journal of Environmental Economics and Management 7, 30−43.

Mendelsohn, R., Olmstead, S., 2009. The economic valuation of environmental amenities and disamenities: methods and applications. Annual Review of Resources 34, 325−347.

McKibbin, W.J., Wilcoxen, P.J., 2002. The role of economics in climate change policy. Journal of Economic Perspectives 16 (2), 107−129.

Montgomery, W.D., 1972. Markets in licenses and efficient pollution control programs. Journal of Economic Theory 5, 395−418.

Muller, N.Z., Mendelsohn, R., 2009. Efficient pollution regulation: getting the prices right. American Economic Review 99, 1714−1739.

Muller, N.Z., Mendelsohn, R., Nordhaus, W., 2011. Environmental accounting for pollution in the United States economy. American Economic Review 101, 1649–1675.

Musgrave, R., 1959. The Theory of Public Finance. McGraw-Hill, New York.

Nash, J., 1950. Equilibrium points in n-person games. Proceedings of the National Academy of Sciences 36 (1), 48–49.

Nash, J., 1951. Non-cooperative games. The Annals of Mathematics 54 (2), 286–295.

Newell, R.G., Pizer, W.A., 2003. Regulating stock pollutants under uncertainty. Journal of Environmental Economics and Management 45, 416–432.

Nordhaus, W., 1982. How fast should we graze the global commons? American Economic Review 72, 242–246.

Nordhaus, W., 1994. Managing the Global Commons. MIT Press, Massachusetts.

Nordhaus, W., 2001. Global warming economics. Science 294, 1283–1284.

Nordhaus, W., 2010. Economic aspects of global warming in a post-Copenhagen environment. Proceedings of the National Academy of Sciences of the United States 107 (26), 11721–11726.

Nordhaus, W.D., 2006. Paul Samuelson and global public goods. In: Szenberg, M., Ramrattan, L., Gottesman, A.A. (Eds.), Samuelsonian Economics and the Twenty-first Century. Oxford Scholarship Online, 2006.

Nordhaus, W.D., Boyer, J.G., 1999. Requiem for Kyoto: an economic analysis of the Kyoto Protocol. Energy Journal 20 (Special Issue), 93–130.

Oates, W., Baumol, W., 1975. The instruments for environmental policy. In: Mills, E.S. (Ed.), Economic Analysis of Environmental Problems. National Bureau of Economic Research, MA.

Ostrom, E., 1990. Governing the Commons: The Evolution of Institutions for Collective Action. Cambridge University Press, Cambridge.

Ostrom, E., 2009. Beyond Markets and States: Polycentric Governance of Complex Economic Systems. Nobel Lecture. The Royal Swedish Academy of the Sciences, Sweden.

Pareto, V., 1906. In: Montesano, A., Zanni, A., Bruni, L., Chipman, J.S., McLure, M. (Eds.), Manual for Political Economy. Oxford University Press, Oxford, 2014.

Pigou, A.C., 1920. Economics of Welfare. Macmillan and Co., London.

Pizer, W., 1997. Prices Vs. Quantities Revisited: The Case of Climate Change. Resources For the Future (RFF), Discussion Paper 98–02. RFF, Washington, DC.

Pope, C.A., Burnett, R.T., Thun, M.J., Calle, E.E., Krewski, D., Ito, K., Thurston, G.D., 2002. Lung cancer, cardiopulmonary mortality, and long-term exposure to fine particulate air pollution. Journal of the American Medical Association 287 (9), 1132–1141.

Posner, R.A., 2004. Catastrophe: Risk and Response. Oxford University Press, New York.

Ridker, R., Henning, J., 1967. The determination of residential property values with special reference to air pollution. Review of Economics and Statistics 48, 246–257.

Rosen, S., 1974. Hedonic prices and implicit markets: product differentiation in pure competition. Journal of Political Economy 82, 34–55.

Samuelson, P., 1954. The pure theory of public expenditure. The Review of Economics and Statistics 36, 387–389.

Samuelson, P., 1955. Diagrammatic exposition of a theory of public expenditure. Review of Economics and Statistics 37, 350–356.

Samuelson, P., Nordhaus, W., 2009. Economics, nineteenth ed. McGraw-Hill Education, New York.

Sandler, T., 1997. Global challenges: an approach to environmental, political, and economic problems. Cambridge University Press, Cambridge.

Seo, S.N., 2012. What eludes global agreements on climate change? Economic Affairs 32, 73–79.

Seo, S.N., 2013. Economics of global warming as a global public good: private incentives and smart adaptations. Regional Science Policy and Practice 5, 83–95.

Seo, S.N., 2015. Adaptation to global warming as an optimal transition process to a greenhouse world. Economic Affairs 35, 272–284.

Seo, S.N., 2016a. Modeling farmer adaptations to climate change in South America: a micro-behavioral economic perspective. Environmental and Ecological Statistics 23, 1–21.

Seo, S.N., 2016b. The micro-behavioral framework for estimating total damage of global warming on natural resource enterprises with full adaptations. Journal of Agricultural, Biological, and Environmental Statistics 21, 328–347.

Seo, S.N., 2016c. A theory of global public goods and their provisions. Journal of Public Affairs 16, 394–405.

Smith, A., 1776. An Inquiry into the Nature and Causes of the Wealth of Nations. In: Cannan, E. (Ed.). University of Chicago Press, Chicago.

Smith, V.K., Huang, J.-C., 1995. Can markets value air quality? A meta-analysis of hedonic property value models. Journal of Political Economy 103, 209–227.

Smith, V.K., 2008. Reflections on the literature. Review of Environmental Economics and Policy 2 (2), 292–308.

Smith, V.K., Desvousges, W.H., 1986. Averting behavior: does it exist? Economics Letters 20, 291–296.

Stavins, R., 1998. What can we learn from the grand policy experiment? Lessons from SO$_2$ allowance trading. Journal of Economic Perspectives 12, 69–88.

Stavins, R., 2007. A US Cap-and-Trade System to Address Global Climate Change. Hamilton Project Discussion Paper 2007–13. The Brookings Institution, Washington, DC.

Thaler, R., Rosen, S., 1976. The value of saving a life: evidence from the market. In: Terleckyj, N. (Ed.), Household Production and Consumption. National Bureau of Economic Research, Cambridge, MA.

Tietenberg, T.H., 2006. Emissions Trading: Principles and Practice, second ed. Resources for the Future, Washington, DC.

Tietenberg, T., 2013. Reflections − carbon pricing in practice. Review of Environmental Economics and Policy 7, 313–329.

Tietenberg, T., Lewis, L., 2014. Environmental & Natural Resource Economics, ninth ed. Routledge, New York.

Tol, R.S.J., 2002. Estimates of the damage costs of climate change—part 1: benchmark estimates. Environmental and Resource Economics 21, 47–73.

United Nations Framework Convention on Climate Change (UNFCCC), 1992. United Nations Framework Convention on Climate Change. New York.

United Nations Framework Convention on Climate Change (UNFCCC), 1998. Kyoto Protocol to the United Nations Framework Convention on Climate Change. UNFCCC, Geneva.

United Nations Framework Convention on Climate Change (UNFCCC), 2015. The Paris Agreement. Conference of the Parties (COP) 21. UNFCCC, New York.

United States House of Representatives, 2009. H.R.2454-American Clean Energy and Security Act of 2009. US House of Representatives, Washington, DC.

United States Environmental Protection Agency (US EPA), 1990. The Clean Air Act Amendments. US EPA, Washington, DC.

United States Environmental Protection Agency, 1999. The Benefits and Costs of the Clean Air Act: 1990–2010. EPA Report to Congress. EPA 410-R-99-001. Washington, DC.

United States Environmental Protection Agency, 2010. The 40th Anniversary of the Clean Air Act. US EPA, Washington, DC. Available at: http://www.epa.gov/airprogm/oar/caa/40th. html.

United States Environmental Protection Agency, 2014. National Emissions Inventory (NEI). Washington, DC.

Viscusi, W.K., 1979. Employment Hazards: An Investigation of Market Performance. Harvard University Press, Cambridge, MA.

Viscusi, W.K., Aldy, J.E., 2003. The value of a statistical life: a critical review of market estimates throughout the world. Journal of Risk and Uncertainty 5, 5−76.

Walras, L., 1954. Elements of Pure Economics (Translated and annotated by William Jaffe). Allen and Unwin, London.

Wang, B., Shugart, H.H., Shuman, J.K., Lerdau, M.T., 2016. Forests and ozone: productivity, carbon storage, and feedbacks. Scientific Reports 6, 22133. http://dx.doi.org/10.1038/srep22133.

Weitzman, M.L., 1974. Prices versus quantities. Review of Economic Studies 41, 477−491.

Weitzman, M.L., 2009. On modeling and interpreting the economics of catastrophic climate change. Review of Economics and Statistics 91, 1−19.

Woodruff, T.J., Parker, J.D., Schoendorf, K.C., 2006. Fine particulate matter (PM2.5) air pollution and selected causes of postneonatal infant mortality in California. Environmental Health Perspectives 114, 786−790.

Further Reading

Hirshleifer, J., 1983. From weakest-link to best-shot: the voluntary provision of public goods. Public Choice 41, 371−386.

Intergovernmental Panel on Climate Change (IPCC), 2014. Climate Change 2014: The Physical Science Basis. The Fifth Assessment Report of the IPCC. Cambridge University Press, Cambridge.

Kotchen, M.J., 2009. Voluntary provision of public goods for bads: a theory of environmental offsets. Economic Journal 119, 883−899.

Designing Global Warming Policies and Major Challenges

Chapter Outline

1. Introduction

The previous chapter provided a comprehensive review of the theory of national (and global) public goods with an array of real-world examples that have received much attention in the literature of environmental policy making. This chapter provides further refinements of our understanding of global warming as a global public good, based upon which a broad review of the literature on challenges and obstacles in designing global warming policies is provided (Nordhaus, 2010b, 2011a; Seo, 2012a, 2016a). The author will leave a rigorous discussion of a carbon price approach to the next chapter because it involves applications of various integrated assessment models of climate change that are analytically complex to be dealt with in this chapter (Nordhaus and Yang, 1996; Manne et al., 1995).

This chapter introduces a number of global public goods that are debated often in an international policy context, including nuclear nonproliferation and global free trade. The problem of global warming—one of the many global public goods—will be viewed in comparison with these other global public good problems through which the author hopes to highlight distinct characteristics of the former. These unique features of the global warming problem, as will be explained throughout this chapter, result in unique great challenges in addressing the problem.

Of these unique features are, inter alia, a truly global scale of the problem, a very long timeframe that must be accounted for, a large disparity across the actors in the impacts of changes, behavioral responses to environmental changes, distinct production technologies involved in the provision of the concerned good, a large number of factors and mechanisms involved in global warming processes and consequently uncertainties in many of them, and possibilities of technological solutions (Seo, 2013, 2015b).

These characteristics lead to scientific and practical challenges in designing global warming policies that have been observed repeatedly in past global warming negotiations. To name a few, difficulty of predicting the degree of global temperature change by the end of this century and the probability of the prediction, differing perspectives between developed nations and developing nations on an international policy, disagreements on the stringency of global warming policy called for, disagreements on the impacts of climate change, disagreements on adaptation possibilities and costs, disagreements on whether certain catastrophic events occurred because of global warming, disagreements on technological possibilities through breakthroughs, and disagreements on the importance of developing alternative low-carbon energy sources (Chan et al., 2016; Mendelsohn, 2016).

In the next section, the author will begin with the description of the unique features of the global warming problem in contrast to other global public goods' problems, which will be followed by examples of global public goods other than the phenomenon of global warming. Then, the author provides a description of the standard-bearer in global warming economics and policy, i.e., the Samuelson–Nordhaus framework. Distinct challenges in designing global warming policies are elaborated subsequently, which are composed of eight subsections: heterogeneity in damage estimate, heterogeneity in economic status of countries, heterogeneity in abatement cost, club provision, a compensation and transfer scheme, uncertainty and extremes, time preference, and governance.

2. Distinct Characteristics of Global Warming

In describing the public goods in the previous chapter, a geopolitical scale of a public good is viewed as an integral element that distinguishes a multitude of public goods. The author introduced the classification of public goods into a local public good, a state public good, and a national public good. A global public good can be considered to be another category in the above-mentioned classification of the public goods (Samuelson and Nordhaus, 2009). The publicness of a global public good has ripple effects on the entire globe.

Let us imagine that a large asteroid that is capable of altering the cyclical route of the Earth around the Sun is rapidly approaching the Earth. The possibility of the Earth going off the route permanently is certain to pose huge risk and may cause a "catastrophic end to the civilizations on Earth." The citizens of the Earth must protect the planet from a collision against the asteroid. The benefits of protecting the Earth fall upon all the communities and nations on the planet. It is not possible to exclude a selected nation from receiving the benefit. The enjoyment by one nation of the benefit does not diminish the benefit available to other nations.

In this asteroid example, looked from the standpoint of a range of spatial scales, a global public good does not seem to differ greatly from a national public good. The only difference seems, at the first glance, to be the size of the concerned (affected) community, which is global. However, when it comes to global warming, the size of the concerned community turns out to be critically important, which will be elaborated shortly.

In the case of global climate changes, we are concerned with the changes in the system that is globally operating, that is, the global climate system. Fundamentally, we are not concerned with the changes in a regional or local climate pattern as long as these changes do not alter the global climate phenomena. That is, if regional changes were to balance out at the global level, we would not be concerned about those changes.

The second distinguishing characteristic, however, presents a major departure from the characteristic of the public goods and in fact appears uniquely in the problem of global warming as well as a global public good. That is, in the problem of global warming, there is no governing body that can determine and enforce any global policy and coordinate the member nations for achieving an agreed goal. There is no political and legal entity that can force nations to act in a certain way.

This is sometimes called the Westphalian dilemma in the literature (Nordhaus, 2006). In the cities of Westphalia in Germany, the present national boundaries were drawn and agreed upon by the European countries in 1648 to stop recurring territorial disputes and violent conflicts in Europe. The Treaty of Westphalia states that an individual nation's sovereignty must be protected. In the system of the Westphalian Treaty, there is no global political entity that can infringe upon an individual nation's sovereign rights.

As we elaborated in the previous chapter, a national public good can be provided only through the intervention of a national government, either through taxation, a permit trading system, or any other regulatory measures. The provision of a global public good runs into a big pothole because of the absence of a so-called global government.

In the example of asteroid collision, the Westphalian dilemma manifests in the question of who should take the burden of protecting the Earth. Should one nation such as the United States take the burden, or China, or Russia? In the problem of global warming, it very often manifests in the debates over who should pay for the mitigation of greenhouse gases (GHGs). It turns out that no country is willing to take the full burden of protecting the climate system. Notwithstanding, there is no government at the global level, either.

The third distinguishing feature of global warming is even more confounding. Although the provision of a global public good, i.e., protection of the global climate system, has to be made over the entire regions of the Earth and by the efforts from the entire communities of the Earth, it turns out that the benefits and costs of provision of the global public good are varied across individual nations and states (Tol, 2002; Mendelsohn et al., 2006). In addition, the benefits and costs of nonprovision of the global public good are disparate across individual nations and states (Seo, 2012a).

This feature makes the provision of the global public good even more challenging. That the benefits and costs of provision of the good are disparate widely across the nations implies that any legally binding agreement among all the nations is almost impossible (Nordhaus, 2001, 2010b). A large number of nations will disagree on any proposal, even though another group of nations enthusiastically supports the proposal (UNFCCC, 1998, 2009).

The large disparity in damages and benefits from a global warming policy turns out to be even more critical when this feature emerges in sync with existing geopolitical divisions across the nations or in clash with them. For example, nations are allied and antagonistic geopolitically against other groups. It may turn out that the existing geopolitical alliances may not align well with the new paradigm that is formed in accordance with the winner-or-loser calculations with regard to the provision of the global public good of protection of the climate system.

Another more prominent example is the divide between rich high-latitude countries and poor low-latitude countries. If the aforementioned disparity emerges in sync with this geoeconomic divide, it would complicate by a great deal the process of making an agreement in global warming policies (Mendelsohn et al., 2006; Seo, 2016d).

The fourth distinguishing feature of the problem of global warming is a very long time horizon that must be taken into consideration in any meaningful attempt to resolve the problem of the global public good. In the problem of global warming, a policy time frame is normally a century (IPCC, 2014). Alternative policies must be compared in consideration of changes in the climate system at least for a century.

With such a long time horizon that must be considered, policies and policy models must answer to many generations of people that will live on Earth (Broome, 1994; Arrow et al., 1996; Kolstad, 1996). In addition, residence times of a variety of GHGs are varied and should be considered. Moreover, the benefit of providing the global public good, that is, reduction in emissions of GHGs today does not materialize for many decades. To put it differently, consequences of not providing the global public good do not come to pass for many decades.

Countries must think with a long-term perspective. Negotiators must resolve the difficult problems that arise because of the long time horizon that must be considered in global warming problems. Given the uncertainty on too many aspects of the future faced by individual nations, analysts and policy makers inevitably rely on many assumptions about the future. These assumptions must be made not only on concrete indicators such as gross domestic product (GDP) growth, but also on more perceptual aspects such as discounting the future (Newell and Pizer, 2001; Stern, 2007; Nordhaus, 2007b).

3. Contrasts With Other Global Public Goods

Other than global warming, often discussed in the context of a global public good are, inter alia, defense against an asteroid collision, prevention of nuclear proliferation, global free trade, fights against transnational terrorism, and development of new knowledge and technologies (Sandler, 1997; Kaul et al., 2003; Posner, 2004;

Nordhaus, 2006). The problem of global warming differs from these other global problems in major ways, which calls for a different policy approach to deal with the problem.

Global warming is a rare and prominent example of a global public good in that a "stable" climate is enjoyed by all the communities on Earth and a state of no global warming, i.e., a state of climate stability, is only attainable by the collective efforts of all the nations on Earth (Nordhaus, 1994). Put differently, a stable global climate system can be destabilized even by a single country, such as the United States, China, India, Russia, or Brazil, if any of these countries does not care about carbon emissions at all.

A stable climate regime is a global public good, whereas a destabilized climate regime, i.e., global warming, is a global public bad. A stable climate regime does not necessarily mean one without any changes at all in climate variables such as temperature normals and precipitation normals. A stable climate regime is one with natural changes where anthropogenic emissions of carbon contribute little to the regime. The states of climate instability or global warming are those with abnormal changes in temperature, precipitation, and other measures of climate that are mainly caused by anthropogenic interventions. A stable climate regime can be destabilized by, inter alia, an excessive pumping out of GHGs into the atmosphere (IPCC, 2014).

Global warming has the canonical characteristics of a global public good (Mas-Colell et al., 1995). Provision of climate stability has the characteristic of nonexcludability. Any nation can enjoy the benefit of climate stability and cannot be excluded from enjoying the benefit of climate stability once it is provided. However, it does not mean that the benefit each nation receives from a stable climate regime is uniform across the nations. Furthermore, it may be argued that a warmer temperature is beneficial to some countries such as Russia. However, instabilities in many other measures of climate are highly likely to turn out to be harmful in these countries with a high degree of warming.

Provision of climate stability has the characteristic of nonrivalry or nondepletability. A nation's enjoyment of climate stability does not diminish the amount of enjoyment of it by other nations. It is neither depleted by a single nation or by a group of nations nor "congested" by the use of a group of nations (Buchanan, 1965; Brown, 1973).

The provision of a stable climate regime can be achieved by many methods, the most discussed of which is the reduction of the emissions of GHGs by a variety of emission sources. GHGs are those gases that, once emitted into the atmosphere, accumulate and form the greenhouse-like blanket that reflects the outgoing long-wave solar radiation, through which they warm the global atmosphere (UNFCCC, 1992). These are carbon dioxide, methane, nitrous oxide, water vapor, ozone, and fluorinated gases such as hydrofluorocarbons and hydrochlorofluorocarbons.

Who will provide the global climate stability? Because of the characteristics of the global public good being nonexcludable and nonrivalrous, each nation has an incentive to free ride on others' sacrifices. That is, each nation would let other nations provide the global public good and then take the benefit from the global public good without paying for it. If all nations become a free rider, there will be no provision of the global public good, that is, a stable global climate regime. If only a group of nations takes the burden of providing climate stability, it is destined to fail because of emissions leakages into the outside of the group. That is, emissions will increase in the nations outside the club.

The negotiations of global warming policies have been led by the United Nations' Framework Convention on Climate Change (UNFCCC) since its establishment in 1992 at the Earth Summit in Rio de Janeiro (UNFCCC, 1992). The twenty-two Conferences of Parties held annually up to the end of 2016 have not yielded a forceful agreement mainly because of the free-rider incentive of participating nations (UNFCCC, 2015). The negotiation experiences for more than two decades have exposed the real conundrum of providing a truly global public good, which is the primary subject that this book set out to address, that is, the problem of free riding on the global public good.

Is the problem of global warming different from other global public goods? Let us consider another global public good problem, that is, the protection of the Earth from so large an asteroid collision that can virtually destroy the Earth (Chapman and Morrison, 1994). The benefit of protection from such a catastrophe is nonexcludable as well as nonrivalrous. But the asteroid problem differs from the global warming problem in several meaningful ways.

Imagine a relatively smaller asteroid that can jolt a single nation, but has only negligible impact on the rest of the nations? In this case, each nation knows that there is some chance of being hit by such an asteroid that devastates the nation, but cannot know the probability of such an event with certainty. Each nation has the incentive to get prepared for such an event and develop an effective strategy to shoot down the asteroid in case it happens. The benefit of protection in this case has some degree of excludability as well as rivalry. The problem in this case becomes less of a global public good.

Even in the case of a very large asteroid that can bring about a global catastrophe, the protection of the Earth against the asteroid does not call for the extensive global collaboration that is envisioned in the solutions of global warming problem. A single country that has the most advanced technological capability would be able to shoot down or blow up the approaching asteroid. In fact, at present, defense against a large asteroid collision is approached at an individual country level, e.g., by the United States (NASA, 2007).

In the economics terminology, the provision of a global public good in the case of asteroid protection is achieved by a best-shot technology (Hirshleifer, 1983). Not every country needs to fire arms to blow up the approaching asteroid; only one country needs to do that to protect the globe. In this sense, the problem of asteroid collision is much easier to be handled than that of global warming.

Let us consider another example of global public goods: prevention of nuclear proliferation. A failure to prevent nuclear proliferation is certain to have dire consequences on the global communities (Turco et al., 1983; Mills et al., 2008). In a scenario in which every nation competes for stockpiling of nuclear arms, the world will turn into a perilous place in which civilizations can be wiped out by nuclear wars.

In a successful scenario in which nuclear proliferation can be deemed eliminated, every nation would reduce the amount of nuclear arms "competitively" step by step.

The success of ending the nuclear arms race would then be measured by the maximum amount of nuclear arms in the largest nuclear nation. In other words, the success is determined by how low the amount of nuclear arms could go in the largest nuclear nation.

In the economics literature, the production technology that provides the solution for nuclear nonproliferation is said to have a weakest link technology (Hirshleifer, 1983). Another example of the weakest link technology is elimination of malaria in sub-Saharan countries. As long as malaria is existent in a country, it will spread quickly to neighboring countries. To eliminate malaria, it should be eliminated at the weakest link.

The success of nuclear nonproliferation does not take all nations on Earth to take part in a coordinated effort. There are fewer than 10 nations in the world that have the capacity to build nuclear bombs and actually own nuclear arms. Five nuclear states are recognized by the United Nations: the United States, Russia, the United Kingdom, France, and China. These nations are also permanent members of the UN Security Council. Four states are known or believed to have nuclear weapons: India, Pakistan, North Korea, and Israel (UNODA, 2015).

The Treaty on Non-proliferation of Nuclear Weapons entered into force in 1970 and was extended indefinitely in 1995. The treaty is signed by 190 nations as of 2015. The treaty establishes a safeguards system under the responsibility of the International Atomic Energy Agency (IAEA). The IAEA verifies compliance with the Treaty through inspections. The Treaty promotes cooperation in the field of peaceful nuclear technology and equal access to this technology for all states parties, while safeguards prevent the diversion of fissile material for weapons use (UNODA, 2015).

Another major world issue that is often discussed in the context of a global public good is global free trade. A global free trade system in its purest form would remove all trade barriers of all the nations on Earth, the result of which would be a Pareto improvement in allocation of resources across the nations. The prices of goods would become lower and the welfare of the world citizens would be enhanced (Ricardo, 1817; Ohlin, 1933; Stolper and Samuelson, 1941; Samuelson, 1949).

However, the expected benefit from a global free trade system to an individual country can be reaped by the country even by a regional free trade system that is well designed to include the groups of nations with a wide range of human and natural resources and with similar political systems. A global free trade may even harm a country if it does not compete well and is dominated in the markets within the global free trade bloc (Stiglitz, 2002; Krugman, 2008). A financial shock in one country may easily spill over to the other nations distressing the whole free trade bloc and beyond, as observed in the global financial crisis since 2008 and the EU debt crisis that followed (Shiller, 2008).

In this context, the free trade system does not fit neatly into the mold of a global public good. Rather, it can be better viewed as a regional public good. To be more specific, it is widely viewed that a global-scale free trade is not as ideal as the pure free market economics would suggest (Ricardo, 1817; Ohlin, 1933), given many complex factors that belong uniquely to individual nations, including politics, culture, and history (Stiglitz, 2002; Krugman, 2008). A well-designed regional free trade system, on the other hand, can be more effective in achieving the gains from free trade as well as avoiding the harms from it.

A similar argument can be applied to the globalized financial system in which capital movements are envisioned to flow freely and regulations are set homogeneously across the nations. The extant example may be found in the Euro Zone in which a single currency is adopted, a single central bank determines money supply and interest rate, and many financial regulations are harmonized within the Euro Zone economies. A globalized financial system may not be feasible nor desirable for the global communities.

Besides the European Union, the Trans-Pacific Partnership (TPP) may turn out to be such a regional trade bloc. It is a trade agreement among 12 Pacific Rim countries signed in February 2016, which has not yet entered into force but whose prospect has dimmed after election of Donald Trump as US President in November 2016. Member countries of the TPP are Brunei, Chile, New Zealand, Singapore, Australia, Canada, Japan, Malaysia, Mexico, Peru, the United States, and Vietnam. Other countries that expressed interests to join the TPP are Colombia, the Philippines, Thailand, Taiwan, South Korea, and Indonesia.

Another good that is often discussed as a global public good is the development of novel knowledge and technologies. Once novel knowledge or a new technology is developed by one country, it spreads to other countries "at the speed of light." A new knowledge benefits the entire global community. A new knowledge is freely available; therefore a single country cannot be excluded from enjoying it. Nor does an individual nation's appreciation and appropriation of the knowledge reduce the amount of knowledge available to other nations. It is nonrivalrous.

Past examples of such knowledge and technologies are numerous, including eradication of small pox, measles, and polio in developed nations (Barrett, 2008). Developing a cure for cancer, Alzheimer disease, or human immunodeficiency virus infection would have similarly large benefits that would spread quickly around the world. Similarly, developments of high-yielding varieties of grains during the Green Revolution era have benefited the global communities (Evenson and Gollin, 2003).

Nonetheless, the global "publicness" of new knowledge and technologies has been constrained by numerous methods. In many breakthrough technologies, the new knowledge and technology is patented by a researcher/developer so that there would be limitations to accessing the knowledge and technology by others and other nations. The property right of a developer is created by the patent system. A perfect patent system, if possible in a certain new technology, would make it a private good, which is both excludable and rivalrous.

An innovative technology or knowledge does not call for an extensive global collaboration that is envisioned in global warming policy negotiations. Many of the breakthrough technologies have been pioneered by an individual scientist/developer. Lighting was pioneered by Thomas Edison, whereas alternating current and radio were pioneered by Nicola Tesla.

A large-scale national as well as international cooperative project is also taking place. Examples abound: the National Aeronautics and Space Administration Mars exploration program, the Conseil Européen pour la Recherche Nucléaire reactor project by the European Union, or the International Thermonuclear Experimental Reactor program for developing a nuclear fusion technology by concerned countries

(CERN, 2015; ITER, 2015; NASA, 2016). But a global participation is neither needed nor feasible in these programs.

Again, production of this global public good, i.e., new knowledge and technologies, is achieved by a best-shot technology. That is, the best individual researcher or institution would first develop this, which then quickly spills over to other researchers and countries (Hirshleifer, 1983).

Furthermore, a specific scientific innovation or knowledge to be discovered is most often unknown before its coming into existence. Because it is difficult to imagine a certain breakthrough technology or knowledge beforehand, an extensive global collaborative project for a certain specific knowledge or technology is harder to realize.

Summing up, the author compared in this section the problem of global warming with the other global problems such as asteroid collision, nuclear proliferation, global free trade, and new knowledge and technology. What this section tells us is that global warming is a truly global public good, for the provision of which calls for an extensive global cooperation.

4. The Standard-Bearer: A Samuelson–Nordhaus Framework

Is there a way to provide efficiently the global public good of climate stability? The answer has been "yes," at least in theory, in the literature (Nordhaus, 1994). This literature views the problem of the global public good as an extension of a national public good problem and applies the solution for provision of a national public good to the provision of the global public good of climate stability.

In this literature, the problem of global warming can be solved efficiently by applying the same approach that is effective in solving the problems of national public goods, i.e., public taxation and expenditure, but only at a global scale (Samuelson, 1954, 1955). A tax (price or penalty) would be imposed at a harmonized level across the globe (Nordhaus, 1994). A "carbon price" would create an incentive for emitters of GHGs to cut the emissions up to the point where a socially optimal level of GHG emissions is achieved. We called this approach as the Samuelson–Nordhaus framework for provision of a global public good. Once the charge (tax) is set at the global level, an efficient removal of the GHGs is achieved by individuals who make optimal decisions under the charge (Nordhaus, 1992).

In the Samuelson–Nordhaus framework, there remains an additional question of how countries should use the tax revenue collected from the charge. To assure social optimality, tax revenue must be spent at least in a (carbon) neutral way (Metcalf, 2009; Nordhaus, 2010a). That is, the public spending should not affect the level of abatement at the global level. Put differently, the distribution of tax revenue should not encourage further emissions by individuals at the global level. We will discuss this issue later in this chapter.

To provide a brief explanation of the Samuelson–Nordhaus framework, let us consider the following simple global economy model. A full description of the framework is the subject of the next chapter of this book. Let q_i be the quantity of GHG emissions from country i and q be the quantity of GHG emissions for the globe. Similarly, let x_i be the quantity of abatement of GHG emissions from country i and x be the quantity of abatement of GHG emissions for the globe. Individual countries' emissions add up to the global emissions and individual countries' abatements add up to the global abatement. That is, the production technology involved is additive (Hirshleifer, 1983; Nordhaus, 2006).

To begin with the simplest case and address increasingly difficult situations, let us assume that there are two countries in the world. Let us assume for the moment that the marginal cost of abatement is equal across the countries, i.e., more of same abatement technology is available to all countries:

$$MC(x) = MC_i = MC_j > 0. \tag{3.1}$$

The damage from a ton of GHGs emitted from each country (and from the other country) on each country varies across the countries:

$$MD_i(q) > \frac{MD(q)}{2} > MD_j(q) > 0. \tag{3.2}$$

In the above-mentioned equation, country i is a high vulnerability agent and country j is a low vulnerability agent. In the public good, the marginal damages of individual countries add up vertically to the social marginal damage:

$$MD(q) = \sum_{k=i,j} MD_k(q). \tag{3.3}$$

On the other hand, because the marginal cost functions add up horizontally to the social marginal cost function:

$$MC^{-1}(P) = \sum_{k=i,j} MC_k^{-1}(P). \tag{3.4}$$

A globally optimal abatement level will be determined at the point at which marginal damage of 1 ton of emissions is equal to the marginal abatement of the ton of emissions:

$$x^* \ s.t. \ MC(x^*) = MD(x^*). \tag{3.5}$$

Because 1 ton of carbon dioxide (and other GHGs) emitted today stays in the atmosphere for more than a century, the marginal damage function must consider the long-term effects of the emissions today. The marginal damage should account for the stream of damage over time caused by 1 ton of emissions today, with applications of appropriate discount rates:

$$MD(q^*) = \sum_{t=0}^{\infty} \frac{MD^t}{(1+\rho_t)^t} \tag{3.6}$$

Note that in the absence of any policy intervention, there is no incentive for a firm (or a country in this simple case) to cut GHG emissions. This means that the marginal abatement cost at the status quo emissions level is zero. To bring the marginal abatement cost to the level of marginal damage caused by 1 ton of emissions, the carbon price (or penalty) should be set at the level of the marginal damage. This creates the artificial marginal damage function for the firms. That is, the marginal damage is the fixed at the carbon price:

$$P^* = MD(q^*). \tag{3.7}$$

If the carbon price can be agreed at the international level and implemented with legal force across the world, the two countries will find themselves to be better off by choosing the levels of abatement that add up to the globally optimal level of abatement in Eq. (3.5):

$$x_k^* \ s.t. \ P^* = MC\left(x_k^*\right), \quad \text{for } k = i, j. \tag{3.8}$$

Broadly speaking, the Emission Trading System (ETS), which has been implemented in the first phase of the Kyoto Protocol within the Annex 1 countries, can be seen as an extension of the carbon price approach described so far if the limit is determined optimally, i.e., at the level that satisfies Eq. (3.5) (Nordhaus, 2007a; Tietenberg, 2013). In this case, most of the difficult issues with regard to the carbon price approach would remain the same in the ETS approach and implementation.

However, in the ETS approach, the limit can be set anywhere else than the optimal level (Montgomery, 1972; Tietenberg, 1980). It may be set at a precautionary level, i.e., at a very high level of price because of the concern for catastrophic consequences beyond a threshold, e.g., "end of civilizations as we know it" (Weitzman, 2009). It is presumed that an agreement on the limit for the ETS system is even more difficult to reach than an agreement on carbon price because there is no known principle in determining the quantity limit of the ETS and because of the high risk involved in the price of emissions permit (Nordhaus, 2007a).

5. Major Challenges to Global Warming Policy

5.1 Situation 1: Heterogeneity in Damage

Now, given the assumed cost and damage structure, the two countries will diverge in approaching a GHG abatement policy. Let us further assume that the two countries are identical except for different degrees of vulnerability to global warming, i.e., the marginal damage functions expressed in Eq. (3.2). In the absence of any global carbon policy, the country i is willing to abate more GHG emissions than the country's fair share of what is needed at the global level, whereas the country j is willing to abate less GHG emissions than the country's fair share of what is needed at the global level:

$$\widetilde{x}_i > \frac{x^*}{2} \quad \text{for country } i,$$

$$\tag{3.9}$$

$$\widetilde{x}_j < \frac{x^*}{2} \quad \text{for country } j.$$

Nonetheless, the world would be able to achieve the optimal level of abatement as some countries do more abatement while other countries do less abatement:

$$\tilde{x}_i + \tilde{x}_j = x^*. \tag{3.10}$$

If each country considers all the damage, not only on the country, from a ton of emissions, then marginal damage will be equal across the countries. Then, each country's abatement will be also equal:

$$\tilde{x}_i = \tilde{x}_j = \frac{x^*}{2} \tag{3.11}$$

Eq. (3.11) is a global (cooperative) solution, whereas Eq. (3.9) is a national (individual) solution to the global warming problem. The Samuelson–Nordhaus solution is expressed in Eqs. (3.11), (3.8) and (3.5). Note that the optimal solution is an equal abatement level between the two countries because we assumed that the two countries are equal except for the different degrees of damage from global warming to each country. More specifically, the abatement cost is assumed to be equal across the two countries.

The discussions of major challenges to making a global warming policy can start from the standard-bearer, i.e., the carbon price approach. In the simple global economy model described earlier, the global cooperative solution, i.e., the Samuelson–Nordhaus solution expressed in Eqs. (3.11), (3.8) and (3.5), is problematic because there is no incentive for country j to cut half of the world's emissions given the smaller impact of GHG emissions and global warming on the country. Global warming may turn out to be even beneficial to some countries, which would make these countries averse to act fast or act at all (Seo, 2015b). That is, country j is better off with a national approach to global warming described in Eq. (3.9).

On the other hand, there is an incentive for country i, without any global cooperative solution, to cut more than half of the world's emissions, as described in Eq. (3.9), because global warming damage falls more heavily on the country. However, country i will soon realize that the damage that befalls the country results from the emissions by country j because carbon dioxide emitted from one place quickly mixes in the atmosphere. Country i will demand that country j should cut at least half of the world's emissions, which country j would certainly reject based on national interest.

5.2   Situation 2: Heterogeneity in Economy

An even more confounding situation arises when country i, the high-damage region, happens to be a poor country and country j, the low-damage region, happens to be a rich country. The situation resembles the current reality in which the United States is a low-damage country and India, Africa, Latin America, China, and South Asia are high-damage countries (Pearce et al., 1996; Tol, 2002; Mendelsohn et al., 2006).

With a global cooperative solution, the two countries in the aforementioned model are required to cut half of the world GHG emissions. This may raise strong discontent from the poor country which views the global solution as lacking fairness and equity, one of the principles stated in the UNFCCC foundation document, because both the poor and rich country are required to abate the same amount of emissions (UNFCCC, 1992).

Furthermore, given that the rich country has a much higher accumulated carbon emissions than the poor country, it is often argued by the poor country that the rich country should do more abatement than the poor country (UNFCCC, 2009, 2011a,b).

The individual solution to the problem described in Eq. (3.9) is also highly unlikely. With no global cooperative solution, the country j, the rich country, does not have an incentive to reduce half of the GHG emissions. With no global cooperative solution, the country i, the poor country, must cut more than half of the world emissions according to the individual solution in Eq. (3.9). The individual solution forces that the poor country bears the burden of cleaning up the mess created by the rich country, which is highly unlikely to occur.

5.3 Situation 3: Heterogeneity in Abatement Cost

Let us further assume that the high-damage country is also a low marginal abatement cost country, whereas the low-damage country is also a high marginal abatement cost country. This means that the high-damage country is at the same time both a poor country and a low marginal abatement cost country, whereas the low-damage country is simultaneously both a rich country and a high marginal abatement cost country.

The rationale for this assumption is that the poor country has more options that are cheaper to abate a ton of emissions than the rich country has. It is easier to cut 1 ton in the poor country than in the rich country. The other aspect is that the rich country has more advanced technological options that make it less costly to cut 1 ton of emissions in the rich country than in the poor country (Fischer and Morgenstern, 2006).

In the former situation, the global cooperative solution results in the poor country doing a majority of the abatement work and the rich country doing a minority of the abatement work needed at the global level. The poor country would certainly reject such an international agreement.

Without the global cooperative agreement and with the individual approach, the poor country has an incentive to do the abatement work that is even greater than that required in situation 2 above where there is no difference in abatement costs of the two countries. This is because the poor country has a lower abatement cost function than the rich country. On the other hand, the rich country has an incentive to do the abatement work that is even smaller than that required in the situation 2 above.

The poor country would certainly express frustrations that such a situation is unfair and unjust, requesting the rich country to take more burden of removing GHGs or to provide the fund needed to cut GHGs.

5.4 Situation 4: Club Provision

A club provision of a global public good is sometimes discussed as a remedy for the conundrum of the Samuelson–Nordhaus solution, that is, noncommitment by many members of the global community (Seo, 2012a). In the club provision framework, a club that supports a global optimal policy is initially formed and the size of the club expands over time by forcing non-club members to join (Nordhaus, 2015).

In the context of a national public good, a club provision can be defined as follows: a group of resourceful individuals may be able to and should provide a public good such as national defense, national public education, or air pollution abatement. A large group of rich individuals may be able to provide national defense or national public education even in a large country like the United States. Individuals who are not in the group would free ride, i.e., enjoy the good without spending fee for utilizing it. We can call this a club provision of a national public good.

A club provision can be seen as a form of a voluntary provision of a public good that may happen in a certain situation (Kotchen and Moore, 2007), albeit to a limited extent, in that a group of individuals bear the responsibility, voluntarily, of cutting GHG emissions, or improving air quality, or providing educational services.

The club provision of a national or a global public good raises three major concerns that are all interwoven: fairness, stability of the club, and trustworthiness/publicness of the club. The first is the issue of fairness, which is rather obvious. It is not fair to the club members who must make such a large sacrifice while others only free ride and enjoy. Under the club solution, wealth is reallocated from the club to the non-club members.

The second is the issue of stability with regard to the club. There may develop over time a strong incentive for a club member to defect because of increasing burden of bearing responsibility. As more members leave the club, the club would become less sustainable and capable. When the club breaks up, the concerned public good will no longer be provided. In this sense, the club is not a stable coalition. In other words, it is not in a Nash equilibrium (Nash, 1950, 1951).

The third is the issue of trustworthiness or publicness of the club. Is the club capable of providing a national public good for the benefit of all members of the nation? Is it willing to do so? It may turn out in the long-term that the club takes advantage of the status as the provider of a public good for promotion of the interests of the club members only.

These problems would persist and could even turn out to be fatal in the case of a global public good, i.e., global warming more specifically, because international interests would diverge more widely and intensely than intranational or club interests within a single country, given a complexity of geopolitical divisions in the world.

In the global warming case, the club provision may be attempted by the European Union or the United States—China partnership. The first implementation phase of the Kyoto Protocol is one form of a club provision because mostly the EU nations were committed to the Protocol, excluding the United States, China, and India, through the EU Emissions Trading System (UNFCCC, 2009; EC, 2016). The United States—China partnership has played a pivotal role in the success of the Paris Agreement (UNFCCC, 2015).

In the club provision of climate stability, the size of the club is critical. A club that is too small to be effective in terms of global GHG abatements will be meaningless for providing the global public good. The Kyoto Protocol was implemented among the group of nations that account for about 20% of the global emissions of carbon (Nordhaus, 2008). Any decrease in the total emissions within the Kyoto club could easily be offset by an increase in the non-Kyoto members (Nordhaus, 2001; Ellerman and Buchner, 2007).

The carbon leakage into non-Kyoto nations can occur directly and indirectly. It occurs through either a direct increase in emissions in non-Kyoto nations or an indirect increase in emissions in non-Kyoto nations because of increased imports by the Kyoto club.

Another criterion for a successful club provision is how to increase participation by nonmembers. A club provision must be complemented by another mechanism that can induce non-club members to join eventually, such as a penalty in the form of trade tariff (Nordhaus, 2015). Otherwise, the burden of responsibility of the club members will keep getting larger, which will eventually turn out to be unsustainable at some point.

5.5 Situation 5: Negotiating a Compensation Scheme

Owing to the global public good characteristics, any global policy that may be agreed upon by the international community is inevitable in leading to winners and losers in the short term and long term. Among them, there will also be big losers as well as big winners. Under such circumstances, the possibility of an international agreement on a global-scale policy by all members is very low.

This negative assessment raises another question of whether a global agreement would be more likely to be achieved with a bundle of monetary transfers from winner nations to loser nations for the purposes of compensating the losses of the latter and encouraging participation of them in the global policy (Carraro et al., 2006).

The rationale for such a transfer is that the global cooperative solution as defined in the Samuelson–Nordhaus framework is maximizing the welfare of the global community under the projected global warming, which means a business-as-usual no action alternative will result in a global welfare loss. The question is then whether it is possible to attempt a monetary transfer from a winner to a loser to induce a global cooperative solution that leads to welfare improvement, even though second best, from the business-as-usual outcome.

The global social welfare, O, at the global cooperative solution (*) is the sum of individual nation's welfare at a certain time (U_t). Let c_t be per capita consumption and L_t be total population. Then, the social welfare without monetary transfer can be expressed as follows (Nordhaus, 1992):

$$O^* = \sum_{t=0}^{\infty} \sum_{k=i,j} \frac{U_{kt}\left(c_{kt}^*, L_{kt}\right) \cdot L_t}{(1+\rho)^t}. \tag{3.12}$$

Let O^{BAU} be the global welfare at the business-as-usual scenario and O^{∇} be the global welfare with a monetary transfer from the global cooperative solution. The transfer mechanism purports to achieve the following:

$$O^* \approx O^{\nabla} > O^{BAU}. \tag{3.13}$$

Let the net monetary transfer to country k at time t be m_{kt}, assuming that the transfer is done annually, which must sum up to zero at the global level:

$$\sum_{k} \sum_{t} m_{kt} = 0. \tag{3.14}$$

The after-transfer global welfare is expressed as follows, assuming independence of the monetary transfers with productions and populations of individual nations:

$$O^{\nabla} = \sum_{t=0}^{\infty} \sum_{k=i,j} \frac{U_{kt}\left(c_{kt}^* + m_{kt}, L_{kt}\right) \cdot L_t}{(1+\rho)^t} \tag{3.15}$$

The question is whether there exists m_{kt} that satisfies Eq. (3.13) and what is the optimal value of the transfer. The difficulty of finding such a transfer is immediately apparent with reference to our rich and poor country example in Section 5.2. That is, because the rich country is a low-damage country and the poor country is a high-damage country, the transfer should be made from the poor country to the rich country to force a global cooperative solution. Such a transfer is politically infeasible nationally.

Even if such a transfer can be made, the increase in the utility of a receiver country that is rich must be smaller than the decrease in the utility of a giver country that is poor, assuming that the individuals in the two countries have more or less the same utility functions, because of the diminishing marginal utility of consumption. Then, the transfer would lead to a decrease in the global social welfare, i.e., a deviation from the Pareto optimality.

A more difficult problem is that a successive transfer of a bundle of wealth alters the trajectories of GHG emissions of the countries as well as the trajectories of consumptions. Given that the trajectories of emissions associated with the global cooperative solution are in a bundle of optimal policy outcomes for the globe, any change in the emissions trajectories of the countries involved in the transfers will lead to reductions of social welfare in the countries. The magnitudes of social welfare loss of the countries involved in the transfers will vary.

What we learn from this analysis of the wealth transfer proposal is that it would be very unlikely that such a transfer can be made if the world community in the first place were to refuse to take a global cooperative action. This is the case even without taking into account the political reality of each individual nation in which sending a constant sum of money to the other countries over a long time period such as many decades is almost not negotiable.

In the next chapter, the author provides a further analysis on the second-best global solution with monetary transfers using empirical data and the integrated assessment models of climate change.

5.6 Situation 6: Uncertainty and Catastrophe

If countries perceive any global legal protocol that may be established to provide a global public good as an uncertain and unreliable international commitment to which countries must lock themselves in for the long term, i.e., as long as a century, then the countries will be reluctant to sign any international agreement on the imposition of carbon penalty (Kolstad, 1996).

The Kolstad's argument can be explained by a simple trade-off model. In the global cooperative solution, the welfare maximization problem is again Eq. (3.12). This problem yields outcome variables: carbon price and control rate of emissions. An optimal choice of these policy variables leads to welfare improvement that is measured by the size of monetary benefit from global warming policy.

Let η^* be the optimal control rates of global emissions if there were to be no uncertainty in global warming policy and ΔO^* the monetary gain from a cooperative global solution over a business-as-usual outcome if there were to be no uncertainty at all.

The reality is that the uncertainty involved in adopting a global warming policy is high. The uncertainty arises from many aspects of the policy making. The first area of uncertainty is future climate predictions (Le Treut et al., 2007). According to the most recent assessment by the Intergovernmental Panel on Climate Change (IPCC), global temperature increase is predicted to range from no change to an 8°C increase by the end of the 21st century. According to the IPCC, global precipitation changes are even more uncertain, with the range from a 7% decrease to an 18% increase by the end of this century (IPCC, 2014).

The uncertainty on the degree of climate change is even further magnified at the regional level. For example, the future change in the Arctic winter temperature is predicted to range from a 5°C decrease to an 18°C increase. Arctic summer precipitation is predicted to range from a 10% decrease to a 70% increase from the baseline precipitation. Antarctic climate changes are equally uncertain in terms of both temperature and precipitation (IPCC, 2014).

The uncertainty on climate change predictions arises from many sources, one of which is an array of existing climate models that rely on different assumptions and relationships among the variables. Climate models are called an AOGCM (Atmospheric Oceanic General Circulation Model) (IPCC, 2014; Le Treut et al., 2007). Because of a large computing capacity and a highly complex modeling program, there are only a handful of AOGCMs available in the world. The collaborative research effort to compare the programs and outcomes across the AOGCMs is called in the literature the Climate Model Intercomparison Project (CMIP). The climate models utilized in the CMIP5 are shown in Table 3.1 (Taylor et al., 2012).

Another source of uncertainty in global warming policy making is future economy of the world by the end of this century. To represent the future economy, society, and technology, the IPCC researchers relied on the storyline (scenario) approach (Nakicenovic et al., 2000). These scenarios are called the "emissions scenarios" by the Special Report on Emissions Scenarios (SRES) by the IPCC. The four storyline families suggested by the IPCC are A1, A2, B1, and B2. The full descriptions of these scenarios are given in Table 3.2.

Of these families of scenarios, the A-versus-B distinction is made with regard to fossil fuel intensity of future economies: The "A" scenario is the storyline in which the world economy grows in the future in more or less the same way as it did in the past, whereas the "B" scenario is the storyline in which the world economy grows in the future in a more environmentally friendly way than it did in the past.

Table 3.1 **Selected Climate Model Intercomparison Project 5 Climate Models**

Modeling Center	Model Name
Canadian Centre for Climate Modelling and Analysis (CCCMA)	CanESM2; CanCM4; CanAM4
National Center for Atmospheric Research (NCAR)	CCSM4
Centro Euro-Mediterraneo per I Cambiamenti Climatici (CMCC)	CMCC-CESM; CMCC-CM; CMCC-CMS
Centre National de Recherches Météorologiques/ Centre Européen de Recherche et Formation Avancée en Calcul Scientifique (CNRM-CERFACS)	CNRM-CM5; CNRM-CM5-2
Commonwealth Scientific and Industrial Research Organization (CSIRO-QCCCE)	CSIRO-Mk3.6.0
NOAA Geophysical Fluid Dynamics Laboratory (NOAA GFDL)	GFDL-CM3; GFDL-ESM2G; GFDL-HIRAM-C180
NASA Goddard Institute for Space Studies (NASA GISS)	GISS-E2-H; GISS-E2-R
Met Office Hadley Centre (MOHC)	HadCM3; HadGEM2-CC; HadGEM2-ES; HadGEM2-A
Atmosphere and Ocean Research Institute (The University of Tokyo), National Institute for Environmental Studies, and Japan Agency for Marine-Earth Science and Technology (MIROC)	MIROC4h; MIROC5
Meteorological Research Institute (MRI)	MRI-AGCM3.2H;MRI-CGCM3; MRI-ESM1

The 1-versus-2 distinction is defined with regard to economic convergence (Barro and Sala-i-Martin, 1992): The "1" scenario is the storyline in which the world's national economies develop in a globally convergent way, whereas the "2" scenario is the storyline in which the world economies develop in a regionally convergent way.

Each of these scenario families is further divided into subscenarios: for example, A1F1, A1T, and A1B for the A1 scenario family. These subscenarios represent alternative directions in technological developments in the energy system. The A1F1 scenario represents high reliance on fossil fuels; the A1T scenario represents high reliance on energy produced from nonfossil energy sources such as solar, wind, hydro, and geothermal; the A1B scenario represents reliance on a balance between fossil and nonfossil energy sources.

The most recent IPCC report, the Fifth Assessment Report, replaces the SRES approach with a Representative Concentration Pathways (RCP) approach (IPCC, 2014). The RCP 2.6, 4.5, 6.0, 8.5 represent the emissions trajectory that results in the Radiative Forcing of

Table 3.2 **Families of Emissions Scenarios by the IPCC**

From the IPCC Assessment Report 2 (1995) to 4 (2007)		From the IPCC Assessment Report 5 (2014)	
Scenario Families		Scenario Families	
A1	Future world: very rapid economic growth; global population that peaks in midcentury and declines thereafter; the rapid introduction of new and more efficient technologies	RCP 2.6	Radiative forcing by the end of the 21st century $= 2.6$ W/m^2
	Major themes: convergence among regions; capacity building; increased cultural and social interactions; a substantial reduction in regional differences in per capita income		
A2	Future world: a very heterogeneous world; self-reliance and preservation of local identities	RCP 4.5	Radiative forcing by the end of the 21st century $= 4.5$ W/m^2
	Fertility patterns across regions converge very slowly; economic development is primarily regionally oriented and per capita economic growth; technological changes are more fragmented and slower than in other storylines		
B1	Future world: a convergent world with the same global population as in the A1 storyline; rapid changes in economic structures toward a service and information economy, with reductions in material intensity, and the introduction of clean and resource-efficient technologies; emphasis on global solutions to economic, social, and environmental sustainability, without additional climate initiatives	RCP 6.0	Radiative forcing by the end of the 21st century $= 6.0$ W/m^2
B2	Future world: a world in which the emphasis is on local solutions to economic, social, and environmental sustainability	RCP 8.5	Radiative forcing by the end of the 21st century $= 8.5$ W/m^2

Continued

Table 3.2 **Families of Emissions Scenarios by the IPCC—cont'd**

From the IPCC Assessment Report 2 (1995) to 4 (2007)		From the IPCC Assessment Report 5 (2014)	
	Major themes: a world with continuously increasing global population at a rate lower than A2; intermediate levels of economic development; less rapid and more diverse technological change than in the B1 and A1 storylines; local and regional solutions to environmental protection and social equity		

IPCC, intergovernmental panel on climate change; *RCP*, representative concentration pathways.

2.6, 4.5, 6.0, and 8.5 W/m^2, respectively. The RCP approach takes the burden of the IPCC researchers off of describing the future worlds through economic growth, regional changes, technological changes, population changes, and social behaviors that characterized the SRES scenarios. To put differently, the RCP approach makes these changes hidden (implicit) to researchers and outsiders.

Underneath the uncertainty of future economies lies the uncertainty of future technologies and innovations in technology. As mentioned earlier, A1F1, A1T, and A1B scenarios are distinguished by future directions in technological developments. An extensive analysis of future technologies and uncertainties of breakthroughs will be provided exclusively in Chapter 5 of this book.

Technological uncertainty is high, especially with regard to breakthrough technologies. Will the nuclear fusion energy production be possible by the middle of this century at a commercial scale (ITER, 2015)? Will solar technology replace conventional fossil fuel–based energy productions (IPCC, 2011, MIT, 2015)? Will a carbon-capture-storage technology become effective to be employed in a large geographical scale such as a country (IPCC, 2005; Lackner et al., 2012)? Will climate engineering provide an effective method at relatively lower costs for reducing the amount of sunlight that falls on the Earth (NRC, 2015)? Will genetic science make it possible for humans to cure human and animal diseases, heat related, that have been regarded fatal until now (Aksoy et al., 2014)?

The fourth major source of uncertainty in adopting a global warming policy lies in the monetary impact of global warming, which again results from the impacts of the change on ecosystems and humans. From the dawn of the literature on global warming policy, the damage estimates that result from global warming varied widely (Cline, 1992; Pearce et al., 1996).

The divergence of impact estimates in turn arises from many sources. The first is the uncertainty on how ecosystems will undergo changes given the manifestations of climate change (Gitay et al., 2001; Ainsworth and Long, 2005). Another is the uncertainty on how individuals and societies will adapt to changes in climate and ecosystems (Mendelsohn, 2000; Seo, 2006, 2012b,c, 2014). The third source of uncertainty lies in the choice of methodologies to study the impacts (Seo, 2015a, 2016b,c,d). The fourth source of uncertainty lies in how to value changes in nonmarket sectors such as individuals' time use changes (Nordhaus and Boyer, 2000).

A study by Tol presents a distribution of global impact estimates from the 14 studies that were selected by the author (Tol, 2009). According to the meta-analysis, in response to global temperature change of 2.5−3.0°C, the impact estimate varies from −4.8% loss of GDP per annum to +2.5% gain of GDP per annum, validating a large uncertainty on the economic impact of climate change.

Taking the large uncertainty that arises from these various aspects of global warming, the welfare improvement achievable by implementing a global cooperative optimal solution as defined by the Samuelson−Nordhaus framework can only be known with a distribution function. As a starting point, let us assume that the welfare improvement follows a normal distribution with a mean and a standard deviation. Continuing with the notations defined earlier,

$$\Delta O^*(\eta^*) = c, \quad \text{with } c \sim N(\bar{c}, \sigma_c). \tag{3.16}$$

The distribution does not have to be normal and will not be the well-defined normal distribution more often than not. It can follow any distribution, which also can be verified through empirical research.

Let us assume that the decision maker is risk averse. A risk-averse decision maker will not accept an offer that is risky over an offer that is riskless if the size of the offer is the same in two situations (Markowitz, 1952; Arrow, 1971). The preference of the risk-averse decision maker can be written as follows:

$$\bar{c} \succ c \sim N(\bar{c}, \sigma_c) \quad \text{for } \sigma_c > 0. \tag{3.17}$$

For the risk-averse decision maker, the optimal control rate of GHG emissions associated with a risky welfare improvement will be lower than the optimal control rate associated with a riskless welfare improvement:

$$\eta^*(c \sim N(\bar{c}, \sigma_c)) < \eta^*(\bar{c}). \tag{3.18}$$

Eq. (3.18) is another way to describe the Kolstad's conclusion on global warming uncertainties (Kolstad, 1996). This states that the high uncertainty existent in many aspects of global warming surveyed in the above will make a global cooperative optimal solution less stringent in terms of mitigation efforts. The larger the risk, the smaller would be the mitigation commitment by the global community. Put differently, global warming uncertainty forces countries to delay actions until the uncertainty is reduced gradually over the course of time.

A starkly different interpretation of global warming uncertainty was propounded by Martin Weitzman (2009). He says that there is a very wide range of predictions of future climate, citing predictions of 10° and 20° in Celsius change in global temperature by the end of this century. He argues that this immense uncertainty on future climate is irreducible even if extensive research and funding were to be directed in the decades to come.

What he arrives at is that the truly catastrophic outcome in which the world civilizations as we know it would be terminated on this Earth cannot be reduced to an event with negligible probability. In a more formal terminology, he argues that the damage of global warming has a fat-tailed distribution, which means that the likelihood of an extremely catastrophic event to occur remains substantial (Cropper, 1976; Schuster, 1984).

With these assumptions, Weitzman proposed a "dismal theorem," which states that the world shall prevent such a catastrophic outcome, i.e., the end of civilizations, at all cost. Under the dismal theorem, he argues policy proposals based on the cost—benefit analysis of alternative policy instruments, including the Samuelson—Nordhaus framework, are misleading. He proposes a precautionary principle as a guiding principle for global warming policy making.

The upshot of the dismal theorem is that in a fat-tailed distribution, the probability of an extreme event remains significantly large forever, in which case the expected value of the extreme outcome is unbounded (Nordhaus, 2011b). According to Martin Weitzman, the dismal theorem is expressed as follows (Weitzman, 2009). For any given n and k,

$$\lim_{\lambda \to \infty} E[M|\lambda] = +\infty \qquad (3.19)$$

Weitzman defines M to be the amount of present consumption that an agent would be willing to give up in the present period to obtain one sure unit of consumption in the future period. Weitzman calls it a "stochastic discounting factor." The parameters n,k are roughly the number of available data (information) and the number of prior data (information), respectively, which are needed to narrow down the uncertainty. The parameter λ is defined to be a Value of Statistical Life—like parameter (Viscusi and Aldy, 2003). It is approximately the value of statistical civilization or the value of statistical life on Earth as we know it. This value is apparently very large. In economic terms, the world would be willing to sacrifice the entire annual income to survive if future global warming were to indeed cause an end of civilizations.

The dismal theorem in Eq. (3.19) can only be derived with several critical assumptions (Nordhaus, 2011b; Yohe and Tol, 2012; Seo, 2010b). First, the dismal theorem assumes that all future climate predictions are equally valid and probable, regardless of whether those predictions are made by a climate expert or a nonexpert, whether with a supercomputer or with a normal-capacity computer, and whether based on more solid assumptions on the future economy or less solid assumptions. Second, scientific endeavors cannot narrow down the probability of even an extremely catastrophic event at all, even with much resources and time devoted to the necessary tasks (NRC, 2013).

Third, the future extreme climate change event will terminate the life on Earth. Fourth, behavioral responses by individuals, communities, governments, and international societies are of no help at all in the context of the climate catastrophe.

The dismal theorem broadly advocates a precautionary principle in global warming policy making. The policy recommendation by the dismal theorem is an immediate end of GHG emissions from human activities. In other words, the control rate of GHG emissions is 100% now and forever.

Although the Weitzman's analysis provides an intriguing analytical result in the context of global warming, policy pertinence of his proposal depends critically on these extreme assumptions on global warming uncertainty. Even in a slightly less extreme view on global warming uncertainty, the benefit−cost analysis will provide a guiding principle that is embodied in the global cooperative solution described in this chapter (Nordhaus, 2011b).

5.7 Situation 7: Time Preference

The problem of global warming cannot be addressed with a short-term outlook. It is not sufficient for a policy maker to take into account a decade or a generation; the policy maker must consider many generations or many centuries. It is less important to know what is in the offing and more important to know what is beyond the horizon. Many aspects in global warming policy decisions have consequences that are felt decades later and even centuries later.

First, carbon dioxide emitted today quickly mixes in the atmosphere and stays in the atmosphere for a long time. Scientists estimate that the residence time of carbon dioxide is up to 50 years for 50% of the emissions today, up to 100 years for 20% of the emissions, up to 300 years for 10% of the emissions, and up to tens of thousands of years for remaining 20% of the emissions (IPCC, 2014). This means that a ton of the emissions today by the current generation would affect the generations to come who have played no part in the accumulation of that ton of emissions of carbon dioxide.

Second, the long residence time of carbon dioxide means that changes in the climate system and the natural ecosystems would unfold a century later in response to today's emissions of carbon dioxide. Researchers and policy makers need to make predictions of the climate system and the natural systems that materialize a century later.

Third, policies that aim to address the problem of global warming must take into account changes in climate and natural systems that would occur in response to carbon dioxide that stays in the atmosphere once emitted today into the atmosphere. In addition, the impacts of global warming, whether beneficial or harmful, felt by future generations must be taken into account by any policy proposal.

A pivotal question in global warming policy making arises with regard to how to value the future consequences. Should policy makers value 1 dollar loss a century later in the same way as they value 1 dollar loss today? Should 1 dollar damage to the future generation that come a century later be valued in the same way as 1 dollar damage to the current generation? This is known as discounting debate (Arrow et al. 1996; Stern, 2007; Nordhaus, 2007b).

One dollar earned 10 years later is not the same as 1 dollar earned today. This difference is captured in the interest one can earn if one saves 1 dollar today for 10 years. Therefore, 1 dollar today is equal to 1 dollar plus interest. With r interest rate, t number of years from today, and q dollars saved today, the value at the future date is as follows, assuming discrete discounting:

$$q\$ \times (1+r)^t. \tag{3.20}$$

What underlies the interest rate are impatience of individuals, alternative ways of production, technological advances over time, and arbitrages in the markets. Financial markets determine the rate of interest through transactions among market participants who value these factors differently (Fisher, 1906, 1930; Bohm-Bawerk, 1959).

The optimization of the social welfare function in a competitive market with a constant rate of consumption growth (g) and a constant elasticity of marginal utility of consumption (α) leads to the standard relationship between the equilibrium real interest rate and other parameters, which is called the "Ramsey equation" (Nordhaus, 2007b; Weitzman, 2009):

$$r^* = \rho + \alpha \cdot g^*. \tag{3.21}$$

Of the three parameters, the elasticity of marginal utility of consumption is also called an inequality aversion parameter. The value of one indicates neutral attitude toward social inequality. The value greater than one implies higher aversion to social inequality, whereas the value smaller than one implies lower aversion to social inequality. Researchers can choose any value but tend to choose 1 or 2 considering different situations (Nordhaus, 1992).

In Eq. (3.21), the most controversial term is ρ, the rate of social time preference. In the climate economics literature, the value of this term varied from 0 to 3% or 4%. A higher rate means that the society is more impatient, preferring strongly the current outcome to future outcomes. A lower rate means that the society is less impatient, preferring not strongly the current outcome to future outcomes.

However, the choice of a social rate of time preference is not entirely arbitrary. It is hinged to the Ramsey equation. For example, 6% real interest rate, 2% consumption growth, and elasticity of marginal utility of consumption of 2 would force the social time preference to 2% to satisfy the Ramsey equation. Alternatively, 4% real interest rate, 2% consumption growth, and elasticity of marginal utility of consumption of 1.5 would force the social rate of time preference to 1%.

It is sometimes suggested that the social rate of time preference should be zero in global warming policy making (Stern, 2007). The main argument for the choice of zero time preference is ethical grounds. Ethicists argue that it is immoral to discount the damage inflicted on future generations because the value of the future generation is not different from the value of the current generation (Broome, 1992, 1994). The damage in the future should be treated in the same way as the damage that is inflicted today.

This morally based view overlooks the other side of morality in discounting (Beckerman and Hepburn, 2007). That is, 1 dollar earned today which is left to the future generation would become in the future 1 dollar plus the interest that will be accrued from today to the future time. A larger sum of money than 1 dollar would be left to the future generation. This is because 1 dollar today can be invested to earn interests (Fisher, 1930).

The social rate of time preference is not known empirically. One can therefore argue in one way or another that it should be set at a high level or at a low level depending upon the situation considered. However, it must be above zero given the overwhelming preference by people of the present income (or living) over the future income (living).

From the modeling perspective, a researcher can set the social rate of time preference to a very small number, perhaps close to zero as some researchers have attempted in the literature (Stern, 2007). However, the social rate of time preference cannot be determined independently of the real interest rate and other parameters of the Ramsey equation in Eq. (3.21).

Another point of contention is what should be the real interest rates today and in the future that enter the social welfare optimization models. Estimated real returns of various capital assets for various time periods that were compiled by Arrow and his coauthors for the IPCC are presented in Table 3.3 (Arrow et al., 1996). The US equities

Table 3.3 Estimated Real Returns to Capital

Asset	Period	Real Return (%)
(1) High-Icome Industrial Countries		
Equities	1960–1984	5.4
Bonds	1960–1984	1.6
Nonresidential capital	1975–1990	15.1
Govt. short-term bonds	1960–1990	0.3
(2) United States		
Equities	1925–1992	6.5
All private capital, pretax	1963–1985	5.7
Corporate capital, capital, posttax	1963–1985	5.7
Real estate	1960–1984	5.5
Farmland	1947–1984	5.5
Treasury bills	1926–1986	0.3
(3) Developing Countries		
Primary education	Various	26
Higher education	Various	13

The data are from Arrow, K.J., Cline, W., Maler, K.G., Munasinghe, M., Squitieri, R., Stiglitz, J., 1996. Intertemporal equity, discounting, and economic efficiency. In: Bruce, J.P., Lee, H., Haites, E.F. (Eds.), Climate Change 1995: Economic and Social Dimensions of Climate Change, Intergovernmental Panel on Climate Change, Cambridge University Press, New York in the IPCC Second Assessment Report.

earned 6.5% real return from 1925 to 1992. Nonresidential capital earned 15.1% in high-income industrial countries during the period from 1975 to 1990. Government bonds in the United States and high-income industrial countries earned the lowest rates, less than 1%. In developing countries, estimated real returns are very high. In developing countries, primary education earned 26% return, whereas higher education earned 13% return.

The estimates of real returns of various assets shown in Table 3.3 should guide researchers in choosing the real interest rate for a global warming policy modeling. A globally averaged return can be calculated. It should be noted, however, that there are assets and investments whose returns are poorly understood, especially in developing countries.

Furthermore, interest rates can be low at some times and high at other times. During the global financial crisis and the European debt crisis, interest rates were extremely low because of a high risk of lending. For a global warming policy modeling, however, appropriate interest rates should be determined from the changes in interest rates over a long period of time.

Another point of contention is whether the real interest rate that is used for future time periods should be the same as that observed in the current period (Ainslie, 1991; Cropper and Laibson, 1999; Nordhaus, 2008). Put differently, will the real interest fall over time or rise? A study by Newell and Pizer presents the 200-year history of the market interest rate for the US long-term government bonds. The US long-term government bonds are chosen by the author because these represent the highest quality, lowest risk market investment consistently available in the United States over the past 200 years (Newell and Pizer, 2001). It shows a steadily declining long-term trend, which started at over 7% interest rate 200 years ago to around 3% by the 1990s. However, the historical rate shows repeated up-and-down swings over the time period, with a peak of over 6% even in the 1980s.

From another point of view, a declining rate of discount is often called a "hyperbolic" discounting in contrast to the conventional discounting called an "exponential" discounting (Ainslie, 1991; Cropper and Laibson, 1999). In an exponential discounting, the dollar in a future period is discounted exponentially, with k being a parameter of the degree of discounting and f a discounting factor:

$$f(t) = \$1 \times e^{-kt}. \tag{3.22}$$

This means that the discounting factor between any two adjacent time periods is constant:

$$\frac{f(t)}{f(t-1)} = \frac{e^{-kt}}{e^{-k(t-1)}} = e^{-k}, \ \forall t. \tag{3.23}$$

By contrast, the discounting factor declines in a hyperbolic discounting as any two adjacent time periods are further away from the present. With g being a discounting factor:

$$g(t) = \frac{1}{1 + kt},$$

$$\frac{g(t+1)}{g(t)} = \frac{1/(1 + k + kt)}{1/(1 + kt)} = \frac{1}{1 + \dfrac{k}{1 + kt}}. \tag{3.24}$$

As is evident in the above-mentioned equation, in a hyperbolic discounting, the discounting factor goes to one when t goes to infinity.

Theorists for hyperbolic discounting argue that individuals make decisions as if the further they look into the future, the lower they choose the discount rate (Ainslie, 1991). However, an individual with hyperbolic preferences should make exactly the same decisions as one with a conventional exponential discounting. They argue that both discounting methods discount the future at the rate equal to the rate of return to capital (Laibson, 1996; Cropper and Laibson, 1999). The only difference is how the two methods understand today's decisions on the event in the far future.

In Fig. 3.1, discounting factors from both exponential discounting and hyperbolic discounting are put together for 100 years from now. In the figure, $k = 0.04$ is assumed

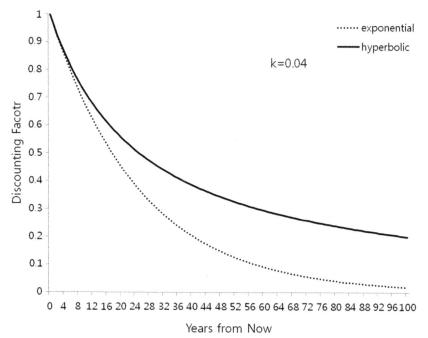

Figure 3.1 Hyperbolic discounting.

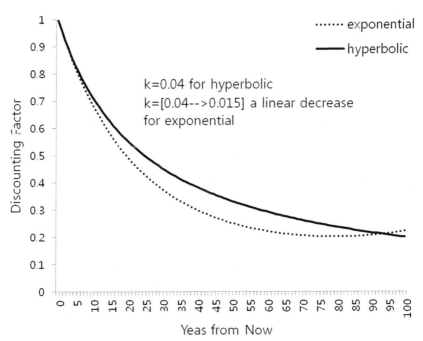

Figure 3.2 A linearly decreasing discount rate for exponential discounting.

for both discounting methods. A stark difference between the two discounting methods is demonstrated. The discounting factor in the exponential discounting declines at a much faster rate and falls to about 0.1 in 50 years and to near zero in 100 years. On the other hand, the discounting factor in the hyperbolic discounting declines at a much slower rate and falls to 0.4 in 50 years and to about 0.25 in 100 years.

The two discounting factors are about the same magnitude in the next 10 years, but depart substantially in the last 50 years of the time period considered. By 100 years, the hyperbolic discounting factor remains high at 0.25, whereas the exponential discounting factor falls to near zero. The two discounting methods have very different implications on the outcomes that occur far in the future.

The two discounting methods, however, can lead to similar trajectories of the discounting factor, which is shown in Fig. 3.2. In the figure, the discounting factor for the hyperbolic discounting is calculated with $k = 0.04$. For the exponential discounting, the discounting factor is calculated with k, which is assumed to decline in a linear trend from 0.04 today to 0.015 by 100 years. This approach has been taken by climate researchers (Nordhaus and Boyer, 2000; Nordhaus, 2008, 2013).

The comparison of Fig. 3.2 with Fig. 3.1 reveals that the two discounting methods can be identical in certain situations. For one example, if the reason behind the hyperbolic discounting is individuals' expectations that the interest rate will fall over time for various reasons, the two methods arrive at the same trajectory of discount rate.

5.8   Situation 8: Governance

Let us assume for a moment that the UNFCCC member nations would succeed in overcoming all these obstacles explained up to this point in this chapter and reach an agreement on a global cooperative solution sketched in Eqs. (3.5) and (3.8). Notwithstanding, it is still possible that the amount of global GHG emissions, carbon dioxide concentration in the atmosphere, and global average temperature continue to increase uncontrollably. This situation can arise from the absence of a global governance structure put in place for provision of a global public good.

Unlike the problems of numerous national public goods, there is no global government that has the same authority and power over all citizens of the world. There is no government that can impose a carbon tax globally, create guidelines, monitor implementations, and punish violators of an international agreement. As explained in the previous chapter, this is known to be a "Westphalian dilemma" in global warming policy making (Nordhaus, 2006). The treaties in the cities of Westphalia ended the wars among European nations but created a basis for self-determination and sovereign states, based upon which international affairs have been approached since then.

Even with a global agreement on a globally optimal climate policy ratified and implemented, carbon tax or emissions trading should be imposed by a national government, guidelines should be created by a national government, monitoring of activities should be performed by a national government, and punishments of violators must be conducted by a national government. In the international system of sovereign states as defined by the Westphalian treaties, it is impossible that a foreign agency intervene and perform these activities. What this means is that a global agreement on a certain policy, e.g., the Paris Agreement by the UNFCCC member nations, does not mean that it will be implemented as agreed (UNFCCC, 2015).

From another angle, governance-related issues are certain to affect the international negotiation process itself. Nations will be reluctant to commit to an international agreement that is sure to result in foreign interferences in national climate policies and programs. The Paris Agreement essentially avoids this issue by letting nations to submit an intended nationally determined commitment, letting monitoring of abatement efforts to be performed by each nation, and removing any penalty/punishment clauses from the agreement (UNFCCC, 2015). A thorough analysis of the Paris and other agreements on global warming will be provided in Chapter 7.

6.   Conclusion and Plans for the Ensuing Chapters

This chapter provided an extensive review of major challenges in global warming policy making as well as defining characteristics of the problem of global warming. The problem of global warming and climate change is salient in that it is a truly global-scale problem; there is a great deal of heterogeneities in many policy-relevant variables across individual nations; a centuries-long time horizon must be considered.

A globally cooperative and optimal policy solution is sketched in this chapter through the Samuelson—Nordhaus framework. Major obstacles and thorny issues are explained against the baseline of the Samuelson—Nordhaus optimal policy framework. These issues are explained through eight major themes: heterogeneity in climate change damage, heterogeneity in national economies, heterogeneity in abatement cost, club provision, a compensation and transfer scheme, uncertainty and catastrophe, time preference, and governance.

Having provided a thorough explanation of a large basket of major obstacles, the ultimate goal of this book is to offer an alternative policy framework that has the chance to overcome these conundrums. The rest of this book, Chapters 4—7, will be devoted to establishing and elucidating this alternative policy paradigm.

The novel policy approach to be presented henceforth is founded on individuals' motives to act upon changing natural and economic conditions (Mendelsohn, 2000; Seo, 2010a, 2015b, 2016b,c). As will be clarified throughout the book, it differs in a major way from the past policy approaches that are based on a top-down perspective. For example, a carbon tax is imposed from the top by the global government and individuals take corrective actions upon seeing the carbon tax.

In the next chapter, the author provides a full description of the carbon tax approach using the Integrated Assessment Models (IAM) of climate change and policy-relevant outcomes of these models. The explanation of the IAMs such as the DICE (Dynamic Integrated Climate and Economy) model will give readers an opportunity to get acquainted with all the major parameters of global warming policy making in an integrated modeling framework as well as an opportunity to assess practical measures that are available for making carbon tax feasible at a global level.

The next chapter will be followed by the chapters, in order, on breakthrough technologies, adaptation paradigm on climate policy, and policy negotiations. An alternative policy framework, which is the primary intended outcome of this book, will be formalized and made clear through these chapters.

References

Ainslie, G., 1991. Derivation of "rational" economic behavior from hyperbolic discount curves. American Economic Review 81, 334—340.

Ainsworth, E.A., Long, S.P., 2005. What have we learned from 15 years of free-air CO_2 enrichment (FACE)? A meta-analysis of the responses of photosynthesis, canopy properties and plant production to rising CO_2. New Phytologist 165, 351—372.

Aksoy, S., Attardo, G., et al., 2014. Genome sequence of the tsetse fly (*Glossina morsitans*): vector of African trypanosomiasis. Science 344 (6182), 380—386.

Arrow, K.J., 1971. Essays in the Theory of Risk Bearing. Markham Publishing Co., Chicago.

Arrow, K.J., Cline, W., Maler, K.G., Munasinghe, M., Squitieri, R., Stiglitz, J., 1996. Intertemporal equity, discounting, and economic efficiency. In: Bruce, J.P., Lee, H., Haites, E.F. (Eds.), Climate Change 1995: Economic and Social Dimensions of Climate Change, Intergovernmental Panel on Climate Change. Cambridge University Press, New York.

Barrett, S., 2008. The incredible economics of geoengineering. Environmental and Resource Economics 39, 45—54.

Barro, R.J., Sala-i-Martin, X., 1992. Convergence. Journal of Political Economy 100, 223—251.

Beckerman, W., Hepburn, C., 2007. Ethics of the discount rate in the Stern review on the economics of climate change. World Economics 8 (1), 187—210.

Bohm-Bawerk, E., 1959. Capital and Interest. Translated by Huncke GD, Sennholz HF. Libertarian Press, South Holland, IL.

Broome, J., 1992. Counting the Cost of Global Warming. The White Horse Press, Cambridge.

Broome, J., 1994. Discounting the future. Philosophy and Public Affairs 23, 128—156.

Brown, K.M., 1973. Welfare implications of congestion in public goods. Review of Social Economy 31, 89—92.

Buchanan, J.M., 1965. An economy theory of clubs. Economica 32, 1—24.

Carraro, C., Eyckmans, J., Finus, N., 2006. Optimal transfers and participation decisions in international environmental agreements. Review of International Organizations 1, 379—396.

Chan, G., Carraro, C., Edenhoffer, O., Kolstad, C., Stavins, R., 2016. Reforming the IPCC's assessment of climate change economics. Climate Change Economics 7. http://dx.doi.org/10.1142/S2010007816400017.

Chapman, C.R., Morrison, D., 1994. Impacts on the earth by asteroids and comets: assessing the hazard. Nature 367, 33—40.

Cline, W., 1992. The Economics of Global Warming. Institute of International Economics, Washington DC.

Conseil Européen pour la Recherche Nucléaire (CERN), 2015. About CERN. Available at: http://home.web.cern.ch/about.

Cropper, M., 1976. Regulating activities with catastrophic environmental effects. Journal of Environmental Economics and Management 3, 1—15.

Cropper, M.L., Laibson, D., 1999. The implications of hyperbolic discounting for project evaluation. In: Portney, P.R., Weyant, J.P. (Eds.), Discounting and Intergenerational Equity. Resources for the Future, Washington, DC.

Ellerman, A.D., Buchner, B.K., 2007. The European Union emissions trading scheme: origins, allocations, and early results. Review of Environmental Economics and Policy 1, 66—87.

European Commission, 2016. EU ETS Handbook. European Commission, Brussels.

Evenson, R., Gollin, D., 2003. Assessing the impact of the green revolution 1960—2000. Science 300, 758—762.

Fischer, C., Morgenstern, R.D., 2006. Carbon abatement costs: why the wide range of estimates? The Energy Journal 27, 73—86.

Fisher, I., 1906. The Nature of Capital and Income. Macmillan, New York.

Fisher, I., 1930. The Theory of Interest. Macmillan, New York.

Gitay, H., Brwon, S., Easterling, W., Jallow, B., 2001. Ecosystems and their goods and services. In: McCarthy, et al. (Eds.), Climate Change 2001: Impacts, Adaptations, and Vulnerabilities. Cambridge University Press, Cambridge, pp. 237—342.

Hirshleifer, J., 1983. From weakest-link to best-shot: the voluntary provision of public goods. Public Choice 41, 371—386.

Intergovernmental Panel on Climate Change (IPCC), 2005. Special Report on Carbon Dioxide Capture and Storage. Cambridge University Press, Cambridge.

Intergovernmental Panel on Climate Change (IPCC), 2011. Special Report on Renewable Energy Sources and Climate Change Mitigation. Cambridge University Press, Cambridge.

Intergovernmental Panel on Climate Change (IPCC), 2014. Climate Change 2014: The Physical Science Basis, The Fifth Assessment Report of the IPCC. Cambridge University Press, Cambridge.

International Thermonuclear Experimental Reactor (ITER), 2015. ITER: The World's Largest Tokamak. Available at: https://www.iter.org/mach.

Kaul, I., Conceicao, P., Goulven, K.L., Mendoza, R.U. (Eds.), 2003. Providing Global Public Goods: Managing Globalization. Oxford University Press, Oxford.

Kolstad, C.D., 1996. Learning and stock effects in environmental pollution: the case of greenhouse gas emissions. Journal of Environmental Economics and Management 31, 1−18.

Kotchen, M., Moore, M.R., 2007. Private provision of environmental public goods: household participation in green-electricity programs. Journal of Environmental Economics and Management 53, 1−16.

Krugman, P., 2008. The Increasing Returns Revolution in Trade and Geography. Nobel Lecture. The Nobel Foundation, Stockholm.

Lackner, K.S., Brennana, S., Matter, J.M., Park, A.A., Wright, A., Zwaan, B.V., 2012. The urgency of the development of CO_2 capture from ambient air. Proceedings of the National Academy of Sciences 109 (33), 13156−13162.

Laibson, D.I., 1996. Hyperbolic Discount Functions, Undersaving, and Savings Policy. National Bureau of Economic Research (NBER) Working Paper 5635, NBER, Cambridge, MA.

Le Treut, H., Somerville, R., Cubasch, U., Ding, Y., Mauritzen, C., Mokssit, A., Peterson, T., Prather, M., 2007. Historical overview of climate change. In: Solomon, S., Qin, D., Manning, M., Chen, Z., Marquis, M., Averyt, K.B., Tignor, M., Miller, H.L. (Eds.), Climate Change 2007: The Physical Science Basis. Contribution of Working Group I to the Fourth Assessment Report of the Intergovernmental Panel on Climate Change. Cambridge University Press, Cambridge.

Manne, A.S., Mendelsohn, R., Richels, R., 1995. MERGE − a model for evaluating regional and global effects of GHG reduction policies. Energy Policy 23 (1), 17−34.

Markowitz, H., 1952. Portfolio selection. The Journal of Finance 7, 77−91.

Mas-Colell, A., Whinston, M.D., Green, J.R., 1995. Microeconomic Theory. Oxford University Press, Oxford.

Massachusetts Institute of Technology (MIT), 2015. The Future of Solar Energy: An Interdisciplinary MIT Study. MIT, MA.

Mendelsohn, R., 2000. Efficient adaptation to climate change. Climatic Change 45, 583−600.

Mendelsohn, R., 2016. Should the IPCC assessment reports be an integrated assessment? Climate Change Economics 7. http://dx.doi.org/10.1142/S2010007816400029.

Mendelsohn, R., Dinar, A., Williams, L., 2006. The distributional impact of climate change on rich and poor countries. Environ Dev Econ 11, 1−20.

Metcalf, G., 2009. Designing a carbon tax to reduce US greenhouse gas emissions. Review of Environmental Economics and Policy 3, 63−83.

Mills, M.J., Toon, O.B., Turco, R.P., Kinnison, D.E., Garcia, R.R., 2008. Massive global ozone loss predicted following regional nuclear conflict. Proceedings of the National Academy of Sciences of the United States of America 105, 5307−5312.

Montgomery, W.D., 1972. Markets in licenses and efficient pollution control programs. Journal of Economic Theory 5, 395−418.

Nakicenovic, N., Davidson, O., Davis, G., Grübler, A., Kram, T., La Rovere, E.L., Metz, B., Morita, T., Pepper, W., Pitcher, H., Sankovski, A., Shukla, P., Swart, R., Watson, R., Dadi, Z., 2000. Emissions Scenarios, a Special Report of Working Group III of the Intergovernmental Panel on Climate Change. IPCC, Geneva.

National Aeronautics and Space Administration (NASA), 2007. Near-Earth Object Survey and Deflection: Analysis of Alternatives. Report to Congress. http://www.nasa.gov/pdf/171331main_NEO_report_march07.pdf.

National Research Council (NRC), 2013. Abrupt Impacts of Climate Change: Anticipating Surprises. Committee on Understanding and Monitoring Abrupt Climate Change and Its Impacts. The National Academies Press, Washington DC.

National Research Council (NRC), 2015. Climate Intervention: Reflecting Sunlight to Cool Earth. Committee on Geoengineering Climate: Technical Evaluation and Discussion of Impacts. The National Academies Press, Washington DC.

NASA, 2016. Mars Exploration. Available at: http://mars.nasa.gov.

Nash, J., 1950. Equilibrium points in n-person games. Proceedings of the National Academy of Sciences 36 (1), 48−49.

Nash, J., 1951. Non-cooperative games. The Annals of Mathematics 54 (2), 286−295.

Newell, R., Pizer, W., 2001. Discounting the Benefits of Climate Change Mitigation: How Much Do Uncertain Rates Increase Valuations? Pew Center, Washington DC.

Nordhaus, W., 1992. An optimal transition path for controlling greenhouse gases. Science 258, 1315−1319.

Nordhaus, W., 1994. Managing the Global Commons. MIT Press, Massachusetts.

Nordhaus, W., 2001. Global warming economics. Science 294, 1283−1284.

Nordhaus, W.D., 2006. Paul Samuelson and global public goods. In: Szenberg, M., Ramrattan, L. (Eds.), Gottesman AA (2006) Samuelsonian Economics and the Twenty-First Century. Oxford Scholarship Online.

Nordhaus, W.D., 2008. A Question of Balance—Weighing the Options on Global Warming Policies. Yale University Press, New Haven.

Nordhaus, W., 2007a. To tax or not to tax: alternative approaches to slowing global warming. Review of Environmental Economics and Policy 1 (1), 26−44.

Nordhaus, W., 2007b. A review of the Stern review on the economics of climate change. Journal of Economic Literature 55, 686−702.

Nordhaus, W., 2010a. Carbon taxes to move toward fiscal sustainability. The Economists' Voice 7 (3), 1−5.

Nordhaus, W., 2010b. Economic aspects of global warming in a post-Copenhagen environment. Proceedings of the U.S. National Academy of Sciences 107 (26), 11721−11726.

Nordhaus, W., 2011a. The architecture of climate economics: designing a global agreement on global warming. Bulletin of Atomic Scientists 67 (1), 9−18.

Nordhaus, W., 2011b. The economics of tail events with an application to climate change. Review of Environmental Economics and Policy 5, 240−257.

Nordhaus, W., 2013. The Climate Casino: Risk, Uncertainty, and Economics for a Warming World. Yale University Press, New Haven, CT.

Nordhaus, W., 2015. Climate clubs: overcoming free-riding in international climate policy, 105 (4), 1339−1370.

Nordhaus, W., Boyer, J., 2000. Warming the World: Economic Models of Global Warming. MIT Press, Cambridge, MA.

Nordhaus, W., Yang, Z., 1996. A regional dynamic general-equilibrium model of alternative climate change strategies. American Economic Review 86, 741−765.

Ohlin, B., 1933. Interregional and International Trade. Harvard University Press, Cambridge, MA.

Pearce, D., Cline, W.R., Achanta, A., Fankhauser, S., Pachauri, R., Tol, R., Vellinga, P., 1996. The social costs of climate change: greenhouse damage and benefits of control. In: Bruce, J., Lee, H., Haites, E. (Eds.), Climate Change 1995: Economic and Social Dimensions of Climate Change. Cambridge University Press, Cambridge.

Posner, R.A., 2004. Catastrophe: Risk and Response. Oxford University Press, New York.

Ricardo, D., 1817. On the Principles of Political Economy and Taxation. John Murray, London.

Samuelson, P.A., 1949. International factor-price equalisation once again. Economic Journal 59, 181−197.

Samuelson, P., 1954. The pure theory of public expenditure. The Review of Economics and Statistics 36, 387−389.

Samuelson, P., 1955. Diagrammatic exposition of a theory of public expenditure. Review of Economics and Statistics 37, 350−356.

Samuelson, P., Nordhaus, W., 2009. Economics, nineteenth ed. McGraw-Hill Education, New York.

Sandler, T., 1997. Global Challenges: An Approach to Environmental, Political, and Economic Problems. Cambridge University Press, Cambridge.

Schuster, E.F., 1984. Classification of probability laws by tail behavior. Journal of the American Statistical Association 79 (388), 936−939.

Seo, S.N., 2006. Modeling Farmer Responses to Climate Change: Climate Change Impacts and Adaptations in Livestock Management in Africa (Ph.D. dissertation). Yale University, New Haven.

Seo, S.N., 2010a. A microeconometric analysis of adapting portfolios to climate change: adoption of agricultural systems in Latin America. Applied Economic Perspectives and Policy 32, 489−514.

Seo, S.N., 2010b. Keys to economics of global warming: a critique of the dismal theorem. Economics Bulletin 30 (1), 130−138.

Seo, S.N., 2012a. What eludes global agreements on climate change? Economic Affairs 32, 73−79.

Seo, S.N., 2012b. Adapting natural resource enterprises under global warming in South America: a mixed logit analysis. Economia. Journal of the Latin American and Caribbean Economic Association 12, 111−135.

Seo, S.N., 2012c. Decision making under climate risks: an analysis of sub-Saharan farmers' adaptation behaviors. Weather, Climate, and Society 4, 285−299.

Seo, S.N., 2013. Economics of global warming as a global public good: private incentives and smart adaptations. Regional Science Policy and Practice 5, 83−95.

Seo, S.N., 2014. Evaluation of Agro-Ecological Zone methods for the study of climate change with micro farming decisions in sub-Saharan Africa. European Journal of Agronomy 52, 157−165.

Seo, S.N., 2015a. Micro-Behavioral Economics of Global Warming: Modeling Adaptation Strategies in Agricultural and Natural Resource Enterprises. Springer International Publishing, Springer.

Seo, S.N., 2015b. Adaptation to global warming as an optimal transition process to a greenhouse world. Economic Affairs 35, 272−284.

Seo, S.N., 2016a. A theory of global public goods and their provisions. Journal of Public Affairs 16, 394−405.

Seo, S.N., 2016b. Modeling farmer adaptations to climate change in South America: a micro-behavioral economic perspective. Environmental and Ecological Statistics 23, 1−21.

Seo, S.N., 2016c. The micro-behavioral framework for estimating total damage of global warming on natural resource enterprises with full adaptations. Journal of Agricultural, Biological, and Environmental Statistics 21, 328−347.

Seo, S.N., 2016d. Microbehavioral Econometric Methods: Theories, Models, and Applications for the Study of Environmental and Natural Resources. Academic Press (Elsevier), Amsterdam, The Netherlands.

Shiller, R., 2008. Subprime Solution: How Today's Global Financial Crisis Happened and What to Do About it. Princeton University Press, Princeton, NJ.

Stern, N., 2007. The Economics of Climate Change: The Stern Review. Cambridge University Press, New York.

Stiglitz, J.E., 2002. Globalization and Its Discontents. W.W. Norton & Company, New York.

Stolper, W.F., Samuelson, P.A., 1941. Protection and real wages. Review of Economic Studies 9, 58−73.

Taylor, K.E., Stouffer, R.J., Meehl, G.A., 2012. An overview of CMIP5 and the experiment design. Bulletin of American Meteorological Society 93, 485−498.

Tietenberg, T., 1980. Transferable discharge permits and the control of stationary source air pollution: a survey and synthesis. Land Economics 56, 391−416.

Tietenberg, T., 2013. Reflections − carbon pricing in practice. Review of Environmental Economics and Policy 7, 313−329.

Tol, R., 2002. Estimates of the damage costs of climate change. Part 1: benchmark estimates. Environmental and Resource Economics 21, 47−73.

Tol, R., 2009. The economic effects of climate change. Journal of Economic Perspectives 23, 29−51.

Turco, R.P., Toon, O.B., Ackerman, T.P., Pollack, J.B., Sagan, C., 1983. Nuclear winter: global consequences of multiple nuclear explosions. Science 222, 1283−1292.

United Nations Framework Convention on Climate Change (UNFCCC), 1992. United Nations Framework Convention on Climate Change. New York.

United Nations Framework Convention on Climate Change (UNFCCC), 1998. Kyoto Protocol to the United Nations Framework Convention on Climate Change. UNFCCC, Geneva.

United Nations Framework Convention on Climate Change (UNFCCC), 2009. Copenhagen Accord. UNFCCC, Geneva.

United Nations Framework Convention on Climate Change (UNFCCC), 2011a. The Durban Platform for Enhanced Action. UNFCCC, Geneva.

United Nations Framework Convention on Climate Change (UNFCCC), 2011b. Report of the Transitional Committee for the Design of Green Climate Fund. UNFCCC, Geneva.

United Nations Framework Convention on Climate Change (UNFCCC), 2015. The Paris Agreement. In: Conference of the Parties (COP) 21. UNFCCC, Geneva.

United Nations Office for Disarmament Affairs (UNODA), 2015. Treaty on the Non-Proliferation of Nuclear Weapons. Available at: http://www.un.org/disarmament/WMD/Nuclear/NPT.shtml.

Viscusi, W.K., Aldy, J.E., 2003. The value of a statistical life: a critical review of market estimates throughout the world. Journal of Risk and Uncertainty 5, 5−76.

Weitzman, M.L., 2009. On modeling and interpreting the economics of catastrophic climate change. Review of Economics and Statistics 91, 1−19.

Yohe, G.W., Tol, R.S.J., 2012. Precaution and a dismal theorem: implications for climate policy and climate research. In: Helyette, G. (Ed.), Risk Management in Commodity Markets. Wiley, New York.

Further Reading

Arrow, K.J., 1999. Discounting, morality, and gaming. In: Portney, P.R., Weyant, J.P. (Eds.), Discounting and Intergenerational Equity. Resources for the Future, Washington, DC.

Denman, K.L., Brasseur, G., Chidthaisong, A., Ciais, P., Cox, P.M., Dickinson, R.E., Hauglustaine, D., Heinze, C., Holland, E., Jacob, D., Lohmann, U., Ramachandran, S., da Silva Dias, P.L., Wofsy, S.C., Zhang, X., 2007. Couplings between changes in the climate system and biogeochemistry. In: Solomon, S., et al. (Eds.), Climate Change 2007: The Physical Science Basis. The Fourth Assessment Report of the Intergovernmental Panel on Climate Change. Cambridge University Press, Cambridge.

Seo, S.N., 2015c. Helping low-latitude poor countries with climate change, Regulation 6−8.

A Globally Optimal Carbon Price Policy From Noncooperative Behavioral Standpoints

Chapter Outline

1. Introduction

The author already explained the gist of a carbon price policy in the previous chapter through the Samuelson–Nordhaus framework (Samuelson, 1954, 1955; Nordhaus, 2006a). The framework has provided the conceptual foundation of the economics and policy of climate change for more than almost 3 decades (Nordhaus, 1991, 1992, 1994). This chapter will begin by providing a full description of a carbon price policy in the Samuelson–Nordhaus framework. This will be followed by a suite of quantitative analyses from the perspectives of behavioral responses of individuals and countries to a carbon price (tax) policy.

The carbon price approach is supported by an integrated assessment model (IAM) such as the DICE/RICE (The Dynamically/Regionally Integrated model of Climate and Economy), MERGE (A Model for Evaluating the Regional and Global Effects of GHG reduction policies), FUND (The Climate Framework for Uncertainty, Negotiation and Distribution), and PAGE (A Policy Analysis of the Greenhouse Effect) (Nordhaus, 1991; Falk and Mendelsohn, 1993; Manne et al., 1995; Tol, 1997; Hope, 2006). This chapter will explain the full set of variables, parameters, equations,

The Behavioral Economics of Climate Change. http://dx.doi.org/10.1016/B978-0-12-811874-0.00004-0

and optimization problems and techniques using one of the IAMs, i.e., the DICE/RICE, as well as the outcome and policy variables of the social welfare optimization program.

This chapter will present readers with an opportunity to appreciate the extensive research efforts for the past 3 decades to build a simple but encompassing physical model of global warming and integrate the changes in the physical model into an economic welfare optimization problem in which policy decision variables are explicitly produced as model outputs (Nordhaus, 1994). Thereby, this chapter provides a right platform from which the author is compelled to elucidate a variety of scientific and economics endeavors with regard to global warming and climate change.

The IAMs of global warming such as the DICE/RICE are well equipped with the tools and capacities of a comparative welfare analysis of a chosen global warming policy across the participating nations (Seo, 2012a). In these models, welfare changes to individual nations due to economic growth, greenhouse gas (GHG) emissions, climate alterations, and global warming policies are computed quantitatively as outcomes of the social welfare optimization problem. This chapter makes use of the changes in these quantitative policy-relevant outcomes to assess divergent responses of participating nations to many phases of global warming policy negotiations and implementations.

As will be highlighted throughout this chapter, a primary conundrum in addressing the problem of global warming consists in a large number of nations that are faced with varied priorities and disparate incentives that arise from climate change as well as from a policy intervention through, e.g., a carbon tax (Nordhaus, 2011; Seo, 2012a). The author shows that the problem of a global public good, i.e., containing inexorable global warming, takes the form of a noncooperative game among the participant nations (Nash, 1950, 1951). In analyzing the noncooperative game of climate negotiations, the focus of the chapter is laid on whether there is no Nash equilibrium in the global warming policy making or there are policy fixes that can correct incentive problems that lead to noncooperation (Carraro et al., 2006; Metcalf, 2009; Barrett, 2010; Nordhaus, 2015).

2. Rolling the DICE: A Dynamic Integrated Model of Climate and Economy

The IAMs developed for a policy analysis of global warming integrates changes in the nature and changes in the economy into a single social welfare optimization decision-making framework. The IAMs trace the entire aspects of global warming: changes in economic activities, changes in emissions of GHGs, changes in the atmosphere, changes in land ecosystems, changes in ocean ecosystems, changes in economic activities, and changes in policy interventions.

This section will describe one of the climate change IAMs developed by William Nordhaus, the DICE/RICE. The DICE (Dynamically Integrated Climate and Economy) model is the first IAM of climate change that was conceived in the late 1970s and completed in the early 1990s by Nordhaus (Nordhaus, 1977, 1982, 1991, 1992). A DICE model with a specification of the world's major regions' economies, carbon emissions, climate change impacts, called the RICE (Regionally Integrated Climate and Economy) model, was developed subsequently (Nordhaus and Yang, 1996).

In addition to being the first IAM of climate change, the DICE/RICE is the most well-documented model of all (Nordhaus, 1994, 2013). All the equations, optimization routines, and parameters were open to the public from the inception of the modeling. Consequently, it has been made use of by numerous researchers in the field including Kolstad (1996), Newell and Pizer (2001), Carraro et al. (2006), and Seo (2007, 2012a).

The description of the DICE/RICE model henceforth relies, above all, on the most recent version of the DICE/RICE models explained in the user's manual while initial versions and subsequent modeling changes are carefully integrated and explained throughout this chapter (Nordhaus and Sztorc, 2013).

In the DICE model, the global society's long-term objective is assumed to be to maximize its welfare, which is expressed as the present value of a stream of social utilities that can be earned now and in the future:

$$\Gamma = \sum_{t=0}^{\infty} U_t \cdot (1 + \rho)^{-t} \tag{4.1}$$

In the aforementioned equation, ρ is a social rate of time preference and U is a utility function (Arrow et al., 1996; Stern, 2007; Nordhaus, 2007a). The higher the rate, the higher the discount rate of the future utilities by the society; the lower the rate, the lower the discount rate of the future utilities by the society. The contentions on the discount rate have been already explained in the previous chapter of this book. It is a positive value that hinges on other factors such as consumption growth, elasticity of marginal utility of consumption, and market interest rates (refer to Chapter 3 for a detailed explanation on discount rate).

The social utility function at time period t is specified as a function of consumption per capita, total population, and inequality aversion (α) (Nordhaus, 2008; Weitzman, 2009):

$$U_t = L_t \cdot \left(\frac{c_t^{1-\alpha}}{1 - \alpha} \right). \tag{4.2}$$

The social utility function is expressed as a function of per capita consumption. The consumption variable is interpreted as "generalized" consumption because it includes not only consumption of goods and services, but also consumption of leisure and nonmarket time uses by individuals (Nordhaus, 2008).

The total population is determined exogenously in the model and its trajectory can be obtained from specialized research centers on population such as the United Nations Population Program and the International Institute for Applied Systems Analysis (IIASA) (IIASA, 2007; Lutz et al., 2014; Gerland et al., 2014). This chapter, following Nordhaus (2008), relies on the probabilistic population projection by the IIASA, which is the most advanced population projection that incorporates many behavioral changes that other projections do not take into account.

The social utility function takes the form of a Bernoulli utility function defined by the inequality aversion parameter, α. The value of one for this parameter means that the society is neutral to inequality; the value greater than one means that the society is averse to inequality; the value smaller than one means that the society is taking inequality (Nordhaus, 1994). Note that neutrality in inequality aversion, i.e., $\alpha = 1$, results in a logarithmic utility function.

The consumption level is determined by total production (Q_t) minus saving (=investment, I_t). Saving (investment) rate is determined exogenously:

$$Q_t = C_t + I_t. \tag{4.3}$$

$$c_t = C_t / L_t. \tag{4.4}$$

The capital of the global economy is assumed to depreciate annually following a perpetual inventory method with an exponential depreciation rate (δ_t) (Kamps, 2004). The capital increases with investment:

$$K_t = I_t + \delta_t \cdot K_{t-1}. \tag{4.5}$$

The production function takes the form of a Cobb Douglas function with labor (L_t) and capital (K_t) as inputs and the Total Factor Productivity (A_t) as a multiplicative factor (Mas-Colell et al., 1995; Hulten, 2000). In the world without climate change, the production takes a simple Cobb–Douglas production form. With climate change, the production function must take into account the damage from climate change on production (O_t) as well as the cost of abatement (Θ_t) of GHGs if a climate policy were to be undertaken:

$$Q_t = [1 - \Theta_t] \cdot A_t \cdot K_t^{\gamma} \cdot L_t^{1-\gamma} \cdot [1 + O_t]^{-1}. \tag{4.6}$$

In the aforementioned equation, the total production with global warming is determined by the damage coefficient, O_t, which is a function of the degree of global warming and climate change. If the degree of global warming becomes larger, the damage from it will increase, which reduces the production of the economy and then the consumption by the economy. A reduced consumption will lead to a decrease in social welfare through Eq. (4.1).

To reduce the damage from global warming, the economy may decide to cut the level of GHG emissions, but the abatement policy is costly. In the aforementioned equation, the total cost of abatement is Θ_t, which is expressed as a fraction of the total economic output. The society should consider the damage from global warming and the total cost of abatement to maximize the economy's output and consumption.

With a global warming policy in place, the amount of carbon emissions from industrial activities (e_t^{Ind}) is determined by the amount of production, carbon intensity of the production, and rate of emissions control. With Q_t^g being the economy's gross total output without global warming damages and carbon abatement, industrial emissions are expressed as:

$$e_t^{Ind} = \phi_t \cdot (1 - \eta_t) \cdot Q_t^g. \tag{4.7}$$

In the aforementioned equation, the carbon intensity parameter ϕ_t is defined by tons of GHG emissions per 1000 dollars of output. The carbon intensity of the advanced economy, e.g., of the United States, has been declining since the 20th century primarily because of technological developments. The carbon intensity of developing countries such as China and India are more than two times greater than that of the United States at present, but is expected to decline following the pattern observed in developed countries.

The key policy variable of the DICE model, along with carbon price, is the control rate chosen by policy makers, η_t, which is expressed as the fraction of gross total emissions of GHGs. The society decides the stream of the control rates to maximize social welfare expressed in Eq. (4.1). Put differently, the control rate is determined by weighing the cost of abatement of each ton of carbon emissions (Θ_t) against the damage caused by each ton of carbon emissions (O_t).

The total amount of carbon emissions that can be emitted by the global society is bounded by the maximum amount of carbon fuels that is available to humanity, i.e., the maximum amount that can be extracted by humanity, in billions of metric tons. This amount is nearly fixed, set to 6000 gtC in the DICE model, because fossil fuels are formed through geological and chemical processes that take millions of years:

$$\sum_{t=0}^{Tmax} e_t^{Ind} \leq C^{Limit} = 6000 \text{ gtC}. \tag{4.8}$$

With a level of abatement chosen by a decision maker, the abatement cost function is specified as a power function of the control rate where the shape of the power function is determined by the exponent, θ_2 (Nordhaus, 2008, 2013):

$$\Theta_t = \theta_t^1 \cdot \eta_t^{\theta_t^2} \tag{4.9}$$

The relationship of the abatement cost function in Eq. (4.9) is largely determined by empirical examinations of the abatement cost data through which the parameters of the equation, θ_1 and θ_2, are estimated. Alternatively, the abatement cost function can be estimated through a bottom-up process with an engineering approach (Nordhaus and Boyer, 2000).

The concept of a backstop technology bounds the abatement cost function (Nordhaus, 2008). A backstop technology is the technology that can provide energy indefinitely with near-zero emissions of carbon. Examples of such a technology may be nuclear fusion energy or solar energy. The marginal cost at 100% abatement of carbon emissions is the marginal cost of a backstop technology. In other words, the marginal cost of abating

1 ton of carbon emissions will keep increasing as additional tons of emissions are cut, but cannot increase beyond the marginal cost of a backstop technology.

The global warming damage function is specified as a quadratic function of the global average atmospheric temperature increase from a preindustrial global average atmospheric temperature (T_t^{AT}):

$$O_t = \tau_1 \cdot T_t^{ATM} + \tau_2 \cdot \left(T_t^{ATM}\right)^2. \tag{4.10}$$

Besides the GHG emissions from industrial activities in Eq. (4.7), carbon dioxide, methane, nitrous oxides, and other GHGs can leak into the atmosphere through land and natural resource uses, such as crop agriculture and forestry (IPCC, 2000). It should be noted that natural resources, e.g., forests and grasslands, are sources of GHG emissions, but they also absorb carbon, i.e., sink carbon from the atmosphere or store carbon under the soils (Schlesinger, 1997; Houghton, 2008).

The total amount of carbon emissions is then the sum of gross carbon emissions from the industrial activities and land use and natural resource activities (e_t^{Natl}), both of which are measured continuously by various sources (Houghton, 2008; GCP, 2014):

$$e_t = e_t^{Ind} + e_t^{Natl}. \tag{4.11}$$

The carbon dioxide emitted from industrial activities and natural resource activities are mixed quickly in the atmosphere, which is one of the prominent and problematic characteristics of carbon dioxide. What it means is that it does not matter where the carbon is emitted, that is, from which country the carbon is released. It is quickly mixed in the atmosphere, which equalizes the atmospheric concentration of carbon dioxide across the globe (Keeling et al., 2005). Furthermore, the carbon dioxide once emitted into the atmosphere stays there for many decades to centuries, and thereby accumulates there. More formally, the residence time of carbon dioxide is from many decades to centuries (Le Treut et al., 2007).

The atmospheric carbon is absorbed in part by oceans and land-based ecosystems, which are again utilized by humans and released into the atmosphere again. This process of carbon moving from one ecosystem to another is called carbon cycle (Schlesinger, 1997). In the DICE/RICE model, the carbon cycle is characterized by a three-reservoir model, which explains the transfer of carbon among the three reservoirs: atmosphere, upper ocean, and deep ocean (Schneider and Thompson, 1981; Schlesinger and Jiang, 1990; MAGICC, 2007). The amounts of carbon in the atmosphere (ATM), upper ocean (UPP), and lower ocean (LOW) are linked through the following equations. With ς_{ij} being flow parameters from one reservoir to another and $i = 1, 2, 3$ being atmosphere, upper ocean, and lower ocean, respectively, the concentration of carbon (Λ) in each reservoir is described as follows:

$$\begin{bmatrix} \Lambda_t^{ATM} \\ \Lambda_t^{UPP} \\ \Lambda_t^{LOW} \end{bmatrix} = \begin{bmatrix} 1 & \varsigma_{11} & \varsigma_{21} & 0 \\ 0 & \varsigma_{12} & \varsigma_{22} & \varsigma_{32} \\ 0 & 0 & \varsigma_{23} & \varsigma_{33} \end{bmatrix} \begin{bmatrix} e_t \\ \Lambda_{t-1}^{ATM} \\ \Lambda_{t-1}^{UPP} \\ \Lambda_{t-1}^{LOW} \end{bmatrix} \tag{4.12}$$

Through the interactions among the three reservoirs, carbon dioxide accumulates in the atmosphere, which then increases the Radiative Forcing (RF) (H) caused by carbon accumulation (IPCC, 1990). The RF is additional radiation incident on the Earth's surface induced by greenhouse effect caused by carbon accumulation. Besides carbon, other factors can increase or decrease the RF, which is denoted by exogenous RF, H_t^{EX}. For example, an increase in aerosols in the atmosphere decreases the exogenous RF, whereas an increase in nitrous oxides or methane increases the exogenous RF.

The RFs of carbon dioxide concentration doubling in the atmosphere (φ) is about 3.8 W/m^2 (Le Treut et al., 2007). Putting together, we get the following RF equation from atmospheric increase in carbon dioxide concentration:

$$H_t = \varphi\{\log_2[\Lambda_t^{ATM}/\Lambda_t^{1750}]\} + H_t^{EX} \tag{4.13}$$

The change in the RF, i.e., the amount of radiation received by the Earth, leads to changes in atmospheric temperature and deep ocean temperature as follows (Nordhaus, 2013):

$$T_t^{ATM} = T_{t-1}^{ATM} + \xi_1\{H_t - \xi_2 T_{t-1}^{ATM} - \xi_3 \cdot \Delta_T\},$$
$$T_t^{LOW} = T_{t-1}^{LOW} + \xi_4 \cdot \Delta_T, \tag{4.14}$$
$$\text{with } \Delta_T = T_{t-1}^{ATM} - T_{t-1}^{LOW}.$$

The parameter ξ_1 is called a diffusion parameter. The parameter ξ_2 is set to satisfy $\Delta T_t^{ATM} = \Delta H_t/\xi_2$ where the equilibrium temperature sensitivity ΔT_t^{ATM} is calibrated to a 3°C increase in global temperature in response to carbon doubling following the climate change literature by the Intergovernmental Panel on Climate Change (IPCC) (Nordhaus, 2008; IPCC, 2014).

This completes the description of the DICE model. The RICE model was soon developed to explain regional differences in preference, economy, technology, and carbon emissions (Nordhaus and Yang, 1996). The two models have the same equations for the geophysical aspects of the models, e.g., the carbon cycle. The world economy in the RICE model is composed of 12 regional economies, which will be explained in the ensuing sections (Nordhaus and Boyer, 2000).

The preference function in the RICE model is a Bergson–Samuelson social welfare function, which encompasses multiple regions, $\Gamma = \Gamma(U^1,...,U^N)$, where U^I is the preference of the I_{th} region (Nordhaus and Yang, 1996). The global welfare function is then specified following the Negishi approach in which regions are aggregated using time- and region-specific Negishi welfare weights:

$$\Gamma = \sum_{t=1}^{T\max} \sum_{I=1}^{N} \vartheta_{I,t} \cdot U^I(c_t^I, L_t^I) \cdot [1 + \rho_t^I]^{-1} \tag{4.15}$$

In the aforementioned equation, $\vartheta_{I,t}$ are the Negishi weights, which are specified for each region and each time period. Consumption and population are specified for each region. The pure rate of time preference is also specified for each region, but it is assumed to be equal in all regions in the RICE model. The Negishi algorithm in the RICE model sets the Negishi weights so that the marginal utility of consumption is equal across all regions and all time periods. This ensures the social welfare function in Eq. (4.15) is maximized in the optimal solution.

The DICE/RICE model is solved by a nonlinear dynamic optimization programming algorithm embedded in a dynamic modeling system such as the General Algebraic Modeling System, which searches for the values of policy variables that maximize the social welfare in Eq. (4.1) or Eq. (4.15) (Arrow and Intriligator, 1981; Dixit, 1990).

3. Calibrations of Major Contentious Parameters of the DICE Model

To complete the DICE/RICE model, values of the parameters in the model must be determined exogenously, that is, outside the model. Many of these parameters are contentiously debated. Some of the parameters are extensively studied by experts in the corresponding fields, whereas other parameters are not known very well by researchers.

An example of the former is population growth. Many organizations are devoted to making future projections of population growth, including the United Nations Population Program and the IIASA. The DICE/RICE model relies on these population projections to specify and calibrate a population growth function, $L_{(t)}$ in Eq. (4.2) (IIASA, 2007; Lutz et al., 2014; Gerland et al., 2014).

Another example is parameters in the production function such as capital elasticity of output and Total Factor Productivity (TPF). These parameters are studied by specialists who work on these subjects (Hulten, 2000; Kamps, 2004). The same goes for an abatement cost function and the price of a backstop technology.

Among the geophysical factors, flow parameters in the three-reservoir model (ς_{ij}), as well as transfer coefficients (ξ_{ij}), are studied by climate scientists. The values of these parameters are calibrated to the scientific model values. Also, the parameters of the RF equation (φ, H_t^{EX}) are calibrated to the scientific conclusions on this relationship. The same is true of the equilibrium temperature sensitivity, which is set to around $3°C$ in response to carbon dioxide doubling in the atmosphere (Wigley et al., 2007; IPCC, 1990, 2014).

Another set of parameters is subject to more controversies: the rate of social time preference, the rate of inequality aversion, and damage function. The debates and theoretical underpinnings of the debates on the rate of social time preference (ρ) were explained in the previous chapter. The takeaway message was that this parameter must be set in accordance with the other parameters in the model such as elasticity of marginal utility of consumption and consumption growth rate (Nordhaus, 2007a). That is, it is not entirely independent of other parameters in the economy.

The rate of social or intergenerational inequality aversion, α in Eq. (4.2), is commonly set to one or two in the literature. The value of one results in the Bernoulli utility function being a logarithmic functional form. The value of two specifies that the society is highly averse to intergenerational inequality. The value of zero specifies that there is no social aversion to inequality, which means the consumptions of different generations are close substitutes with no aversion to inequality (Nordhaus, 2013).

The inequality aversion parameter is also a measure of elasticity of marginal utility of consumption. As explained in the previous chapter, the setting of this value must be in accordance with the other parameters in the model such as real interest rates, social time preference, and consumption growth.

Another contentious parameter is the climate damage function, O_t in Eq. (4.10). As shown earlier, it is calibrated to be a quadratic function of global atmospheric temperature increase. Recent DICE/RICE models calibrate that the parameter value for the linear term (τ_1) in Eq. (4.10) is set to zero while the parameter value for the quadratic term (τ_2) is set to 0.002388 (Nordhaus, 2008, 2013). This means that the climate damage that results from 2.5°C increase in temperature is around $0.00266375 \times (2.5)^2 = 0.0166$, i.e., 1.66% loss of gross domestic product (GDP) per year.

The quadratic damage function in Eq. (4.10) traces the means of the point estimates made by numerous researchers on different degrees of global temperature change (Mendelsohn and Williams, 2007; Tol, 2009; Seo, 2016a,b,d). The damage function must be understood with reference to a probability distribution. That is, the variance of the point estimate on a given temperature increase can be large or small. In IAMs such as the DICE/RICE, the climate damage function is interpreted as the best-guess estimates of climate change damages from certain degrees of changes in global temperature.

4. Future Trajectories of Climate Change and Policy Variables

Having explained the theoretical foundation and the IAMs of climate change with the DICE/RICE model, the author will henceforth provide a range of quantitative analyses on climate policy interventions with a particular emphasis on behavioral incentives and consequences.

To compare climate and policy outcomes from a certain policy intervention across the world regions, the author makes a number of modifications to the DICE/RICE model, explained earlier. First, the author calibrates a regional DICE model with 13 world regions (Seo, 2012a): the United States, European Union, China, India, Africa, Latin America, Russia, Japan, Middle East, Eurasia, Other High-Income countries, Other Asian countries, and Oceania.

Then the climate change damage function for each of the 13 world regions is specified based on the regional climate change impact literature (Mendelsohn et al., 2000, 2006; Mendelsohn and Williams, 2007; Tol, 2002, 2009; Nordhaus, 2006b, 2008). Roughly, middle-of-the-range estimate of economic damage given a degree of climate change is used for approximating a quadratic damage function in Eq. (4.10).

In Table 4.1, parameters of a regional climate damage function are presented for the world 13 regions. High-damage regions such as Africa, Latin America, India, Middle

Table 4.1 **Parameters for Region-Specific Climate Damage Functions**

World Regions	Vulnerability Classification	Damage From Carbon Doubling (% of GDP)	Quadratic Coefficient of Damage Function	Exponent of Damage Function
USA	Medium damage	1.25% loss	0.00139	2
EU	High damage	2.5% loss	0.00278	2
China	Low damage	0.4% loss	0.00037	2
India	High damage	2.5% loss	0.00278	2
Africa	High damage	2.5% loss	0.00278	2
Latin America	High damage	2.5% loss	0.00278	2
Russia	Beneficiary	1.25% gain	−0.00139	2
Japan	Medium damage	1.25% loss	0.00139	2
Middle East	High damage	2.5% loss	0.00278	2
Eurasia	Low damage	0.4% loss	0.00037	2
Other high-income countries	Medium damage	1.25% loss	0.00139	2
Other Asian countries	High damage	2.5% loss	0.00278	2
Oceania	High damage	2.5% loss	0.00278	2

GDP, gross domestic product.

East, Other Asia, European Union, and Oceania are calibrated to lose around 2.5% of annual GDP from a 3°C increase in temperature, i.e., an equilibrium climate sensitivity to carbon dioxide doubling. Medium-damage regions such as the United States, Japan, and Other High-Income countries are calibrated to lose only half of that, i.e., 1.25% of the annual GDP. Low-damage regions such as China and Eurasia are calibrated to lose a third of the damage predicted in the medium-damage countries, i.e., 0.4% loss of the annual GDP. Russia is calibrated to be a beneficiary country from global warming because of thawing of permafrost zones: 1.25% gain due to a 3°C increase in temperature. Note that a quadratic specification of the damage function means that economic damage is assumed to increase nonlinearly at a faster rate at temperature increases beyond 3°C.

Table 4.2 **Parameters for Region-Specific Abatement Cost Functions**

World Regions	Exponent of a Regional Abatement Cost Function	Cost of a Backstop Technology ($/tC)	Ratio of Asymptotic Price to Current Backstop Price
USA	2.8	1200	1/2
EU	2.8	1200	1/2
China	2.8	720	1/2
India	2.8	792	1/2
Africa	2.8	792	1/2
Latin America	2.8	792	1/2
Russia	2.8	600	1/2
Japan	2.8	1200	1/2
Middle East	2.8	1200	1/2
Eurasia	2.8	720	1/2
Other high-income countries	2.8	792	1/2
Other Asian countries	2.8	792	1/2
Oceania	2.8	792	1/2

Another modification is made to the abatement cost function shown in Eq. (4.9). A region-specific abatement cost function is calibrated based on varied costs of the backstop technology across the world regions. Regions are faced with different prices of the backstop technology because a zero-carbon-emitting economy is easier to achieve for some countries and harder for other countries. A highly industrial country may be deeply trenched in fossil-fuel-based economic activities; hence, a total decoupling of its economy from fossil fuels is more costly to achieve.

In calibrating the region-specific abatement cost functions, the author follows the estimates by Nordhaus and the IPCC, which are in turn based on the range of estimates from different estimation methodologies (Nordhaus, 1994, 2008). As shown in Table 4.2, the backstop price is estimated to be 1200$ per ton of carbon removal for developed regions (Nordhaus, 2010b; IPCC, 2007). What this means is that the last ton of carbon can be removed, given current technologies, at the cost of 1200$. This is more than 10 times larger than the range of estimate of the current social cost of carbon (Mendelsohn and Williams, 2007; Tol, 2009; Nordhaus, 2013).

Table 4.3 **Parameters for Region-Specific Carbon Intensity Parameters and Land Use Emissions**

World Regions	Carbon Emissions per $1000 GDP at Present	Growth Rate of Carbon Intensity per Decade	Land Use Emissions at Present (GtC/ Decade)
USA	0.133	−0.1748	−0.320
EU	0.090	−0.1196	−0.180
China	0.305	−0.2286	−0.129
India	0.142	−0.2458	0
Africa	0.141	−0.2212	2.624
Latin America	0.093	−0.1397	6.064
Russia	0.280	−0.2727	0.200
Japan	0.091	−0.2249	0
Middle East	0.210	−0.1263	0
Eurasia	0.268	−0.2800	0
Other high-income countries	0.176	−0.1368	0.176
Other Asian countries	0.128	−0.1469	6.197
Oceania	0.176	−0.1368	0

The backstop price for developing regions is calibrated to be lower with 790$ per ton of carbon removal. The backstop price is lowest in Russia with 600$ per ton of carbon removal. The present cost of backstop technology is assumed to decline, because of technological developments, asymptotically to the half of the present level by the end of the 21st century. For example, the cost of solar panels or nuclear energy will fall over time.

Regional differences are also captured in Table 4.3 by carbon intensity, the amount of carbon dioxide emissions per $1000 GDP produced. For developed regions, carbon intensity is lower. That is, developed economies emit less carbon per dollar of production. As of 2005, carbon intensity of the United States is 0.133 tons of carbon dioxide per $1000 GDP, whereas it is as high as 0.305 tons of carbon dioxide per $1000 GDP in China. It is the lowest in the European Union and Japan with 0.090 tons of carbon dioxide per $1000 GDP (Nordhaus and Boyer, 2000).

The carbon intensity of a developed economy such as the European Union and the United States has fallen steadily since the early 20th century as its economy has grown.

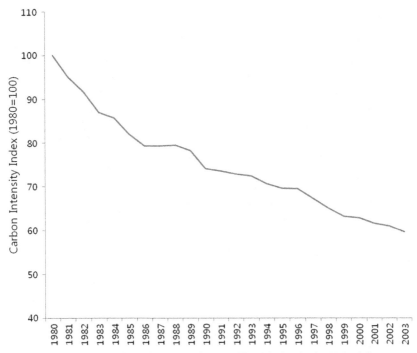

Figure 4.1 Carbon intensity (tons of carbon/GDP) index in the United States.

In Fig. 4.1, a time series of carbon intensity of the United States from 1980 to 2003 is drawn, with the index set to 100 in 1980. It shows a rapid decrease in the carbon intensity, tons of carbon emissions per GDP, during this time period. During the decade of the 1970s, carbon intensity fell by 18%; during the decade of the 1980s, it fell by 26%, during the decade of the 1990s, it fell by 17% (EIA, 2004, 2014). It is expected to fall even further, albeit with a reduced rate, as the economy further expands in the future.

Similarly, the carbon intensities of developing countries such as China, India, and Russia have declined in the past decades, especially in the case of China, and are expected to decline further as these economies continue to grow in the upcoming decades (Fan et al., 2007).

The third column of Table 4.3 shows different (negative) growth rates of carbon intensity for the 13 world regions. It is expected to decline at a faster rate in developing regions than in developed regions. Although not shown in the table, it is further assumed that the decline rate of carbon intensity will decline over time (Nordhaus and Boyer, 2000).

Table 4.3 also shows varied land use and ecosystem emissions of carbon across the world regions (Denman et al., 2007; Houghton, 2008). Per decade, the amount of carbon emissions from changes in land use and ecosystems is as high as 6 GtC in Latin America where about half of the entire continent is densely forested (WRI, 2005). It is also high with 6.2 GtC per decade in Other Asian Countries, in which major timber exporting countries such as Indonesia are located. The amount of carbon emissions that originate from land uses and ecosystem changes is 2.6 GtC for Africa.

In the table, the amount of carbon emissions from land uses and ecosystem changes is negative for the United States, European Union, and China. It is negative because forests and grasslands absorb carbon dioxide from the atmosphere, a phenomenon called carbon sink (US EPA, 2015). In these regions, carbon sinks resulting from increased forests and grasslands exceed carbon emissions from deforestation during the past several decades. On the other hand, in Latin America and Indonesia, the amount of carbon emissions due to deforestation is far greater than carbon sinks from additional forests and ecosystems (Houghton, 2008).

Large differences in the amount of carbon emissions from land uses and ecosystem changes across the regions, shown in Table 4.3, showcase a remarkable reality of global warming in which countries must confront disparate incentives where some countries may turn out to be a loser and other countries may turn out to be a winner, which is one of the aspects that this chapter will highlight.

With these region-specific calibrations of economies, emissions, and technologies, the modified DICE model is equipped to produce as model outputs a trajectory of the climate change variable for many centuries ahead as well as those of climate policy variables such as emissions control rates, carbon price, welfare changes. First, let us set the control rate of carbon emissions to zero throughout the entire time period in the modified DICE model. Put differently, this is a no policy intervention scenario in response to unfolding inexorable global warming in the centuries to come. In Fig. 4.2, we call this a business-as-usual (BAU) scenario. In this scenario, as shown

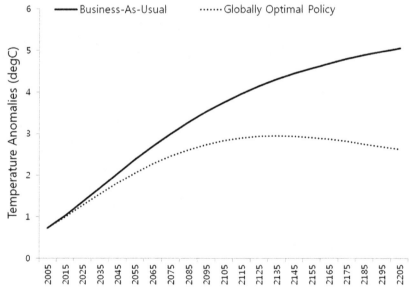

Figure 4.2 Global warming predictions with an optimal carbon policy versus a business-as-usual scenario.

in Fig. 4.2, global average temperature is projected to increase by 1°C by 2015, 2.3°C by 2055, and 3.7°C by the end of the 21st century from the 20th century average global temperature. The global temperature will keep rising beyond this century. By the 2200s, the temperature is projected to have increased by more than 5°C, that is, without any policy intervention to cut emissions of GHGs.

If the global community were to agree on a global cooperative solution according to the Samuelson–Nordhaus framework and the DICE model, which we call a globally optimal policy (GOP) in Fig. 4.2, an efficient carbon price (or tax) shall be set at 35$ per ton of carbon in 2015, as shown in Table 4.4. The carbon price should be harmonized and implemented across the world. As global warming would unfold ever more severely in the future, an optimal carbon tax should increase to 144$ per ton by the middle of this century, and to 361$ per ton of carbon by the end of this century.

Under this trajectory of carbon price imposed globally by a potentially grand global policy agreement, the world community will have achieved the rate of reduction of carbon emissions at the level of 17% by 2015, 39% by the 2050s, and 67% by the 2100s. This is the trajectory of carbon emissions control rate at the global level, that is, regional emissions control rates will diverge even under the GOP scenario.

With the optimal trajectory of carbon price thus determined and imposed, the amount of global carbon emissions in the atmosphere would increase from 11 GtC/year in the 2010s to 12.6 GtC/year in the 2030s. Note that this amount includes all GHG emissions converted to a carbon unit. The amount of global carbon emissions is projected to reach a peak in the 2030s and decline thereafter gradually to 7.5 GtC/year at the end of this century.

Will the GOP be sufficient to halt global warming? With the implementation of the globally optimal carbon policy, the Earth's temperature is projected to increase throughout this century, but the rate of increase will be slowed down decade by decade. Global temperature is projected to increase by 2°C by the middle of this century and by 2.8°C by the end of this century.

The effectiveness of the GOP will manifest unequivocally in the next century through global temperature change, which is depicted in Fig. 4.1. With the GOP policy intervention, global temperature increase would peak at 2.9°C during the first decade of the next century and thereafter would start to fall slowly throughout the centuries.

The GOP temperature trajectory in Fig. 4.2 is in stark contrast to the temperature trajectory under the BAU scenario. In the no policy intervention scenario, i.e., the BAU scenario, global temperature is projected to increase by as much as 5°C in two centuries. We can interpret the contrasting outcomes as the rationale that a policy response through the Samuelson–Nordhaus carbon tax framework will accomplish the monumental task of turning around the trend of global warming and stabilizing the global climate system.

5. Diverging Behavioral Incentives for Actions Under a Business-as-Usual Scenario

The optimal carbon price policy, as captured by the policy-relevant outcome variables in the previous section, would do the job of slowing down the rate of global warming and

Table 4.4 **Trajectories of Global Climate and Policy Variables Under a Globally Optimal Policy**

	2005	2015	2025	2035	2045	2055	2065	2075	2085	2095	2105
Carbon tax ($/tC)	19	35	54	78	109	144	183	224	269	314	361
Control rate (%)	12.1	17.3	22.1	27.5	33.2	39.0	44.8	50.5	56.2	61.6	67.0
Temperature anomalies (°C)	0.73	0.99	1.27	1.55	1.81	2.06	2.27	2.46	2.61	2.74	2.84

eventually stabilizing the climate system, and further with the lowest cost possible globally. However, this does not mean that participant countries in the global climate efforts have the incentives to agree on and adopt the DICE optimal carbon price policy. Rather, the analysis in the previous section only demonstrates, without equivocation, that it is indeed the best course of action for the global community as a whole for stopping global warming.

As the first step to unravel what is not explained in the earlier analysis, we can ask whether, given the climate changes observed recently and projected in the future, countries have the incentive to act to combat climatic changes and further to agree on a globally optimal carbon price policy such as the DICE-based carbon price policy described in the previous section.

What forces a country to act to address global warming? To begin with, a country would have the incentive to act if projected climatic changes would harm the country significantly. On the other hand, the country would have no incentive to act if such changes in climate would benefit the country in a significant way.

In Table 4.5, assuming the trajectory of projected climate change by the modified DICE model under the BAU scenario shown in Fig. 4.1, a trajectory of global warming damage from the projected climate change is presented for each of the major world regions throughout the 21st century. The economic damage to region j at time period t under the BAU scenario, $\Pi_t^{j,\text{BAU}}$, is expressed as follows:

$$\Pi_t^{j,\text{BAU}} = O_t^{j,\text{BAU}} = \tau_1^j \cdot T_t^{ATM,\text{BAU}} + \tau_2^j \cdot \left(T_t^{ATM,\text{BAU}} \right)^2 \tag{4.16}$$

The damage from future climate changes is large for Europe, with $666 billion loss of income per year by the middle of this century and $3.07 trillion loss of income per year by the end of this century. By contrast, the damage on the United States is relatively smaller with $326 billion annual loss by the middle of this century and $1.44 trillion annual loss per year by the end of this century. The large expected damage in Europe owes to the potential slowdown of the thermohaline circulation in the oceans and many countries in low-lying areas, which are vulnerable to sea level rise (Nordhaus and Boyer, 2000).

Among the developing regions in the modified DICE model, damages on China and Russia are projected to be small. For China, it would reach $99 billion by the middle of this century and $391 billion by the century's end. Note that this is despite the fact that China is projected to grow rapidly throughout the century to become the largest economy in the world along with the United States.

For Russia, the damage is projected to be negative, i.e., the country is projected to benefit from the warming world, which is due mainly to the thawing of the large land masses of permafrost zones and decreased human mortality from cold weather (Tol, 2002; Barreca et al., 2016). The benefit would amount to only $57 billion annual income by midcentury and $271 billion annual income by the century's end.

The biggest losers from climate change are Africa, Latin America, and India. Africa is predicted to suffer $1.8 trillion loss of income , Latin America $1.5 trillion, India $1.5 trillion per year by the end of this century. The absolute damages in these regions are as large as that projected for the United States, although these regions have incomes far less than 10% of the US income.

Table 4.5 Region-Specific Damages From Global Warming Under the Business-as-Usual Scenario ($US billion)

	2005	2015	2025	2035	2045	2055	2065	2075	2085	2095	2105
USA	12	28	61	117	204	326	485	681	908	1164	1442
EU	26	61	128	242	417	666	993	1401	1886	2446	3074
China	1	5	15	33	60	99	146	201	262	326	391
India	5	16	42	93	180	311	487	708	966	1254	1563
Africa	4	14	39	90	182	325	525	785	1100	1462	1861
Latin America	9	24	57	117	213	351	530	749	999	1274	1565
Russia	-2	-4	-10	-19	-35	-57	-87	-124	-168	-217	-271
Japan	4	9	18	35	60	96	144	203	274	356	447
Middle East	4	10	25	54	101	173	270	395	546	721	916
Eurasia	0	1	2	4	6	11	16	24	32	43	54
Other high-income countries	2	6	13	25	45	74	114	164	227	300	385
Other Asian countries	5	13	32	69	134	237	390	603	883	1239	1676
Oceania	1	4	10	22	42	71	112	166	232	312	403

These damage estimates under the BAU scenario reveal that climate changes will have varied impacts on the world's regions. Some regions might not suffer much or even get better off with global warming. For example, thawing of the permafrost zones in Russia and Canada might result in increased land areas for cultivation and residing of their peoples. The biggest losers are the European Union and the low-latitude regions such as Africa, Latin America, and India. The relative winners of the BAU scenario under climate change are Russia and China. The impact on the United States would be larger than that on China and Russia, but smaller than that on the hardest-hit regions.

These projections imply that there is stronger incentive to take actions to battle climate change in the hardest-hit regions such as the European Union, Africa, India, Latin America, Other Asian Countries, and Middle East. These regions are expected to suffer a great deal owing to unfolding climatic changes, and therefore would be inclined to take whatever necessary actions to avoid such harmful consequences.

Nonetheless, the strong incentive for these regions may not be sufficient to have a globally cooperative action to deal with global warming. This is because there are regions that are relative beneficiaries from global warming such as Russia, Canada, China, and Eurasia. If global warming were to result in relative (or absolute) gains to these regions against the hardest-hit regions, these winner regions will feel little motivation to take costly actions to combat global warming.

Table 4.5 leads us to the platform of behavioral economics of global warming policy making. More specifically, at the level of the world's 13 regions, there is divergence among them in incentives to take costly actions. Then, at an even finer level of the world's sovereign countries in which most political decisions are made, there will be even greater disparities among the sovereign nations in motivations to take costly measures to slow down global warming.

As a matter of fact, this conclusion does not stop at national borders. Analyses have shown that there are winners and losers from global warming even within the national border. Various sectors of the economy would be affected by climate change disparately (Seo, 2010b, 2012b, 2016b). Also, municipalities within the national border would be unequally impacted by changes in climate.

An inevitable policy question is thus: Given the wide range of incentives among the playmakers of global warming policy, does the DICE optimal carbon price policy have a shot at being agreed upon at a global conference and further implemented in a harmonized way across the world? Is it reasonable to assume that global cooperation for combating climate change would arise through the trajectory of carbon price or through other policy instruments?

6. Alterations of Behavioral Incentives Under an Optimal Climate Policy Scenario

A globally optimal carbon price policy as prescribed by the DICE model would bring about global welfare improvement over the BAU scenario in the world where climate is changing inexorably, which has been proved both theoretically and empirically (Nordhaus, 1991). However, this does not mean that all countries of the world or sectors of the society will reap the benefit from the GOP policy.

The welfare improvement that results from the GOP would not be uniformly distributed across the world regions and countries. Winning regions and losing regions would reemerge with the implementation of the optimal policy. Furthermore, a transition from the BAU policy to the GOP would lead to rearrangements of the winners and losers from climate change.

In Tables 4.6 and 4.7, the author calculates the total cost of the GOP for each region as the sum of the damage from climate change, abatement cost, and cost of emissions permits. A region complying with an international protocol on climate change that requires all regions (countries) to implement a globally harmonized carbon tax should "pay" the three costs: damages, abatement cost, emissions permits (or carbon tax).

As shown in the previous section, an optimal climate policy is projected to slow down the rate of increase in global temperature. Under the altered temperature trajectory under the GOP, the regional damages that result from unfolding climatic changes would become smaller than those expected from the BAU policy scenario. For instance, the European Union's climate damage is reduced from $3.1 trillion per year in the BAU scenario to $1.8 trillion per year in the GOP scenario at the end of this century.

A reduction of climate damage owing to a slower temperature increase because of the implementation of the GOP policy is also large in India, Africa, and Latin America. The damage in Africa is reduced from almost $1.9 trillion per year to $1.1 trillion per year. The loss from climate change in India is reduced from $1.6 trillion annually to $0.9 trillion annually. A similarly large reduction in the expected damage from climate change with the GOP scenario can be seen in Latin America.

In these regions, a large reduction in the expected damage justifies a strong push for an internationally agreed optimal policy such as the DICE carbon price policy. However, not all the regions feel the same urge for an aggressive push for an international agreement. For example, the reduction in damage is much more modest in China: $160 billion reduction annually in the climate-induced damage for China. For Russia, the GOP scenario leads to a decrease in the benefit from climate change by $120 billion annually by the end of the 21st century. In other words, a GOP intervention makes Russia worse off. Given these expected outcomes, it would be reasonable to think that these regions will be less enthusiastic about a global climate policy.

The analysis of the changes in expected climate change damages arising from a globally optimal climate policy gives us the first glimpse into distributional consequences of a climate policy. A full picture of the distributional impacts of a climate policy, however, cannot be gained without considerations of other costs from a global carbon policy.

What are the other costs of implementing the carbon price policy? An implementation of a globally harmonized carbon tax (price) by a country in an effort to comply with an international protocol requires two simultaneous actions. On the one side, an emitter of carbon should reduce the amount of carbon as long as it is cheaper per unit to do so than paying the carbon price (tax) per unit of carbon. This is the cost

Table 4.6 Costs of the Globally Optimal Carbon Policy: Damage + Abatement Cost

	2005	2015	2025	2035	2045	2055	2065	2075	2085	2095	2105
(1) Damage ($US billion)											
USA	12	26	54	98	162	246	348	463	587	713	836
EU	26	57	113	203	332	503	714	957	1225	1508	1797
China	1	5	13	27	48	74	105	137	168	198	226
India	5	15	37	78	144	235	350	484	627	773	914
Africa	4	13	34	76	145	245	378	536	714	901	1088
Latin America	9	22	50	98	169	265	381	512	649	785	915
Russia	−2	−4	−8	−16	−28	−43	−62	−84	−107	−131	−155
Japan	4	8	16	29	48	73	103	138	177	218	260
Middle East	4	10	23	45	81	131	194	270	355	444	535
Eurasia	0	1	2	3	5	8	12	16	21	26	31
Other high-income	2	6	11	21	36	56	81	112	146	184	224
Other Asian	5	13	29	58	107	180	281	412	573	764	980
Oceania	1	4	9	18	33	54	81	113	151	192	236
(2) Abatement Cost ($US billion)											
USA	1	4	8	16	29	47	70	98	130	166	204
EU	1	3	7	13	24	40	63	92	129	173	223

Continued

Table 4.6 Costs of the Globally Optimal Carbon Policy: Damage + Abatement Cost—cont'd

	2005	2015	2025	2035	2045	2055	2065	2075	2085	2095	2105
China	2	8	21	46	83	132	191	256	324	392	459
India	0	1	3	7	14	23	36	50	66	83	100
Africa	0	1	3	7	15	25	39	57	76	97	118
Latin America	0	2	4	8	15	25	38	55	75	97	120
Russia	1	2	3	6	11	17	23	31	38	46	52
Japan	0	1	2	3	5	8	12	16	21	27	33
Middle East	0	1	3	7	13	23	38	57	81	109	141
Eurasia	0	1	2	4	7	11	16	21	26	31	36
Other high-income	0	1	3	5	10	17	26	39	56	76	100
Other Asian	0	1	3	6	12	22	38	59	87	123	167
Oceania	0	0	1	2	4	8	13	20	29	40	53

Table 4.7 Costs of the Globally Optimal Carbon Policy: Carbon Tax or Cost of Permits

	2005	2015	2025	2035	2045	2055	2065	2075	2085	2095	2105
Cost of Permit Purchase ($US billion)											
USA	34	65	102	150	204	259	310	351	380	396	398
EU	26	50	80	121	170	225	280	332	378	413	437
China	33	98	186	293	397	479	526	537	512	459	383
India	7	18	32	51	73	93	108	117	119	114	103
Africa	10	23	39	62	88	113	134	147	150	145	130
Latin America	19	35	54	78	104	128	148	160	163	158	143
Russia	10	18	27	36	45	51	53	51	45	36	26
Japan	7	13	20	28	36	45	52	58	62	65	65
Middle East	9	20	37	62	94	131	170	206	237	261	276
Eurasia	7	12	17	23	29	33	35	34	30	25	18
Other high income	10	19	32	49	70	94	118	143	165	183	196
Other Asian	17	31	47	68	93	120	146	169	186	195	192
Oceania	3	7	12	21	32	45	59	72	85	96	104

of abatement. The emitter is better off by cutting down emissions, i.e., paying for the abatement.

On the other side, an emitter of carbon should pay the carbon tax for the emissions of carbon, i.e., unabated emissions of carbon because of too high cost of cutting them. For these unabated emissions, the emitter is better of paying the carbon tax than abating the emissions. This is the cost of carbon tax that must be paid by an emitter of carbon. Alternatively, the emitter may need to purchase the permits, given the policy instrument chosen by the government, for the emissions of carbon, in which case the cost is the cost of permits.

The bottom panel of Table 4.6 shows the cost of abatement for each region. It is the annual cost of each region calculated as the sum of the marginal cost for each ton of carbon emissions abated. The total abatement cost for the United States is about $4 billion per year by 2015, $47 billion by midcentury, and $200 billion by the century's end. A similar trajectory is seen in the abatement cost for the European Union.

In comparison, abatement costs of the low-latitude regions of Africa, Latin America, and India are shown to be about half of that of the United States with about $100 billion per annum at the end of this century for India and $120 billion for Africa and Latin America. The reason for this lower cost of abatement is that cheaper options for cutting carbon emissions are available in these low-latitude regions, such as changes in land uses and agricultural practices, a decrease in deforestation, more efficient buildings and plants, and more efficient power productions.

The abatement cost of China is shown to be the largest among the world regions. It amounts to only $8 billion per annum at present, but quickly rises to $132 billion annually by midcentury and $459 billion annually by the end of this century. For Russia, the abatement cost amounts to $8 billion per annum by the middle of this century and $52 billion per annum in a century. The abatement cost of China is larger than that of the other regions because of a higher rate of economic growth in China through the 21st century. The country runs out of cheaper options in the near term and must resort to ever more costly options in the longer term to reduce emissions of carbon, which is projected to increase rapidly through the 21st century.

The third component of the cost of a global climate policy, shown in Table 4.7, is the cost of carbon emissions permits, in other words, the amount of carbon tax to be paid by emitters (Tietenberg, 2006, 2013; Ellerman and Buchner, 2007; Nordhaus, 2007b). This is the cost that must be paid by emitters such as businesses, households, and public sectors. The cost of permits can be best imagined as the cost that accrues to the country if such permits must be purchased from low carbon companies located in foreign countries, which is unavoidable to ensure the efficiency of the program at the global level.

The carbon penalty, i.e., the cost of permits, of the United States increases from $65 billion per annum today, to $259 billion by midcentury, and to $398 billion per annum in a century. The permit cost for the European Union shows an analogous trajectory until the end of this century.

For Africa, the cost of permits is equivalent to $23 billion per annum in 2015, $113 billion by the 2050s, and $130 billion by the end of the 21st century. For India, the cost of permits increases from $18 billion annually in 2015, to $92 billion per year by 2055, and to $103 billion per annum in a century. The relatively lower cost of permits in these low-latitude developing regions is because these regions are better off by cutting carbon emissions than paying for additional permits as there are many less costly mitigation options found there.

In China, the cost of permits increases from $98 billion in 2015 to peak at $537 billion by the 2070s and thenceforth declines to $383 billion by the 2100s. The cost of permits by Russia is estimated to be $18 billion in 2015, to peak at $53 billion by the 2060s, and then to decline to $24 billion by the end of this century. For these regions, the cost of carbon tax (or carbon permits) reaches the peak at the latter half of this century because the rate of control increases sharply in these countries. The actual amount of carbon tax per annum starts to decline when the amount of carbon emissions per annum starts to fall, offsetting an ever higher price of carbon through this century.

We can alternatively think of the cost of purchasing permits as the carbon tax to be paid to the government by carbon emitting businesses, households, and public sectors. Because there is no global government to collect the tax, the carbon tax will be collected by the national government. Because national governments face different challenges and have divergent incentives with regards to climate change, the carbon tax revenue may be used to promote national governments' agendas, which may lead to even larger carbon emissions.

From one point of view, the collected tax revenue by the national government can be given back to the individuals in a carbon neutral way, i.e., in a way that does not cause any additional carbon emissions. For example, the US federal government may give back the tax revenue to solar energy enterprises (White House, 2013; US EPA, 2014). However, the subsidy given to solar energy industry can lead to additional distortions in natural resource uses, which may further increase energy bills in the economy and increase the stress of fossil-fuel-dependent state economies. Furthermore, it may not turn out to be carbon neutral. That is, the solar industry may become a major carbon emitter because of the processes involved in constructing and maintaining solar panels.

Alternatively, the carbon revenue may be held by the national government for eternity. In that case, it may be permanently lost from the economy. Or it may be used to address the problem of a large government budget deficit, i.e., debts (Nordhaus, 2010a). The government may use it for other nonclimate projects such as military buildup and improvements. Or the government may use the revenue for supporting low-income families (Metcalf, 2009). These reallocations can lead, however, to additional carbon emissions, e.g., by military and low-income families.

From a national government perspective, a carbon tax or a carbon emissions permit trading is likely to be favored by a nondemocratic or an authoritarian regime. For the authoritarian government, a carbon tax system provides another avenue of government revenue approved legally by the international community. For example, the carbon tax system may turn out to be a boon to the Chinese communist party or the Russian government in maintaining the government resources and political power.

Another way to reason about the cost of carbon tax or emissions permits is that the government revenue can be used to support the implementation of a carbon tax program nationally, or an emission trading system, or any cost of participation in an international protocol. A carbon tax program is costly as it calls for new institutions, physical infrastructure, operating costs, and human resources to manage and monitor the program.

The author calculates the sum of total damage, total abatement cost, and cost of permits as the total cost of a globally optimal carbon policy. This sum is the most immediate and direct burden of a policy to the national economy. The total cost under the GOP scenario is expressed as follows, with Q^g gross GDP, i.e., the GDP under no global warming constraints, and P_t price of carbon tax optimally determined:

$$\Pi_t^{j,\text{GOP}} = O_t^{j,\text{GOP}} \cdot Q_t^{g,j} + \Theta_t^{j,\text{GOP}} \cdot Q_t^{g,j} + \left(1 - \eta_t^{j,\text{GOP}}\right) \cdot e_t^{j,\text{BAU}} \cdot P_t \tag{4.17}$$

Then, the net cost from a globally optimal carbon policy is calculated as the difference between the total cost from the optional GOP policy and the total cost from the BAU policy. The net cost is the additional cost required to adopt the global optimal policy over the BAU no action policy:

$$\Delta\Pi_t^j = \Pi_t^{j,\text{GOP}} - \Pi_t^{j,\text{BAU}}. \tag{4.18}$$

The net cost will be positive for the country that is worse off under the global policy and negative for the country that is better off under the global policy. Bear in mind that the true cost of a global optimal policy is the net cost in Eq. (4.18), not the total cost in Eq. (4.17), assuming that global warming will manifest as predicted by the DICE model.

The trajectory of the net cost for each of the world major regions is drawn in Fig. 4.3. To avoid cluttering in the figure, the results for only seven major regions are depicted. The net cost is large in the near term and keeps increasing throughout the 21st century for China. By the middle of this century, the net cost reaches $600 billion per annum and reaches the peak at $800 billion annually by the 2080s, both of which are expressed in 2005 US$. For Russia, the net cost keeps increasing steadily until the end of this century at which point it reaches $200 billion per year.

For the United States, the net cost remains positive throughout the century. The net cost increases linearly until 2070 by which time the net cost is as large as $250 billion per annum. Thenceforth, the net cost declines steadily to zero by the century's end. The decline of the net cost during the after-2080 period is due to a nonlinear increase in climate damage for the United States in the BAU policy. The net cost for Japan is more muted throughout the century: it is slightly positive in the first half of the century and slightly negative in the second half of the century.

The trajectories for the European Union, Africa, Latin America, and India take on an analogous shape, with the European Union having the largest curvature. The net cost for the European Union increases to about $100 billion by the middle of this century, and thenceforth falls rapidly through the rest of the century. By the end of the century, the net cost is negative for the European Union with $650 billion per annum. That is, a large gain from a globally optimal carbon policy is expected for the European

Union. The large gain is attributable to a globally cooperative climate policy and the emissions control, which, as a consequence, reduces the expected damage from global warming on the region substantially. Note that the damage to the European Union under the BAU policy, i.e., a no-intervention scenario, is as large as $3.1 trillion annually by the 2100s, as shown in Table 4.5.

The trajectories for Africa, Latin America, and India take on a similar shape to that of the European Union but with a smaller curvature. The net cost of a global carbon policy is positive through 2060, after which point it becomes negative through the rest of the century. The net cost rises steadily to $50 billion, then declines to negative $300 billion per annum in Latin America, negative $400 billion per annum for India, and negative $500 billion per annum for Africa. This means that there would be a large financial gain to these poor regions in the long term, despite a much smaller loss in the near term, if a global carbon tax were to be adopted and implemented, thereby to slow-down the rate of climate change at the global level.

The analysis of the regional net costs tells us that some regions are better off with a globally optimal carbon policy, whereas other regions are worse off with it. The losing regions are China, Russia, Canada (not shown here), and the United States and the winning regions are the European Union, Africa, India, and Latin America. The losing regions become worse off under a globally welfare maximizing solution because they have to cut carbon emissions substantially, whereas the benefits of such efforts are not sufficiently large to these regions.

Another way to examine the burden of a global climate policy is the rate of control of carbon emissions required of each region/country under the adopted policy. In fact, the regional control rates are one of the components that account for the regional net costs in Fig. 4.3. As shown in Fig. 4.4, the optimal control rate of carbon today is about 14% for the United States and the European Union. The control rate increases steadily to about 33% by midcentury, and to 59% by the end of this century for the two regions.

By contrast, the control rate required for China under the GOP scenario is today about 19%, which increases to 44% by midcentury, and to 77% by the end of the century. The control rate is even larger for Russia, with 48% by midcentury and 85% by the end of the century. The trajectory of the carbon control rate for Latin America, Africa, and India is similar to that of China, but slightly lower.

Why are Russia, China, and other developing regions required to cut a higher percentage of GHG emissions under the implementation of the GOP? The answer lies in the lower marginal cost of abatement in these regions than those in the advanced regions, which are trenched in carbon-based economies. Note that the emissions reduction rates are determined by the regions for their benefits, i.e., not forced, given the global climate policy through the GOP.

The series of analyses up to now reveal many important distributional consequences of a global climate policy making. The first observation is that the world regions that are predicted to suffer substantially from global warming have an economic incentive to support an optimal global climate policy through an international agreement. The policy, if implemented as designed, will benefit these countries in the long term because it will reduce the large damage from global warming projected in these regions under a BAU policy.

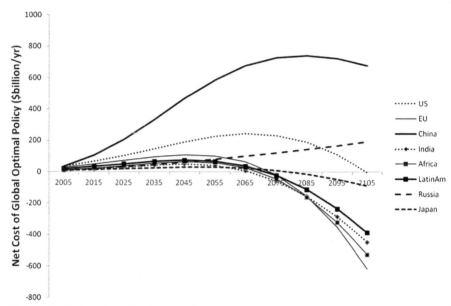

Figure 4.3 Trajectories of region-specific net costs of the globally optimal policy through the 21st century.

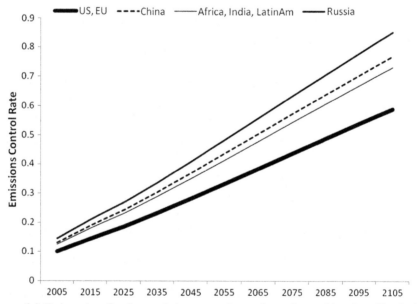

Figure 4.4 Trajectories of carbon emissions control rates for major world regions (fraction).

Second, many regions will pay a significant cost during the first half of the 21st century. For most world regions, the net cost, i.e., the additional cost over the cost of a no action climate change scenario, will exceed $100 billion per year by the middle of this century. Adoption of a GOP would mean that the world regions are making a very-long-term investment into climate mitigation in which the cost is incurred now and in the near future and the benefit is accrued by the latter half of this century or by the end of the century for some regions.

Third, losers of a global climate policy will be those regions located in temperate and colder regions that are projected to grow at a higher rate economically throughout the 21st century. China, Russia, East Asia, Oceania, North America, and some European countries are likely to fall into this category. They will be the losers from a global climate policy. If there is no other noneconomic and/or nonclimate motivation for these countries, they will likely reject any proposal of a global climate policy protocol.

7. Alterations of Behavioral Incentives Through Monetary Transfers

As explained in the previous chapter, one potential way to overcome the disparate incentive problem in the framework of a global cooperative optimal policy is to negotiate transfers of wealth from winner countries to loser countries or in other ways (Carraro et al., 2006). This would create an incentive for a loser country to join an international agreement and/or protocol while a winner country still benefits from a global optimal policy even with monetary transfers to loser countries.

In the DICE/RICE optimization framework in Eq. (4.15), a global policy maker should maximize the following, with $\omega_{t,K}^I$ being the amount of wealth transfer per capita from region K to region I at time period t, which can be positive or negative:

$$\Gamma = \sum_{t=1}^{Tmax} \sum_{I=1}^{N} \vartheta_{I,t} \cdot U^I \left(c_t^I + \sum_{K \neq I} \omega_{t,K}^I, L_t^I \right) [1 + \rho_t^I]^{-1} \tag{4.19}$$

Does a solution exist for Eq. (4.19)? Note that the wealth transfer $\omega_{t,K}^I$ can be determined endogenously, i.e., within the model. To be more specific, it can be determined following a certain functional relationship with the policy variables in the model such as temperature (T^{ATM}), damage cost (O), abatement cost (Θ), or control rate (η).

Alternatively, $\omega_{t,K}^I$ may be determined exogenously of the model, i.e., outside the model. This means that the array of parameters is determined politically, without any formal rule, in an ad hoc manner to force an individual nation to join an agreement.

To explain the rationale of monetary transfers and answer whether a solution exists to Eq. (4.19) or not, the author will proceed with the quantitative results from the modified DICE model presented up to this point in this chapter. As shown, the winner region from a GOP is the European Union. Hence, as long as the European Union is expected to have a welfare improvement from the implementation of the optimal global climate policy, it would be willing to offer monetary transfers to other regions/ countries to urge the loser countries such as China and Russia to join an international protocol. On the other hand, it may not be realistic to expect that the other winner countries, such as Africa, Latin America, and India, would offer any wealth transfer to China or Russia.

How much money has to be transferred to induce an agreement from disadvantaged countries, e.g., China or Russia? It would be determined at the amount of money upon which all countries can agree. The transfer of wealth should lead to a state in which all nations gain some benefit from an optimal global policy over a BAU policy.

Does the solution exist in this wealth transfer scheme? In other words, is there an array of wealth transfers among the countries that guarantee the state in which all countries gain welfare improvement from a global climate policy? Alternatively, is there more than one array of wealth transfers among the countries that satisfies all participating countries?

Will there "always" be an array of wealth transfers among the participant countries upon which they would all agree? Put differently, will there always be an array of mutually beneficial wealth transfers among the countries? The answer is no. The reason for this negative answer can be provided through Fig. 4.2. In the figure, the sum of net costs to China, Russia, Japan, and the United States in the 2070s far exceeds the net gains to the other regions. In this situation, there does not exist an array of wealth transfers that results in a state in which social welfare is improved in all countries. In fact, there does not exist such an array of mutually beneficial transfers through the 2090s as shown in Fig. 4.2.

Interestingly, however, such an array of transfers appears to emerge at the end of the 21st century. By the 2100s, the net benefits that accrue to the European Union, Africa, India, and Latin America sum up to exceed the net costs to China, Russia, and the United States. This is because, by that point in time, the damage from unmitigated global warming in any region will have become so large that it will outweigh all the costs of a global climate policy intervention in the region.

Nonetheless, even by the 2100s, the expected loss to China is much larger than the gain that would occur to the European Union. As long as China is not willing to accept any loss from a global climate policy, there should be a country or a region that can transfer money to China if an international climate protocol were to be established. However, as is shown in Fig. 4.2, there is no country or region that can match what China is seeking without incurring a loss from a global policy.

There are other winners besides the European Union. However, it is near impossible to argue that the wealth transfer be done by African, Latin American, and South Asian regions to China. In addition to China, the United States and Russia are losing from a global optimal climate policy throughout this century. It is not realistic to argue that the wealth transfer be done to the United States from Africa, Latin America, and South Asia.

The empirical results presented in this chapter show that there are many occasions and reasons to believe that a global agreement would not be reached on a GOP as laid out by the Samuelson–Nordhaus framework and the modified DICE model, even with an additional option of the transfers of wealth considered.

Although the analysis so far is not a categorical rejection of the possibility of a globally agreed optimal carbon policy with wealth transfers, it does forcefully demonstrate that the obstacles are high and many. Furthermore, the quantitative results presented in this chapter do not take into account a political reality in which a wealth transfer from one country to another is a sensitive political subject. That is, a wealth transfer in the size of $100 billion per annum from the United States to China and Russia that would occur annually for the entire 21st century is hard to imagine.

8. Conclusion and Moving Forward

Through the looking glass of behavioral economics, the author presented an analysis of a Samuelson—Nordhaus framework explained in the previous chapter relying on the DICE/RICE model developed by William Nordhaus. The DICE/RICE model is an IAM that strings together economies, emissions, atmosphere, oceans, climate, and ecosystems into a global welfare optimization framework. In the DICE/RICE model, all the complexities in global warming are finely integrated with representative functional relationships, at the level of world major regions.

The optimization model produces outcomes of policy variables such as carbon tax and an emissions control rate, which can be adopted by the global community for a long-term time horizon. The trajectory of carbon penalties that is needed to fend off a run-away global warming and control emissions optimally is a powerful intellectual accomplishment by the DICE/RICE model and other IAMs of climate change.

What have been underexamined in the literature are behavioral consequences of the Samuelson—Nordhaus framework and the DICE/RICE model (Seo, 2012a, 2013, 2015). This chapter provides a set of analysis on behavioral aspects of the DICE/RICE framework: diverging behavioral incentives under the BAU policy, alterations of behavioral incentives under the globally optimal carbon policy, and alterations of behavioral incentives through monetary transfers.

A series of empirical analyses conducted in this chapter provides a conceptual foundation for why there could be no globally cooperative solution for the global warming problem. Almost 3 decades of negotiations at the UN level and mutual negotiations among concerned nations have also demonstrated that a GOP or any policy close to it may not materialize at present and in the future (Nordhaus, 2010b, 2011; Barrett, 2010). The UN-level negotiations and intercountry negotiations will be further explained later in this book in the chapters on technological breakthroughs, adaptation strategies, and global policy negotiations (UNFCCC, 1998, 2009, 2011, 2015).

The analyses of the behavioral aspects of climate change economics provided in this chapter are undertaken at the level of a country or a region. That is, the basis for analysis is diverging incentives across the nations or the regions. However, an analysis at a finer level is also possible. For example, disparate incentives among different industries within a country can be empirically studied and presented (Seo, 2010b, 2012b, 2016a,b). Winners and losers, in other words, are diverging even within a national boundary or a regional boundary. For example, a specialized crop system may suffer the most among the natural resource intensive enterprises (Seo, 2010a, 2014). This will be the topic in the ensuing chapters of this book, especially in Chapter 6 on an adaptation paradigm for climate policy.

The quantitative results presented in this chapter should not, however, be interpreted without qualifications. To be more specific, the results in this chapter rely on many functions and relationships that are subject to uncertainty (Kolstad, 1996; Weitzman, 2009). For example, the results and conclusions can be shifted if damage functions specified in this chapter are modified. A damage function with a larger negative value for the second-order term would force a country to be more inclined to adopt an international protocol to control the rate of carbon emissions. This chapter shows the quantitative results assuming the best-guess estimates of many parameters and functions (Mendelsohn et al., 2006; Mendelsohn and Williams, 2007; Tol, 2009; Nordhaus, 2008).

At this point, the author would like to and is ready to lead the readers who have been patient to read the book up to this point to a set of alternative options and frameworks to deal with the problems of global warming and climatic changes. Again, these options will be presented with a focus on behavioral implications and consequences of adopting and moving forward with one of these alternatives.

In the next chapter, the author will delineate an alternative approach that is based on technological innovations and breakthroughs in which a multitude of technologies that are existent or suggested to be developed will be explained in comparison with a GOP scenario described in this chapter (IPCC, 2011; Lackner et al., 2012; NRC, 2015; MIT, 2015). This will be followed by Chapter 6, which focuses on the concept of adaptation paradigm to global warming and climatic changes (Mendelsohn, 2000; Seo, 2015, 2016c). The chapter will present the readers with an opportunity to go through a whole array of adaptation strategies and measures that can be taken to address climatic changes in a meaningful way and by an individual decision maker who experiences gains and losses directly from such changes.

References

Arrow, K.J., Intriligator, M.D., 1981. Handbook of Mathematical Economics, vol. 1. Elsevier, Amsterdam.

Arrow, K.J., Cline, W., Maler, K.G., Munasinghe, M., Squitieri, R., Stiglitz, J., 1996. Intertemporal equity, discounting, and economic efficiency. In: Bruce, J.P., Lee, H., Haites, E.F. (Eds.), Climate Change 1995: Economic and Social Dimensions of Climate Change, Intergovernmental Panel on Climate Change. Cambridge University Press, New York.

Barreca, A., Clay, K., Deschenes, O., Greenstone, M., Shapiro, J.S., 2016. Adapting to climate change: the remarkable decline in the US temperature-mortality relationship over the twentieth century. Journal of Political Economy 124 (1). http://dx.doi.org/10.1086/684582.

Barrett, S., 2010. Why Cooperate?: The Incentive to Supply Global Public Goods. Oxford University Press, Oxford.

Carraro, C., Eyckmans, J., Finus, N., 2006. Optimal transfers and participation decisions in international environmental agreements. Review of International Organizations 1, 379–396.

Denman, K.L., Brasseur, G., Chidthaisong, A., Ciais, P., Cox, P.M., Dickinson, R.E., Hauglustaine, D., Heinze, C., Holland, E., Jacob, D., Lohmann, U., Ramachandran, S., da

Silva Dias, P.L., Wofsy, S.C., Zhang, X., 2007. Couplings between changes in the climate system and biogeochemistry. In: Solomon, S., et al. (Eds.), Climate Change 2007: The Physical Science Basis. The Fourth Assessment Report of the Intergovernmental Panel on Climate Change. Cambridge University Press, Cambridge.

Dixit, A.K., 1990. Optimization in Economic Theory, second ed. Oxford University Press, Oxford.

Ellerman, A.D., Buchner, B.K., 2007. The European Union Emissions Trading Scheme: origins, allocations, and early results. Review of Environmental Economics and Policy 1, 66–87.

Falk, I., Mendelsohn, R., 1993. The economics of controlling stock pollution: an efficient strategy for greenhouse gases. Journal of Environmental Economics and Management 25, 76–88.

Fan, Y., Liu, L., Wu, G., Tsai, H., Wei, Y., 2007. Changes in carbon intensity in China. Empirical findings from 1980–2003. Ecological Economics 62, 683–691.

Gerland, P., Raftery, A.E., Sevcikova, H., Li, N., Gu, D., Spoorenberg, T., Alkema, L., Fosdick, B.K., Chunn, J., Lalic, N., Bay, G., Buettner, T., Heilig, G.K., Wilmoth, J., 2014. World population stabilization unlikely this century. Science 1257469.

Global Carbon Project, 2014. Global Carbon Budget 2014. Available at: http://cdiac.ornl.gov/GCP/.

Hope, C., 2006. The marginal impact of CO_2 from PAGE2002: an integrated assessment model incorporating the IPCC's five reasons for concern. The Integrated Assessment Journal 6, 19–56.

Houghton, R.A., 2008. Carbon flux to the atmosphere from land-use changes: 1850–2005. In: Trends: A Compendium of Data on Global Change. Carbon Dioxide Information Analysis Center, Oak Ridge National Laboratory, U.S. Department of Energy, Oak Ridge, TN.

Hulten, C.R., 2000. Total Factor Productivity: A Short Biography. National Bureau of Economic Research (NBER) Working Paper Series 7471, Cambridge, MA.

International Institute of Applied Systems Analysis (IIASA), 2007. Probabilistic Projections by 13 World Regions, Forecast Period 2000–2100, 2001 revision. Available online at: http://www.iiasa.ac.at/Research/POP/proj01/.

Intergovernmental Panel on Climate Change (IPCC), 1990. Climate Change: The IPCC Scientific Assessment. Cambridge University Press, Cambridge.

Intergovernmental Panel on Climate Change (IPCC), 2000. Special Report on Land Use, Land-Use Change, and Forestry. Cambridge University Press, Cambridge.

Intergovernmental Panel on Climate Change (IPCC), 2007. Climate Change 2007: The Physical Science Basis. The Fifth Assessment Report of the IPCC. Cambridge University Press, Cambridge.

Intergovernmental Panel on Climate Change (IPCC), 2011. Special Report on Renewable Energy Sources and Climate Change Mitigation. Cambridge University Press, Cambridge.

Intergovernmental Panel on Climate Change (IPCC), 2014. Climate Change 2014: The Physical Science Basis, The Fifth Assessment Report of the IPCC. Cambridge University Press, Cambridge.

Kamps, C., 2004. New Estimates of Government Net Capital Stocks for 22 OECD Countries 1961–2001. IMF Working Paper 04/67. Washington, DC.

Keeling, C.D., Piper, S.C., Bacastow, R.B., Wahlen, M., Whorf, T.P., Heimann, M., Meijer, H.A., 2005. Atmospheric CO_2 and $^{13}CO_2$ exchange with the terrestrial biosphere and oceans from 1978 to 2000: observations and carbon cycle implications. In: Ehleringer, J.R., Cerling, T.E., Dearing, M.D. (Eds.), A History of Atmospheric CO_2 and Its Effects on Plants, Animals, and Ecosystems, Pages 83–113. SpringerVerlag, New York.

Kolstad, C.D., 1996. Learning and stock effects in environmental pollution: the case of greenhouse gas emissions. Journal of Environmental Economics and Management 31, 1–18.

Lackner, K.S., Brennana, S., Matter, J.M., Park, A.A., Wright, A., Zwaan, B.V., 2012. The urgency of the development of CO_2 capture from ambient air. Proceedings of the National Academy of Sciences 109 (33), 13156–13162.

Le Treut, H., Somerville, R., Cubasch, U., Ding, Y., Mauritzen, C., Mokssit, A., Peterson, T., Prather, M., 2007. Historical overview of climate change. In: Solomon, S., et al. (Eds.), Climate Change 2007: The Physical Science Basis. The Fourth Assessment Report of the Intergovernmental Panel on Climate Change. Cambridge University Press, Cambridge.

Lutz, W., Butz, W., Samir, K.C. (Eds.), 2014. World Population and Global Human Capital in the 21st Century. Oxford University Press, Oxford.

Wigley, T., Raper, S., Salmon, M., Osborn, T (developers), 2007. MAGICC (Model for the Assessment of Greenhouse-Gas Induced Climate Change). Available online at: http://www.cgd.ucar.edu/cas/wigley/magicc/index.html.

Manne, A.S., Mendelsohn, R., Richels, R., 1995. MERGE — a model for evaluating regional and global effects of GHG reduction policies. Energy Policy 23 (1), 17–34.

Mas-Colell, A., Whinston, M.D., Green, J.R., 1995. Microeconomic Theory. Oxford University Press, Oxford.

Massachusetts Institute of Technology (MIT), 2015. The Future of Solar Energy: An Interdisciplinary MIT Study. MIT, MA.

Mendelsohn, R., 2000. Efficient adaptation to climate change. Climatic Change 45, 583–600.

Mendelsohn, R.O., Morrison, W.N., Schlesinger, M.E., Andronova, N.G., 2000. Country-specific market impacts of climate change. Climatic Change 45, 553–569.

Mendelsohn, R., Dinar, A., Williams, L., 2006. The distributional impact of climate change on rich and poor countries. Environment and Development Economics 11, 1–20.

Mendelsohn, R., Williams, L., 2007. Dynamic forecasts of the sectoral impacts of climate change. In: Schlesinger, M., Kheshgi, H., Smith, J., de la Chesnaye, F., Reilly, J.M., Wilson, T., Kolstad, C. (Eds.), Human-Induced Climate Change: An Interdisciplinary Assessment. Cambridge University Press, Cambridge.

Metcalf, G., 2009. Designing a carbon tax to reduce US greenhouse gas emissions. Review of Environmental Economics and Policy 3, 63–83.

National Research Council (NRC), 2015. Climate Intervention: Reflecting Sunlight to Cool Earth. Committee on Geoengineering Climate: Technical Evaluation and Discussion of Impacts. National Academies Press, Washington, DC.

Nash, J., 1950. Equilibrium points in n-person games. Proceedings of the National Academy of Sciences 36 (1), 48–49.

Nash, J., 1951. Non-cooperative games. The Annals of Mathematics 54 (2), 286–295.

Newell, R., Pizer, W., 2001. Discounting the Benefits of Climate Change Mitigation: How Much Do Uncertain Rates Increase Valuations? Pew Center, Washington, DC.

Nordhaus, W., 1982. How fast should we graze the global commons? American Economic Review 72, 242–246.

Nordhaus, W., 1991. To slow or not to slow: the economics of the greenhouse effects. The Economic Journal 101, 920–937.

Nordhaus, W., 1992. An optimal transition path for controlling greenhouse gases. Science 258, 1315–1319.

Nordhaus, W., 1994. Managing the Global Commons. MIT Press, Massachusetts.

Nordhaus, W.D., 1977. Economic growth and climate: the carbon dioxide problem. American Economic Review 67, 341–346.

Nordhaus, W.D., 2006a. Paul Samuelson and global public goods. In: Szenberg, M., Ramrattan, L., Gottesman, A.A. (Eds.), Samuelsonian Economics and the Twenty-first Century. Oxford Scholarship Online.

Nordhaus, W.D., 2006b. Geography and macroeconomics: new data and new findings. Proceedings of the National Academy of Science 103 (10), 3510−3517.

Nordhaus, W., 2007a. A review of the Stern Review on the economics of climate change. Journal of Economic Literature 55, 686−702.

Nordhaus, W., 2007b. To tax or not to tax: alternative approaches to slowing global warming. Review of Environmental Economics and Policy 1 (1), 26−44.

Nordhaus, W.D., 2008. A Question of Balance—Weighing the Options on Global Warming Policies. Yale University Press, New Haven.

Nordhaus, W., 2010a. Carbon taxes to move toward fiscal sustainability. The Economists' Voice 7 (3), 1−5.

Nordhaus, W., 2010b. Economic aspects of global warming in a post-Copenhagen environment. Proceedings of the U.S. National Academy of Sciences 107 (26), 11721−11726.

Nordhaus, W., 2011. The architecture of climate economics: designing a global agreement on global warming. Bulletin of Atomic Scientists 67 (1), 9−18.

Nordhaus, W., 2013. The Climate Casino: Risk, Uncertainty, and Economics for a Warming World. Yale University Press, New Haven, CT.

Nordhaus, W., 2015. Climate clubs: overcoming free-riding in international climate policy, 105 (4), 1339−1370.

Nordhaus, W., Yang, Z., 1996. A regional dynamic general-equilibrium model of alternative climate change strategies. American Economic Review 86, 741−765.

Nordhaus, W., Boyer, J., 2000. Warming the World: Economic Models of Global Warming. MIT Press, Cambridge, MA.

Nordhaus, W., Sztorc, P., 2013. DICE 2013: Introduction and User's Manual. Yale University, New Haven.

Samuelson, P., 1954. The pure theory of public expenditure. The Review of Economics and Statistics 36, 387−389.

Samuelson, P., 1955. Diagrammatic exposition of a theory of public expenditure. Review of Economics and Statistics 37, 350−356.

Schlesinger, W.H., 1997. Biogeochemistry: An Analysis of Global Change, second ed. Academic Press, San Diego, CA.

Schlesinger, M.E., Jiang, X., December 1990. Simple model representation of atmosphere-ocean GCMs and estimation of the timescale of CO_2-induced climate change. Journal of Climate 12−15.

Schneider, S.H., Thompson, S.L., 1981. Atmospheric CO_2 and climate: importance of the transient response. Journal of Geophysical Research 86, 3135−3147.

Seo, S.N., 2007. Is Stern Review on climate change alarmist? Energy and Environment 18, 521−532.

Seo, S.N., 2010a. A microeconometric analysis of adapting portfolios to climate change: adoption of agricultural systems in Latin America. Applied Economic Perspectives and Policy 32, 489−514.

Seo, S.N., 2010b. Managing forests, livestock, and crops under global warming: a microeconometric analysis of land use changes in Africa. Australian Journal of Agricultural and Resource Economics 54 (2), 239−258.

Seo, S.N., 2012a. What eludes global agreements on climate change? Economic Affairs 32, 73−79.

Seo, S.N., 2012b. Adapting natural resource enterprises under global warming in South America: a mixed logit analysis. Economia: The Journal of the Latin American and Caribbean Economic Association 12, 111−135.

Seo, S.N., 2013. Economics of global warming as a global public good: private incentives and smart adaptations. Regional Science Policy and Practice 5, 83−95.

Seo, S.N., 2014. Evaluation of Agro-Ecological Zone methods for the study of climate change with micro farming decisions in sub-Saharan Africa. European Journal of Agronomy 52, 157—165.

Seo, S.N., 2015. Adaptation to global warming as an optimal transition process to a greenhouse world. Economic Affairs 35, 272—284.

Seo, S.N., 2016a. Modeling farmer adaptations to climate change in South America: a micro-behavioral economic perspective. Environmental and Ecological Statistics 23, 1—21.

Seo, S.N., 2016b. The micro-behavioral framework for estimating total damage of global warming on natural resource enterprises with full adaptations. Journal of Agricultural, Biological, and Environmental Statistics 21, 328—347.

Seo, S.N., 2016c. A theory of global public goods and their provisions. Journal of Public Affairs 16, 394—405.

Seo, S.N., 2016d. Microbehavioral Econometric Methods: Theories, Models, and Applications for the Study of Environmental and Natural Resources. Academic Press (Elsevier), Amsterdam, the Netherlands.

Stern, N., 2007. The Economics of Climate Change: The Stern Review. Cambridge University Press, New York.

Tietenberg, T.H., 2006. Emissions Trading: Principles and Practice, second ed. Resources for the Future, Washington, DC.

Tietenberg, T., 2013. Reflections — carbon pricing in practice. Review of Environmental Economics and Policy 7, 313—329.

Tol, R.S.J., 1997. On the optimal control of carbon dioxide emissions: an application of FUND. Environmental Modeling and Assessment 2, 151—163.

Tol, R.S.J., 2002. Estimates of the damage costs of climate change—Part 1: benchmark estimates. Environmental and Resource Economics 21 (1), 47—73.

Tol, R., 2009. The economic effects of climate change. Journal of Economic Perspectives 23, 29—51.

United Nations Framework Convention on Climate Change (UNFCCC), 1998. Kyoto Protocol to the United Nations Framework Convention on Climate Change. UNFCCC, New York.

United Nations Framework Convention on Climate Change (UNFCCC), 2009. Copenhagen Accord. UNFCCC, New York.

United Nations Framework Convention on Climate Change (UNFCCC), 2011. The Durban Platform for Enhanced Action. UNFCCC, New York.

United Nations Framework Convention on Climate Change (UNFCCC), 2015. The Paris Agreement. Conference of the Parties (COP) 21. UNFCCC, New York.

United States Environmental Protection Agency (US EPA), 2014. Carbon Pollution Emission Guidelines for Existing Stationary Sources: Electric Utility Generating Units. USEPA, Washington, DC, USA.

United States Environmental Protection Agency (US EPA), 2015. Inventory of US Greenhouse Gas Emissions and Sinks: 1990—2013. EPA, Washington, DC.

United States Energy Information Administration (EIA), 2004. Emissions of Greenhouse Gases in the United States 2003. DOE/EIA-0573. Department of Energy (DOE), Washington, DC.

United States Energy Information Administration (EIA), 2014. Annual Energy Outlook 2014. US EIA, Department of Energy, Washington, DC.

Weitzman, M.L., 2009. On modeling and interpreting the economics of catastrophic climate change. Review of Economics and Statistics 91, 1—19.

White House, 2013. The President's Climate Action Plan. Executive Office of the President. The White House, Washington, DC.

World Resources Institute (WRI), 2005. World Resources 2005. The Wealth of the Poor: Managing Ecosystems to Fight Poverty. WRI, Washington, DC.

Further Reading

Nakicenovic, N., Davidson, O., Davis, G., Grübler, A., Kram, T., La Rovere, E.L., Metz, B., Morita, T., Pepper, W., Pitcher, H., Sankovski, A., Shukla, P., Swart, R., Watson, R., Dadi, Z., 2000. Emissions Scenarios. A Special Report of Working Group III of the Intergovernmental Panel on Climate Change. IPCC, Geneva.

Schultz, P.A., Kasting, J.F., 1997. Optimal reductions in CO_2 emissions. Energy Policy 25, 491–500.

Stouffer, R.J., Manabe, S., Bryan, K., 1989. Interhemispheric asymmetry in climate response to a gradual increase of atmospheric CO_2. Nature 342, 660–662.

Breakthrough Technologies: Technological Innovations as an Alternative Global Warming Solution

Chapter Outline

1. Introduction

In the literature of global warming and policy options to contain global warming and stabilize the climate system, technological options and breakthroughs have long been viewed as one of the most pivotal unknowns, let alone one of the most optimistic options (Nordhaus, 1973, 1977, 1992; IPCC, 2005b, 2011). Since the earliest years of global warming debates in the late 1970s, a basket of technological options has expanded over the course of time while knowledge and research on each of these options have been refined and accumulated. The portfolio of technological options includes currently available technologies as well as future anticipated technologies

The Behavioral Economics of Climate Change. http://dx.doi.org/10.1016/B978-0-12-811874-0.00005-2

that are predicted to be introduced at some point in the future. Some of these technologies are regarded as a breakthrough technology, which can offer a quick fix of the climate problem at a much lower cost than the lowest cost possible in the absence of it.

In this chapter, the author shifts the focus of the book away from the theories and instruments for an economically optimal provision of containing global warming to a large array of technological solutions that has held high promises and large sways in global warming research and debates. If materialized in the future, any one of the breakthrough technologies should alter the trajectories of numerous climate policy variables and outcomes substantially.

This chapter provides a wide-ranging survey of technological options that can play a major role in dealing with global warming challenges (IPCC, 2005a, 2005b, 2011; NRC, 2013, 2015; MIT, 2015). There are two types of technological options surveyed in this chapter: breakthrough technologies and incremental technologies (Seo, 2016). A breakthrough technology is loosely defined as one that is revolutionary in the sense that it reduces the cost of addressing global warming by more than, say, an order of magnitude from that attainable in the absence of it. An incremental technological advance is one that does little to affect the global cost of containing global warming but has the potential to become a pivotal cooperative tool for individuals and businesses who must make adaptive adjustments in response to the reality of global warming.

The portfolio of breakthrough technologies includes carbon-capture-and-storage and geoengineering (Lackner et al., 2012), reflecting sunlight from the space (NRC, 2015), nuclear fission with an enhanced safety and storage of wastes (US DOE, 2016a), a nuclear fusion energy production technology (ITER, 2015), ocean iron fertilization (Martin et al., 1994), solar energy (MIT, 2015), electric vehicles (EVs) (NRC, 2013), and new lighting methods such as the light-emitting diodes (LEDs) (Akasaki et al., 2014). Other major technological innovations include wind energy, geothermal energy, bioenergy, hydroelectricity, and electricity storage systems (IPCC, 2011).

The portfolio of incremental technologies includes, inter alia, methane reduction technologies from animals as well as from oil and gas extractions (US EPA, 2006; Brandt et al., 2014), new varieties of crops and animals that are resilient to climatic changes (Evenson and Gollin, 2003), cures for animal and human diseases that are susceptible to global warming (Aksoy et al., 2014), hurricane projection technologies (Seo, 2015b), replacements of refrigerants such as hydrofluorocarbons (HFCs) and hydrochlorofluorocarbons (HCFCs) (EC, 2016), mobile communication technologies, and advances in the energy sector such as the smart grid system (Sims et al., 2007; Joskow, 2012).

This chapter will provide an introduction to the basic physics and engineering that underlie each of these technological options. A number of fundamental economic questions are raised with regard to technological innovations. First, an economic interpretation of these technological options will be made by comparing across these options costs and benefits of employing them by referring to various economic indicators as well as by comparing against the global cost of an optimal economic policy (Nordhaus, 1994; Manne and Richels, 1999; Heal, 2010; IPCC, 2011). Second, the author will quantify the significance of some of these breakthroughs by the changes in the carbon tax and the changes in the global emissions trajectories in the

Samuelson—Nordhaus framework with the introduction of each of these options (Nordhaus, 2008). Third, it will be asked whether a certain policy instrument, e.g., carbon tax or other policy options, is preferable to another policy option because the former is likely to be more effective in inducing future technological innovations (Goulder and Mathai, 2000; Nordhaus, 2002; Popp, 2004).

There are a number of more pertinent questions raised with regard to behavioral aspects of technological solutions. First, the times of introduction and the effectiveness of these technological breakthroughs are not known with certainty. This has major implications on individual nations' taking climate actions and participating in a global protocol. A country will be more likely to wait for the introductions of these technologies because the option value of no action increases and because the country can learn about these technological options (Arrow and Fisher, 1974; Kolstad, 1996; Manne and Richels, 2004). For a business owner, a major capital investment into a climate project will lead to the loss of a larger option value of the current capital.

The second behavioral aspect of technological remedies is their roles in climate actors' adaptation behaviors. Many existing technological options and highly anticipated new options are playing major roles in choices of individuals and businesses in making numerous decisions now and in the future, given the global warming trend and projections (Seo, 2015a, 2016).

This chapter proceeds as follows. In the next section, the author provides a survey of breakthrough technologies. It is followed by a survey of microincremental technologies in Section 3. The fourth section describes quantitatively economic significances of these technologies. Section 5 explains the literature on induced technological innovations. Section 6 discusses technological uncertainties and option values that influence individuals' choices of adaptation measures and strategies. The chapter concludes with discussions in Section 7 on how numerous technological advances would affect adaptation behaviors.

2. A Survey of Breakthrough Technologies

Breakthrough technologies are those technologies that, once developed, have the potential to enable humanity to contain global warming and solve the problems caused by global warming with a much lower cost than that in the absence of such technologies. A more formal definition can be given with reference to a backstop technology, which is done later in this section.

Some of these breakthroughs are aimed at altering the climate system directly, whereas the others are aimed at influencing the climate system indirectly, that is, by cutting carbon emissions at the points of release. An example of the former is geoengineering of the climate system and an example of the latter is nuclear fusion or solar energy.

2.1 Carbon Capture, Storage, and Reuse

A carbon-capture-storage-reuse (CCSR) technology is conceptually simple: a machine will suck the carbon from the atmosphere and store it somewhere for other commercial uses later in time (Lackner et al., 1999, 2012; IEA, 2013). The captured carbon, for example, can be bought by commercial farms and can be used as an input for the process that enhances photosynthesis of crops, plants, and trees. Or the captured CO_2 can be buried deep underground.

Broadly speaking, the CO_2 capture and storage techniques include a bioenergy production with a carbon capture and sequestration technology and a direct air capture and sequestration technology. The former relies on plants and trees to remove the CO_2 from the air, much like naturally occurring sinks of carbon by various ecosystems (Denman et al., 2007). The latter includes various techniques to scrub CO_2 directly from ambient air (NRC, 2015).

The CCSR technology is already available and has been adopted at a local scale by various actors. Many of the large-scale carbon-capture-storage (CCS) projects will be introduced shortly. The big hurdle that lies ahead is how to scale up the technology. That is, will it be possible to apply the CCSR technology at a global scale or a national scale in a way that can alter the atmospheric concentration of carbon dioxide and ultimately global temperature?

Another major concern with regard to the CCSR technology is whether and in what types a global-scale application of the CCSR technology will have unintended consequences on the global atmosphere and consequently the earth systems. Is it acceptable by the nations that an application of the CCSR technology in the United States, for example, leads to unexpected changes in weather patterns and climate in other countries upon which many economic and social activities depend?

According to the International Energy Agency, the CCSR technologies can be grouped into the following categories based on the ways the energy production process is modified to enable CO_2 separation: postprocess or postcombustion capture, syngas/hydrogen capture or precombustion capture, oxyfuel combustion, and inherent separation (IEA, 2013):

1. Postprocess capture or postcombustion capture: It simply means that CO_2 is taken out after fuel combustion. At the end of the energy production process, CO_2 is separated from the mixture of gases, e.g., from combustion flue gases.
2. Syngas/hydrogen capture or precombustion capture: This method is based on the creation of syngas, a mixture of gases composed of hydrogen, carbon monoxide, and carbon dioxide. From burning fossil fuels or biomass, syngas is generated. Then, CO_2 is removed from the syngas. In addition, in the cases in which pure hydrogen is needed or additional emission reduction is required, the syngas can be shifted to hydrogen by converting the carbon monoxide to CO_2. Then, CO_2 is separated from hydrogen.
3. Oxyfuel combustion: This process adds pure oxygen in the combustion process instead of air, which then yields a flue gas of high-concentration CO_2. Therefore this process does not call for a specific CO_2 separation step, either postcombustion or precombustion. Nevertheless, to extract oxygen from the air, an initial separation step is needed.
4. Inherent separation: This method refers to the cases in which generation of concentrated CO_2 is an intrinsic part of the energy production process. As such, there is no separate method required for separating CO_2. Examples include gas processing and fermentation-based biofuels. In these processes, the generated CO_2 is released into the atmosphere. This CO_2 can be captured.

As of 2012, there are 16 large-scale CCS projects worldwide in either an "operate" stage or an "execute" stage (GCCSI, 2012). An "execute" stage refers to the project in which construction of a CCS facility has begun. The total capacity of these CCS projects is said to be 36 million tons of carbon dioxide per annum (MTPA) of which 23 MTPA is in an "operate" stage and 13 MTPA is in an "execute" stage, as shown in Table 5.1.

As such, the current total capacity of the CCS technology, being less than one-tenth of 1% of the total annual carbon dioxide emissions, is not sufficiently large to be a meaningful strategy for cutting carbon dioxide globally (GCP, 2014). Furthermore,

Table 5.1 Large-Scale Integrated Projects Active as of 2012

Project Name, Country	Type of Capture	Volume of CO_2 Captured (MTPA)	Storage Type	Date of Operation
(1) Stage: Operate				
Val Verde Gas Plants, USA	Precombustion: gas processing	1.3	EOR	1972
Enid Fertilizer CO_2-EOR Project, USA	Precombustion: fertilizer	0.68	EOR	1982
Shute Creek Gas Processing Facility, USA	Precombustion: gas processing	7	EOR	1986
Sleipner CO_2 Injection, Norway	Precombustion: gas processing	1 (+0.2)	DSF	1996
Great Plains Synfuel Plant and Weyburn–Midale Project, USA/Canada	Precombustion: synfuels	3	EOR	2000
In Salah CO_2 Injection, Algeria	Precombustion: gas processing	1	DSF	2004
Snøhvit CO_2 Injection, Norway	Precombustion: gas processing	0.7	DSF	2008
Century Plant, USA	Precombustion: gas processing	5 (+3.5)	EOR	2010
Total capacity		**19.68 (+3.7) MTPA**		
(2) Stage: Execute				
Air Products Steam Methane Reformer EOR Project, USA	Postcombustion: hydrogen production	1	EOR	2012

Continued

Table 5.1 **Large-Scale Integrated Projects Active as of 2012—cont'd**

Project Name, Country	Type of Capture	Volume of CO$_2$ Captured (MTPA)	Storage Type	Date of Operation
Lost Cabin Gas Plant, USA	Precombustion: gas processing	1	EOR	2012
Illinois Industrial CCS Project, USA	Industrial separation: ethanol	1	DSF	2013
ACTL with Agrium CO$_2$ Stream, Canada	Precombustion: fertilizer	0.59	EOR	2014
Boundary Dam Integrated CCS Demonstration Project, Canada	Postcombustion: power generation	1	EOR	2014
Kemper County IGCC Project, USA	Precombustion: power generation	3.5	EOR	2014
Gorgon Carbon Dioxide Injection Project, Australia	Precombustion: gas processing	3.4—4.1	DSF	2015
Quest, Canada	Precombustion: hydrogen production	1.08	DSF	2015
Total capacity		**12.57 (+0.7) MTPA**		

DSF, deep saline formation; *EOR*, enhanced oil recovery; *MTPA*, million tons per annum.
Adapted from Global Carbon Capture and Storage Institute (GCCSI), 2012. The Global Status of the CCS. Canberra, Australia.

most CCS projects in an "operate" stage are geographically concentrated in the United States. There are 59 other large-scale CCS projects in a planning stage with the total capacity of 110 MTPA. These projects are summarized in Table 5.1.

How costly are these CCS technologies relative to the costs of the conventional non-CCS power productions? The levelized cost of electricity with a CCS technology for each of the energy production processes can be compared across different CCS technologies (GCCSI, 2012). According to one estimate of the levelized cost, which includes capital cost, fuel cost, operating and maintenance cost, transportation cost, and storage cost, the cost estimate ranges from US\$114/MWh (in 2010 US dollars) in the oxyfuel process, to 120/MWh in the Natural Gas Combined Cycle (NGCC), to 125/MWh in the Integrated Gasification Combined Cycle (IGCC), and 130/MWh in the postcombustion process at a supercritical pulverized coal plant.

A cost increase of employing each of these technologies with the CCS facility over the total cost of power generation from each of these technologies without the CCS facility can be calculated with several assumptions, which is shown in Table 5.2. The cost increase amounts to 40% for the NGCC, the IGCC, and the oxyfuel plants. It amounts to over 60% for the postcombustion approach in the supercritical black coal plants (GCCSI, 2012).

2.2 Geoengineering of the Climate System: Climate Engineering

There are two types of climate intervention that are commonly referred to as geoengineering in the climate literature. One is Carbon Dioxide Removal (CDR) strategies and the other is Albedo Modification (AM) strategies (NRC, 2015). The CDR strategies refer to the strategies to sequester carbon in the terrestrial biosphere or the ocean by accelerating processes that are already occurring as part of the natural carbon cycle and that already remove significant quantities of CO_2 from the atmosphere. The CDR strategies include the CCSR techniques explained in Section 2.1. Climate engineering to be elaborated in this section is narrowly defined to mean the AM strategies.

The CDR strategies include a variety of land and ecosystems management practices, such as reforestation, ocean iron fertilization, and capturing CO_2 from the atmosphere. The CO_2 capture-storage-reuse techniques are as explained earlier. The ocean fertilization will be explained in a later subsection.

The AM technology is a set of strategies designed to reduce the amount of solar energy from the Sun that is absorbed by the Earth system, which cools the temperature of the Earth on average. Albedo is a measure of reflectivity of solar radiation by the Earth's surface. It is defined as the fraction of solar radiation reflected by the Earth's surface, which ranges from zero to one. The National Research Council (NRC)

Table 5.2 Increases in Production Costs of Electricity for Different Generation Plants Due to the Carbon Capture and Storage

	Natural Gas Combined Cycle ($/MWh)	Pulverized Coal ($/MWh)	Integrated Gasification Combined Cycle ($/MWh)
Without capture (reference point)	30−50	40−50	40−60
With capture and geological storage	40−80	60−100	50−90
With capture and EOR	40−70	50−80	40−70

Based on oil prices of 15−20$ per barrel. Expressed in 2002 US$. *EOR*, enhanced oil recovery.
Adapted from the Global Carbon Capture and Storage Institute (GCCSI), 2012. The Global Status of the CCS. Canberra, Australia.

committee suggests that there are strong reasons to believe that the AM strategy has the potential to rapidly counter the warming effects of increased carbon dioxide and other greenhouse gases (GHGs) at an affordable cost (NRC, 2015).

The observational evidence for the effectiveness of the AM strategy is, according to the NRC committee, the volcano eruption of Mount Pinatubo in the Philippines in 1991, which released 20 million tons of sulfur dioxide into the stratosphere. It is reported that the increase in the Earth's Albedo caused by the eruption led to a decrease of Earth's surface temperature by 0.3°C for the subsequent 3-year period. By injecting additional materials, such an effect can be made sustained for the purpose of cooling the Earth (NRC, 2015).

Specific techniques of the AM strategy include an enhancement in the reflectivity of low clouds, injection of aerosols into the stratosphere, and installations of space reflectors, so-called smart mirrors, outside the atmosphere. According to the NRC committee, the injection of aerosols into the stratosphere can reduce incoming solar radiation by 1 W/m^2 or more with existing technologies.

In the injection-of-aerosols method, engineers insert aerosols, i.e., fine solid particles or liquid droplets, into the atmosphere, which then reflect incoming solar radiation into the atmosphere, thereby lowering Radiative Forcing (RF) of the Sun. Furthermore, an increase in aerosols leads to interaction with the water contents to increase the formations of clouds, which again has the potential to reflect incoming solar radiation into the space.

Scientists estimate that the cost of deployment of a stratospheric aerosol layer of sufficient magnitude to offset the global mean RF caused by a CO_2 increase by human activities is at least an order of magnitude less than the economic cost of decarbonization through existing options (NRC, 2015). The cost of installations of space reflectors, another AM strategy, outside the Earth is not projected to be high.

However, the AM strategies are yet untested at a large geographical scale to be effective at least at the national level; therefore side effects of a large-scale experiment are not fully known. Past experiences from volcanic eruptions showed that the AM experiments can lead to stratospheric ozone loss, changes in precipitation amounts and patterns, and increased growth rates of forests due to an increase in diffuse solar radiation.

A geoengineering solution was foreseen from the very early literature on global warming policy as a potential scientific panacea for climate problems (Nordhaus, 1977). It would provide an easy fix of one of the most challenging problems that humanity has ever faced, if all things would unfold as expected. The humanity's ability of climate engineering attests to the human race's power to manipulate the Earth's climate system.

2.3   Nuclear Fusion Energy

A nuclear fusion energy technology is a technology that produces energy through the process of nuclear fusion. Unlike the nuclear fission energy production, which generates energy in the process of splitting atoms, a nuclear fusion technology harnesses the energy that is generated in the process of two atoms merging (fusing) together.

A nuclear fusion process is conducted with hydrogen atoms. Hydrogen is the simplest element in the universe and also the most abundant gas in the universe. Given atomic number 1, each atom of hydrogen has only one proton and one electron.

A nuclear fusion technology aims to imitate the process in which the Sun emits sunlight. The Sun is a giant ball composed of hydrogen and helium gases. The process in which hydrogen atoms in the Sun combine to form helium atoms is called a fusion process, which gives off the radiant energy of the Sun (US EIA, 2016).

Because hydrogen gas by itself is very much lighter than the air and quickly ejected from the atmosphere, it is found only in a compound form with other elements such as water (H_2O) and methane (CH_4). Hydrogen is found in all growing things and is also abundant in the Earth's crust.

As hydrogen exists only in a compound form, to obtain hydrogen gases, it must be separated from other elements such as water, natural gas molecules, or biomass (US EIA, 2016). The most common methods are steam reforming and electrolysis (water splitting). The steam reforming method is the least expensive method that separates hydrogen atoms from carbon atoms in methane (CH_4). The process results in carbon dioxide emissions. Electrolysis (water splitting) is a process that splits hydrogen from water. One advantage of the electrolysis method is that the process does not emit carbon dioxide. Other methods for obtaining hydrogen gases are being researched, including microbes, biomass, or solar technologies.

Almost all hydrogen in the United States is used by the industries for refining petroleum, for treating metals, for producing fertilizer, and for processing foods. Hydrogen fuel cells are used on spacecraft run by the National Aeronautics and Space Administration and for zero-emission fuel cell vehicles.

Research on nuclear fusion technology has been ongoing at the National Ignition Facility in the Lawrence Livermore National Laboratory in California (LLNL, 2015). The National Ignition Facility is the world's largest and most energetic laser facility ever built. The giant laser has nearly 40,000 optics that focus 192 laser beams onto a fusion target that is about the size of a pencil eraser. The process creates a temperature of 100 million degrees Celsius, about seven times hotter than the Sun's surface.

Another nuclear fusion research is an international collaborative project called the International Thermonuclear Experimental Reactor (ITER) project created in 2007 (ITER, 2015). Located in southern France, it is a collaboration of 35 nations: China, the European Union member countries, India, Japan, Korea, Russia, and the United States. The ITER project has been building a giant tokamak machine in which heat is created at the temperature of 150 million degrees Celsius, about 10 times the Sun's core temperature. It is predicted to produce 500 MW of fusion power for 50 MW input power. Various facts of the ITER project are summarized in Table 5.3.

It is claimed by many that the nuclear fusion technology, if successful on a large scale, can provide humanity with almost unlimited energy simply because hydrogen is abundant. In other words, the nuclear fusion energy has the potential to become a backstop technology that can supply energy indefinitely at a fixed price and thereby replace other methods of energy productions (Nordhaus, 1973; Hartwick and Olewiler, 1997).

Table 5.3 Statistics on the International Thermonuclear Experimental Reactor (ITER) Nuclear Fusion Project

	Statistics	Notes
Location	Saint Paul-lez-Durance, France	
Members of the ITER Project	China, the European Union, India, Japan, Korea, Russia, and the United States	
The ITER's toroidal field magnets	100,000 km of niobium-tin (Nb$_3$Sn) superconducting strands	
The ITER Tokamak, temperatures	150 million°C	The temperature at our Sun's surface is 6000°C, and at its core—15 million°C
The ITER Tokamak, weight	23,000 tons	The metal contained in the Eiffel Tower (7300 tons)
Energy produced	500 MW of output power for 50 MW of input power	
The Tokamak Seismic Isolation Pit	400,000 tons	The weight of New York's Empire State Building

Adapted from ITER (2016).

The critical advantage of a nuclear fusion energy production over a nuclear fission energy production, to be explained shortly, comes from the absence of adverse safety, environmental, and health risks in the former. Although the nuclear fission technology can also provide abundant energy as long as source materials are available, it has suffered from multiple catastrophic nuclear accidents and has the unresolved problem of radioactive wastes, e.g., spent uranium/plutonium rods (Slovic, 1987; NEI, 2016). By contrast, a nuclear fusion energy production does not result in nuclear waste materials.

Both nuclear fission and nuclear fusion are a zero-carbon energy production technology (Heal, 2010; IPCC, 2011). A nuclear fusion energy production with electrolysis does not result in direct (smokestack or tailpipe) emissions of carbon dioxide. However, a nuclear fission technology is firmly established and widely adopted, whereas a nuclear fusion technology is only in the phase of research and experiments. There is still a high degree of uncertainty about the possibility of a nuclear fusion energy production becoming a dominant method of energy production as well as about the time when such a potential transition to nuclear fusion would occur at a future time.

2.4   Nuclear Fission With Safe Waste Disposal

Nuclear fission is a process in which atoms are split apart, resulting in the release of energy. All nuclear power plants operating now in the world rely on a nuclear fission technology. In the nuclear fission process, a neutron strikes and splits a uranium atom, i.e., separates electrons from the nucleus, which releases energy in the form of heat and radiation. This process is repeated by the neutrons that are released by the initial split of the atom but strike other atoms, known as a nuclear chain reaction. The fission process is controlled inside nuclear reactors (MIT, 2003).

The most widely used nuclear fuel by nuclear power plants in the world is uranium (U-235), followed by plutonium (P-239). Uranium is a common metal found in rocks worldwide, 100 times more common than silver. U-235, a special kind of uranium, is most widely used because its atoms are easily split apart. U-235 is extracted from uranium, which is mined mostly in the western United States (US EIA, 2016).

The United States is the largest producer of nuclear fission energy, with 799 billion KWh produced, followed by France, Russia, South Korea, and China. In 2012, nuclear power plants provided 10.9% of the world's electricity production. Reliance on nuclear energy is by far the largest in France, with 77% of the total energy production. The reliance on nuclear energy exceeds 25% of the total energy production in 13 countries in the world: most of them are eastern European countries. In South Korea, reliance on nuclear energy is 30.4%, whereas it is 8% in the United States (NEI, 2016).

Unlike power productions from fossil fuels such as coal and natural gas, nuclear reactors do not produce carbon dioxide emissions during the nuclear fission process. Nuclear energy production can result in carbon dioxide emissions during the mining and refining process of uranium, which require a large amount of energy, if fossil fuels are used to produce the required energy. Furthermore, a construction of nuclear power plants requires a large amount of cement and metal, productions of which entail heavy emissions of carbon dioxide through excess burning of fossil fuels to produce the necessary heat energy.

Despite near-zero emissions of carbon dioxide during the nuclear fission process, concerns on safety, environmental, and health effects have played a dominant role in the adoption and expansion decisions of nuclear energy (Turco et al., 1983; Slovic, 1987). The public's primary hesitation to expand nuclear power has been that the nuclear production results in radioactive wastes, such as uranium mill tailings, spent reactor fuel, and other radioactive wastes. Major or catastrophic events such as the Three Mile Island accident in Pennsylvania in 1979, the Chernobyl nuclear disaster in the former Soviet Union in 1986, and the Fukushima nuclear disaster in 2011 have swayed the public perception on nuclear energy greatly (see Table 5.4).

A nuclear fission technology has yet unresolved challenges in the management of radioactive waste materials for the very long term, which may span as long as many millenniums. Spent fuel rods and high-level radioactive nuclear waste streams created at various stages of the nuclear fuel cycle pose some risk to present and future generations (MIT, 2003). The Project for the Yucca Mountain Nuclear Waste Repository, designated by the Nuclear Waste Policy Act amendments, to establish a permanent deep geological repository storage facility for the United States in Nye County,

Table 5.4 **Nuclear Energy Statistics**

	Statistics	Notes
Top generating countries, billion KWh	USA (798), France (418), Russia (169), South Korea (149), China (123), Canada, Germany, Ukraine, Sweden, UK	
Reliance on nuclear energy	10.9% worldwide in 2012	
Countries relied on nuclear energy to supply at least one-quarter of their total electricity	France 76.9%, Slovakia 56.8%, Hungary 53.6%, Ukraine 49.4%, Belgium 47.5%, Sweden 41.5%, Switzerland 37.9%, Slovenia 37.2%, Czech Republic 35.8%, Finland 34.6%, Bulgaria 31.8%, Armenia 30.7%, South Korea 30.4%	USA (19.5%), China (2.4%), Germany (15.8%), Spain (20%), Russia (18%), UK (17%)
Major nuclear accidents	Chernobyl disaster, Ukrainian SSR (1986); 56 direct death; 4000–985,000 cancer; cost 6.7 billion USD (in 2006)	INES level 7
	Fukushima, Japan (2011); a tsunami flooded and damaged the five active reactor plants drowning two workers. Loss of backup electrical power led to overheating, meltdowns, and evacuations; two dead	INES level 7

Adapted from Nuclear Energy Institute (nei.org); International Nuclear and Radiological Event Scale (INES).

Nevada, was approved by the US Congress in 2002, but Federal funding ended in 2011 under the Obama Administration for political reasons (NYT, 2011).

Scientific research to develop a deep geological safe repository of nuclear wastes called the Waste Isolation Pilot Plant (WIPP) has been ongoing by the United States Department of Energy in southwest New Mexico (US DOE, 2016a). The repository is carved out of a salt bed, formed 250 million years ago. The salt beds are known to have ideal characteristics for a safe repository because the salt is free of flowing water, can be carved out easily, impermeable, and geologically stable. Furthermore, salt rock naturally seals fractures and closes openings.

The underground repository in the WIPP plant is carved out of a 2000-ft-thick salt bed formed 250 million years ago. Transuranic waste is disposed of 2150 ft underground in rooms mined from the salt bed. Deep geologic disposal in salt beds was chosen because the salt is free of flowing water, easily mined, impermeable, and geologically stable. Salt rock also naturally seals fractures and closes openings. Constructed for a repository of the by-product of the nuclear defense program of the United States, the WIPP has been disposing nuclear waste since 1999 and cleaning up 22 generation sites.

At present, nuclear power is not competitive against the fossil fuel—based energy productions. Table 5.5 compares the cost of nuclear power against the costs of electricity based on fossil fuels using the concept of levelized costs of electricity (LCOEs) in 2002$ (MIT), with several assumptions explained beneath the table. The LCOE of nuclear power is 6.7 cents/KWh equivalent electricity in contrast to 4.2 cents for coal and 4.1 cents for natural gas with a combined cycle (CC) turbine technology assuming a moderate gas price (MIT, 2003).

The higher LCOE of nuclear power is attributable to a higher cost of construction of a nuclear plant, in other words, a higher capital cost. The reduction of construction cost by 25% would reduce the LCOE of nuclear power to 5.5 cents/KWh equivalent electricity. There are other ways to cut the cost of nuclear energy.

As shown in the table, nuclear power becomes competitive with an imposition of carbon tax as a form of internalization of negative externalities from the use of fossil fuels. Nuclear power becomes competitive against coal with about $100 per ton of carbon tax, against natural gas with about $250 per ton of carbon tax (MIT, 2003).

2.5 Ocean Fertilization

The possibility of ocean fertilization as a way to increase carbon absorption by the sea was put forward by John Martin, an oceanographer at the Moss Landing Marine Laboratories in California, who proposed the iron hypothesis (Martin et al., 1994; Weier, 2001). Through the experiment in the surface waters of Antarctica where phytoplankton is absent (Martin and Fitzwater, 1988), Martin and his team reported that iron deficiency is limiting the growth of phytoplankton (microscopic marine plants) in nutrient-rich major waters. Owing to the absence of a trace amount of iron, vast areas of the world's oceans are devoid of phytoplankton despite adequate amounts of necessary nutrients such as phosphorous and nitrogen for phytoplankton growth.

Martin and his team's subsequent works suggested that the trend of global warming may be stopped by adding a trace amount of iron into major ocean waters (Martin et al., 1994; Weier, 2001). By simply adding a small amount of iron into high-nutrient, low-chlorophyll zones of oceans, scientists could create large blooms of algae. The growth of algae could then take in a large amount of carbon from the atmosphere, which could reverse the growth of carbon in the atmosphere and consequently cool the Earth.

An analysis of an ocean iron fertilization experiment by the European Iron Fertilization Experiment (EIFEX) showed that stimulating the growth of algae in oceans

Table 5.5 **Comparative Cost of Nuclear Energy Against Energy Productions From Fossil Fuels (2002 US$)**

Fuel Type	Levelized Costs of Electricity Without Carbon Tax (cents/KWh equivalent electricity)	Levelized Costs of Electricity with $50 per ton of Carbon	Levelized Costs of Electricity with $100 per ton of Carbon	Levelized Costs of Electricity with $200 per ton of Carbon
		With Carbon Tax (cents/KWh equivalent electricity)		
Nuclear fission	6.7			
Pulverized coal	4.2	5.4	6.6	9.0
Natural gas (low gas prices, $3.77/MCF)	3.8			
Natural gas (moderate gas prices, $4.42/MCF)	4.1	4.7	5.2	6.2
Natural gas (high gas prices, $6.72/MCF)	5.6			

Assuming an 85% capacity factor, a 40-year economic life for the nuclear plant, and a combined cycle turbine technology.
MCF, million cubic feet.
Adapted from Massachusetts Institute of Technology (MIT), 2003. The Future of Nuclear Power: An Interdisciplinary MIT Study. MIT, MA.

by adding iron is an effective way to remove carbon dioxide from the atmosphere (Smetacek et al., 2012). In Feb. 2004, EIFEX researchers fertilized the 167 km^2 area of Southern Ocean with several tons of iron sulfate. The researchers reported that each atom of added iron pulls at least 13,000 atoms of carbon out of the atmosphere through algal growth through the process of photosynthesis of phytoplankton, which captures carbon. Much of the captured carbon by phytoplankton was transported to deep ocean when the algae die and would remain there for centuries (Smetacek et al., 2012).

Despite the progress in an experimental setting, citing the gaps in the scientific knowledge about ocean iron fertilization, the parties of the Convention on the

Prevention of Marine Pollution by Dumping Wastes and Other Matter agreed that commercial ocean fertilization is not justifiable (IMO, 2006). Even for an ocean fertilization experiment for public benefits, major concerns of side effects remain strong on potentially harmful consequences of ocean fertilization on marine ecosystems and ocean chemistry. Ocean fertilization in a massive scale, some scientists fear, might result in toxic algal blooms or depleted oxygen levels (Schiermeier, 2012).

Owing to limited research, especially on a large scale, we are not yet able to compare the cost of removing carbon dioxide through ocean iron fertilization with the cost of removing the same amount through other methods such as CCS, AM through injection of aerosols into the atmosphere, installations of solar reflectors, nuclear fusion, and other methods. The literature does seem to suggest that the ocean fertilization strategy poses higher risk than a CCS technology or space reflectors.

2.6 Natural Geoengineering

Natural geoengineering is the nomenclature suggested by ecologist Oswald Schmitz to refer to a range of techniques for reducing carbon from the atmosphere by intentionally managing natural ecosystems, particularly an array of predator–prey relationships in the natural world (Schmitz, 2016). The cornerstone scientific evidence of natural geoengineering is that a decrease in a predator animal may lead to an increase in the population of the prey, which feeds on certain types of plants, and the changes in the predator–prey relations would lead to changes in carbon storages and emissions from plants and soils (Strickland et al., 2013).

Schmitz cites illustrative examples of wolves in boreal forests and sharks in seagrass meadows, two important predators in the natural ecosystem. The loss of these predators can result in increases in populations of terrestrial and marine herbivores whose wider grazing will weaken the capacity of natural ecosystems to sink carbon dioxide from the atmosphere. Put differently, restorations of these predators would then lead to increased capability of natural ecosystems to absorb carbon dioxide (Schmitz, 2016).

In Schmitz's examples, biodiversity loss is associated with accumulation of carbon dioxide in the atmosphere. An increase in biodiversity through restorations of wolves in boreal forests and sharks in seagrass meadows is proposed as an effective technique for removing carbon dioxide from the atmosphere and therefore for slowing down global warming. However, an increase in biodiversity through restorations of wolves and sharks can also lead to biodiversity loss in the prey animals.

In the climate literature, natural ecosystems have long been recognized as sources of carbon dioxide sinks and tested through extensive field experiments (Ainsworth and Long, 2005). The process of photosynthesis by plants and trees absorb carbon dioxide and cutting of trees and grasses releases carbon dioxide from biomass and soils (Denman et al., 2007; Houghton, 2008). More than half of additional CO_2 released into the atmosphere is dissolved annually in the surface waters of the oceans (Schlesinger, 1997). The process of photosynthesis by phytoplankton in the oceans stores carbon into phytoplankton (Martin et al., 1994).

Many of these naturally occurring carbon sinks in the carbon cycle have already been integrated, albeit not tightly, as a policy option for global warming or a GHG abatement option in many countries at the national or subnational level, e.g., the

Global Warming Solutions Act in California (AB 32) or the Climate Action Plan by the Obama Administration (ARB, 2006; White House, 2013). These processes are also seriously discussed as an important policy option to be negotiated at bilateral and international climate conferences (UNFCCC, 1998, 2015).

What is unique in the "natural geoengineering" approach is that the predator—prey relationships in the natural ecosystems are carefully managed in ways to increase absorption of carbon dioxide from the atmosphere. However, the literature on natural geoengineering is only beginning to emerge and we have to wait and see whether it can be developed to be widely recognized as a breakthrough technology for solving global warming problems.

2.7 Solar Energy

Solar energy is produced directly by making use of sunlight. The generation of solar energy does not produce air pollutants or carbon dioxide and sunlight is abundant and permanent, which provides the solar technology necessary qualifications for a breakthrough energy technology for containing the trend of global warming.

There are two solar-to-electricity technologies: Photovoltaics (PV) and Concentrated Solar Power (CSP). The PV technology directly converts sunlight to electricity, whereas the CSP technology does so indirectly. The solar PV is the dominant solar technology accounting for 98% of global solar energy generation capacity in 2013 (MIT, 2015).

In the CSP technology, solar energy is be converted to heat (thermal energy), which is then converted to electricity. The solar thermal energy can be used to heat water for various purposes, e.g., for use in homes, buildings, and swimming pools. The solar thermal energy can also be used to heat spaces inside homes, greenhouses, and buildings. Alternatively, the solar thermal energy can be utilized to heat water to high temperatures to produce steam energy, which then turns turbines to generate electricity (MIT, 2015).

In the solar PV technology, PV cells, also called solar cells, convert sunlight directly into electricity, through the mechanics explained momentarily. PV cells are put together to form a solar module. Solar models are bundled together to form a solar panel. Solar panels are bunched together to form a solar array. The array of solar panels is then placed on the roofs of houses and buildings in urban areas or where sunlight can be received with little interference, e.g., desert areas. PV cell technologies are classified into either wafer-based PV technologies or thin-film PV technologies based on the primary light-absorbing material. The vast majority of commercial PV module production, whether wafer based or thin film, has been silicon based (MIT, 2015).

An introductory understanding of the mechanics of the solar PV technology will be worthwhile to the readers of this chapter. A PV cell is made of a semiconductor material, which is silicon-based in most cases. When photons, i.e., elementary or smallest particles, of sunlight strike a solar cell, they are either reflected, or pass right through the cell, or are absorbed by the semiconductor material. When a sufficient amount of photons is absorbed, it dislodges electrons from the atoms of the semiconductor material. The freed electrons are then made to flow to the surface of the semiconductor material through a special treatment of the surface. With many electrons moving from the back surface to the front surface of the semiconductor, a differential of electrical charge between the two surfaces creates a voltage potential like the two positively and negatively charged terminals of a battery. Electrical conductors placed on the PV cell absorb the electrons. The electrons then flow through an electrical circuit to an external appliance (US EIA, 2016).

With regards to climate change, attractiveness of the solar PV technology lies in its low CO_2 emissions rate in comparison with those from energy productions by other conventional fossil fuels. In Fig. 5.1, additional CO_2 emissions by various fossil fuels with reference to that from the solar PV technology are presented per million British thermal units (Btu) of energy produced. Against the reference case of the solar PV technology, which emits near-zero CO_2, coal (anthracite) emits 228.6 pounds, diesel fuel 161 pounds, gasoline 157 pounds, and natural gas 117 pounds of CO_2 to produce 1 million Btu of energy (US EIA, 2015b).

Despite being touted as a zero-carbon energy source, solar energy has several limitations too (Heal, 2010; Schmalensee, 2015). First, supply of sunlight or solar radiation is not constant, i.e., intermittent, and quickly changeable. The amount of sunlight that is received varies across the Earth's surface; some places receive more sunlight than others. The amount of sunlight varies across the day as well as across the year. There is no sunlight at night. The amount of sunlight is smaller in winter times.

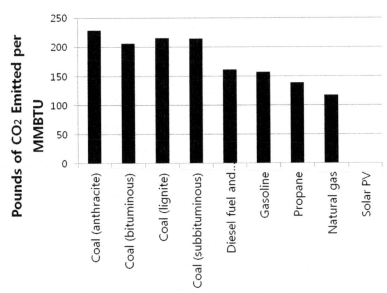

Figure 5.1 Pounds of additional CO_2 emitted per million British thermal units (Btu) of energy produced for various fuels with reference to that from the solar photovoltaic (PV) technology. Based on United States Energy Information Administration (US EIA), 2015b. U.S. Energy-Related Carbon Dioxide Emissions, 2014. EIA, US DOE, Washington, DC.

Furthermore, the amount of sunlight depends on weather conditions, which can change abruptly. For example, in rainy or snowy days, there is little sunlight. Because of these characteristics, the solar PV or thermal technology is therefore nondispatchable, i.e., cannot be turned on and off on demand.

Second, because the amount of solar radiation falling on a spot is not large, mass production of solar energy requires a large surface area for installations of a large number of arrays of solar panels to produce a sufficiently large amount of electricity, which could turn out to be costly. Solar arrays may be installed on land areas where there is no hindrance to sunlight and land values are low, e.g., Mojave Desert in the United States and arid/desert outbacks of Australia.

At present, the cost of electricity generation by solar PV technologies is far higher than that from alternative conventional technologies. Table 5.6 compares the LCOEs of different energy sources and technologies (US EIA, 2014). The LCOE is the average total cost of a power-generation plant, including both capital cost and operational cost, over the lifetime of the plant divided by the total energy produced over that lifetime (Borenstein, 2012).

The solar PV technology has the LCOE of 125 US$/MWh, whereas the solar thermal technology has the LCOE of 239$/MWh. It is notable that the LCOEs of the solar technologies are much higher than the LCOE of conventional coal at 95$/MWh and the LCOE of conventional natural gas at 75$/MWh.

The LCOEs of the solar technologies are also much higher than alternative low-carbon energy technologies. The LCOE of wind turbines is 73$/MWh, but the LCOE increases sharply for offshore wind generations to 196$/MWh. The LCOE of a hydroelectricity plant is 83$/MWh, that of a geothermal energy plant is 47$/MWh, that of a biomass energy generation is 100$/MWh, and that of an advanced nuclear energy plant is 95$/MWh.

The cost of electricity generation by the solar PV technology is higher than that by conventional fossil fuels combined with advanced technologies. The LCOE of an advanced coal technology, e.g., adding wood chips to burning coal, which reduces CO_2 emissions, is 115$/MWh, but the LCOE of an advanced coal technology with carbon-capture-and-storage is 144$/MWh.

Against the LCOE of the solar PV, those of advanced natural gas technologies are significantly lower. The natural gas energy production with an advanced CC has the LCOE of 72$/MWh, whereas the natural gas energy production with an advanced CC with carbon-capture-and-storage (CCS) has the LCOE of 100$/MWh.

The natural gas energy production with both CC and CCS is likely on par with the solar PV technologies in terms of carbon emissions, but the latter is 25$ more expensive per megawatt hour of electricity. This explains the attractiveness of the natural gas energy production embodied in the Clean Power Plan by the Obama Administration in the United States (US EPA, 2014). The large abundance of natural gas supply in the next several decades in the United States and other countries mean that the natural gas technology is likely to be a competitive CO_2 emissions reduction strategy for many countries (Joskow, 2013).

Table 5.6 US Average Levelized Costs (2013$/MWh) for Plants Entering Service in 2020

Plant Type		Capacity Factor (%)	Levelized Capital Cost ($/MWh)	Total System LCOE ($/MWh)
Dispatchable Technologies				
Coal fired	Conventional coal	85	60.4	95.1
	Advanced coal	85	76.9	115.7
	Advanced coal with carbon-capture-storage (CCS)	85	97.3	144.4
Natural gas fired	Conventional combined cycle (CC)	87	14.4	75.2
	Advanced combined cycle	87	15.9	72.6
	Advanced CC with CCS	87	30.1	100.2
	Conventional combustion turbine	30	40.7	141.5
	Advanced combustion turbine	30	27.8	113.5
Advanced nuclear		90	70.1	95.2
Geothermal		92	34.1	47.8
Biomass		83	47.1	100.5
Nondispatchable Technologies				
Wind	Wind	36	57.7	73.6
	Wind, offshore	38	168.6	196.9
Solar	Solar PV	25	109.8	125.3
	Solar thermal	20	191.6	239.7
Hydroelectric		54	70.7	83.5

Modified from United States Energy Information Administration (US EIA), 2015b. U.S. Energy-Related Carbon Dioxide Emissions, 2014. EIA, US DOE, Washington, DC.

The high cost of solar technologies is due to high capital costs and low capacity factors (Heal, 2010). The capacity factor of the solar PV technologies is only 25%, which can be contrasted to 85% capacity factor of coal, 87% of natural gas, and 90% of nuclear energy. On average, solar PV technologies produce only 25% of electricity to the potential capacity owing to the intermittent and changeable characteristics of solar radiation.

Another reason for the high cost of solar PV technologies is the large capital cost. The levelized capital cost of the solar PV is 110$/MWh, which is contrasted with 60$/MWh for coal and 30$/MWh for advanced natural gas with both a CC and a CCS. The capital cost of the solar PV is due to the high cost for manufacturing the solar panels and the cost of lands.

2.8 Electric Vehicles

The transportation sector is responsible for about one-third of the total global carbon dioxide emissions annually (GCP, 2014). An automobile with an internal combustion engine burns fossil fuels to produce energy that is needed to propel itself, in which process it emits carbon dioxide. Gasoline, liquefied petroleum gas, compressed natural gas, and natural gas are the most commonly used fossil fuels for automobiles.

Several alternatives to the internal combustion engines that burn fossil fuels were developed to reduce the amount of carbon dioxide emissions: diesel cars, hybrid vehicles, EVs, and hydrogen fuel cell vehicles (NRC, 2013). These alternative vehicles have significantly higher mileages that can be driven per gallon of gasoline used as well as per kilogram of carbon dioxide emitted (McConnell, 2013).

Diesel cars, named after a German inventor, run on diesel fuels. Diesel cars have an internal combustion engine that is run by a compression-ignition method rather than a spark-ignition method, which is used for the other internal combustion engines. The ignition of a diesel fuel is initiated by a high temperature within the chamber caused by high pressure on the diesel fuel. Diesel fuels include not only distillate fuels from crude oil but also vegetable oils and biodiesel.

Diesel vehicles were advertised and road-tested as a clean vehicle that emits much less carbon dioxide than the other internal combustion engines. A Volkswagen scandal in the latter half of 2015 revealed that emissions tests were manipulated by the company. The company admitted that more than 11 million vehicles were equipped with software that was used to cheat on emissions tests, especially on nitrogen oxides (NO_x) (NYT, 2015).

A hybrid vehicle runs alternately on an internal combustion engine and an electric motor. For example, it can run on a battery-powered electric motor for the first couple hours of drive and switches to an internal combustion engine when the battery runs low (Yale Environment 360 2013b). The hybrid vehicles became successful and popular in the automobile markets by Prius made by the Toyota Company. A hybrid vehicle lowers the emissions of carbon dioxide per mile driven, but still relies on fossil fuels for running.

An EV is run solely on motors operated by electric batteries, i.e., without reliance on fossil fuels (NRC, 2013). Therefore there is no tailpipe release of carbon dioxide during driving. However, manufacturing of aluminum, batteries, and vehicle parts requires a large amount of energy, which must be generated from fossil fuels, if not renewable sources, which emit carbon dioxide (Time, 2014).

The biggest obstacle to the competitiveness of EVs is battery life, weight, and costs. At \$450 per kWh of energy in the battery pack, which is the NRC's current battery pack cost estimate, a 78-kWh battery pack, which is needed for about 300 driving miles per charge, would cost \$35,000 (NRC, 2013). This means that with the current technology and costs a battery should be recharged multiple times during the day for many hours of driving. Recharge stations can be built, but should be built in a very large number across a country. Building recharge stations in a sufficient number turns out to be costly for remote regions or rural areas where population is sparse.

Even if recharge stations can be built in a sufficiently large number, the long hours required for fully recharging a battery is still a big problem. Replacement stations can be built instead of recharge stations. That is, a run-out battery is simply replaced with a new battery at the replacement stations. It is still very cumbersome to replace a battery every 2 h because it takes time to find replacement stations and replace batteries, in addition to being charged a price for replacement. A driver may decide to carry more than one battery in the car, but it adds significantly to the weight of the car. A driver may purchase a supercharger and recharge at home during the night in the same way consumers recharge mobile phones these days. But the cost of a super-charger is as expensive as the EV itself (Yale Environment 360, 2013a; Bloomberg, 2016).

EV producers have had little commercial success around the world. In the United States, the Obama administration has given a large amount of subsidies to start-up EV companies (White House, 2013). Nonetheless, many of these start-ups faced financial difficulties and failed (Yale Environment 360 2013a). By contrast, Tesla motor company has enjoyed a large commercial success, primarily through a steep increase in the value of its public equities, especially in the low-end luxury markets.

In Table 5.7, the author provides a number of comparative statistics between a hybrid vehicle, Toyota Prius, and an EV, Tesla Model S, based on the two sources noted underneath the table. The Toyota hybrid is the most fuel-efficient car excluding the EVs, with 54 miles driven per gallon of gasoline (mpg). The Tesla EV is as high as 101 mpg in fuel efficiency, almost doubling the hybrid's fuel efficiency. For comparison, Ford Mustang's fuel efficiency is 22 mpg and Honda Accord's is 27 mpg in 2016. According to the sources, the Tesla EV can run 264 miles/charge, although the NRC argues that a range of 300 miles/charge is prohibitively expensive with current battery technology and costs (NRC, 2013). It can accelerate in 3 s to 60 mph and its top speed is 155 mph.

The big weakness of the Tesla EV against the Toyota hybrid is an overwhelmingly higher purchase price: \$110K versus \$18K. The former is more than eight times more expensive than the latter. This means that the CO_2 emissions reduction by the EV is achieved with a much higher cost than that by the hybrid. The hybrid is at least at present a more economical and efficient way to reduce the CO_2 emissions from automobiles (Yale Environment 360 2013b).

Table 5.7 Electric Vehicles Versus Hybrids

Vehicles	Variables	Statistics	Notes for Comparisons
Tesla Model S (P90D)	Range per charge	264 miles	65 mph, 70°F, AC on, 21 in. wheels
	Acceleration	3.1 s for 0–60 mph	
	Top speed	155 mph	
	Fuel efficiency	101 mpg˜	
	Price	About 110,000$	Toyota Camry: 26,000$*
Toyota Prius (fourth generation)	Fuel efficiency	54 mpg (EPA)	The most fuel efficient car in 2015 excluding EVs Ford Mustang 2016: 22 mpg Honda Accord 2016: 27 mpg
	Price	2 million yen (18,000$)	

AC, air conditioning; *EPA*, Environmental Protection Agency
* denotes Kelly Blue Book (http://www.kbb.com); ˜ denotes fueleconomy.gov.

In addition to the first big obstacle, which is battery life, the second big question for the EV is how much the cost and sale price of the EV can be lowered. At present, EVs cannot compete against the hybrids or against other advanced conventional fuel energy production options, such as natural gas—based power generations in cutting CO_2 emissions economically.

In any way, the potential for the EVs to achieve CO_2 emissions reduction in the future is large (McConnell, 2013). If the world can replace all fossil fuel—based internal combustion engines with EVs, the world will be able to reduce more than 10 giga - tons of CO_2 annually at the current automobile consumption/usage level and even more in the future consumption/usage level. This means that the EV technology alone, if successful, may be able to contain the inexorable global warming.

2.9 Lighting Revolutions: LEDs, compact fluorescent lights, Incandescents

Electrical lighting for homes and buildings was made possible by the invention of an incandescent light bulb in the late 19th century by Thomas Edison and the subsequent invention of alternating currents (AC) by Nicola Tesla for long-distance transmission of electricity (Nordhaus, 1996). In an incandescent lighting, electric current passes through a wire carbon filament, which is heated because of resistance in the filament, which produces glow and heat. The process of incandescent lighting requires production of energy and electricity most often by burning fossil fuels in which process carbon dioxide is released (US EIA, 2016).

Increasingly, novel lighting methods such as compact fluorescent light (CFL) and LEDs have begun to slowly replace incandescent light bulbs (Levitan, 2012). In a CFL, electric current sparks argon and mercury vapor inside a tube, which generates invisible ultraviolet light, which excites the fluorescent coating (phosphor) on the inside of the tube, which emits visible light. As will be explained shortly, the CFL improves energy efficiency substantially. The downside of the CFL lighting is that it contains toxic mercury, which is potentially hazardous and hard to dispose of.

An LED is illuminated by the movement of electrons in a semiconductor material called a diode. The conductor material is typically aluminum-gallium-arsenide (AlGaAs). The scientific principle that makes an LED possible is that when electrons move, photons (light) are released. When an electron in an atom drops from a higher (greater energy) orbital to a lower (smaller energy) orbital, the electron releases energy in the form of a photon. The larger the orbital difference, the larger the energy produced. The LEDs are lighted by manipulating the electron movement in the diode (Akasaki et al., 2014).

For comparisons of the three lighting systems to be followed, let me first remind you of the basic units of electricity and light. A Watt (W) is the standard unit of power, i.e., energy per unit time, and is defined by joules per second. In turn, 1 J is the amount of energy exerted when a force of 1 N is applied on an object over a distance of 1 m (US EIA, 2016). Lumen is the unit of light flux or flow, i.e., the rate of emissions of light from a source. For reference, a wax candle emits about 13 lumens of light. Lux is the unit of illuminance, i.e., the amount of light per unit area. One lux equals one lumen per square meter (Nordhaus, 1996).

First, the LED technology vastly improves the lifetime of a light bulb over the CFL technology and the incandescent light bulbs. As shown in Table 5.8, a traditional 60-W incandescent light bulb lasts on average 1000 h. A CFL light bulb can last 10 times longer with 10,000 h of lifetime. An LED light bulb can last as many as 25,000−50,000 h (US DOE, 2016b). A halogen incandescent bulb can last up to 3000 h.

Second, the LED technology vastly improves energy efficiency and consequently significantly saves energy needed to produce the same amount of light as incandescent light bulbs or CFLs. A 60-W incandescent light bulb uses more than $300 worth of electricity per year while it provides about 800 lumens of light. To produce the same amount of light for a year, a CFL bulb uses less than 15 W of energy and costs about 75$/year. As in Table 5.8, this amounts to 75% energy saving. Again, to produce the same lumens of light, an LED bulb uses less than 8 W of energy and costs only 30$/year (Levitan, 2012).

An LED lamp saves 80% of the energy that is required in a traditional incandescent light bulb to produce the same amount of light and lasts at most 50 times more hours than the latter. The lighting revolution holds a promise of a revolutionary cut in energy and electricity consumption for the sake of lighting. Given that the amount of carbon dioxide emissions from electricity production by power plants accounts for more than

Table 5.8 Comparisons Between Traditional Incandescents, Halogen Incandescents, CFLs, and LEDs

	Incandescents		15 W CFL		12 W LED	
	60-W traditional incandescent	43-W energy-saving halogen incandescent	Against 60-W traditional	Against 43-W halogen	Against 60-W traditional	Against 43-W halogen
Energy $ saved (%)	–	~25%	~75%	~65%	~75%–80%	~72%
Annual energy cost[a]	$4.80	$3.50	$1.20		$1.00	
Bulb life	1000 h	1000–3000 h	10,000 h		25,000 h	

CFL, compact fluorescent light; LED, light-emitting diode.
[a]Based on 2 h/day of usage, an electricity rate of 11 cents/KWh, shown in US dollars.
Adapted from the United States Department of Energy (US DOE), 2016b. How Energy Efficient Light Bulbs Compare with Traditional Incandescent. US DOE, Washington DC. Available at: http://energy.gov/energysaver/how-energy-efficient-light-bulbs-compare-traditional-incandescents.

30% of the total carbon dioxide emissions in the United States in 2013 (US EPA, 2015), an advance of the LED lighting is expected to contribute substantially to the total amount of abatement of carbon dioxide in developed countries.

The impact of the LED lighting is expected to be especially large in rapidly growing economies now and in the future, such as China, India, South Asian nations, Brazil, Russia, South Africa, and others. Spurred by economic growth, consumption of electricity and lighting will grow at a high rate in these countries in this century. Against the baseline scenario of future lighting with the incandescent lighting technology, which is the predominant technology of lighting in these countries at present, the LED lighting in the future will lead to a sizable reduction of carbon dioxide emissions from lighting.

An advantage of the LED lighting against the other breakthrough technologies presented in this section is that it is even less costly than the currently predominant technology, i.e., incandescents. In fact, it costs only one-fifth of the incandescent technology (Table 5.8). This is in sharp contrast to the fact that the other breakthrough technologies are substantially more costly, sometimes many times, than the existing technologies.

People are, however, averse to adopting a new technology, which has also been the case in the LED adoption. A new technology, including the LED, often faces a series of glitches, which are overcome one by one over time. That is, it takes time to perfect the LED technology. Second, the sale cost of an incandescent light bulb is lower than that of an LED lamp. The LED lamp becomes cheaper only when the full lifetime of the lamp is considered. For wider adoptions of the LED lamps, consumers should be made far sighted, which may be accomplished through education, contract designs, and other means.

3. A Survey of Microincremental Technologies

Besides these breakthrough technologies, there are numerous other technologies that by themselves are not viewed as a breakthrough technology, but nonetheless could strongly influence individuals' behaviors that lead to GHG emissions and sinks as well as adjustments of practices to changing climates. In this section, the author explains selected, although not intended to be comprehensive, technological innovations that could incrementally affect global warming behaviors and decisions.

3.1 Improvements in Natural Resources Sectors

Crop varieties that are more heat tolerant, more drought tolerant, or more moisture tolerant may become practical in the future through genetic research and developments (Evenson and Gollin, 2003; James, 2012). Advances in developing and making such varieties practical can make low-latitude developing countries, which are expected to bear the brunt of global warming, far more resilient to climatic changes. A high-yielding rice variety innovated during the Green Revolution is one such example of the past.

Advances in genetic studies may uncover ways to control a variety of livestock diseases that tend to become prevalent during humid seasons and kill sometimes millions of cattle in sub-Saharan Africa. For example, nagana disease (trypanosomiasis) transmitted by Tsetse flies kills millions of cattle in West Africa (Ford and Katondo, 1977; Seo and Mendelsohn, 2008).

One study was able to fully record the genome of the Tsetse flies (Aksoy et al., 2014). This advance in genomic science has the potential to reduce significantly the rate of transmission of nagana disease by altering the genome of the tsetse fly, thereby making livestock management more resilient to climatic changes.

Another example is technological advances in reducing methane (CH_4) emissions. Methane is a powerful GHG, more than 80 times more potent, for a 20-year global warming potential (GWP), than carbon dioxide (IPCC, 2014). A large amount of methane is emitted annually through burping and farting from ruminant animals, such as cattle, sheep, and goats (Seo, 2015a; Schaefer et al., 2016). Another major source of methane is leakages from extracting and refining shale gas and oil through hydraulic fracturing (Turner et al., 2016). Landfill waste and coal production account for the remaining methane emissions.

Methane emissions from ruminant animals can be significantly reduced by various changes such as adding feed additives and changing diets of animals (US EPA, 2006). Methane emissions can be also captured from natural gas productions or landfill waste to be reused to generate heat and electricity.

A third example of technological innovations in natural resource uses is a desalination plant. A desalination plant is a plant that removes salt and minerals from the sea water to supply the desalinized water to water users such as agricultural farms and humans. It was built by countries in frequently drought-stricken zones or arid/semiarid zones such as Israel and California (USDA, 2016). A severe drought in California during the period leading up to the very strong El Niño years through the end of 2016 motivated the State to build a number of desalination plants (Carlsbad, 2016; USDA, 2016).

The desalination plant holds promise to frequently drought-hit areas or arid zones for cultivating lands that are often left unmanaged as a result of rainfall shortages or volatile rainfall regimes. The existence of the plants will make farming, besides human consumption, more resilient to climatic changes and global warming, which may manifest through drastically reduced rainfall or more volatile rainfall regimes.

Furthermore, it will contribute significantly to GHG mitigations if desalinized water can be directed to grassland managements in arid and semiarid areas. Grasses and pastures absorb atmospheric carbon dioxide and at the same time keep soil organic carbon underground (Ainsworth and Long, 2005; Soussana et al., 2010).

3.2   Improvements in Energy Sectors

Besides numerous innovations in agricultural and natural resources industries, a variety of incremental technological innovations is found in various improvements in the energy system, which enhances energy efficiency (Sims et al., 2007; Joskow, 2012). For example, a smart meter for gas and electricity use can digitally send meter readings to the energy supplier. This enables more accurate and real-time readings of energy use by the supplier than the conventional meters, which are checked once a month by a technician. Real-time and accurate readings make it possible that the price of energy be reflective of the real-time use of energy. That is, when real-time energy use is high, price of electricity can go up real time, thereby sending a real-time signal to consumers to reduce electricity/gas consumption.

A smart meter is one component of the smart grid initiative that refers to the "modernization of the electricity delivery system" in the ways that the system "monitors, protects, and optimizes the operation of its interconnected elements" from electricity generators to high-voltage transmission systems, local distribution networks, industrial users, end-use consumers, solar PV technologies, plug-in EVs, thermostats, and household devices (EPRI, 2011). The smart grid technologies include enhancing high-voltage AC transmission systems, automating local distribution networks, and smart meters and dynamic pricing incentives (Joskow, 2012).

These improvements in the energy system have the potential to reduce substantially the amount of CO_2-spewing fossil fuels burned to produce the required amount of energy for numerous activities (Joskow, 2012). In the United States, energy-related CO_2 emissions amount to 5.4 billion metric tons ($gtCO_2$) from about 7 billion metric tons emitted from all sources (US EIA, 2015a, 2015b). Energy intensity, defined as the amount of energy (in British thermal units) used per dollar of gross domestic product (GDP) produced, declined by 1.2% in 2014. According to the Annual Energy Outlook from the United States, from 1950 to 2011, energy intensity in the United States has declined by 60% and is projected to decline by 80% by 2040 (US EIA, 2014).

The projected decrease in the energy intensity in the United States will lower the amount of carbon dioxide emissions through 2040 by 80% for producing the same level of GDP. This projected decrease is due to numerous "micro" innovations in the smart grid, including a smart meter, as well as other predicted changes in the energy system such as switching of fuels.

The huge significance of these energy innovations lies in the fast developing countries such as China, India, Brazil, Russia, and South Africa. Fig. 5.2 shows the changes in energy intensity since 1980 for the United States and those for India and China are shown in Fig. 5.3 (US EIA, 2014). China's energy intensity has declined from 80,000 Btu of energy per dollar of GDP in 1980 to 25,000 in 2011. The United States' energy intensity has declined during the same period to 7300 Btu per dollar of GDP in 2011, which is projected further to decline to around 5000 Btu of energy by 2020.

If the pattern of energy intensity observed and projected in the United States were to manifest in the developing countries in the same way, it will significantly lower the projected increase in future emissions of carbon dioxide there, even without additional climate mitigation measures and policies taken in China and India (Nakicenovic et al., 2000; IPCC, 2014).

Hydraulic fracturing and horizontal drilling technology is another example of an innovation in the energy sector. Hydraulic fracturing, known as fracking, is a technique for extracting natural gas and oil by injection of water under high pressure to fracture low-permeability shale. A surge in the extraction of natural gas in the United States was made possible by the hydraulic fracturing technique along with horizontal

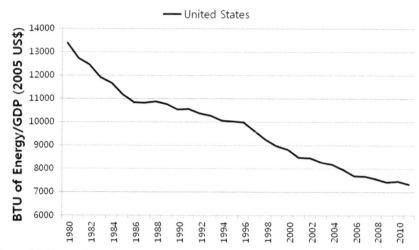

Figure 5.2 Energy intensity changes since 1980 in the United States.

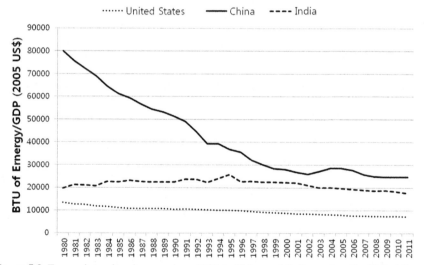

Figure 5.3 Energy intensity changes since 1980 in China and India against the United States.

drilling (Joskow, 2013). Shale gas and shale (tight) oil, which have been extremely difficult to extract in the past, are now extracted in almost all cases using this technique. Annual shale gas production stood at 1 trillion cubic feet (Tcf) in 2006 and surged to 9.7 Tcf in 2012. It is predicted to continue to increase to reach 19.8 Tcf by 2040 (US EIA, 2014).

Per unit of energy produced, natural gas emits only half the amount of emissions of carbon dioxide by coal, as already shown in Fig. 5.1. In addition, an increase in the supply of shale gas for electricity generation and home heating lowers the electricity and heating prices to consumers, which also would increase the demand for natural gas (Mason et al., 2015). Replacing coal-fired power plants with natural gas—fired power plants, as envisioned in the Clean Power Plan by the Obama administration, is widely perceived in many countries as a cost-effective strategy to cut carbon dioxide emissions to meet the long-term international commitments made through, e.g., the Paris Agreement (Krupnick et al., 2013; US EPA, 2014; UNFCCC, 2015). Note that natural gas production is projected to continue to expand in the next several decades in the United States (US EIA, 2014).

On the negative environmental effects, the hydraulic fracturing technique leads to an increase in methane leakages from the wells as well as quality deteriorations of aquifers, rivers, and streams because of a large amount of a combination of water, sands, and chemicals that must be pumped in to break underground rocks (Kuwayama et al., 2015; Mason et al., 2015). A methane capture and reuse facility should be required for natural gas wells if natural gas—-fired power generations would be a credible GHG mitigation option (US EPA, 2006; Brandt et al., 2014).

Another example of technological developments in the energy system is replacement of coolants such as HFCs and HCFCs (IPCC, 2005a). HFCs and HCFCs have been widely adopted as a refrigerant in the refrigerator and air conditioner as an alternative to chlorofluorcarbons after the Montreal Protocol, which banned the ozone-depleting material (UNEP, 1987). However, the HFCs and HCFCs are GHGs with a very high GWP.

The GWP is a relative measure of how much heat the emissions of 1 ton of a GHG will trap in the atmosphere over a certain period of time, usually 100 years, relative to the emissions of 1 ton of carbon dioxide (CO_2). HFCs (HFC-134a) have a GWP of 3790 for 20 years and 1550 for 100 years (IPCC, 2014). By contrast, the GWP of carbon dioxide is one.

A climate-friendly alternative to these chemicals are shown in Table 5.9 (EC, 2016). Most of these alternatives are available immediately. In comparisons with HFCs (R32) and HCFCs (R22), the GWPs of many alternatives are more than two orders of magnitude smaller. For example, hydrocarbons have a GWP in the range from three to five. Hydrocarbons are, however, flammable, as are other alternatives, and so must be handled with certain safety measures. R744 (carbon dioxide) is another alternative with a low GWP of one.

Replacing HFCs and HCFCs with alternative refrigerants has been a focus of bilateral talks in the Obama administration between the United States and China and between the United States and Canada (White House, 2013, 2016). Because of the immediate availability of many alternatives that are highly effective, many politicians and scientists consider this as a low-hanging fruit in the policy efforts to lower GHGs.

The list of incremental technological innovations is lengthy and the earlier description is not meant to be comprehensive, but rather illustrative of the concept and examples of incremental technologies. Incremental technologies would not by themselves make a breakthrough in combating global warming in the future, but have the potential to enhance the capacity of individuals and various climate actors to deal with the globally warming world. At the same time, these technologies have the potential to help individuals and businesses reduce carbon dioxide in the atmosphere.

Table 5.9 **Alternatives to HFCs and HCFCs**

Alternative Refrigerants	Global Warming Potential	Major Issues	Commercially Available?
Hydrocarbons	3–5	Flammable	Immediately
CO2 (R744)	1	High pressure	Immediately
Ammonia (NH3, R717)	1	Toxic	Immediately
Water (R718)	1	No risks	Immediately
R32 (an HFC)	675	Mildly flammable	Immediately
HFOs	4–9	Mildly flammable	Immediately/short term
R32-HFO blends	200–400	Mildly flammable	Midterm

HCFC, hydrochlorofluorocarbons; HFC, hydrofluorocarbons, HFOs, hydrofluoro-olefins.
Adapted from European Commission (EC), 2016. Climate-Friendly Alternatives to HFCs and HCFCs. EC, Brussels, Belgium. Available at: http://ec.europa.eu/clima/policies/f-gas/alternatives/index_en.htm

Will an individual or a business choose these technologies, taking into consideration the rising temperature and other climatic changes? We will come back to some of these incremental technologies in the next chapter when we discuss adaptation strategies to answer this question.

4. Adopt Now? The Cost of Backstop Technologies

The whole set of existing and potential technologies reviewed up to this point make it pertinent for us to ask "what would be the total cost of removing all emissions of CO_2 from industrial and land use activities, given technological options, now and in the future?" This concept was formalized by William Nordhaus as a "backstop" technology (Nordhaus, 1973, 1994).

A backstop technology is a technology that can replace permanently all fossil fuels used for energy production (Nordhaus, 1973). It can be a zero-carbon energy technology such as solar energy, nuclear fusion, or a future technology that has not yet been discovered. Alternatively, loosely speaking, it can be a technology that can remove all excessive carbon dioxide from the atmosphere, e.g., the CCS technologies and climate engineering explained earlier. As Nordhaus puts it, the backstop technology is "the ultimate technology, resting on a very abundant resource base" (Nordhaus, 1973).

In an oversimplified model with inelastic demand for electricity and a finite amount of fossil fuel resources for electricity production, the price of electricity (p) at the time of switch (t^*) to a backstop technology is defined by the cost of the backstop technology (Nordhaus, 1973):

$$p(t^*) = (\gamma + \delta) \cdot K^b, \tag{5.1}$$

where γ is the rate of interest, δ is the depreciation rate, and K^b is the capital requirement of the backstop technology per unit of electricity output.

The concept of a backstop technology can be illustrated with an example of a nuclear fusion technology. It is a future technology and, if realized, would become an energy source that emits no carbon dioxide for energy productions. If the world were to adopt the fusion technology for removing carbon dioxide, how much would it cost to remove that last ton of emissions per year? Nuclear fusion would provide all energy required for human activities without any emissions of carbon dioxide permanently.

Many technologies explained in the previous section have the potential to become a backstop technology in the future, which is why they are called a breakthrough technology. However, backstop costs, to be defined shortly, of these technologies would be different. The technology with the lowest backstop cost would be chosen by the society for energy production.

A backstop price can be defined as the marginal cost of removing the final ton of carbon dioxide from human activities, given the existing economic structures and technologies. Put differently, it is the marginal cost of producing energy from the backstop technology, which is equal at the point of transition to the marginal cost of producing energy from the conventional energy source that is replaced.

As potential technologies would become materialized and adopted by users over time one by one, the backstop price would decline over time as well. Furthermore, it can be said that the backstop price of a region, i.e., the cost of removing the last ton of carbon dioxide in a region, would differ across the world regions because of varied economic structures at the present time. That is, the backstop price of sub-Sahara would be lower than the backstop price of the United States because the latter's economy is far more heavily loaded with carbon-intensive industries. It is costlier to remove the last ton of carbon dioxide in the United States.

Based on the Intergovernmental Panel on Climate Change report on sequestration (IPCC, 2005b), Nordhaus suggests that the cost of a backstop technology today would be around US$1200 per on of carbon or about US$320 per ton of carbon dioxide. It would decline over time to $950 per ton of carbon by the end of the 21st century (Nordhaus, 2008, 2013). Note that the cost of backstop is more than an order of magnitude larger than the efficient carbon price, which was explained extensively in the previous chapter.

Is it rational for the world to become carbon-free now, given the array of current and future backstop technologies and projected fuel prices? Simply, it is not rational. First, future backstop technologies are much more cost-effective, i.e., can reduce the unit of emissions of carbon dioxide at a much lower cost. It is cheaper and rational to abate some of the carbon dioxide emissions today and increase the level of abatement over time.

Second, the current emissions of carbon dioxide make much less impact on the Earth's climate than the future emissions of carbon dioxide. Carbon emissions at 400 ppm (parts per million) of carbon dioxide concentration in the atmosphere are less harmful than carbon emissions at 600 ppm of carbon dioxide concentration. It is rational and cheaper to cut carbon more in the future when it is more harmful than in the present.

5. Inducing Technological Innovations: Subsidy or Tax?

A technological change (TC) can be defined as an increase in the outputs possible with a given level of inputs through the processes of invention, innovation, and diffusion. A technological breakthrough can be defined as an instantaneous jump in the outputs possible with a given level of inputs. What induces technological changes and break-throughs? Is a certain policy more likely than others to induce TCs?

In the Integrated Assessment Models of climate change elaborated in the previous section, TCs are modeled either exogenously or endogenously. A review of this literature tells how TCs occur and what policies might be needed to induce these changes.

A model of exogenous TCs incorporates TCs as a function of time using a number of TC variables. One is an energy efficiency indicator, such as carbon intensity of outputs, i.e., the amount of carbon emissions per $1000 outputs (Nordhaus, 1991). Another is the change in the price of a backstop technology explained in the previous section (Nordhaus, 2008).

When TCs are accounted for endogenously, production possibilities are modeled to depend on past, present, and future expected prices and policy variables. Researchers explain TCs in one of the following three ways: direct price-induced TC, research and development (R&D)-induced TC, and learning-by-doing (LBD)-induced TC (Gillingham et al., 2008).

In the direct price-induced TC, changes in relative prices are modeled to induce technological innovations in a way that economizes the use of a factor that has become more expensive, such as energy (Popp, 2002, 2006a,b). This approach was developed by inspiration from the Hicks' price-induced innovation hypothesis (Hicks, 1932). If the price of energy rises, price-induced TC will lead to increased energy efficiency (Nordhaus and Boyer, 2000).

However, there are only a few examples of a climate policy model with the price-induced TC (Jakeman et al., 2004). In this approach, the relationship between price and TC is determined in a rather ad hoc, reduced-form manner. In addition, there is no accounting for the cost of achieving changes.

The second approach is the R&D-induced TC model in which the R&D investment influences the rate and direction of TC (Sue Wing, 2006; Popp, 2004; Nordhaus, 2002; Goulder and Schneider, 1999). The R&D investment is quantified by the size of a knowledge capital stock. The R&D-induced TC can be embedded into the structure of a neoclassical growth model or into a multisector general equilibrium model.

A researcher may add the R&D-induced TC to the production function of the DICE (Dynamic Integrated model of Climate and Economy) model introduced in Chapter 4 in the form of a knowledge capital as follows (Buonanno et al., 2003):

$$Y = A K_{R\&D}^{\beta} \left(L^{\gamma} K^{1-\gamma} \right), \tag{5.2}$$

where A is the total factor productivity, $K_{R\&D}$ is the knowledge capital, L is the labor, K is the capital, and Greek letters are elasticity parameters.

Alternatively, carbon intensity can be modeled as a function of knowledge stock (Nordhaus, 2002):

$$\dot{\sigma}_t / \sigma_t = \Psi_1 R_t^{\Psi_2} - \Psi_3, \tag{5.3}$$

where σ is the carbon intensity, R is the knowledge capital, and $\Psi_i's$ are parameters.

From another angle, the R&D-induced TC can be entered into a cost minimization framework as follows (Goulder and Mathai, 2000):

$$\underset{a_t, R_t}{\text{MIN}} \int_0^{\infty} \left(C(a_t, H_t) + p(R_t) R_t \right) e^{-rt} dt, \tag{5.4}$$

where $C(\cdot)$ is the cost function, a_t is the level of abatement at time t, H_t is the stock of knowledge, $p(\cdot)$ is the real price of investment resources, and R_t is the investment in knowledge, i.e., R&D investment.

This minimization is subject to two constraints. One is a constraint governing the change in concentration of CO_2 in the atmosphere. The other is a constraint governing the change in the knowledge stock:

$$\dot{H}_t = \alpha_t H_t + \Psi(R_t, H_t), \tag{5.5}$$

where α is the rate of exogenous TC, e.g., change in the carbon intensity, and Ψ is the knowledge accumulation function.

A number of critiques were leveled against the R&D-induced TC modeling, which are all pertinent to the question posed in the beginning of this section, i.e., what induces technological innovations (Gillingham et al., 2008)? First, it is not well settled on how the knowledge capital accumulates and affects productions. Second, it is not well understood whether R&D investment is associated with market imperfections in the innovation market due to spillovers. Third, it is not well understood whether carbon-saving R&D investment crowds out the R&D in the other sectors. Fourth, it is not well established whether there is a substitutability or complementarity between the generation of output (production) and the generation of knowledge (R&D).

Nordhaus validates the above-mentioned critiques with empirical data plugged into the DICE model. After comparing the DICE model with the R&D-induced TC and exogenous TCs, he concludes that induced innovation is less powerful a factor in reducing emissions than substitution of abatement for consumption (Nordhaus, 2002).

This is because the returns to R&D equal the opportunity costs, crowding out other investments.

The third way for explaining TCs and modeling TCs endogenously is learning-induced TC. It is based on the concept that the unit cost of a particular technology declines with the experience with that technology (Grubler and Messner, 1998; Goulder and Mathai, 2000; Manne and Richels, 2004). The most common method for modeling learning-induced TC is LBD. In the LBD method, the unit cost of a particular technology is modeled as a decreasing function of the cumulative output of the technology.

In a simple model of LBD TCs, the unit cost of a technology (C) is defined as follows:

$$C(K_I) = \varsigma \cdot K_I^{-\vartheta}, \tag{5.6}$$

where K_I is the cumulative installed capacity (or output), ς is the normalization parameter, and ϑ is the learning elasticity.

The formulation by Goulder and Mathai for the R&D-induced TC using the cost minimization problem expressed in Eqs. (5.4) and (5.5) can be modified to capture a LBD process (Goulder and Mathai, 2000):

$$\dot{H}_t = \alpha_t H_t + \Psi(a_t, H_t). \tag{5.7}$$

In the aforementioned equation, the R&D investment is replaced by the level of abatement (a_t). The higher the abatement level, the higher the LBD.

Although the rationale of LBD is sound, it is not possible to identify the mechanisms behind the LBD. Empirically, one may not even be confident about the causality between LBD and the unit cost of a concerned technology. A learning function may be estimated statistically by researchers without much difficulty, which may turn out to be a false representation of something else, e.g., the R&D investment or other resources that are directed to the technology development (Clarke and Weyant, 2002).

An important policy question is whether a certain policy instrument is more likely to spur technological changes and innovations than others. A policy maker may choose one of the numerous policy instruments: giving subsidy to new technologies, removing subsidies given to carbon-heavy industries and power plants, creating and charging a carbon tax, initiating carbon tradable permits, research grants, divestments from fossil fuels, etc. Indeed, any climate policy can alter the incentive, whether in a right direction or not, to develop new low-carbon technologies or climate engineering technologies.

The subsidy given to developing a new low-carbon technology has been a focus of international climate debates for quite a while. For example, one of the pillars of the Obama Administration's carbon policy has been an array of subsidies to renewable resource companies, such as solar startup companies, EVs, wind farms, and ethanol producers (White House, 2013). During his administration, many renewable energy companies or low-carbon energy companies have made great commercial success and technological innovations, one example of which is Tesla Motors.

It is rather straightforward to understand the concept of inducing technological innovations in the renewable energy subsidy. A subsidy gives an incentive to develop a renewable energy technology by lowering its cost with reference to the costs of other high-carbon technologies. A removal of subsidies given to high-carbon technologies gives developers an incentive to develop new low-carbon technologies by making high-carbon technologies more costly to build and produce. At present, a large amount of subsidies is given to fossil-based energy productions, e.g., coal-fired, oil-fired, and natural gas–fired power plants in the United States.

An array of subsidies given to renewable energy developers will, however, crowd out investments into other areas, thereby slowing down the rate of technological innovations elsewhere (Nordhaus, 2002). An abrupt ending of a subsidy program as a result of various unexpected causes such as a global financial meltdown can lead to bankruptcies of many renewable energy firms, as experienced in the United States and elsewhere.

In a carbon tax system, another climate policy instrument, which is suggested to be implemented globally at a harmonized price level (Nordhaus, 1994), a carbon emitter, whether an individual or an enterprise, should make a decision to pay the price for each ton of emissions or abate that unit by employing various abatement measures. Without carbon tax imposed, the firm has no incentive to adopt a new technological measure, but with carbon tax, it is rational for the firm to employ a new technological measure(s) as long as it costs less to abate than the carbon tax per unit of carbon emissions. Carbon emitters are forced to seek and innovate various low-carbon measures to lower the cost of complying with the carbon tax policy.

A second avenue of inducing TCs under the carbon tax system is through tax revenue (Nordhaus, 2010). If the tax revenue were to be given out to renewable and low-carbon energy firms, the carbon tax system will further induce technological innovations. On the other hand, if the tax revenue were to be given out to low-income families, the carbon tax system can lead to an increase in carbon emissions from the low-income families through increased consumption (Metcalf, 2009).

A third policy instrument to be considered here is a tradable permit system or a cap-and-trade system. With carbon permits traded among the firms, a high-abatement-cost firm makes a rational decision to purchase a permit from a low-abatement-cost firm for each ton of emissions of carbon. For the high-abatement-cost firm, it costs less to purchase a permit than to abate that unit of emissions. For the low-abatement-cost firm, it is more profitable to sell a permit and abate that unit of emissions by itself (Tietenberg, 2006; Stavins, 2007).

With the introduction of the cap-and-trade system, a high-abatement-cost firm has an incentive to employ a set of technological measures and innovate them to reduce the marginal abatement cost of the firm for complying with the policy. However, a large price volatility in the permit market due to various nonclimate change reasons, such as real estate and financial market volatilities, can significantly weaken the incentive to innovate the carbon-emitting production processes (Nordhaus, 2007).

In addition, a cap-and-trade policy is implemented in almost all cases by handing out permits freely, without charge, to the firms included in the policy. Consequently, in contrast to the carbon tax policy, there is no room for the government to redirect carbon tax revenue to renewable and low-carbon energy developers (Stavins, 2007).

6. Technological Uncertainties and Option Value

Many of the breakthrough technologies surveyed in this chapter are not yet applicable, or not applicable on a global scale, or not competitive in the markets. There is a high degree of uncertainty with regard to the times when these technologies become practical for wide adoptions across the society. A high degree of uncertainty sways many climate-related decisions by individuals and various climatic actors.

If the global community believes that a nuclear fusion technology or a solar technology will soon provide at a future time nearly unlimited energy with no emissions of carbon dioxide at a fixed cost and it will make a transition to the backstop technology, the world would be better off by holding off in slashing extensively carbon emissions now. The world would be better off by waiting until the backstop technology replaces other technologies (Kolstad, 1996). The higher the probability of the backstop technology to become practical, the greater the world's incentive to wait.

In the presence of a large uncertainty with regard to the feasibility and introduction of a backstop technology, e.g., a nuclear fusion technology, the global community cannot rely on the future technology with a large uncertainty. The cost of waiting for the introduction of the backstop technology increases. The world community would be better off by shifting the burden of cutting down carbon emissions from the future date to the earlier dates. The larger the uncertainty, the larger should the shifts of burden to the earlier dates. The smaller the uncertainty, the smaller should be the shifts of burden to the earlier dates.

From another perspective, advances of technological capabilities over time in the future force another decision to a climate actor who is planning to implement policies to deal with GHG emissions. That is, today's capital investments into mitigation of GHGs could quickly become outdated as new breakthrough and incremental technologies become introduced and practical, replacing the currently most advanced technologies.

Let us consider a company's construction today of a large number of wind turbines across a large land area as a low-carbon energy technology. If a solar technology were to be advanced rapidly and become a backstop technology in 10 years, the company's capital investments on wind turbines today could turn out to be pretty meaningless in 10 years as a low-carbon energy source. Furthermore, once built, it would take many years and large cost to replace the wind turbines with other capital investments such as solar panels.

In this simple scenario, the option value is lost when the wind turbines are built today (Arrow and Fisher, 1974). When wind turbines are built across a large land area or even offshore, it removes the option for the society to use the land and sea areas for other purposes such as crop agriculture, animal grazing, forests, and even wildlife reserves.

The option value is the value attached to the land (asset) because of the options the land (asset) has for future uses. There is no option value in the asset whose usage is fixed and immutable. The possibility of breakthrough technologies in the near future increases the option value of land and other assets today. Fixing the use for the land today gets rid of the option value of the land (asset).

The option value of an asset can be traded in the markets, i.e., purchased and sold at an agreed price. An option contract is one of the derivatives traded in financial markets. An option contact specifies the right of the option owner for the option to buy or sell a specified asset at a specified price at a specified future date. A call option is a contract that specifies the right for the option to buy an asset, whereas a put option is a contract that specifies the right for the option to sell an asset, at an agreed date for an American option (Fabozzi et al., 2009).

If an investor believes that there is a natural gas reservoir under a certain tract of land, he/she may buy a call option, i.e., an option to buy the land at a certain price at a future specified date. By buying an option instead of buying the land directly, the investor can decide not to exercise the option at the exercise date if the market price of the land at the exercise date is below the price specified in the option contract. If the market price is higher than the exercise price, then the investor will exercise the option and purchase the land at the exercise date (Shiller, 2008).

For the seller of the option, the value of the option he/she earns is the value of making the tract of land available for alternative uses. If the use of the land were fixed permanently for wind turbines, the option value of the land that arises from the possibility of a natural gas reservoir underneath would be completely lost. This is because the land cannot be used for other purposes than the wind turbines.

How is the price (value) of an option contract (to buy or sell something in a future date) determined? Let T be the time to exercise date, σ^2 the variance of price change of an underlying asset, γ the risk-free interest rate, and $\Phi(\cdot)$ the standard normal cumulative distribution function. Furthermore, let P_0 be the current price of the asset and P_{EX} the exercise (strike) price of the option. Then, according to the Black–Sholes model, the fair market value (price) of the call option is determined by the following equations and variables (Black and Scholes, 1973; Fabozzi et al., 2009):

$$P_C = P_0 \cdot \Phi(q_1) - e^{-\gamma \cdot T} \cdot P_{EX} \cdot \Phi(q_2), \tag{5.8}$$

where

$$q_1 = \frac{\ln\left(\dfrac{P_0}{P_{EX}}\right) + \gamma \cdot T + \sigma^2 \cdot \left(\dfrac{T}{2}\right)}{\sigma\sqrt{T}},$$

$$q_2 = \frac{\ln\left(\dfrac{P_0}{P_{EX}}\right) + \gamma \cdot T - \sigma^2 \cdot \left(\dfrac{T}{2}\right)}{\sigma\sqrt{T}}. \tag{5.9}$$

Note in the aforementioned equations that the value of the option is determined by the magnitude of uncertainty captured by Φ and σ, given the current price of the asset and the exercise price. The larger the volatility in the price of the asset σ^2, of concern, the higher the price of the call option because a high volatility leads to an increase in q_1 and a decrease in q_2. When there is near-zero volatility, the optional value will be close to zero. Note also that the price of the call option becomes larger as the time to exercise date T becomes larger.

A high degree of technological uncertainty increases the option value of a natural resource asset, such as land, water, forests, and ecosystems. Fixing the use of the natural resource asset to a specific usage decreases the value of option attributed to the asset. The lost option value is a welfare loss to the society in making the best use of the resource.

7. Conclusion

This chapter provided a broad review of breakthrough and incremental technologies as an alternative way to address the problems that arise from global warming and climatic changes. A breakthrough technology is one that enables the world to cut GHG emissions from the atmosphere or to engineer the Earth's climate at a substantially lower cost than the current cost of global abatement. The list of breakthrough technologies surveyed in this chapter includes nuclear fusion, nuclear fission with an improved safety and storage system, solar energy, climate engineering, carbon-capture-and-storage, ocean iron fertilization, EVs, and revolutions in lighting methods.

An incremental microtechnological advance is, although it does not provide a dramatic cut in the cost of addressing climatic changes, such an advance that enhances private actors' abilities to adapt to climatic changes. The list of incremental technologies surveyed in this chapter includes technological developments in the natural sources' sectors, such as crop variety improvements, genetic science advances, methane reduction technologies, and desalination plants; and technological developments in the energy system, such as a smart grid, hydraulic fracturing, and replacements of Earth-warming coolants such as HFCs and HCFCs.

Economic aspects of current and future technological innovations as a policy for fighting global warming are analyzed through the following economic concepts: a backstop technology and its cost; inducing technological innovations through the mechanism of price changes, or R&D investments, or LBD; and the option value attributable to technological possibilities and uncertainties.

There are two major drawbacks of relying on technological breakthroughs for a global climate remedy. First, there is large uncertainty with regard to feasibilities, potentials, side effects, and times of introduction of many breakthrough technologies surveyed in this chapter. Furthermore, the world's policy makers and researchers are not well equipped to answer how to make many of these technological breakthroughs come to be eventually realized. Under such circumstances, the world community may not be too patient to simply wait for a magical technology to come along while global temperature and atmospheric concentration of carbon dioxide keep climbing.

The second weakness of an exclusive reliance on technological solutions is that technological innovations themselves cannot make explicit and disentangle a large array of complex incentives faced by individuals, businesses, public sectors, and international organizations for the purpose of slowing down global warming. A climate actor may even appropriate breakthrough or incremental technologies for deterioration and destabilization of the world's climate system.

This leads us to the next chapter, which is devoted to an adaptation paradigm for addressing the problems of global warming. As an alternative climate policy solution, the adaptation paradigm will be developed to provide an answer to the major drawbacks identified in the carbon price approach of the Samuelson—Nordhaus framework in Chapter 4 and the technological solutions described in this chapter.

References

Akasaki, I., Amano, H., Nakamura, S., 2014. Blue LEDs — Filling the World with New Light. Nobel Prize Lecture. The Nobel Foundation, Stockholm. Available at: http://www. nobelprize.org/nobel_prizes/physics/laureates/2014/popular-physicsprize2014.pdf.

Aksoy, S., Attardo, G., et al., 2014. Genome sequence of the tsetse fly (*Glossina morsitans*): vector of African trypanosomiasis. Science 344 (6182), 380—386.

Ainsworth, E.A., Long, S.P., 2005. What have we learned from 15 years of free-air CO_2 enrichment (FACE)? A meta-analysis of the responses of photosynthesis, canopy properties and plant production to rising CO_2. New Phytologist 165, 351—372.

Air Resources Board (ARB), 2006. Assembly Bill No. 32. Air Resources Board, California Environmental Protection Agency, Sacramento, California.

Arrow, K.J., Fisher, A.C., 1974. Environmental preservation, uncertainty, and irreversibility. Quarterly Journal of Economics 88 (2), 312—319.

Black, F., Scholes, M., 1973. The pricing of options and corporate liabilities. The Journal of Political Economy 81 (3), 637—654.

Bloomberg, 2016. Musk Says It's Obvious Model 3 Owners to Pay for Superchargers. Available at: http://www.bloomberg.com/news/articles/2016-06-01/musk-says-it-s-obvious-model-3-owners-to-pay-for-superchargers.

Borenstein, S., 2012. The private and public economics of electricity generation. Journal of Economic Perspectives 26 (1), 67—92.

Brandt, A.R., Heath, G.A., Kort, E.A., O'Sullivan, F., Petron, G., et al., 2014. Methane leaks from North American natural gas systems. Science 343 (6172), 733—735.

Buonanno, P., Carraro, C., Galeotti, M., 2003. Endogenous induced technical change and the costs of Kyoto. Resource and Energy Economics 25, 11—34.

Carlsbad Desalination Plant, 2016. DESAL-101. Claude "Bud" Lewis Carlsbad Desalination Plant, San Diego, CA.

Clarke, L., Weyant, J., 2002. Modeling induced technological change: an overview. In: Grubler, A., Nakicenovic, N., Nordhaus, W. (Eds.), Technological Change and the Environment. Resources for the Future Press, Washington DC.

Denman, K.L., Brasseur, G., Chidthaisong, A., Ciais, P., Cox, P.M., Dickinson, R.E., Hauglustaine, D., Heinze, C., Holland, E., Jacob, D., Lohmann, U., Ramachandran, S., da Silva Dias, P.L., Wofsy, S.C., Zhang, X., 2007. Couplings between changes in the climate system and biogeochemistry. In: Solomon, S., et al. (Eds.), Climate Change 2007: The Physical Science Basis. The Fourth Assessment Report of the Intergovernmental Panel on Climate Change. Cambridge University Press, Cambridge.

Electric Power Research Institute (EPRI), 2011. Estimating the Costs and Benefits of the Smart Grid: A Preliminary Estimate of the Investment Requirements and Resultant Benefits of a Fully Functioning Smart Grid. Technical Report 1022519. Electric Power Research Institute, Palo Alto, CA.

European Commission (EC), 2016. Climate-friendly Alternatives to HFCs and HCFCs. EC, Brussels, Belgium. Available at: http://ec.europa.eu/clima/policies/f-gas/alternatives/index_en.htm.

Evenson, R., Gollin, D., 2003. Assessing the impact of the green revolution 1960−2000. Science 300, 758−762.

Fabozzi, F.J., Modigliani, F.G., Jones, F.J., 2009. Foundations of Financial Markets and Institutions, fourth ed. Prentice Hall, New York.

Ford, J., Katondo, K.M., 1977. Maps of tsetse fly (*Glossina*) distribution in Africa, 1973, according to subgeneric groups on a scale of 1: 5000000. Bulletin of Animal Health and Production in Africa 15, 187−193.

Gillingham, K., Newell, R.G., Pizer, W.A., 2008. Modeling endogenous technological changes for climate policy analysis. Energy Economics 30, 2734−2753.

Global Carbon Capture and Storage Institute (GCCSI), 2012. The Global Status of the CCS. Canberra, Australia.

Global Carbon Project (GCP), 2014. Global Carbon Budget 2014. Available at: http://cdiac.ornl.gov/GCP/.

Goulder, L., Mathai, K., 2000. Optimal CO_2 abatement in the presence of induced technological change. Journal of Environmental Economics and Management 39, 1−38.

Goulder, L., Schneider, S., 1999. Induced technological change and the attractiveness of CO_2 abatement policies. Resource and Energy Economics 21, 211−253.

Grubler, A., Messner, S., 1998. Technological change and the timing of mitigation measures. Energy Economics 20, 495−512.

Hartwick, J.M., Olewiler, N.D., 1997. The Economics of Natural Resource Use, second ed. Pearson, New York.

Heal, G., 2010. Reflections: the economics of renewable energy in the United States. Review of Environmental Economics and Policy 4, 139−154.

Hicks, J., 1932. The Theory of Wages. Macmillan, London, UK.

Houghton, R.A., 2008. Carbon flux to the atmosphere from land-use changes: 1850−2005. In: TRENDS: A Compendium of Data on Global Change. Carbon Dioxide Information Analysis Center, Oak Ridge National Laboratory, U.S. Department of Energy, Oak Ridge, TN.

International Energy Agency (IEA), 2013. Technology Roadmap: Carbon Capture and Storage. IEA, France.

International Maritime Organization (IMO), 2006. 1996 Protocol to the Convention on the Prevention of Marine Pollution by Dumping Wastes and Other Matter 1972. IMO, London.

Intergovernmental Panel on Climate Change (IPCC), 2005a. Special Report on Safeguarding the Ozone Layer and the Global Climate System: Issues Related to Hydrofluorocarbons and Perfluorocarbons. Cambridge University Press, Cambridge.

Intergovernmental Panel on Climate Change (IPCC), 2005b. Special Report on Carbon Dioxide Capture and Storage. Cambridge University Press, Cambridge.

Intergovernmental Panel on Climate Change (IPCC), 2011. Special Report on Renewable Energy Sources and Climate Change Mitigation. Cambridge University Press, Cambridge.

Intergovernmental Panel on Climate Change (IPCC), 2014. Climate Change 2014: The Physical Science Basis. The Fifth Assessment Report of the IPCC. Cambridge University Press, Cambridge.

International Thermonuclear Experimental Reactor (ITER), 2015. ITER: The World's Largest Tokamak. Available at: https://www.iter.org/mach.

Jakeman, G., Hanslow, K., Hinchy, M., Fisher, B., Woffenden, K., 2004. Induced innovations and climate change policy. Energy Economics 26, 937−960.

James, C., 2012. Global Status of Commercialized Biotech/GM Crops: 2012. ISAAA (The International Service for the Acquisition of Agri-biotech Applications) Brief No. 44. ISAAA, Ithaca, NY.

Joskow, P.L., 2012. Creating a smarter U.S. electricity grid. Journal of Economic Perspectives 26, 29−48.

Joskow, P.L., 2013. Natural gas: from shortages to abundance in the United States. American Economic Review 103, 338−343.

Kolstad, C.D., 1996. Learning and stock effects in environmental pollution: the case of greenhouse gas emissions. Journal of Environmental Economics and Management 31, 1−18.

Krupnick, A., Wang, Z., Wang, Y., 2013. Sector Effects of the Shale Gas Revolution in the United States. Resources for the Future (RFF) Discussion Paper. RFF, Washington DC.

Kuwayama, Y., Olmstead, S., Krupnick, A., 2015. Water quality and quantity impacts of hydraulic fracturing. Current Sustainable/Renewable Energy Reports 2, 17−24.

Lackner, K.S., Ziock, H.J., Grimes, P., 1999. Carbon dioxide extraction from air: is it an option?. In: Proceedings of the 24th International Conference on Coal Utilization & Fuel Systems. Clearwater, Florida, 8−11 March.

Lackner, K.S., Brennana, S., Matter, J.M., Park, A.A., Wright, A., Zwaan, B.V., 2012. The urgency of the development of CO_2 capture from ambient air. Proceedings of the National Academy of Sciences 109 (33), 13156−13162.

Lawrence Livermore National Laboratory (LLNL), 2015. How NIF Works. Available at: https://lasers.llnl.gov/about/how-nif-works.

Levitan, D., January 24, 2012. Building a Better Bulb: Lighting Revolution Advances. Yale Environment 360. Yale University, New Haven.

Manne, A.S., Richels, R.G., 1999. The Kyoto Protocol: a cost-effective strategy for meeting environmental objectives? The Energy Journal 20 (Special Issue), 1−23.

Manne, A., Richels, R., 2004. The impact of learning-by-doing on the timing and costs of CO_2 abatement. Energy Economics 26, 603−619.

Martin, J.H., Fitzwater, S.E., 1988. Iron-deficiency limits phytoplankton growth in the Northeast Pacific Subarctic. Nature 331, 341−343.

Martin, J.H., Coale, K.H., Johnson, K.S., Fitzwater, S.E., et al., 1994. Testing the iron hypothesis in ecosystems of the equatorial Pacific ocean. Nature 371, 123−129.

Massachusetts Institute of Technology (MIT), 2003. The Future of Nuclear Power: An Interdisciplinary MIT Study. MIT, MA.

Massachusetts Institute of Technology (MIT), 2015. The Future of Solar Energy: An Interdisciplinary MIT Study. MIT, MA.

Mason, C.F., Muehlenbachs, L.A., Olmstead, S.A., 2015. Economics of Shale Gas Development. Resources for the Future Discussion Paper. RFF, Washington DC.

McConnell, V., 2013. The New CAFÉ Standards: Are They Enough on Their Own? Resources for the Future Discussion Paper 13−14. Washington DC.

Metcalf, G., 2009. Designing a carbon tax to reduce US greenhouse gas emissions. Review of Environmental Economics and Policy 3, 63−83.

Nakicenovic, N., Davidson, O., Davis, G., Grübler, A., Kram, T., La Rovere, E.L., Metz, B., Morita, T., Pepper, W., Pitcher, H., Sankovski, A., Shukla, P., Swart, R., Watson, R., Dadi, Z., 2000. Emissions Scenarios, A Special Report of Working Group III of the Intergovernmental Panel on Climate Change. Geneva, IPCC.

National Research Council (NRC), 2013. Transitions to Alternative Vehicles and Fuels. National Academies Press, Washington DC.

National Research Council (NRC), 2015. Climate Intervention: Reflecting Sunlight to Cool Earth. Committee on Geoengineering Climate: Technical Evaluation and Discussion of Impacts. National Academies Press, Washington DC.

New York Times (NYT), May 10, 2011. GAO: Death of Yucca Mountain Caused by Political Maneuvering. NYT, New York.

New York Times (NYT), 2015. Explaining Volkswagen's Emissions Scandal. http://www. nytimes.com/interactive/2015/business/international/vw-diesel-emissions-scandal-explained. html?_r=0.

Nuclear Energy Institute (NEI), 2016. Energy Statistics. NEI, Washington DC. Accessed from: http://www.nei.org/Knowledge-Center/Nuclear-Statistics.

Nordhaus, W., 1973. The Allocation of Energy Resources. Brookings Papers on Economic Activities, pp. 529–576.

Nordhaus, W., 1977. Economic growth and climate: the Carbon Dioxide problem. American Economic Review 67, 341–346.

Nordhaus, W., 1991. To slow or not to slow: the economics of the greenhouse effects. The Economic Journal 101, 920–937.

Nordhaus, W., 1992. An optimal transition path for controlling greenhouse gases. Science 258, 1315–1319.

Nordhaus, W., 1994. Managing the Global Commons. MIT Press, Massachusetts.

Nordhaus, W.D., 1996. Do real-output and real-wage measures capture reality? The history of lighting suggests not. In: Bresnahan, T.F., Gordon, R.J. (Eds.), The Economics of New Goods. University of Chicago Press, Chicago, pp. 27–70.

Nordhaus, W., 2002. Modeling induced innovation in climate change policy. In: Grubler, A., Nakicenovic, N., Nordhaus, W. (Eds.), Technological Change and the Environment. Resources for the Future Press, Washington, DC.

Nordhaus, W.D., 2006. Paul Samuelson and global public goods. In: Szenberg, M., Ramrattan, L., Gottesman, A.A. (Eds.), Samuelsonian Economics and the Twenty-first Century. Oxford Scholarship Online, 2006.

Nordhaus, W., 2007. To tax or not to tax: alternative approaches to slowing global warming. Review of Environmental Economics and Policy 1 (1), 26–44.

Nordhaus, W.D., 2008. A Question of Balance—Weighing the Options on Global Warming Policies. Yale University Press, New Haven, CT.

Nordhaus, W., 2010. Carbon taxes to move toward fiscal sustainability. The Economists' Voice 7 (3), 1–5.

Nordhaus, W., 2013. The climate casino: risk, uncertainty, and economics for a warming world. Yale University Press, New Haven, CT.

Nordhaus, W.D., Boyer, J., 2000. Warming the World: Economic Models of Global Warming. MIT Press, Cambridge, MA.

Popp, D., 2002. Induced innovation and energy prices. American Economic Review 92, 160–180.

Popp, D., 2004. ENTICE: endogenous technological change in the DICE model of global warming. Journal of Environmental Economics and Management 48, 742–768.

Popp, D., 2006a. ENTICE-BR: the effects of backstop technology R&D on climate policy models. Energy Economics 28, 188–222.

Popp, D., 2006b. Innovation in climate policy models: implementing lessons from the economics of R&D. Energy Economics 28 (5–6), 596–609.

Schaefer, H., Fletcher, S.E.M., Veidt, C., et al., 2016. A 21st century shift from fossil-fuel to biogenic methane emissions indicated by $^{13}CH_4$. Science 352, 80–84.

Schlesinger, W.H., 1997. Biogeochemistry: An Analysis of Global Change, second ed. Academic Press, San Diego, CA.

Schmalensee, R., 2015. The future of solar energy: a personal assessment. Energy Economics 52, S142–S148.

Schmitz, O.J., 2016. How 'Natural Geoengineering' Can Help Slow Global Warming. Yale Environment 360. Yale School of Forestry & Environmental Studies, New Haven, CT.

Schiermeier, Q., 2012. Dumping iron at sea does sink carbon. Nature News. http://dx.doi.org/10.1038/nature.2012.11028.

Shiller, R.J., 2008. The Subprime Solution: How Today's Global Financial Crisis Happened, and What to Do about it. Princeton University Press, Princeton, NJ.

Seo, S.N., 2015a. Adaptation to global warming as an optimal transition process to a greenhouse world. Economic Affairs 35, 272–284.

Seo, S.N., 2015b. Fatalities of neglect: adapt to more intense hurricanes? International Journal of Climatology 35, 3505–3514.

Seo, S.N., 2016. A theory of global public goods and their provisions. Journal of Public Affairs 16, 394–405.

Seo, S.N., Mendelsohn, R., 2008. Measuring impacts and adaptations to climate change: a structural Ricardian model of African livestock management. Agricultural Economics 38, 151–165.

Sims, R.E.H., Schock, R.N., Adegbululgbe, A., et al., 2007. Energy supply. In: Climate Change 2007: Mitigation. Cambridge University Press, Cambridge, UK. The Fourth Assessment Report of the Intergovernmental Panel on Climate Change.

Slovic, P., 1987. Perception of risk. Science 236, 280–285.

Smetacek, V., Klaas, C., Strass, V.H., et al., 2012. Deep carbon export from a Southern Ocean iron-fertilized diatom bloom. Nature 487, 313–319.

Soussana, J.F., Tallec, Blanfort, V., 2010. Mitigating the greenhouse gas balance of ruminant production systems through carbon sequestration in grasslands. Animal 4, 334–350.

Stavins, R., 2007. A US Cap-and-Trade System to Address Global Climate Change. Hamilton Project Discussion Paper 2007–13. The Brookings Institution, Washington, DC.

Strickland, M.S., Hawlena, D., Reese, A., Bradford, M.A., Schmitz, O.Z., 2013. Trophic cascade alters ecosystem Carbon exchange. Proceedings of the National Academy of Sciences of the United States of America 110, 11035–11038.

Sue Wing, I., 2006. Representing induced technological change in models for climate policy. Energy Economics 28, 539–562.

Tietenberg, T.H., 2006. Emissions Trading: Principles and Practice, second ed. Resources For the Future, Washington, DC.

Time, 2014. Why "green" Cars Are Still Destroying the Earth. Time Magazine. Available at: http://time.com/money/3432529/tesla-electric-environmentally-friendly-aluminum/.

Turco, R.P., Toon, O.B., Ackerman, T.P., Pollack, J.B., Sagan, C., 1983. Nuclear winter: global consequences of multiple nuclear explosions. Science 222, 1283–1292.

Turner, A.J., Jacob, D.J., Benmergui, J., Wofsy, S.C., Maasakkers, J.D., Butz, A., Hasekamp, O., Biraud, S.C., 2016. A large increase in U.S. methane emissions over the past decade inferred from satellite data and surface observations. Geophysical Research Letters 43, 2218–2224.

United Nations Environmental Programme (UNEP), 1987. The Montreal Protocol on Substances that Deplete the Ozone Layer. UNEP, Nairobi, Kenya.

United Nations Framework Convention on Climate Change (UNFCCC), 1998. Kyoto Protocol to the United Nations Framework Convention on Climate Change. UNFCCC, New York.

United Nations Framework Convention on Climate Change (UNFCCC), 2015. The Paris Agreement. Conference of the Parties (COP) 21. UNFCCC, New York.

United States Department of Agriculture (USDA), 2016. California drought: Farm and Food Impacts. USDA, Washington DC. Available at: https://www.ers.usda.gov/topics/in-the-news/california-drought-farm-and-food-impacts/.

United States Department of Energy (US DOE), 2016a. Waste Isolation Pilot Project (WIPP) Recovery. US DOE, Washington DC. Available at: http://www.wipp.energy.gov/.

United States Department of Energy (US DOE), 2016b. How Energy Efficient Light Bulbs Compare with Traditional Incandescent. US DOE, Washington DC. Available at: http://energy.gov/energysaver/how-energy-efficient-light-bulbs-compare-traditional-incandescents.

United States Energy Information Administration (US EIA), 2014. Annual Energy Outlook 2014. EIA, US DOE, Washington DC.

United States Energy Information Administration (US EIA), 2015a. Monthly Power Sector Carbon Dioxide Emissions Reach 27-year Low in April. Today in Energy. EIA, US DOE, Washington DC.

United States Energy Information Administration (US EIA), 2015b. U.S. Energy-related Carbon Dioxide Emissions, 2014. EIA, US DOE, Washington DC.

United States Energy Information Administration (US EIA), 2016. Energy Explained. US EIA, Department of Energy, Washington DC.

United States Environmental Protection Agency (US EPA), 2006. Global Mitigation of Non-CO_2 Greenhouse Gases. US EPA, Washington DC.

United States Environmental Protection Agency (US EPA), 2014. Carbon Pollution Emission Guidelines for Existing Stationary Sources: Electric Utility Generating Units. US EPA, Washington DC.

United States Environmental Protection Agency (US EPA), 2015. Inventory of US Greenhouse Gas Emissions and Sinks: 1990–2013. US EPA, Washington DC.

Weier, J., 2001. John Martin (1935–1993). Earth Observatory, National Aeronautics and Space Administration, USA.

White House, 2013. The President's Climate Action Plan. Executive Office of the President, The White House, Washington DC.

White House, 2016. U.S.-Canada Joint Statement on Climate, Energy, and Arctic Leadership. The White House, Washington DC.

Yale Environment 360, 2013a. Why a Highly Promising Electric Car Start-up Is Failing by Gunther. M. Yale University, New Haven, CT.

Yale Environment 360, 2013b. Interview with Bill Reinert: He's Still Bullish on Hybrids, but Skeptical of Electric Cars by McDonald K. Yale University, New Haven, CT.

Further Reading

Barrett, S., 2008. The incredible economics of geoengineering. Environmental and Resource Economics 39, 45–54.

Intergovernmental Panel on Climate Change (IPCC), 1990. Climate Change: The IPCC Scientific Assessment. Cambridge University Press, Cambridge.

Kaul, I., Conceicao, P., Goulven, K.L., Mendoza, R.U. (Eds.), 2003. Providing Global Public Goods: Managing Globalization. Oxford University Press, Oxford.

Adaptation Paradigm as an Alternative Global Warming Policy

Chapter Outline

1. Inevitability of Adapting to Global Warming

The previous two chapters described two policy approaches to global warming: a carbon pricing approach in Chapter 4 and a technological innovation approach in Chapter 5. A major challenge in the former is disparate impacts and a strong incentive to noncooperation, whereas a major challenge in the latter is uncertainties and inducing innovations and adoptions of new technologies. This chapter presents an adaptation paradigm as an alternative policy paradigm that has the potential to overcome major conundrums of both policy approaches.

An atmospheric increase in the concentration of carbon dioxide and changes in the global climate system, including the observed trend of global warming, compels people to adapt. The changes in the climate system are to bring about changes in natural ecosystems and the amenities that directly or indirectly alter personal welfare through a multitude of changes that will occur through the market and outside the market (Pearce et al., 1996; Schlesinger, 1997).

The Behavioral Economics of Climate Change. http://dx.doi.org/10.1016/B978-0-12-811874-0.00006-4

At the personal level, there is no need for a government to intervene to force an individual to take adaptation measures. An individual will compare the costs and benefits of multiple options that are available to him/her in the current and altered climate conditions (Mendelsohn, 2000; Hanemann, 2000). The individual will make a transition from one enterprise to another, relocate from one location to another, and take up one task against another, considering relevant costs and benefits involved (Seo and Mendelsohn, 2008; Seo, 2010b, 2015a).

A variety of communities in varied sizes and characteristics also have an incentive to adapt to climatic changes and global warming. A village in a rural area, for example, will need to adapt to the changes caused by global warming if village members cannot individually adapt. The same is true of a local government. A local government that is given the responsibility for managing public resources and money on behalf of its residents will be forced to take efficient adaptation measures if the constituents cannot do so individually (Seo, 2011a). The author will call the former a community adaptation and the latter a public adaptation. Both types of adaptations are taken by a community composed of a group, whether large or small, of individuals. By contrast, a private adaptation is an adaptation behavior undertaken by an individual.

A unique feature in public adaptation and community adaptation is the need for coordination of its members. A community of concern may have to coordinate the members to accomplish the adaptation task that is to be implemented. Coordination is costly. As such, the cost of coordination can be made one component of the adaptation cost that is shared by the members or an informal arrangement may arise among the members with regard to the completion of the adaptation task (Coase, 1960; Ostrom, 2009; Seo, 2011a).

In the sections that ensue, the author establishes the adaptation paradigm as an alternative global warming policy by answering the thorny questions on global warming policy challenges elaborated in Chapters 3−5. In the next section, a conceptual framework of the adaptation paradigm is laid out. Section 3 describes distinguishing features of the adaptation paradigm from other policy approaches. An array of adaptation measures and strategies that constitute the adaptation paradigm are explained through Sections 4−6: Section 4 by economic agents and sectors, Section 5 with a focus on natural resource enterprises, and Section 6 with a focus on ocean environments. A time line of the adaptation paradigm is presented in Section 7 with specific short-, medium-, and long-term adaptation strategies. Finally, the author offers an assessment of short-, medium-, and long-term carbon abatement potentials as well as an assessment of a future temperature trajectory under the projected mitigation efforts through the adaptation paradigm.

2. Adaptation Paradigm as an Alternative Global Warming Policy

That there is an incentive for both an individual and a community of individuals to adapt to global climatic changes is an aspect of global warming that is shared by a vast majority of people concerned on the warming planet (Seo, 2013a, 2015a). This consensus is the foundation for the adaptation paradigm, to be defined shortly, as an alternative global warming policy.

An illustrative example of the empirical evidence of an individual's adaptation behaviors is presented graphically in Fig. 6.1 (Seo, 2016a). In an agricultural study of South America using the farm household survey data collected from Argentina, Brazil, Chile, Uruguay, Colombia, Venezuela, and Ecuador, farmers are found to switch agricultural systems in response to changes in the climate system. Assuming that climate change would unfold according to the GISS-ER (Goddard Institute of Space Studies Model E-R) scenario by the middle of this century (Schmidt et al., 2005), South African farmers switch away from a specialized crop system (−9.5% from the baseline) and switch into livestock-based systems, such as a mixed crops—livestock system (+4.5% from the baseline) and a specialized livestock system (+9% from the baseline) (Seo, 2016a).

Such changes are driven by private incentives. As illustrated in Fig. 6.2, the specialized crop system is the most vulnerable system to the climate change forecast by the GISS scenario. The land value of the specialized crop system is observed to decrease by about 9% from the baseline land value of the system. On the other hand, the mixed system is relatively more resilient, the land value of which is observed to decrease by only 4% under the same scenario. The specialized livestock system benefits from the

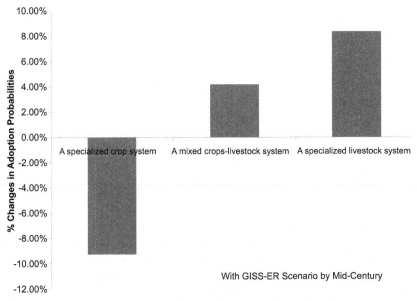

Figure 6.1 Evidence of adaptation behaviors: percentage changes in adoption probabilities of agricultural systems in South America. *GISS-ER*, Goddard Institute of Space Studies Model E-R. Based on Seo, S.N., 2016a. Modeling farmer adaptations to climate change in South America: a micro-behavioral economic perspective. Environmental and Ecological Statistics 23, 1−21.

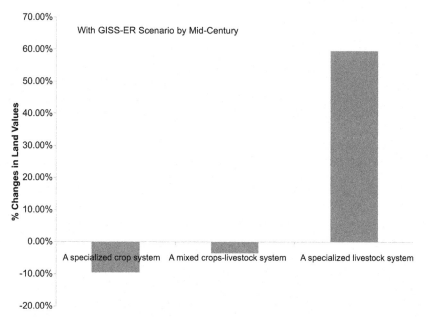

Figure 6.2 Monetary incentives for adaptation: percentage changes in land values of agricultural systems in South America. *GISS-ER*, Goddard Institute of Space Studies Model E-R.
Based on Seo, S.N., 2016a. Modeling farmer adaptations to climate change in South America: a micro-behavioral economic perspective. Environmental and Ecological Statistics 23, 1−21.

GISS climate scenario by the middle of this century, the land value of which increases by 60% (Seo, 2016a).

Therefore it is profitable for a South American farmer to switch from a crops-only system to a mixed system or a livestock-only system, taking into consideration the current climate, future climates, soils, geography, geology, markets, and family characteristics of his/her farm. Put differently, a farmer who fails to adapt or maladapts will suffer monetary loss in comparison with a farmer who adapts efficiently as needed.

The possibility and capability of individuals and communities to adapt to global climatic shifts makes the problem of global warming a two-way mutual relationship. In the one way which has been predominantly emphasized by climate communities, human activities lead to alterations of the climate system. In the other way, changes in the climate system force humanity to adjust behaviors of individuals and businesses.

The mutual relationship between natural changes and anthropogenic changes is the foundation of the adaptation paradigm. From the perspective of the mutual relationship, the adaptation paradigm takes into account changes in anthropogenic behaviors caused by climatic changes as well as changes in anthropogenic behaviors that cause climatic changes.

In the adaptation paradigm, an adaptation strategy is taken by a climate actor, i.e., an individual, a business, or a community, by considering the benefits and costs that are incurred from both changes in behaviors in response to climatic changes and changes in behaviors that lead to climatic changes.

Let us consider the following three cases to elucidate the mutual relationship: a farmer in the Pampas grasslands in South America, a business company in the United States, and a local government in the United States. For a farmer in the Pampas grasslands, he/she will adapt to the changes in the climate system considering the benefits and costs of available options. Will the farmer change his/her current farming behaviors that lead to emissions of greenhouse gases? For example, cultivating soils lead to emissions of soil organic carbon; flooded rice fields emit methane (CH_4); burning crop residues emit nitrous oxides (N_2O); raising ruminant animals, such as cattle, sheep, and goats, lead to methane emissions; cutting trees lead to emissions of carbon dioxide (US EPA, 2006; Smith et al., 2008).

There is no incentive for the farmer to take actions solely to reduce voluntarily emissions of greenhouse gases from numerous farming activities, without any government policy to support such activities. Nonetheless, changes in farming activities for the purpose of adaptation to climatic changes that are inevitable, as described earlier, have consequences on numerous emission-generating activities by the farmer.

A switch of an enterprise from a crops-only enterprise to a crops—forests enterprise can reduce the emissions of soil carbon and increase the absorption of carbon dioxide in the atmosphere (Houghton, 2008; Seo, 2010c, 2012a). For another example, a switch from a crops-only enterprise to a crops—livestock enterprise can lead to a decrease in the soil carbon emissions, an increase or decrease in methane emissions, and an increase in carbon sinks from grasslands (Seo, 2010a,b; Soussana et al., 2010).

A farmer's adoption of emission-cutting activities such as forestry and grassland management is motivated by faster growth and higher qualities of grasslands, trees, and forest products under a warmer carbon-rich atmosphere (Schlesinger, 1997; Ainsworth and Long, 2005). Although motivated solely by private monetary gains, a farmer's adaptation behaviors can have positive externalities on the society, that is, carbon removal and storage.

On the other hand, growth in the management of ruminant livestock, such as cattle, sheep, and goats, because of increased productivity of grasslands would lead to an increase in methane emissions, without any additional measures undertaken (Schaefer et al., 2016). In other words, there can be also negative externalities in the farmer's adaptation behavior. A switch to nonruminant animals, such as chickens, pigs, turkeys, and kangaroos, does not lead to an increase in methane emissions.

However, there exists a third dimension of adaptation behaviors: there may be handy ways to cut methane emissions from ruminant animals, such as cattle, sheep, and goats, at low cost (US EPA, 2006). Changes in feed additives and animal diets are known to reduce methane emissions from burping, farting, and defecations from ruminant animals (Gerber et al., 2013). Furthermore, a mask placed on a ruminant animal or an indoor absorption facility can effectively capture methane, which can be reused for profitable activities.

Changes in agricultural practices, natural resource uses, and land uses for adaptation to climatic changes can result in reduction of carbon dioxide emissions, but how much? A meaningful benchmark for how much carbon reduction can be achieved is changes in the annual net carbon flux into the atmosphere from land use changes in the United States since 1850 (Houghton, 1999, 2008; Denman et al., 2007). As shown in Fig. 6.3, the carbon emissions from land uses peaked in the late 19th century at 350 Tg carbon (million tons of carbon) per year, which then declined to −100 Tg carbon emissions in the late 20th century. Put differently, by the late 20th century, land and ecosystems are a source of carbon sink of about 100 million tons of carbon. The emission reduction from the peak year amounts to 450 million tons of carbon per year.

A similar historical pattern is also observed in China where the peak of annual net carbon flux occurred only in the first decade of the 21st century (Houghton, 2008). What this statistic tells us is that adaptive changes in agricultural and natural resource enterprises in China can have a major implication on annual global level of carbon emissions. Although not attempted at this point, it is also possible to associate each adaptation strategy with a differential in carbon emissions at a local context through locally explicit studies of ecosystems and changes (Ainsworth and Long, 2005; Seo, 2013b; Crowther et al., 2015; Van Pelt et al., 2016).

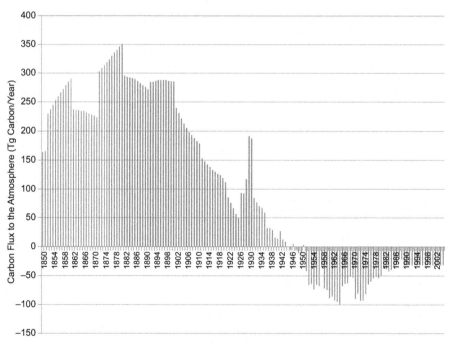

Figure 6.3 Reductions in carbon emissions from land use changes in the United States since 1850.
Based on Houghton, R.A., 1999. The annual net flux of carbon to the atmosphere from changes in land use 1850−1990. Tellus 51B, 298−313; Houghton, R.A., 2008. Carbon flux to the atmosphere from land-use changes: 1850−2005. In: TRENDS: A Compendium of Data on Global Change. Carbon Dioxide Information Analysis Center, Oak Ridge National Laboratory, U.S. Department of Energy, Oak Ridge, TN.

With regard to the adaptation paradigm as an alternative global warming policy, the discussion up to this point brings up two cooperative components of the adaptation paradigm. One is technological developments. That is, although the author provided an extensive review of potential breakthrough technologies in the previous chapter, incremental technological advances, e.g., methane capturing from animals or cures for animal diseases, can also make a significant contribution to the policy efforts for greenhouse gas emission reductions (US EPA, 2006; Aksoy et al., 2014).

The second component is the role of governments. An individual farmer may have no incentive to take some emission reduction measures such as methane capturing from ruminant animals, whereas a government has the incentive to nudge a farmer to adopt these measures (Thaler and Sunstein, 2009; Seo, 2015c). This is especially so when the cost of these measures gets lower because of technological innovations. Although a farmer may have no reason to act solely to cut carbon emissions, a government may have the reason, as an organization that is entrusted to provide various public goods, to act if the general public believes climate change is real, harms and will harm people and natural systems, and can be catastrophic in the far future (White House, 2013; US EPA, 2014). The general public will force, through a legislative body, the public sector to take appropriate measures within the limits of the relevant public sector, which will be further explained in this chapter (WSJ, 2017).

This completes the description of an adaptation paradigm explained in the context of a natural resource manager who adopts the above-described adaptation strategies. Many remaining questions including whether this paradigm can be extended to other sectors such as a business and energy producers, whether the adaptation paradigm will provide sufficient amount of emission reductions will be answered throughout this chapter.

3. Distinguishing Features From Other Approaches

A variety of climate policy proposals, agreements, and protocols can be categorized into one of the four approaches: scientific, economic, technological, and behavioral. In Table 6.1, the author provides a list of policy instruments and policy experiences/ examples for each of these policy approaches.

The scientific policy approach directly targets CO_2 emissions or temperature increase. An emissions limit set in Kyoto Protocol, a temperature ceiling proposed in the Cancun Agreements, and the nationally determined contributions in the Paris Agreement are examples of the scientific approach (UNFCCC, 1998, 2010). The term "scientific" can be justified because policy proposals by climate scientists are predominantly rooted on the concern on a critical threshold or a tipping point (Mann et al., 1999; Lenton et al., 2008).

The economic policy approach is focused on creating the price of carbon efficiently or the price of an emissions permit of carbon (Nordhaus, 1994, 2006). A carbon tax program adopted in several countries, the EU Emissions Trading System program, the cap-and-trade proposal in the United States, and the US SO_2 allowance trading

Table 6.1 **Alternative Policy Approaches to Global Warming**

	Scientific	Economic	Technological	Behavioral
Instruments	Command and control; emissions limit; temperature ceiling	Pricing carbon emissions	Breakthrough technologies	Adaptation paradigm
Examples	1. Kyoto Protocol: limit carbon dioxide emissions at 1990 level; 2. Cancun Agreements: temperature ceiling of 2°C; 3. Paris Agreement; Intended nationally determined contributions	1. Carbon tax adopted in several countries Tietenberg (2013); 2. EU emissions trading system (EC, 2015); 3. Cap-and-trade proposed in the USA Stavins (2007)	1. Carbon-capture-storage; 2. Nuclear fusion/fission energy; 3. Solar energy; 4. Climate engineering; 5. Ocean fertilization; 6. New lighting methods; 7. Electric vehicles; 8. Replacing hydrofluoro-carbons EC (2016)	

system belong to the economic policy approach (Stavins, 1998, 2007; Ellerman and Buchner, 2007; Tietenberg, 2013).

The technological policy approach, which was covered exclusively in the previous chapter, pins hope on breakthrough technologies such as a carbon-capture-storage, nuclear fusion energy, solar energy, climate engineering, ocean fertilization, and others (Martin et al., 1994; Lackner et al., 1999; IPCC, 2005b, 2011; ITER, 2015; MIT, 2015; NRC, 2015).

The fourth policy approach is a microbehavioral approach, which is encapsulated in the adaptation paradigm developed in this chapter (Seo, 2015c, 2016b). How does the adaptation paradigm differ from the other policy approaches? The author considers two policy frameworks for comparison: the mitigation-focused, complemented by adaptation, approach by the United Nations and the social welfare optimization framework such as the DICE/RICE (Dynamically/Regionally Integrated model of Climate and Economy) model.

Why is the adaptation paradigm distinct from the mitigation-focused, complemented by adaptation, approach purposed by the Intergovernmental Panel on Climate Change (IPCC) and the United Nations Framework Convention on Climate Change (UNFCCC)? To begin with, neither the IPCC nor the UNFCCC explicitly supports this approach, but only implicitly so. From now on, the author will call this approach the mitigation-plus approach.

Evidences of the mitigation-plus approach are handily found. The agreements of the UNFCCC since the Copenhagen Conference of the Parties in 2009 include separate subcommittee documents on mitigation and adaptation: one called the Durban Platform for Enhanced Action and the other called the Green Climate Fund (UNFCCC, 2011a,b). In addition, the IPCC assessment is composed of three separate reports: scientific basis, impacts and adaptation, and mitigation (IPCC, 2014a,b,c). However, the agreements in Kyoto Protocol, Copenhagen Accord, Durban Platform, and Paris Agreements all are concentrated on achieving mitigation targets agreed by the members.

The mitigation-plus approach puts together two distinct components, i.e., mitigation and adaptation, into one framework, if we can call it a framework. There is no unifying principle of the two components. In the mitigation-plus approach, the principle for mitigation has been to keep the global temperature below $2°C$ or to prevent a dangerous anthropogenic interference with the climate system (UNFCCC, 1992, 2010).

The principle for adaptation has never been stated, but a straightforward interpretation of the above-mentioned mitigation principle would mean that the guiding principle of adaptation is to protect humanity from the dangerous consequences of climate change. A careful reading of the early reports by the UN organizations reveals that an implicit principle has been to protect low-latitude poor countries from the worst impacts of climate change (IPCC, 1990; UNFCCC, 1992).

How does the adaptation paradigm developed in this chapter differ? The adaptation paradigm integrates both human influences on the climate system and human responses to changes in the climate system into a unified framework of behavioral adaptations. Adaptation measures and strategies are taken in consideration of the benefits and costs of both adaptation and mitigation options.

To give an example, a natural resource manager will choose a strategy from the available alternatives to adapt to changes in the climate system and at the same time will choose a portfolio of income-generating activities that has a distinct emissions profile (Seo, 2015a). The manager will make the two decisions simultaneously considering total benefits and costs.

In this paradigm, a natural resource manager can choose a portfolio of income-generating activities that produces a larger amount of emissions of greenhouse gases if it is more beneficial to his/her enterprise. Alternatively, she can also choose a portfolio of activities that produces a smaller amount of emissions.

Two additional policy dimensions would make an individual's adaptation choices a carbon-reducing behavior (Seo, 2015c, 2016b). First, numerous technological innovations surveyed in the previous chapter provide an individual low-cost options for reducing emissions of greenhouse gases from the chosen adaptation portfolio. Second, all natural resource managers are compelled, in one way or another, by the public sector to take emission-cutting measures and strategies with the assistance of the public sector if the rate of global warming does indeed become an ever bigger threat to the public. Under the public sector's roles, an individual will choose a low-carbon portfolio over a high-carbon portfolio if all other aspects of available options are similar.

In the adaptation paradigm, the guiding rule is that an individual decision maker chooses the bundle of behavioral adjustments that lead to the maximum net benefit, i.e., total benefit minus total cost, given the unfolding climate change. In the adaptation paradigm, therefore, a primary decision criterion can be transparently established.

A surprising aspect of the adaptation paradigm is, in contrast to the other approaches, that the benefits and costs of actions need not be social benefits and costs. It is sufficient that only private benefits and costs are considered by an individual in making optimal adaptation decisions. A natural resource manager makes adaptation decisions considering only private benefits and costs that accrue to him/her.

The adaptation paradigm can be compared meaningfully with a social welfare optimization framework in which a social planner chooses an optimal greenhouse gas level or an optimal price of carbon. There is the need for intervention because markets fail to achieve optimality in resource uses because of the characteristics of public goods in global warming (Samuelson, 1954, 1955). Broadly speaking, models of a social welfare optimization modeling framework, often cited, include the DICE/RICE, MERGE (A Model for Evaluating the Regional and Global Effects of GHG Reduction Policies), FUND (The Climate Framework for Uncertainty, Negotiation and Distribution), and PAGE (A Policy Analysis of the Greenhouse Effect) (Nordhaus, 1994; Manne et al., 1995; Tol, 1997; Hope, 2006). In the social welfare maximization framework, a global society or a global planner, not individuals, chooses the level of greenhouse gases or prices of carbon dioxide optimal for the society.

In the DICE/RICE model, for example, the level of greenhouse gases and the level of carbon price are determined by a global decision maker assuming that individuals will take all actions necessary to cope with climatic changes. Adaptation by individuals and businesses reduces the damage from global warming, and consequently reduces the level of greenhouse gases to be abated, which is calculated from the DICE/RICE model. The only decision variable in the model is the level of carbon in the atmosphere or the level of carbon price, which is chosen by the global decision maker. Adaptation measures and strategies are inside the black box, i.e., left to individuals.

Furthermore, the social welfare maximization framework such as the DICE/RICE relies on the concept of a global decision maker. There is one decision-making person or body who makes the decisions on behalf of the whole world. The global planner makes decisions based on the variables of global benefits and costs. A globally beneficial path of greenhouse gases, i.e., a single trajectory, is determined and implemented in a harmonized way across all countries and individuals.

In the adaptation paradigm, decisions are made at the microlevel, i.e., by individuals who are affected by climatic changes and global warming. In this paradigm, there is no central authority on global warming responses (Ostrom, 2009), although the public sector plays pertinent roles, which will be clarified later in this chapter. An individual is the basis of policy responses to global warming; therefore the adaptation paradigm is a polycentric policy approach.

4. Adaptation Paradigms Explained by Agents and Sectors

4.1 Adaptation by Businesses

Is the adaptation paradigm pertinent for businesses that must rely heavily on energy and electricity produced from fossil fuels for numerous operations and productions? How does a business make a portfolio of adaptation decisions taking into consideration both the impacts of climate change on the business and its contribution to the buildup of greenhouse gases?

Let us consider a steel manufacturing company, one of the most carbon-intensive industries that have received much attention from global climate conferences from the earliest days (UNFCCC, 1992, 1998). Steel manufacturing activities are conducted, by and large, indoors. Hence, changes in the climate system are not expected to cause large changes in the indoor manufacturing processes. However, a higher degree of warming and a more volatile precipitation pattern can increase the demand for steels to construct sturdier houses and buildings that could withstand more adverse climate conditions. The company will adapt to the higher demand by increasing the production of steels and steel products.

How does the steel company take into account the impacts of its operations on the global climate system? Steel production is highly carbon intensive (UNFCCC, 1998). Steel production requires the furnace temperature extremely high for which a large amount of coal must be burned. An increased production of steels and steel products will lead to even more emissions of carbon into the atmosphere.

On the other hand, a higher temperature and a more volatile precipitation pattern make the company's operations more costly and difficult. A warmer world will force the company to increase air conditioning for its factories and increase indoor climate controls. In addition, a carbon-enriched world makes it more costly for the firm to procure iron ores for steel productions as outdoor activities would become more difficult and unpredictable. Because of these impacts of climate change on the firm, which add to production costs, the firm will reduce the production of steels, *ceteris paribus*, which would lower the emissions of carbon dioxide by the company.

In the longer term at which the realizations of the global warming predictions made at the present time by climate modelers would become more evident to the public, harmful consequences of such climate realizations on various sectors of the society will give local and federal governments a strong rationale to charge carbon-intensive industries, such as steel manufacturing, for the damages on the society caused by carbon emissions by numerous emitters, including the steel company.

The steel company must make a decision on whether to pay such penalty imposed by the government or develop and adopt low-carbon measures to avoid the penalty. The company should choose a bundle of actions considering net benefits of available options as well as net benefits of adaptation strategies. The company makes its decisions for the company's benefits only. That is, it does not make decisions for social benefits.

What carbon-cutting measures can the steel company adopt? It can reduce carbon emissions from steel making by employing one of the carbon-capture-storage techniques explained in detail in the previous chapter, which is more cost-effective: postcombustion capture, precombustion capture, and oxyfuel capture (IPCC, 2005b; IEA, 2013). Second, it may opt for a cleaner coal, i.e., high-quality coals, such as anthracite and bituminous, instead of peat and lignite coals, which emit more carbon dioxide per unit of energy produced (US EIA, 2014). A third option is to shift out of coal to an alternative method to heat the furnace, e.g., natural gas, solar energy, or nuclear energy (Heal, 2010; IPCC, 2011).

The steel company can also reduce greenhouse gas emissions from the extraction process of iron ores and other operations. It can adopt electric vehicles for various transportation works, deploy methane-capturing technologies, change refrigerants from hydrofluorocarbons (HFCs) and hydrochlorofluorocarbons (HCFCs) to alternative refrigerants such as hydrocarbons, and change lighting methods from incandescent light bulbs to compact fluorescent lamps (CFLs) or light-emitting diode (LED) lamps (IPCC, 2005a; Akasaki et al., 2014; EC, 2016).

The steel company's decisions to cut greenhouse gases from production and operation processes can be forced by consumer reactions. If global warming damages were to become more evident over time, consumers and the general public would increasingly force steel companies to adopt low-carbon measures. Consumer actions will push the company to make innovative changes to minimize the cost of greenhouse gas abatement, which is called for by the consumers.

4.2 Adaptation by Governments

Let us consider a local government, say, a county in the United States or a district in South America. Changes in the climate system affect various assets and activities of the local government. For example, public parks, rivers, wetlands, grasslands, deserts, and mountains that are managed by the local government are influenced by climatic changes. The local government should adapt to these changes to manage these resources optimally.

In managing national parks, mountains, and other ecosystems, some species of animals and plants may decline while others increase owing to climate changes. This will have consequences on emissions of greenhouse gases from the government's resources. For example, an increased forest coverage in the government-owned land would increase absorption of carbon dioxide.

Another area of concern is the flooding of coastal zones of the county by storm surges, the heights of which are expected to rise because of global warming and sea level rise (Dube et al., 2009; Seo and Bakkensen, 2016). The government should decide how to protect coastal zones from flooding and inundation. The cost for building protective systems and increasing resilience of coastal communities may be financed by imposing charges on heavy carbon-emitting industries, such as power plants, steel and cement producers, and other businesses.

On the other side, a large variety of the government's activities lead to emissions of greenhouse gases as well as sinks of greenhouse gases. Various offices and operations consume electricity and transportation vehicles of the local government burn fossil fuels. Managing national parks, mountains, and rivers can help reduce greenhouse gases, but also increase them.

As the detrimental impacts of global warming manifest ever more clearly over time on the communities within the government, the local government will be asked by its constituents to adopt carbon-cutting measures. This means that the government's activities will be the first that will be forced to adopt low-carbon measures before it can impose a penalty on private firms and enterprises (White House, 2013).

The local and federal governments have the power to force technological innovations and breakthroughs in dealing with global warming. The imposition of penalties on firms and enterprises will force them to search for lower-cost means of achieving reductions of greenhouse gas emissions. Furthermore, research grants and subsidies by the governments for developing a certain technology can increase the odds and reduce the waiting time for the sought-after technology.

4.3 Adaptation by Power Plants

Power plants are a major source of greenhouse gas emissions, mainly carbon dioxide (Muller and Mendelsohn, 2009; Muller et al., 2011). Power plants may be coal fired, natural gas fired, oil fired, solar, wind, hydroelectric, geothermal, or nuclear, depending on how heat is generated. How does the adaptation paradigm apply to power plants, the heaviest emitter of carbon?

Changes in the climate system would influence various operations of power plants. Let us start with a coal-fired power plant. For example, under climate stress, increased costs for air conditioning in the offices, increased efforts are needed to extract coals. The power plant should adapt to these changes accordingly, which may or may not have consequences on the amount of carbon dioxide it emits.

Through excessive burning of coals, a coal-fired power plant is the largest as well as the heaviest emitter of carbon dioxide. As explained in the previous chapter, one MMBTU (Million British Thermal Unit) of energy is produced by burning anthracite coal with accompanying 228.6 pounds of carbon dioxide release. In comparison, the same amount of energy can be produced with accompanying only 117 pounds of carbon dioxide emissions by a natural gas-fired power plant (US EIA, 2015).

The coal-fired power plant does not have any incentive for cutting carbon dioxide emissions from its production activities. A government imposition of carbon penalty on the power plant will force it to change its behaviors to reduce emissions. The power plant may switch to cleaner coals. That is, it may switch from anthracite coals to bituminous coals, which emit slightly lower level of carbon dioxide per unit energy production, i.e., 205 pounds of CO_2 emissions per MMBTU of energy produced.

The coal switch, however, may turn out to be insufficient to meet the abatement requirement set by the government. Then, the power plant may shut down the coal-fired productions and open a natural gas–fired operation, complemented with a methane detection and capture facility, which also reaps the benefits of a large increase in shale gas productions in the recent and upcoming decades (Joskow, 2013; Brandt et al., 2014). Alternatively, the power plant may opt for a carbon-capture-storage facility to reduce the emissions while it maintains coal-fired productions. Still another option for the power plant is to close the coal-fired power plant and open low-carbon operations, e.g., solar energy plants.

As is clear from the description so far, a coal-fired power plant does have little motivation to act to cut emissions because of its concern on global warming. For the power plant to take costly abatement measures, the government must be involved in forcing it to act. As long as the rise in carbon dioxide concentration in the global atmosphere continues and the increase in global temperature is not slowing down, there is a strong reason for the governments to intervene through legislation by the Congress (USEPA, 2014; WSJ, 2017).

However, if the increase in carbon dioxide concentration as well as the temperature increase were to slow down in upcoming decades, it would be very difficult for the government to force them to cut emissions. The observed trends in these measures, which have been monitored by scientists closely for decades, will play a critical role in deciding whether the governments should intervene or not (NCEI, 2016).

Energy productions in general will adapt to changes in the climate regime. A warmer temperature is, more often than not, associated with a larger amount of rainfall as well as melting of glaciers and ice sheets in high mountains (IPCC, 2014a). An increase in rainfall increases the amount of water that can be used for hydroelectric energy productions. Large-scale hydroelectric projects such as those currently pursued in the river of Congo (Inga Falls hydroelectric dams) and in China (the Three Gorges Dam Project and the Yarlung Tsangpo River Dam Project in Tibet) are what we may see more often in the future because of more rainfall or melting of glaciers due to global warming in selected locations (Seo, 2016b). Energy suppliers may find that hydroelectric energy productions have relatively become more economical against other methods of energy production such as coal-fired power plants.

Such increases in hydroelectric plants are expected to contribute significantly to greenhouse gas mitigation efforts. Of the 62,500 power plants worldwide, as of 2016, the world's nine largest operating power plants are hydroelectric power plants. Four of the nine largest operating power plants are located in China and began operating in the past 13 years. Hydroelectric power is the second largest source of electricity, accounting for 20% of the total electricity generation of China in 2015 (US EIA, 2016).

This adaptation behavior would arise solely from the energy producer's private incentives created by the changes in the climate system, i.e., increased rainfall or melting of glaciers and ice sheets. The adaptation strategy then leads to mitigation of greenhouse gases. An increased energy supply from hydroelectric power generations means reduction in carbon dioxide emissions per unit of energy produced for the energy sector as a whole, given the total amount of energy consumption is unchanged.

A warmer climate regime may mean less solar radiation that is received on Earth that can be utilized for solar energy productions. This may occur primarily because of increased clouds in the atmosphere that result from increased evapotranspiration from water bodies and vegetation. This means that heavy investments today into solar panels may turn out to be less effective in producing energy per day in some regions, but not all, in the future.

The critical role of another cooperative component of the adaptation paradigm, i.e., technological developments, is well demonstrated in the power sector's potential strategies discussed earlier to cut carbon emissions. A switch to a natural gas−fired power production is made possible in part by the hydrofracturing technology; a carbon-capture-storage facility can be employed more widely if the cost of the technology falls significantly; a transition to low-carbon energy productions such as solar energy can be fast-tracked if the costs of these technologies fall (Heal, 2010; Krupnick et al., 2013; MIT, 2015).

4.4 Adaptation by Consumers and Households

Households emit a large amount of carbon dioxide annually. Of the 5.2 giga tons of carbon dioxide emitted in the United States in 2013, the residential sector accounted for 20.6% and the transportation sector accounted for 33.8% of the total emissions. Of the total emissions of carbon dioxide from the residential sector, electricity consumption accounted for about three-quarters (US EPA, 2015).

Consumers and households are not immune to the changes in the global climate system and they will also adapt to these changes. A shift of the climate system to a hotter and a more variable precipitation pattern motivates consumers to seek a climatically pleasant residential location as well as a well-climate-controlled housing. In the northern states of the United States, we may see an increase in population as temperature becomes less cold. Similarly, we may see a decrease in population in the southern states of the United States.

In the areas in the globe where there is currently no need for climate controls, such as air conditioning, heating, and improved sunlight blocking because of a temperate friendly climate, global warming will necessitate an increase in the installations of the climate control measures. In the areas where heating need is very high currently, we may see a decrease in the need for heating due to a warmer climate condition in the future. Furthermore, developers and municipalities will increase investments to make residential areas more climate friendly by planting more trees around the residential areas to provide coolness in the summer and warmness in the winter provided by groves of trees.

These adaptive behaviors have consequences on carbon emissions at present. Planting trees around residential areas would increase absorption of carbon dioxide from the atmosphere. An increase in climate-controlled houses and offices increases the emissions of carbon dioxide and HFCs. A decrease in heating would decrease carbon emissions.

As mentioned earlier, three-quarters of the residential sector emissions of carbon dioxide come from electricity consumption. If climate change were to become ever more evident in the future and its damaging effects were to be experienced by individuals and households, a motivation for relying on low-carbon energy and products would increase on the consumer side.

Even without such a motivation, switching incandescent light bulbs to CFLs or LEDs is economically sensible to consumers at the present time if long-term costs of these lighting methods are compared. As explained in detail in the previous chapter, an LED lamp can last up to 50 times more hours than an incandescent light bulb and saves almost 80% of energy in producing the same amount of light as the incandescent bulbs (US DOE, 2016). Such a change in the consumer choice among lighting technologies will make a very substantial contribution to reducing the carbon dioxide emissions from the residential and consumer sector.

This is another example that highlights the intersection between the adaptation paradigm and technological innovations. As novel technologies become practical and competitive over time, they will be a part of the adaptation paradigm of the society. This in return demonstrates the theoretical strength of the adaptation paradigm. It incorporates all existing approaches to a global warming policy response such as individual actions, carbon tax, emissions trading, and technologies.

Another important technological development that strongly influences decisions by consumers and households is technological advances in automobile manufacturing. Automobiles are increasingly made with improved fuel efficiency, i.e., a higher mileage per gallon of gasoline burned, as a hybrid vehicle, and as an electric vehicle (McConnell, 2013). If technological innovations were to make these alternative vehicles cost competitive against low-fuel-efficiency vehicles, consumers will replace the latter with the low-carbon vehicles. In addition, if global warming were to unfold ever more severely with ever-increasing damages on people and ecosystems, consumers can have motivation to switch to low-carbon vehicles, even at a higher cost of these vehicles.

Another adaptation strategy by households and consumers will lie in replacing the coolant for air conditioners and refrigerators (EC, 2016). The currently most widely used coolant, HFCs, has a 100-year global warming potential (GWP) that is more than 1000 times that of carbon dioxide. According to the Kigali amendment to the Montreal Protocol agreed in Kigali, Rwanda, an alternative climate-friendly coolant such as hydrocarbons is expected to replace the HFCs by 2028 at the latest on new machines, which is anticipated to have a substantial contribution to climate change mitigation efforts (UNEP, 2016).

But a more incisive perspective from the adaptation paradigm is that, even without the Kigali amendment, HFC replacements, such as hydrocarbons, are already a cost-competitive alternative against the HFCs and HCFCs, owing to technological innovations. Technological innovations make it easier for producers and consumers to replace the high-GWP coolants with the low-GWP coolants.

These changes in behaviors by consumers and households will result in changes in the amount of emissions of greenhouse gases. In all these behavioral changes, adaptation measures and strategies are taken by individuals taking into consideration both reducing harmful effects of global warming and lowering emissions of greenhouse gases.

5. Adaptation Strategies in Natural Resource Enterprises

In the development of the conceptual framework for the adaptation paradigm as an alternative global warming policy, individual behaviors in agricultural and natural resource intensive sectors have played a crucial role (IPCC, 1990; Rosenberg, 1992; Seo, 2006, 2010b, 2016a,d; Mendelsohn, 2012). Adaptation strategies in these sectors have been studied for the past one and half decades. Studies examined low-latitude developing countries in Africa, Latin America, and South Asia (Seo, 2015a). As demonstrated by these studies, adaptation strategies observed in these sectors provide important insights and solutions on how the society should cope with global warming that unfolds in the future. This section provides a review of this literature in the context of the adaptation paradigm developed in this chapter.

Agriculture and natural resource enterprises are the dominant form of land use in low-latitude countries in sub-Sahara, Latin America, and South Asia. In many subsistent sub-Saharan countries, agriculture alone employs more than 80% of the country's economically active population (World Bank, 2008). In Latin America, agriculture employs 50%–60% of the economically active population in the Andean region (Baethgen, 1997). In South Asia, agricultural employment accounts for 51% of the country's total employment in India in the year 2010 and 36% of the total employment in Thailand in the same year.

In these regions, forest coverage accounts for a high percentage of the total land area (Crowther et al., 2015). A forest-covered area, defined as >50% coverage of the land area, accounts for 44% in South America and 36% in sub-Saharan Africa. In South Asia, the forest cover accounts for 78% of the total land area in Indonesia, 61% in Myanmar, and 43% in Vietnam (WRI, 2005).

In addition, grasslands are a major form of land cover in sub-Sahara and South America. In sub-Sahara, semiarid savannahs expand across the Sahelian region, the eastern highlands, and the east coasts of Africa (Seo et al., 2009). In South America, the Pampas grasslands occupy a vast land area in southern South America, the Llanos grasslands are expansive in the Andean highlands such as Colombia and Venezuela, and the Cerrado grasslands are expansive in southern Brazil (Seo, 2016a).

These land and ecosystem characteristics of the low-latitude developing regions have big implications on designing global warming policies there, especially on developing an adaptation paradigm. Furthermore, because agricultural and natural resource enterprises are managed mostly outdoors exposed directly to changing weather and climate conditions, it has been shown that there is much to learn from the experiences of these enterprises in the past and present in ways to adapt to changing conditions.

A change in the climate regime to a warmer and drier regime makes grasslands more competitive against various grains and crops and may make animals more resilient than crops (Ainsworth and Long, 2005; Hahn et al., 2009), which forces a farmer to increase adoptions of various animals against grains and crops in sub-Saharan Africa (Seo, 2010a). Farmers are found to switch from a specialized crop enterprise to a mixed crops−livestock enterprise in a hotter and drier condition. A similar switch is also observed in South America in which a farmer increases adoption of a mixed crops−livestock enterprise and a specialized livestock enterprise in a warmer and more arid condition (Seo, 2010b). A livestock enterprise can adjust numerous practices, including replacing one animal species with another, to minimize the net cost from global warming (Hahn, 1981; Seo and Mendelsohn, 2008; Seo et al., 2010; Seo, 2015e).

An increase in grassland productivities under a warmer climate with elevated CO_2 makes it possible for farmers to switch to these animals-based enterprises (Shaw et al., 2002; Ainsworth and Long, 2005). At the same time, grassland managements make it possible for carbon absorptions through grasslands (Ainsworth and Long, 2005; Soussana et al., 2010). In addition, a switch from crop management to grassland management results in reduced soil carbon and nitrous oxides emissions from crop agriculture (Smith et al., 2008). On the other hand, increases in ruminant animals, such as cattle, sheep, and goats, make methane emissions from burping, farting, and manure a more serious concern in mitigation efforts (US EPA, 2006; Schaefer et al., 2016).

In a hotter and wetter climate regime, rural residents adopt increasingly forest-based activities in South America, e.g., a crops−forest enterprise, a crops−livestock−forests enterprise, a forests-only enterprise (Seo, 2012a,b). A large number of farmers make this switch in South America where forests already play a major, if not dominant, role in rural income and livelihoods. A great diversity of forests exists in the continent and covers densely about half of the continent (WRI, 2005).

Forest income is responsible for, on average, more than 20% of the rural income in South America (Vedeld et al., 2004, 2007). A dominant forest type varies across the continent: tropical rainforests in the Amazon basin, xeromorphic forests in arid zones, cold-deciduous forests in highland Andes zones, subtropical temperate forests, and xeromorphic woodlands (Matthews, 1983; Seo, 2012b).

An adaptive switch to forest-based activities is also found in sub-Sahara, although not as dramatic as that observed in South America. Hot and humid equatorial countries are found to have huge resources of tropical rainforests, such as Cameroon, Nigeria, and Republic of Congo. In a hotter and wetter climate, farmers resort increasingly more to forest activities such as a mixed crops−forests enterprise (Seo, 2010c). A forest enterprise can adjust numerous practices, including replacing one type of forest with another, to minimize the loss and maximize the benefit from climate change (Joyce et al., 1995; Sohngen and Mendelsohn, 1998).

In South Asia, Sri Lankan farmers are found to make a transition from paddy-based agriculture to forest-based activities. They are found to switch increasingly to forests and forest products, such as tea, rubber, and coconut, in a higher temperature, major export commodities of the country (Seo et al., 2005).

The climate literature has shed light on behavioral adjustments to climatic changes by individuals through such changes as diversifying a portfolio of assets managed by an individual (Seo, 2010b, 2011b). In a hotter climate regime, a farmer in Africa is found to switch from a specialized crop portfolio to a diversified portfolio of both crops and livestock. A more arid condition also motivates farmers to switch from a crops-only portfolio to a mixed crops—livestock portfolio.

In South America, farmers diversify an exclusive portfolio of crops into a crops—forests enterprise in a hotter and wetter climate regime. They diversify into a crops—livestock—forests enterprise in a more daunting climate, e.g., a hotter and more arid climate regime (Seo, 2012a,b).

These behavioral changes through diversification again offer fresh insights on how an individual will make adaptation decisions in consideration of both responses to changes in climate and carbon-emitting behaviors, which alter the climate system. To be more specific, a farmer will switch to a crops—forests enterprise in efforts not only to adapt to changes in the climate system, but also to reduce the emissions or increase the absorptions of carbon. The diversification decision into both crops and forests has implications on both sides of the adaptation paradigm.

An increase in the adoption of a crops—livestock—forests enterprise would have similar consequences on both responses to changed climates and carbon-releasing behaviors that alter the climate system (Seo, 2016d). An increase in grasslands and forests as a part of the rural economy implies that such changes will bring reduction of climate-altering emissions.

A switch from a crops-only system of agriculture to a crops—livestock system of agriculture would also have consequences on emissions of greenhouse gases. A conversion of croplands to grasslands for animals to feed on would preserve soil carbon and increase absorption of carbon dioxide from the atmosphere (Soussana et al., 2010). Again, an increase in livestock management leads to an increase in the emission of methane, another potent greenhouse gas.

Diversification is found to be one of the most effective strategies to cope with risks and extremes caused by climatic changes and global warming (Seo, 2012c, 2015d, 2016c). The scientific literature indicates that extreme weather events may increase in the future as a result of greenhouse effects (Hansen et al., 2012; Titley et al., 2016). The behavioral adaptation through diversification of a portfolio to climate risks and extremes is consistent with the finance literature, which is concerned on an investor's motivation to diversify one's portfolio to reduce the risk in the returns earned from the portfolio (Markowitz, 1952, 1959; Modigliani and Pogue, 1974). By diversifying the portfolio, investors can better cope with the volatility created by numerous factors in the financial markets.

In a more risky or volatile climate regime, rainfall fluctuations from a year to another year are expected to increase. In an increased volatility regime, farmers adapt by diversifying their portfolios with both crops and livestock, as observed in sub-Saharan Africa (Seo, 2012c). This switch is found in places such as sub-Saharan Africa where volatility at present and in the future is much larger than that in South America where long-term rainfall fluctuations are less severe (Seo, 2014b).

As such, an individual's diversification decisions made to cope with expected increased risk and extremes can be associated explicitly with greenhouse gas reduction efforts. Farmers make the system more resilient to risk and extremes, but at the same time make it more climate friendly, i.e., less carbon intensive and more carbon absorptive.

Another risk that is most predominant in South Asia is a monsoon climate (Meehl and Hu, 2006; Ueda et al., 2006). The risk of the monsoon climate is characterized by an extremely heavy rainfall in the monsoon season and an extremely scarce rainfall in the nonmonsoon season. The ratio of the monsoon rainfall to nonmonsoon rainfall, called the Monsoon Severity Index (MSI), is very high in many South Asian regions. Furthermore, these regions are characterized by the high variability of the ratio of the monsoon rainfall to nonmonsoon season rainfall, called the Monsoon Variability Index (MVI) (Seo, 2016c).

An increase in the long-term MVI means that the monsoon risk is increasing. In regions of high monsoon risk, farmers in India are observed to increase the number of goats (Seo, 2016c). Because a high monsoon risk is very adverse to crop agriculture, Indian farmers tend to survive through the monsoons by raising a larger number of goats, which are also productive animals that can easily multiply through reproduction. Furthermore, goats are traded with ease among the villagers when cash income is needed. This may or may not hold for other animals such as cattle or sheep or pigs, which are held with religious value in India.

In Sri Lanka, an island nation below the Indian continent, farmers are indeed found to increase the number of cattle/buffaloes owned in high-monsoon-risk zones, i.e., high-MVI zones (Seo, 2017a). It is reported that Sri Lanka is exceptionally vulnerable to monsoon risks in that the MVI is exceptionally high, compared with other countries. The study also reports that a high ratio of monsoon rainfall to nonmonsoon rainfall, a high MSI, motivates farmers to increase the number of chickens and ducks.

Experiences of India and Sri Lanka show that goats, water buffaloes, and chickens may turn out to be effective adaptation strategies to shifts in the monsoon climate regime. Examinations of whether global warming and greenhouse effects will lead to changes in the monsoon climate regime of India and Sri Lanka and, if so, how are on-going research areas (IPCC, 2014a). However, it should be noted that these observed changes in farmers' behaviors offer valuable clues on how societies should cope with the calls for reductions in greenhouse gases in these monsoon-dominated regions.

From the mitigation standpoint, chickens, turkeys, pigs, ducks, and kangaroos are not ruminant animals that are major sources of emissions of methane in the process of digestion and manure. Ruminant animals are animals that have a rumen with billions of microorganisms to break down grasses and vegetation to make "cud," which is then chewed again by the ruminant animals. Therefore an increased consumption of these nonruminant animals can lead to reductions of greenhouse gases, methane more specifically.

6. Adaptation Strategies in Changes in Ocean Environments

Besides the land-based ecosystems, ocean ecosystems and biogeochemistry will be altered as a result of global warming (Denman et al., 2007). Ocean temperature will rise; sea level will rise; ocean currents such as thermohaline circulation may slow down; ocean oscillations such as El Niño Southern Oscillation, Atlantic Multidecadal Oscillation, and Pacific Decadal Oscillation may be altered; ocean salinity and oxygen level can be altered; fisheries catch and distribution will be altered under warmer oceans (Pratchett et al., 2011; Cheung et al., 2013); conditions for genesis, frequency, intensity of hurricanes will be altered (Emanuel, 2005, 2008).

One of the communities that will be affected strongly from global warming is low-lying coastal zones, especially in the low latitude. A coastal community in the United States is likely to have resources to make whatever efficient decisions and implement them to cope with the sea level rise and changes in hurricane frequency and intensity (Yohe and Schlesinger, 1998; Nicholls et al., 2007). It may decide to build sea walls collectively as a community or retreat from the vulnerable coastal zones. There is no doubt that such decisions will have carbon emissions implications, even though how much can be debated.

Particularly vulnerable are those coastal communities in South Asia, e.g., Bangladesh, India, Myanmar, and Sri Lanka. In these nations from 1990 to 2014, a tropical storm killed on average 4000 people annually but a single tropical cyclone often killed more than 10,000 people and sometimes 100,000 people about once per decade (Seo and Bakkensen, 2016). Besides hurricane intensity indicators such as wind speeds and central minimum pressure, the large number of fatalities arises because of low-lying lands, high population density, and low income in these countries.

Although fewer hurricanes hit annually South Asian nations than other parts of the world, the number of cyclone fatalities is more than two orders of magnitude larger there than in the advanced countries such as the United States and Australia (Seo, 2015b). Unlike other parts of the world, a large number of people in these countries die because of high storm surge, in addition to high hurricane intensity (Seo and Bakkensen, 2017).

Adaptation measures and strategies have been effective in reducing the number of fatalities from tropical cyclones and will play critical roles in future adaptations under a warmer world (Paul, 2009; Seo, 2015b; Seo and Bakkensen, 2016). One of the options is to build a wall of forests in a polder structure, along the coastal lines that are often inundated by sea surges (Seo, 2017b). At present, some areas are effectively protected by mangrove forests. A polder planted with carbon-absorbing trees or seagrass meadows would fend off storm surges during tropical cyclone events. The forest polder has the advantage of giving protection to coastal communities both from storm winds and from storm surges.

Adapting through the forest or seagrass polder leads to the additional benefit of increased carbon absorption through the forest of trees or seagrass meadows. For a reference, California red woods (Sequoia) planted on 1 ha of land may absorb as much as 2600 metric tons of carbon, whereas ancient conifer forests and Australian eucalyptus store about 1000 metric tons of carbon on the same size land (Kindermann et al., 2008; Van Pelt et al., 2016). Carbon absorption by seagrass meadows may result in as much as 27,000 g of carbon per square meter (Rohr et al., 2016).

The polder with trees or seagrass meadows can survive occasional inundations from the sea surge while coastal communities can take the benefit of fruits and other tree products produced within the polder. With the protective polder system, currently fertile lands along the low-lying coastal zones, e.g., the fertile Bangladesh Delta, which is currently used mainly for rice and jute productions, can be continued to be utilized for the same purposes by coastal residents.

The polder of forests or seagrass meadows can be seen as one option for protecting the coastal zones by building a special protective structure. Another structure that is more often discussed is a dam structure, which could be built considering geographic and hydrologic conditions of a coastal region. In addition to protecting from the sea surge or sea level rise, a coastal dam may be utilized for hydroelectric energy production. It may be utilized as a desalination plant from which salty water is processed and provided to various users for growing grasslands and trees, which absorb carbon. Furthermore, it may have the potential to be utilized for the facility to experiment on ocean iron fertilization through which carbon can be absorbed by microscopic phytoplanktons (Martin et al., 1994; Weier, 2001; Smetacek et al., 2012).

Coastal communities that are threatened by changes in the climate system certainly have the incentive to build one or more of these protective structures. However, because of substantial cost, some communities can take a less expensive option such as relocation, i.e., retreat from a costal line. For other communities, a timely evacuation temporarily may turn out to be the best option, making use of early predictions and warning systems.

A shift in ocean climate is predicted to affect fisheries and aquaculture around the world (Cochrane et al., 2009). An increase in the total fish catch due to a warmer ocean is projected by some researchers (Pratchett et al., 2011). Furthermore, changes in the distribution of fish catch may occur, e.g., an increase in the fish catch in high-latitude oceans and a decrease in the fish catch in low-latitude oceans (Cheung et al., 2010).

These changes may result in major changes in food consumption of the world population. For example, it may mean a decrease in grain/meat consumption, which is offset by an increase in fish consumption. This may reduce the amount of carbon emissions from cultivating soils and managing animals. On the other hand, this may increase the amount of carbon emissions by an increased energy production for fisheries.

Coastal and ocean adaptation measures and strategies would again have consequences on carbon abatement efforts (Seo, 2016b). A polder with forests or seagrass meadows would absorb carbon dioxide; increased grasslands and forests from water provided by a desalination plant would capture carbon dioxide; an ocean fertilization facility may be used to increase the capacity to absorb carbon by the ocean; an increase in hydroelectric energy production would lower the demand for energy produced from fossil fuels, reducing the amount of emissions of carbon dioxide from energy production; an increase in fish consumption, which replaces grain consumption, may result in the reduction of carbon emissions.

7. A Time Line of Adaptation Paradigm With Mitigation Potentials

Adaptation measures and strategies must be timely adopted over the course of time in response to and in anticipation of a gradually rising temperature and gradual changes in existing local precipitation patterns. In addition, some of the future adaptation options described in this chapter have not yet been materialized as a practical and competitive option, e.g., a nuclear fusion technology or a climate engineering technology.

In Table 6.2, the author tabulates the aforementioned adaptation measures and strategies by the time of adoption and an economic agent who adopts them: individuals and communities, consumers, businesses, power plants, natural resource enterprises, coastal and ocean communities, and local and federal governments.

Table 6.2 assumes that the phenomena of global warming will unfold throughout the 21st century with an ever higher global temperature and changes in precipitation patterns. Table 6.2 also assumes that at some point in the 21st century, local and federal governments should intervene directly and indirectly in the adaptation paradigm of the society, which may call for levying penalties on heavy carbon emitters. The penalty may be charged on the grounds of the observed harmful effects to other constituents of the relevant municipality if such harms should become more evident and larger in the coming decades.

As can be seen from the time line of adaptation strategies in the table, the adaptation paradigm takes advantage of technological advances over the course of the 21st century. Novel technologies such as a carbon-capture-storage, climate engineering, solar energy, and nuclear fusion are expected to play major roles in the adaptation paradigm. These technologies are shown to be relied upon in the latter half of the 21st century as a dominant adaptation strategy. That is, these technologies need not be applied at a large scale immediately or in the near future.

Furthermore, the adaptation paradigm makes use of the fundamental theory of public goods and the government's role to provide them (Samuelson, 1954; Baumol and Oates, 1988). Governments are expected to play a major role in pushing heavy carbon emitters to adopt carbon-abating measures and strategies in the production processes in the latter half of this century. However, governments need not play a forceful role right now. For now and in the near future, governments are envisioned to play soft roles in developing collaborative partnerships with private individuals and sectors in adaptation efforts.

How much carbon can be abated by the realizations of the adaptation paradigm through the course of time as a global climate change policy? The author provides rough estimates of mitigation potentials by the time frame of short term, medium term, and long term in Table 6.3 based on the existing climate literature.

Table 6.2 A Time Line of the Adaptation Paradigm by Climate Actors

Climate Actors	Short-Term: Within a Decade	Medium-Term: In a Half Century	Long-term: In a Century
Individuals and communities	1. Increases in energy-saving efforts, e.g., turning off lights, taking public transportations, reducing indoor temperature in winter	1. Migration into forested zones	
Consumers	1. Increases in adoptions of new lighting appliances such as CFLs and LEDs; 2. Increases in purchases of higher-mileage cars; 3. Replace HFCs in refrigerators, air-conditioners, etc.	1. Increases in purchases of hybrid, electric, hydrogen vehicles; 2. An increase in consumption of nonruminant meats; 3. Increases in purchases of low-carbon energy, e.g., solar energy	
Businesses	1. An increase in forest cover by property developers; 2. Improvements in energy efficiency in the energy system through, e.g., smart grid (Joskow (2012) and Sims et al. (2007))	1. Increases in sea water treatment, which is directed to grasslands and forest managements; 2. Set up carbon-capture-storage facilities	
Power plants	1. Use of cleaner, high-quality coals; 2. Transitions to natural gas—fired power productions (Krupnick et al. (2013) and Brandt et al. (2014))	1. Increases in low-carbon energy generations, such as nuclear, solar, wind, geothermal; 2. Increases in hydroelectric energy generation due to rainfall increase; 3. Increases in carbon-capture-and-storage facilities	1. Nuclear fusion energy generations (ITER 2015)
Natural resource enterprises	1. Increases in grassland managements; 2. Increases in forestry activities; 3. Increases in soil carbon conservation techniques	1. Methane emissions reductions from cattle and other ruminants;	1. Frozen lands turned into

		2. Prevention and cure of livestock diseases (Aksoy et al. (2014)); 3. Expansion of grasslands and forests resulting from precipitation increase	grasslands and vegetation
Coastal and ocean communities	1. Construct a polder of forests and seagrass meadows on coastal lands	1. Construct a dam structure and use it for hydroelectric energy production; 2. Construct a dam structure for desalinization plants for vegetation growth; 3. Increased fish consumption	1. Construct a structure for ocean fertilization
Local and federal governments	1. Disseminate knowledge and expertise on adaptation; 2. Manage public natural resources optimally; 3. Communicate across stakeholders	1. Penalty on heavy carbon emitters; 2. Afforestation and reforestation on public lands	1. Climate engineering, e.g., solar reflection; 2. Carbon capture and storage

CFL, compact fluorescent lamp; HFC, hydrofluorocarbon; LED, light-emitting diode.

Table 6.3 **Approximate Abatement Targets in the Adaptation Paradigm**

	Short-Term: Within a Decade	**Medium-Term: In Half a Century**	**Long-Term: In a Century**
Approximate abatement targets	15% of baseline emissions	50% of baseline emissions	90% of baseline emissions
Ad hoc evidence	Houghton (2008), Denman et al. (2007), USEPA (2011), Soussana et al. (2010), Van Pelt et al. (2016)	Ainsworth and Long (2005), USEPA (2006), NRC (2013b), MIT (2015) Nordhaus (2008), Smith et al. (2008), Lackner et al. (2012), Akasaki et al. (2014), EC (2016)	Owe to backstop technologies: Nordhaus (1994), MIT (2003, 2015), Lackner et al. (2012), ITER (2015) NRC (2015)

In the short term, the adaptation paradigm is predicted to cut annually 15% of the greenhouse gas emissions from the baseline economy, i.e., the economy without any climate adaptations and any policy interventions. In other words, the baseline economy is a business-as-usual economy. In the medium term, the projected mitigation potential is 50% reduction of carbon from the baseline economy's emissions. In the long term, which sets in 100 years later, the adaptation paradigm is projected to achieve 90% reduction of the greenhouse gas emissions from the baseline economy.

Although these projections are the author's one-person committee assessment at least at the moment, it is possible that future studies can validate and provide accurate projections of these mitigation potentials. Furthermore, these estimates are not arbitrarily provided. The short-term estimates are based on the mitigation efforts of international communities in the recent decades (Denman et al., 2007; Houghton, 2008; Soussana et al., 2010; GCP, 2014; US EPA, 2011; Van Pelt et al., 2016).

The medium-term projection is approximately in the range of international ambitions for greenhouse gas mitigations as expressed in Intended Nationally Determined Commitments (INDC) in the Paris Agreements (UNFCCC, 2015). For example, the US commitment is 26% reduction by 2025 from the 2005 level of emissions of carbon dioxide, whereas neither India nor China provides a specific INDC target. There is no INDC commitment by any country beyond 2030.

The midterm projection is based on ecosystem sinks, agricultural sinks, forestry sinks, new lighting methods, solar energy, electric vehicles, replacements of HFCs, improved fuel economy standards, carbon capture, and carbon penalty available from various sources (USEPA, 2006; NRC, 2013b, 2015; Nordhaus, 2008; Lackner et al., 2012; Akasaki et al., 2014; McConnell, 2013; EC, 2016).

The long-term projection is owed to the backstop technology, an energy source that can provide energy at a fixed cost indefinitely and without carbon emissions (Nordhaus, 1994). It might be nuclear fusion, solar energy, nuclear fission, or climate engineering techniques (MIT, 2015; ITER, 2015; NRC, 2015).

With the unfolding of the adaptation paradigm throughout this century as suggested in Table 6.2, a trajectory of the emission control rate will be materialized as that in Fig. 6.4. The rate of control at the present time stands at around 10% from the baseline economy emissions, i.e., the amount of emissions in the business-as-usual economy. Over the next century, the control rate will rise gradually decade by decade to reach about 50% reduction from the baseline in about five decades. It will reach about 90% reduction from the baseline economy emissions in a century. The emission control rate will remain above 90% through the 22nd century and increase incrementally decade by decade.

Will the projected reductions of greenhouse gases according to the trajectory of emission control rate in Fig. 6.4 be sufficient to prevent a dangerous global warming that results in a global catastrophic event (Weitzman, 2009; Nordhaus, 2011; Titley et al., 2016)? Can catastrophic events such as a runaway global warming, a halt in the global thermohaline circulation, and an ocean anoxia (devoid of oxygen) be prevented through the adaptation paradigm (Mann et al., 1999; Lenton et al., 2008)?

The answer is positive. The grounds for the positive answer come from both scientific assessments and economic assessments. Among the Representative Concentration Pathway scenarios relied upon by the IPCC, these projected reductions in greenhouse gas emissions likely correspond to a mild increase or a weak increase scenario of

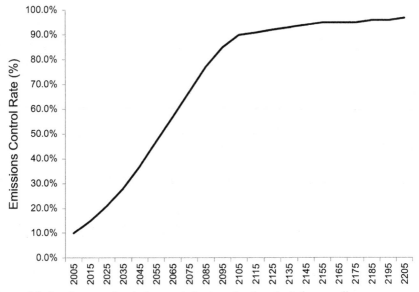

Figure 6.4 A trajectory of emission control rate under the adaptation paradigm.

carbon concentration (IPCC, 2014a). In this mild scenario by the IPCC, global temperature is projected to stay below a 2°C increase from the long-term climate.

As far as economic assessments are concerned, the Integrated Assessment Models of climate change policy, such as the DICE/RICE, MERGE, and others, predict that the projected emissions reduction schedule of Fig. 6.4 would lead to temperature increases around 2°C by the end of this century (Nordhaus, 1994, 2013; Manne et al., 1995).

The author plugged the trajectory of emission control rate shown in Fig. 6.4 into the modified DICE/RICE model and simulated the trajectory of global average temperature through the next two centuries (Nordhaus, 2013; Nordhaus and Sztorc, 2013). For the modified DICE/RICE model, refer to Chapter 4, which provided the full description of the model and outcomes. As shown in Fig. 6.5, the global average temperature or global normal climate is projected to rise gradually at a decreasing rate to peak at around 2.5°C above the 20th century average temperature by the end of this century and thereafter start declining incrementally over the 22nd century. By the end of the 22nd century, the global temperature increase is projected to fall below 2°C.

Under this trajectory of global temperature, the world will fend off challenges of global warming, including many catastrophic events mentioned earlier (Broecker, 1997; Mann et al., 1999; Meyer and Kump, 2008; Weitzman, 2009; NRC, 2013a). Agricultural and natural resource sectors will be able to adjust an array of practices and systems given the rate of change in global average temperature and associated changes in climate risk (Mendelsohn et al., 1994; Adams et al., 1999; Seo, 2016a,d,e).

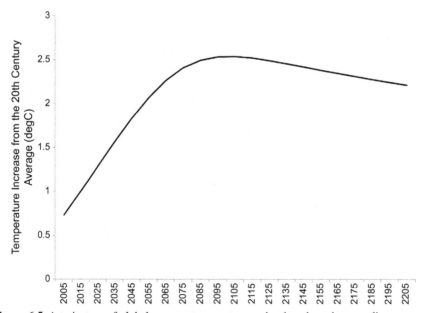

Figure 6.5 A trajectory of global average temperature under the adaptation paradigm.

Many sectors of the global economy and numerous regions of the world will experience the impacts of global warming and there will be winners and losers, but the aggregate impact on the global economy will be modest given the rate of change shown in Fig. 6.5 (Mendelsohn et al., 2006; Tol, 2009).

8. Conclusion

This chapter provided a full account of the adaptation paradigm for global warming policy making as an alternative conceptual policy framework. In the adaptation paradigm, economic agents make decisions simultaneously on both adaptive responses to the changes brought about by global warming and consequences of their actions on greenhouse gas emissions and global warming. An individual acts in consideration of private benefits and costs of available options in making adaptation decisions. After presenting the conceptual foundation of the adaptation paradigm and contrasting it with other policy approaches, the author described, based on the empirical adaptation research literature, an array of adaptation portfolios pertinent to economic sectors and climate actors tailored to certain contexts and time periods.

With a number of qualifying statements and additional clarifications, the author is ready to close this key chapter of the book. First, that an individual does not have an incentive to reduce voluntarily greenhouse gas emissions must be heeded and comprehended carefully. The adaptation paradigm sees that, in certain activities and enterprises, there is a strong incentive to take various adaptive measures to cope with changes in the climate system (Mendelsohn, 2000; Seo, 2006, 2015a). Adaptation behaviors in agricultural and natural resource enterprises are presented in this chapter as representative examples of adaptation changes attributable to changes in such private incentives. In these enterprises, changes in behaviors by individuals to cope with changes in the climate system result in changes in greenhouse gas emissions. That is, an adaptation decision has consequences on carbon emissions and abatements by an agricultural and natural resource manager. In certain situations, a natural resource manager will most likely take an adaptation strategy that will also reduce greenhouse gas emissions from a natural resource enterprise (Seo, 2015c). Increases in economic activities based on grasslands and forests, natural gas—fired power plants, hydroelectric power productions, and seagrass meadows are some of the examples highlighted throughout this chapter.

Second, such adaptation changes with carbon-reducing consequences can be enhanced by technological innovations and breakthroughs. In the adaptation paradigm, incremental technological innovations play a major role in global warming policy efforts. This means that technological uncertainties that are deemed very large with regard to breakthrough technologies, such as nuclear fusion and climate engineering, are made less of critical importance in the adaptation paradigm (NRC, 2015). Methane capture technologies, various improvements in the energy grid system, new lighting methods such as the LEDs, replacing HFCs with hydrocarbons as a coolant for air conditioners and refrigerators, and advances in electric vehicles are some examples of such incremental technological innovations.

Third, the adaptation paradigm elucidates and reinterprets the role of governments in the global warming policy making. The governments still play an important role, but a much softer role especially in the near and medium terms. In the adaptation paradigm, the governments do not attempt to design, implement, and monitor an economy-wide price or quantity regulation (Nordhaus, 1994; Stavins, 2007). Rather, the governments coordinate exchanges of information and technologies, manage public resources, and nudge individuals and enterprises to adopt climate-friendly practices. In the longer term, however, governments are envisioned in the adaptation paradigm to play a more forceful role such as charging heaviest polluters to protect or compensate victims from climate change in a high degree warming future.

This chapter also answered some of the important policy questions with regard to global warming. Among them are whether and how societies will cope with extremes and catastrophic climatic changes; whether the adaptation paradigm will be effective in preventing such dangerous consequences of global warming; and what roles and responsibilities different climate actors such as individuals, communities, businesses, public sectors, and international communities should bear.

The author leaves out discussions of the roles of international communities from this chapter because the next chapter is entirely devoted to international negotiations on global warming. The history of international policy negotiations and numerous international organizational frameworks created by such negotiations will be reviewed in the historical contexts. The author will also offer a number of prospects of and suggestions for future international policy negotiations and research collaborations.

References

Adams, R., McCarl, B.A., Segerson, K., Rosenzweig, C., Bryant, K., Dixon, B.L., Conner, R., Evenson, R.E., Ojima, D., 1999. The economic effects of climate change on US agriculture. In: Mendelsohn, R., Neumann, J. (Eds.), The Impact of Climate Change on the United States Economy. Cambridge University Press, Cambridge.

Ainsworth, E.A., Long, S.P., 2005. What have we learned from 15 years of free-air CO_2 enrichment (FACE)? A meta-analysis of the responses of photosynthesis, canopy properties and plant production to rising CO_2. New Phytologist 165, 351–372.

Akasaki, I., Amano, H., Nakamura, S., 2014. Blue LEDs – Filling the World with New Light. Nobel Prize Lecture. The Nobel Foundation, Stockholm. Available at: http://www.nobelprize.org/nobel_prizes/physics/laureates/2014/popular-physicsprize2014.pdf.

Aksoy, S., Attardo, G., et al., 2014. Genome sequence of the tsetse fly (*Glossina* morsitans): vector of African trypanosomiasis. Science 344, 380–386.

Baethgen, W.E., 1997. Vulnerability of agricultural sector of Latin America to climate change. Climate Research 9, 1–7.

Baumol, W.J., Oates, O.A., 1988. The Theory of Environmental Policy, second ed. Cambridge University Press, Cambridge.

Brandt, A.R., Heath, G.A., Kort, E.A., O'Sullivan, F., Petron, G., et al., 2014. Methane leaks from North American natural gas systems. Science 343 (6172), 733–735.

Broecker, W.S., 1997. Thermohaline circulation, the Achilles heel of our climate system: will man-made CO_2 upset the current balance? Science 278, 1582−1588.

Cheung, W., Lam, V., Sarmiento, J., Kearney, K., Watson, R., Zeller, D., Pauly, D., 2010. Large scale redistribution of maximum fisheries catch in the global ocean under climate change. Global Change Biology 16 (1), 24−35.

Cheung, W.L., Watson, R., Pauly, D., 2013. Signature of ocean warming in global fisheries catch. Nature 497, 365−368.

Coase, R., 1960. The problem of social costs. Journal of Law and Economics 3, 1−44.

Crowther, T.W., Glick, H.B., Covey, K.R., et al., 2015. Mapping tree density at a global scale. Nature 525, 201−205.

Denman, K.L., Brasseur, G., Chidthaisong, A., Ciais, P., Cox, P.M., Dickinson, R.E., Hauglustaine, D., Heinze, C., Holland, E., Jacob, D., Lohmann, U., Ramachandran, S., da Silva Dias, P.L., Wofsy, S.C., Zhang, X., 2007. Couplings between changes in the climate system and biogeochemistry. In: Solomon, S., et al. (Eds.), Climate Change 2007: The Physical Science Basis. The Fourth Assessment Report of the Intergovernmental Panel on Climate Change. Cambridge University Press, Cambridge.

Dube, S.K., Jain, I., Rao, A.D., Murty, T.S., 2009. Storm surge modelling for the Bay of Bengal and Arabian Sea. Natural Hazards 51, 3−27.

Ellerman, A.D., Buchner, B.K., 2007. The European Union emissions trading scheme: origins, allocations, and early results. Review of Environmental Economics and Policy 1, 66−87.

Emanuel, K., 2005. Increasing destructiveness of tropical cyclones over the past 30 years. Nature 436, 686−688.

Emanuel, K., 2008. The hurricane-climate connection. Bulletin of the American Meteorological Society 89, ES10−ES20.

European Commission (EC), 2015. Carbon Market Report 2015. EC, Brussels.

European Commission (EC), 2016. Climate-Friendly Alternatives to HFCs and HCFCs. EC, Brussels, Belgium. Available at: http://ec.europa.eu/clima/policies/f-gas/alternatives/index_en.htm.

FAO Fisheries and Aquaculture Technical Paper. No. 530. In: Cochrane, K., Young, C.D., Soto, D., Bahri, T. (Eds.), 2009. Climate change implications for fisheries and aquaculture: overview of current scientific knowledge. FAO, Rome.

Gerber, P.J., Steinfeld, H., Henderson, B., Mottet, A., Opio, C., Dijkman, J., Falcucci, A., Tempio, G., 2013. Tackling Climate Change Through Livestock − A Global Assessment of Emissions and Mitigation Opportunities. Food and Agriculture Organization of the United Nations (FAO), Rome.

Global Carbon Project, 2014. Global Carbon Budget 2014. Available at: http://cdiac.ornl.gov/GCP/.

Hahn, G.L., 1981. Housing and management to reduce climate impacts on livestock. Journal of Animal Science 52, 175−186.

Hahn, G.L., Gaughan, J.B., Mader, T.L., Eigenberg, R.A., 2009. Thermal indices and their applications for livestock environments (Chapter 5). In: DeShazer, J.A. (Ed.), Livestock Energetics and Thermal Environmental Management. ASABE. Copyright 2009 American Society of Agricultural and Biological Engineers, St. Joseph, Mich., pp. 113−130

Hanemann, W.M., 2000. Adaptation and its management. Climatic Change 45, 511−581.

Hansen, J., Sato, M., Reudy, R., Lo, K., Lea, D.W., Medina-Elizade, M., 2012. Perception of climate change. In: Proc.Natl. Acad. Sci. USA, vol. 109, pp. E2415−E2423. http://dx.doi.org/10.1073/pnas.1205276109.

Heal, G., 2010. Reflections: the economics of renewable energy in the United States. Review of Environmental Economics and Policy 4, 139–154.

Hope, C., 2006. The marginal impact of CO_2 from PAGE2002: an integrated assessment model incorporating the IPCC's five reasons for concern. The Integrated Assessment Journal 6, 19–56.

Houghton, R.A., 1999. The annual net flux of carbon to the atmosphere from changes in land use 1850–1990. Tellus 51B, 298–313.

Houghton, R.A., 2008. Carbon flux to the atmosphere from land-use changes: 1850–2005. In: TRENDS: A Compendium of Data on Global Change. Carbon Dioxide Information Analysis Center. Oak Ridge National Laboratory, U.S. Department of Energy, Oak Ridge, TN.

International Energy Agency (IEA), 2013. Technology Roadmap: Carbon Capture and Storage. IEA, Paris, France.

Intergovernmental Panel on Climate Change (IPCC), 1990. Climate Change: The IPCC Scientific Assessment. Cambridge University Press, Cambridge.

Intergovernmental Panel on Climate Change (IPCC), 2005a. Special Report on Safeguarding the Ozone Layer and the Global Climate System: Issues Related to Hydrofluorocarbons and Perfluorocarbons. Cambridge University Press, Cambridge.

Intergovernmental Panel on Climate Change (IPCC), 2005b. Special Report on Carbon Dioxide Capture and Storage. Cambridge University Press, Cambridge.

Intergovernmental Panel on Climate Change (IPCC), 2011. Special Report on Renewable Energy Sources and Climate Change Mitigation. Cambridge University Press, Cambridge.

Intergovernmental Panel on Climate Change (IPCC), 2014a. Climate Change 2013: The Physical Science Basis. The Fifth Assessment Report of the IPCC. Cambridge University Press, Cambridge.

Intergovernmental Panel on Climate Change (IPCC), 2014b. Climate Change 2014: Impacts, Adaptation, and Vulnerability. The Fifth Assessment Report of the IPCC. Cambridge University Press, Cambridge.

Intergovernmental Panel on Climate Change (IPCC), 2014c. Climate Change 2014: Mitigation of Climate Change. The Fifth Assessment Report of the IPCC. Cambridge University Press, Cambridge.

International Thermonuclear Experimental Reactor (ITER), 2015. ITER: The World's Largest Tokamak. Available at: https://www.iter.org/mach.

Joskow, P.L., 2012. Creating a smarter U.S. electricity grid. Journal of Economic Perspectives 26 (1), 29–48.

Joskow, P.L., 2013. Natural gas: from shortages to abundance in the United States. American Economic Review 103 (3), 338–343.

Joyce, L.A., Mills, J.R., Heath, L.S., McGuire, A.D., Haynes, R.W., Birdsey, R.A., 1995. Forest sector impacts from changes in forest productivity under climate change. Journal of Biogeography 22, 703–713.

Kindermann, G., Obersteiner, M., Sohngen, B., Sathaye, J., Andrasko, K., Rametsteiner, E., Schlamadinger, B., Wunder, S., Beach, R., 2008. Global cost estimates of reducing carbon emissions through avoided deforestation. Proceedings of the National Academy of Science 105, 10302–10307.

Krupnick, A., Wang, Z., Wang, Y., 2013. Sector Effects of the Shale Gas Revolution in the United States. Resources For the Future Discussion Paper. RFF, Washington DC.

Lackner, K.S., Ziock, H.J., Grimes, P., 1999. Carbon dioxide extraction from air: is it an option?. In: Proceedings of the 24th International Conference on Coal Utilization & Fuel Systems. Florida, Clearwater.

Lackner, K.S., Brennana, S., Matter, J.M., Park, A.A., Wright, A., Zwaan, B.V., 2012. The urgency of the development of CO_2 capture from ambient air. Proceedings of the National Academy of Sciences 109 (33), 13156–13162.

Lenton, T.M., Held, H., Kriegler, E., Hall, J.W., Lucht, W., Rahmstorf, S., Schellnhuber, H.J., 2008. Tipping elements in the earth's climate system. Proceedings of National Academy of Science 105, 1786–1793.

Mann, M.E., Bradley, R.S., Hughes, M.K., 1999. Northern hemisphere temperatures during the past millennium: inferences, uncertainties, and limitations. Geophysical Research Letters 26, 759–762.

Manne, A.S., Mendelsohn, R., Richels, R., 1995. MERGE – a model for evaluating regional and global effects of GHG reduction policies. Energy Policy 23 (1), 17–34.

Markowitz, H., 1952. Portfolio selection. Journal of Finance 7, 77–91.

Markowitz, H., 1959. Portfolio Selection: Efficient Diversification of Investments. John Wiley & Sons, New York.

Martin, J.H., Coale, K.H., Johnson, K.S., Fitzwater, S.E., et al., 1994. Testing the iron hypothesis in ecosystems of the equatorial Pacific Ocean. Nature 371, 123–129.

Massachusetts Institute of Technology (MIT), 2003. The Future of Nuclear Power: An Interdisciplinary MIT Study. MIT, MA.

Massachusetts Institute of Technology (MIT), 2015. The Future of Solar Energy: An Interdisciplinary MIT Study. MIT, MA.

Matthews, E., 1983. Global vegetation and land use: new high-resolution data bases for climate studies. Journal of Climate and Applied Meteorology 22, 474–487.

McConnell, V., 2013. The New CAFE Standards: Are They Enough on Their Own? Resources For the Future Discussion Paper 13–14 RFF, Washington DC.

Meehl, G.A., Hu, A., 2006. Megadroughts in the Indian monsoon region and southwest North America and a mechanism for associated multidecadal Pacific sea surface temperature anomalies. Journal of Climate 19, 1605–1623.

Mendelsohn, R., 2000. Efficient adaptation to climate change. Climatic Change 45, 583–600.

Mendelsohn, R., 2012. The economics of adaptation to climate change in developing countries. Climate Change Economics 3, 1–21.

Mendelsohn, R., Nordhaus, W., Shaw, D., 1994. The impact of global warming on agriculture: a Ricardian analysis. American Economic Review 84, 753–771.

Mendelsohn, R., Dinar, A., Williams, L., 2006. The distributional impact of climate change on rich and poor countries. Environment and Development Economics 11, 1–20.

Meyer, K.M., Kump, L.R., 2008. Oceanic euxinia in earth history: causes and consequences. Annual Review of Earth and Planetary Sciences 36, 251–288.

Modigliani, F., Pogue, G.A., May–June 1974. An introduction to risk and return: concepts and evidence. Financial Analysts Journal 69–86.

Muller, N.Z., Mendelsohn, R., 2009. Efficient pollution regulation: getting the prices right. American Economic Review 99, 1714–1739.

Muller, N.A., Mendelsohn, R., Nordhaus, W., 2011. Environmental accounting for pollution in the United States economy. American Economic Review 101, 1649–1675.

National Research Council (NRC), 2013a. Abrupt Impacts of Climate Change: Anticipating Surprises. Committee on Understanding and Monitoring Abrupt Climate Change and Its Impacts. The National Academies Press, Washington DC.

National Research Council (NRC), 2013b. Transitions to Alternative Vehicles and Fuels. The National Academies Press, Washington DC.

National Research Council (NRC), 2015. Climate Intervention: Reflecting Sunlight to Cool Earth. Committee on Geoengineering Climate: Technical Evaluation and Discussion of Impacts. The National Academies Press, Washington DC.

National Centers for Environmental Information (NCEI), 2016. Climate Monitoring. National Oceanic and Atmospheric Administration (NOAA), US. Available at: http://www.ncdc. noaa.gov/climate-monitoring/.

Nicholls, R.J., Wong, P.P., Burkett, V.R., Codignotto, J.O., Hay, J.E., McLean, R.F., Ragoonaden, S., Woodroffe, C.D., 2007. Coastal systems and low-lying areas. In: Parry, M.L., Canziani, O.F., Palutikof, J.P., van der Linden, P.J., Hanson, C.E. (Eds.), Climate Change 2007: Impacts, Adaptation and Vulnerability. Contribution of Working Group II to the Fourth Assessment Report of the Intergovernmental Panel on Climate Change. Cambridge University Press, Cambridge, UK, pp. 315–356.

Nordhaus, W., 1994. Managing the Global Commons. MIT Press, Massachusetts.

Nordhaus, W.D., 2006. Paul Samuelson and global public goods. In: Szenberg, M., Ramrattan, L. (Eds.), Gottesman AA (2006) Samuelsonian Economics and the Twenty-First Century. Oxford Scholarship Online.

Nordhaus, W.D., 2008. A Question of Balance—Weighing the Options on Global Warming Policies. Yale University Press, New Haven.

Nordhaus, W., 2011. The economics of tail events with an application to climate change. Review of Environmental Economics and Policy 5, 240–257.

Nordhaus, W., 2013. The Climate Casino: Risk, Uncertainty, and Economics for a Warming World. Yale University Press, New Haven, CT.

Nordhaus, W., Sztorc, P., 2013. DICE 2013: Introduction and User's Manual. Yale University, New Haven.

Ostrom, E., 2009. Beyond Markets and States: Polycentric Governance of Complex Economic Systems. Nobel Lecture. The Royal Swedish Academy of the Sciences, Sweden.

Paul, B.K., 2009. Why relatively fewer people died? The case of Bangladesh's Cyclone Sidr. Natural Hazards 50, 289–304.

Pearce, D., Cline, W.R., Achanta, A., Fankhauser, S., Pachauri, R., Tol, R., Vellinga, P., 1996. The social costs of climate change: greenhouse damage and benefits of control. In: Bruce, J., Lee, H., Haites, E. (Eds.), Climate Change 1995: Economic and Social Dimensions of Climate Change. Cambridge University Press, Cambridge.

Pratchett, M.S., Munday, P.L., Graham, N.A.J., et al., 2011. Vulnerability of coastal fisheries in the tropical Pacific to climate change. In: Bell, J.D., Johnson, J.E., Hobday, A.J. (Eds.), Vulnerability of Tropical Pacific Fisheries and Aquaculture to Climate Change. Secretariat of the Pacific Community, Noumea, New Caledonia, pp. 493–573.

Rohr, M.E., Bostrom, C., Canal-Verges, P., Holmer, M., 2016. Blue carbon stocks in Baltic Sea eelgrass (*Zostera marina*) meadows. Biogeosciences 13, 6139–6153.

Rosenberg, N.J., 1992. Adaptation of agriculture to climate change. Climate Change 21, 385–405.

Samuelson, P., 1954. The pure theory of public expenditure. The Review of Economics and Statistics 36, 387–389.

Samuelson, P., 1955. Diagrammatic exposition of a theory of public expenditure. Review of Economics and Statistics 37, 350–356.

Schaefer, H., Fletcher, S.E.M., Veidt, C., et al., 2016. A 21st century shift from fossil-fuel to biogenic methane emissions indicated by $^{13}CH_4$. Science 352, 80–84.

Schlesinger, W.H., 1997. Biogeochemistry: An Analysis of Global Change, second ed. Academic Press, San Diego, CA.

Schmidt, G.A., Ruedy, R., Hansen, J.E., et al., 2005. Present day atmospheric simulations using GISS ModelE: comparison to in-situ, satellite and reanalysis data. Journal of Climate 19, 153—192.

Seo, S.N., 2006. Modeling Farmer Responses to Climate Change: Climate Change Impacts and Adaptations in Livestock Management in Africa (Ph.D. dissertation). Yale University, New Haven.

Seo, S.N., 2010a. Is an integrated farm more resilient against climate change?: a microeconometric analysis of portfolio diversification in African agriculture? Food Policy 35, 32—40.

Seo, S.N., 2010b. A microeconometric analysis of adapting portfolios to climate change: adoption of agricultural systems in Latin America. Applied Economic Perspectives and Policy 32, 489—514.

Seo, S.N., 2010c. Managing forests, livestock, and crops under global warming: a microeconometric analysis of land use changes in Africa. Australian Journal of Agricultural and Resource Economics 54 (2), 239—258.

Seo, S.N., 2011a. An analysis of public adaptation to climate change using agricultural water schemes in South America. Ecological Economics 70, 825—834.

Seo, S.N., 2011b. A geographically scaled analysis of adaptation to climate change with spatial models using agricultural systems in Africa. Journal of Agricultural Science 149, 437—449.

Seo, S.N., 2012a. Adapting natural resource enterprises under global warming in South America: a mixed logit analysis. Economia: Journal of the Latin American and Caribbean Economic Association 12, 111—135.

Seo, S.N., 2012b. Adaptation behaviors across ecosystems under global warming: a spatial microeconometric model of the rural economy in South America. Papers in Regional Science 91, 849—871.

Seo, S.N., 2012c. Decision making under climate risks: an analysis of sub-Saharan farmers' adaptation behaviors. Weather, Climate and Society 4, 285—299.

Seo, S.N., 2013a. An essay on the impact of climate change on US agriculture: weather fluctuations, climatic shifts, and adaptation strategies. Climatic Change 121, 115—124.

Seo, S.N., 2013b. Refining spatial resolution and spillovers of a microeconometric model of adapting portfolios to climate change. Mitigation and Adaptation Strategies for Global Change 18, 1019—1034.

Seo, S.N., 2014b. Coupling climate risks, eco-systems, anthropogenic decisions using South American and Sub-Saharan farming activities. Meteorological Applications 21, 848—858.

Seo, S.N., 2015a. Micro-Behavioral Economics of Global Warming: Modeling Adaptation Strategies in Agricultural and Natural Resource Enterprises. Springer, Cham, Switzerland.

Seo, S.N., 2015b. Fatalities of neglect: adapt to more intense hurricanes? International Journal of Climatology 35, 3505—3514.

Seo, S.N., 2015c. Adaptation to global warming as an optimal transition process to a greenhouse world. Economic Affairs 35, 272—284.

Seo, S.N., 2015d. Helping low-latitude, poor countries with climate change. Winter 2015—2016 Regulation (6—8).

Seo, S.N., 2015e. Adapting to extreme climates: raising animals in hot and arid ecosystems in Australia. International Journal of Biometeorology 59, 541—550.

Seo, S.N., 2016a. Modeling farmer adaptations to climate change in South America: a microbehavioral economic perspective. Environmental and Ecological Statistics 23, 1—21.

Seo, S.N., 2016b. A theory of global public goods and their provisions. Journal of Public Affairs 16, 394−405.

Seo, S.N., 2016c. Untold tales of goats in deadly Indian monsoons: adapt or rain-retreat under global warming? Journal of Extreme Events 3. http://dx.doi.org/10.1142/S2345737616500019.

Seo, S.N., 2016d. The micro-behavioral framework for estimating total damage of global warming on natural resource enterprises with full adaptations. Journal of Agricultural, Biological, and Environmental Statistics 21, 328−347.

Seo, S.N., 2016e. Microbehavioral Econometric Methods: Theories, Models, and Applications for the Study of Environmental and Natural Resources. Academic Press (Elsevier), Amsterdam.

Seo, S.N., 2017a. Adapting to a Monsoon Climate Regime in Sri Lanka Through Animal Husbandry. Working Paper, Muaebak Institute of Global Warming Studies, Seoul.

Seo, S.N., 2017b. Measuring Policy Benefits of the Cyclone Shelter Program in the North Indian Ocean: Protection from Intense Winds or High Storm Surges? Working Paper, Muaebak Institute of Global Warming Studies, Seoul.

Seo, S.N., Mendelsohn, R., Munasinghe, M., 2005. Climate change and agriculture in Sri Lanka: a Ricardian valuation. Environment and Development Economics 10, 581−596.

Seo, S.N., Mendelsohn, R., 2008. Measuring impacts and adaptations to climate change: a structural Ricardian model of African livestock management. Agricultural Economics 38, 151−165.

Seo, S.N., Mendelsohn, R., Dinar, A., Hassan, R., Kurukulasuriya, P., 2009. A Ricardian analysis of the distribution of climate change impacts on agriculture across Agro-Ecological Zones in Africa. Environmental and Resource Economics 43, 313−332.

Seo, S.N., McCarl, B., Mendelsohn, R., 2010. From beef cattle to sheep under global warming? An analysis of adaptation by livestock species choice in South America. Ecological Economics 69, 2486−2494.

Seo, S.N., Bakkensen, L.A., 2016. Did adaptation strategies work? High fatalities from tropical cyclones in the North Indian Ocean and future vulnerability under global warming. Natural Hazards 82, 1341−1355.

Seo, S.N., Bakkensen, L.A., 2017. Is tropical cyclone surge, not intensity, what kills so many people in South Asia? Weather, Climate, and Society 9, 71−81.

Shaw, M.R., Zavaleta, E.S., Chiariello, N.R., Cleland, E.E., Mooney, H.A., Field, C.B., 2002. Grassland responses to global environmental changes suppressed by elevated CO_2. Science 298, 1987−1990.

Sims, R.E.H., Schock, R.N., Adegbululgbe, A., Fenhann, J., Konstantinaviciute, I., Moomaw, W., Nimir, H.B., Schlamadinger, B., Torres-Martínez, J., Turner, C., Uchiyama, Y., Vuori, S.J.V., Wamukonya, N., Zhang, X., 2007. Energy supply. In: Climate Change 2007: Mitigation. The Fourth Assessment Report of the Intergovernmental Panel on Climate Change. Cambridge University Press, Cambridge.

Smetacek, V., Klaas, C., Strass, V.H., et al., 2012. Deep carbon export from a Southern Ocean iron-fertilized diatom bloom. Nature 487, 313−319.

Smith, P., Martino, D., Cai, Z., Gwary, D., Janzen, H., Kumar, P., McCarl, B., Ogle, S., O'Mara, F., Rice, C., Scholes, B., Sirotenko, O., Howden, M., McAllister, T., Pan, G., Romanenkov, V., Schneider, U., Towprayoon, S., Wattenbach, M., Smith, J., 2008. Greenhouse gas mitigation in agriculture. Philosophical Transactions of the Royal Society B 363, 789−813.

Sohngen, B., Mendelsohn, R., 1998. Valuing the impact of large-scale ecological change in a market: the effect of climate change on US timber. American Economic Review 88, 686−710.

Soussana, J.F., Tallec, T., Blanfort, V., 2010. Mitigating the greenhouse gas balance of ruminant production systems through carbon sequestration in grasslands. Animal 4, 334−350.

Stavins, R., 1998. What can we learn from the grand policy experiment? Lessons from SO_2 allowance trading. Journal of Economic Perspectives 12, 69−88.

Stavins, R., 2007. A US Cap-and-Trade System to Address Global Climate Change. Hamilton Project Discussion Paper 2007−13. The Brookings Institution, Washington, DC.

Thaler, R.H., Sunstein, C.R., 2009. Nudge: Improving Decisions About Health, Wealth and Happiness. Yale University Press, New Haven.

Tietenberg, T., 2013. Reflections - carbon pricing in practice. Review of Environmental Economics and Policy 7, 313−329.

Titley, D.W., Hegerl, G., Jacobs, K.L., Mote, P.W., Paciorek, C.J., Shepherd, J.M., Shepherd, T.G., Sobel, A.H., Walsh, J., Zwiers, F.W., Thomas, K., Everett, L., Purcell, A., Gaskins, R., Markovich, E., 2016. Attribution of Extreme Weather Events in the Context of Climate Change. National Academies of Sciences, Engineering, and Medicine. The National Academies Press, Washington DC.

Tol, R.S.J., 1997. On the optimal control of carbon dioxide emissions: an application of FUND. Environmental Modeling and Assessment 2, 151−163.

Tol, R., 2009. The economic effects of climate change. Journal of Economic Perspectives 23, 29−51.

Ueda, H., Iwai, A., Kuwako, K., Hori, M.E., 2006. Impact of anthropogenic forcing on the Asian summer monsoon as simulated by eight GCMs. Geophysical Research Letter 33. http://dx.doi.org/10.1029/2005gl025336.

United Nations Environmental Programme (UNEP), 2016. The Montreal Protocol on Substances that Deplete the Ozone Layer. UNEP, Kigali, Rwanda.

United Nations Framework Convention on Climate Change (UNFCCC), 1992. United Nations Framework Convention on Climate Change. New York.

United Nations Framework Convention on Climate Change (UNFCCC), 1998. Kyoto Protocol to the United Nations Framework Convention on Climate Change. UNFCCC, New York.

United Nations Framework Convention on Climate Change (UNFCCC), 2010. Cancun Agreements. UNFCCC, New York.

United Nations Framework Convention on Climate Change (UNFCCC), 2011a. The Durban Platform for Enhanced Action. UNFCCC, New York.

United Nations Framework Convention on Climate Change (UNFCCC), 2011b. Report of the Transitional Committee for the Design of Green Climate Fund. UNFCCC, New York.

United Nations Framework Convention on Climate Change (UNFCCC), 2015. The Paris agreement. In: Conference of the Parties (COP) 21. UNFCCC, New York.

United States Department of Energy (US DOE), 2016. How Energy Efficient Light Bulbs Compare with Traditional Incandescent. US DOE, Washington DC. Available at: http://energy.gov/energysaver/how-energy-efficient-light-bulbs-compare-traditional-incandescents.

United States Environmental Protection Agency (US EPA), 2006. Global Mitigation of Non-CO_2 Greenhouse Gases. US EPA, Washington DC.

United States Environmental Protection Agency (US EPA), 2011. Inventory of US Greenhouse Gas Emissions and Sinks: 1990−2009. US EPA, Washington, DC.

United States Environmental Protection Agency (US EPA), 2014. Carbon Pollution Emission Guidelines for Existing Stationary Sources: Electric Utility Generating Units. US EPA, Washington DC.

United States Environmental Protection Agency (US EPA), 2015. Inventory of US Greenhouse Gas Emissions and Sinks: 1990–2013. US EPA, Washington, DC.

United States Energy Information Administration (US EIA), 2014. Annual Energy Outlook 2014. US EIA, Department of Energy, Washington DC.

United States Energy Information Administration (US EIA), 2015. Monthly Power Sector Carbon Dioxide Emissions Reach 27-year Low in April. Today in Energy. US EIA, Department of Energy, Washington DC.

United States Energy Information Administration (US EIA), 2016. The World's Nine Largest Operating Power Plants Are Hydroelectric Facilities. Today in Energy. US EIA, Department of Energy, Washington DC.

Van Pelt, R., Sillett, S.C., Kruse, W.A., Freund, J.A., Kramer, R.D., 2016. Emergent crowns and light-use complementarity lead to global maximum biomass and leaf area in *Sequoia sempervirens* forests. Forest Ecology and Management 375, 279–308.

Vedeld, P., Angelsen, A., Sjaastad, E., Berg, G.K., 2004. Counting on the Environment – Forest Incomes and the Rural Poor. Environmental Economics Series, Paper # 98. World Bank, Washington DC.

Vedeld, P., Angelsen, A., Bojø, J., Sjaastad, E., Berg, G.K., 2007. Forest environmental incomes and the rural poor. Forest Policy and Economics 9, 869–879.

Wall Street Journal (WSJ), 2017. Scott Pruitt's Back-to- Basics Agenda for the EPA. By Strassel KA. On February 17, 2017. Available at: https://www.wsj.com/articles/scott-pruitts-back-to-basics-agenda-for-the-epa-1487375872.

Weier, J., 2001. John Martin (1935–1993). Earth Observatory. National Aeronautics and Space Administration (NASA), Washington DC.

Weitzman, M.L., 2009. On modeling and interpreting the economics of catastrophic climate change. Review of Economics and Statistics 91, 1–19.

White House, 2013. The President's Climate Action Plan. Executive Office of the President. The White House, Washington DC.

World Bank, 2008. World Development Report 2008: Agriculture for Development. World Bank, Washington DC.

World Resources Institute (WRI), 2005. World Resources 2005: The Wealth of the Poor: Managing Ecosystems to Fight Poverty. WRI, Washington DC.

Yohe, G.W., Schlesinger, M.E., 1998. Sea level change: the expected economic cost of protection or abandonment in the United States. Climatic Change 38, 337–342.

Further Reading

Nordhaus, W., 1992. An optimal transition path for controlling greenhouse gases. Science 258, 1315–1319.

Seo, S.N., 2014a. Evaluation of Agro-Ecological Zone methods for the study of climate change with micro farming decisions in sub-Saharan Africa. European Journal of Agronomy 52, 157–165.

Seo, S.N., 2014c. Adapting sensibly when global warming turns the field brown or blue: a comment on the 2014 IPCC Report. Economic Affairs 34, 399–401.

Negotiating a Global Public Good: Lessons From Global Warming Conferences and Future Directions

7

Chapter Outline

1.   Introduction

The final chapter of this book is devoted to international policy negotiations on global warming and climate change. The author aims to unravel both conceptual aspects of policy making on global public goods and empirical experiences on various policy instruments by the international community since the establishments of the Intergovernmental Panel on Climate Change (IPCC) in 1988 (IPCC, 1990).

At the conclusion of the 21st Conference of the Parties (COP) in Paris at the end of 2015, there emerged renewed enthusiasm toward a global cooperative climate change policy protocol as well as a number of new directions in global climate negotiations (UNFCCC, 2015). At one of the pivotal crossroads of international policy endeavors, the author will provide a review of historical climate change negotiations, with an emphasis on a critical examination of the frontiers of the not-a-few policy instruments

The Behavioral Economics of Climate Change. http://dx.doi.org/10.1016/B978-0-12-811874-0.00007-6

and agreements that emerged from the past conferences as well as their prospects in future conferences.

Global atmospheric temperature has risen steadily, with fluctuations, during the past century, and the 3 years of 2014, 2015, and 2016, according to many sources, are the hottest years in the historical record of global temperature available from 1880 as well as the highest years of carbon concentration since the 1950s when the measurement began (Keeling et al., 2005; NOAA, 2016).

Global policy efforts to address the trend of global temperature increase and the buildup of carbon dioxide in the atmosphere began in the late 1980s. In 1988, the United Nations (UN) and the World Meteorological Organization (WMO) jointly established the IPCC, which was soon followed by the establishment of the United Nations Framework Convention on Climate Change (UNFCCC) at the Rio de Janeiro Earth Summit in 1992 (IPCC, 1990; UNFCCC, 1992). The IPCC was intended as a scientific body that reports on the progresses in the science of climate change. On the other hand, the UNFCCC was intended to be an administrative body that oversees meetings and negotiations among the member nations on the policy measures that are aimed at addressing the problems of global warming.

One would be surprised to find out that these systematic and organizational efforts to deal with global warming began at the global stage even when there were so little done at the national level both in terms of scientific knowledge on global warming and climate policies adopted at the national level. This is despite the fact that a large basket of national laws and regulations on numerous environmental pollution problems were being designed and implemented at the national level by the early 1990s (US EPA, 2014; Tietenberg and Lewis, 2014).

This chapter provides a review of the international negotiations on climate change since the establishments of the two foundational institutions, the IPCC and the UNFCCC. Major works of the two institutions and critical concerns on these institutions are reviewed (IPCC, 1990, 1995, 2001, 2007, 2014). Major outcomes from the past 22 COPs are summarized, including those from the Rio Earth Summit, the Kyoto Protocol, the Copenhagen Accord, the Durban Platform, and the Paris Agreement (UNFCCC, 1992, 1998, 2009, 2010, 2011a, 2015).

A major international push to put into action the Paris Agreement, which is scheduled to enter into force in November 2016, by the "ratification" of countries covering 55% of the world greenhouse gas (GHG) emissions and be "enforced" from 2020 are under way (UNFCCC, 2015). This chapter critically reviews the agreements at the Paris COP with particular attention to the Intended Nationally Determined Contributions (INDCs), which were set voluntarily by participating nations and hence were varied widely across the countries.

Furthermore, one of the most important policy developments that emerged from the UN COPs is the creation of and conflicts around the Green Climate Fund (GCF) (UNFCCC, 2010, 2011b, 2015). Through the GCF, rich countries have promised to raise over US$100 billion annually to support adaptation and mitigation efforts in developing countries. This chapter summarizes the developments, unresolved issues, and future prospects with regards to the GCF.

Besides the international processes led by the IPCC and the UNFCCC, two international treaties have gained importance in international climate talks: the Montreal Protocol (UNEP, 2016) and the Carbon Offsetting and Reduction Scheme for International Aviation (ICAO, 2016). The former commits member countries to ban the use of Earth-heating hydrofluorocarbons (HFCs), a coolant in refrigerators and air conditioners. The latter commits member countries of the International Civil Aviation Organization (ICAO) to reduce GHG emissions from airplanes. These two treaties, which were agreed at the latter half of 2016 after the Paris Agreement, will be reviewed in this chapter.

This chapter comprises the following sections. Section 2 explains the institutional foundations for international negotiations of climate change: the IPCC and the UNFCCC. Section 3 summarizes the major outcomes from the most prominent COPs. Section 4 is devoted to the descriptions of the GCF. Section 5 explains other, mostly nonclimate, international treaties and agreements relevant to climate policy making. The chapter concludes with Section 6 with discussions of future directions of global warming negotiations.

2. Institutional Foundations

2.1 Intergovernmental Panel on Climate Change

Global policy efforts to deal with challenges of climate change and global warming began by the establishment of the IPCC in 1988. It was established jointly by the WMO and the United Nations Environmental Programme. The IPCC is intended as an international body that assesses the science of climate change (IPCC, 2016):

> The initial task for the IPCC…was to prepare a comprehensive review and recommendations with respect to the state of knowledge of the science of climate change; the social and economic impact of climate change, and possible response strategies and elements for inclusion in a possible future international convention on climate.

As of 2016, the IPCC has 195 members. Participation is open to all member countries of the WMO and the UN. The Panel, made up of representatives of the member states, meets in plenary sessions to take major decisions. The IPCC Bureau, elected by member governments, provides guidance to the Panel on the scientific and technical aspects of the Panel's work and advises the Panel on related management and strategic issues (IPCC, 2016).

The primary work of the IPCC is the publication of the assessment reports once every 5 years or so (IPCC, 1990, 1995, 2001, 2007, 2014). The assessment reports are written by hundreds of scientists who are classified into coordinating lead authors, lead authors, and contributing authors. The authors are selected in a way that the world major regions and member countries are all represented in a balanced way.

The IPCC assessment reports are prepared by three independent working groups. Working Group 1 is responsible for a report on the physical science basis of climate change. Working Group 2 is charged with a report on climate change impacts, adaptation, and vulnerability. Working Group 3 has responsibility for a report on mitigation of climate change.

One of the conspicuous issues in the publications of the IPCC reports has been the difficult task of coordinating a large number of authors/scientists, often thousands of them, to produce a single consensus document. Occasionally, it was reported that many authors of the report disagreed on a final draft. A finalized report was then criticized by the participating scientists as a political statement rather than a scientific consensus report. Some authors of the report are also reported to have withdrawn from the panel of authors citing irreconcilable differences.

The IPCC has published five sets of assessment reports since 1990: the first assessment report in 1990, the second in 1996, the third in 2001, the fourth in 2007, and the fifth in 2013 (IPCC, 1990, 1995, 2001, 2007, 2014). Each assessment report is composed of the three separate reports that are submitted by the aforementioned three working groups, in addition to a document entitled "Synthesis Report."

In addition to the assessment reports, the IPCC has published numerous special reports on various major aspects of climate change and policy. Published special reports are Aviation and Global Atmosphere in 1999 (IPCC, 1999); Land Use, Land-use Change, and Forestry in 2000 (IPCC, 2000a); Emissions Scenarios in 2000 (IPCC, 2000b); Safeguarding the Ozone Layer and the Global Climate System: Issues related to HydroFluoroCarbons and PerFluoroCarbons in 2005 (IPCC, 2005a); Carbon Dioxide Capture and Storage in 2005 (IPCC, 2005b); Renewable Energy Sources and Climate Change Mitigation in 2011 (IPCC, 2011); Managing the Risks of Extreme Events and Disasters to Advance Climate Change Mitigation in 2012 (IPCC, 2012).

With regards to the publications of the IPCC, a number of criticisms have been leveled (Chan et al., 2016). First, as pointed out earlier, whether there is indeed a consensus among a large number of authors in the report was occasionally questioned, as evidenced by the authors who withdrew. Some researchers noted that there are differences in the tones and contents of the three related documents of the same report: the summary for policy makers, the technical report, and the full report. The summary report for policy makers tends to be more politically and policy motivated and consequently obscures some of the details of the technical report and the full report.

Second, there has been little economic analysis across all the IPCC reports (Tol, 2016). In the second assessment report, the IPCC reported a chapter on the social costs of climate change and a chapter on intergenerational equity in Volume 3 of the report entitled "Economic Dimensions of Climate Change" (Pearce et al., 1996; Arrow et al., 1996). These chapters have since then become widely controversial. The IPCC dropped these chapters from the publications that followed. Furthermore, economic analyses of adaptation behaviors have been largely unreported by the IPCC reports (Seo, 2014, 2015b).

Third, the IPCC assessment report puts together a large number of articles and papers, but does not attempt to understand the differences and similarities among them. Especially, there has been little effort to synthesize them using, for example, an integrated assessment method. There is indeed a treasure trove of information in the IPCC assessment reports, but the trade-offs and conflicts among a large number of priorities and options are not largely attempted to be understood (Mendelsohn, 2016).

Fourth, the "Climategate" after the publication of the fourth assessment report by the IPCC gained much attention and media coverage (IPCC, 2007). The scandal revealed a number of cases that the findings that are scientifically weak or even baseless are reported. One example was the report on the Himalayan glaciers in which the assessment report, relying on an unpublished paper, concluded that the entire Himalayan glaciers will disappear completely in 20 years, i.e., by 2025.

2.2 United Nations Framework Convention on Climate Change

The UNFCCC is an international environmental treaty negotiated at the Earth Summit in Rio de Janeiro in 1992. As of May 2016, it has 197 members. Article 2 of the UNFCCC states that the objective of the treaty is "to stabilize greenhouse gas concentrations in the atmosphere at a level that would prevent dangerous anthropogenic interference with the climate system" (UNFCCC, 1992):

> *The ultimate objective of this Convention and any related legal instruments that the Conference of the Parties may adopt is to achieve, in accordance with the relevant provisions of the Convention, <u>stabilization of greenhouse gas concentrations in the atmosphere at a level that would prevent dangerous anthropogenic interference with the climate system</u>. Such a level should be achieved within a time-frame sufficient to allow ecosystems to adapt naturally to climate change, to ensure that food production is not threatened and to enable economic development to proceed in a sustainable manner.*

In Article 3 of the UNFCCC, principles of the convention are stated, which would become the recurring and contentious talking points between rich and poor countries in the 21 COPs held through the end of 2015. The article declares the "common but differentiated" responsibilities in addressing the global warming problems:

> *In their actions to achieve the objective of the Convention and to implement its provisions, the Parties shall be guided, inter alia, by the following: 1. The Parties should protect the climate system for the benefit of present and future generations of humankind, on the basis of equity and in accordance with their <u>common but differentiated responsibilities</u> and respective capabilities. Accordingly, the developed country Parties should take the lead in combating climate change and the adverse effects thereof.*

The parties of the convention regularly, normally annually, hold the COP to discuss and negotiate various policy instruments and issues on climate change. Of the 21 COPs held through the end of 2015, major progresses were made in Kyoto, Japan, in 1998; Bali, Indonesia, in 2007; Copenhagen, Denmark, in 2009; Cancun, Mexico, in 2010; Durban, South Africa, in 2011; and Paris, France, in 2015. The author will describe major outcomes from these COPs in the next section.

A major breakthrough in global climate negotiations was accomplished in Kyoto in 1998, which is known as the Kyoto Protocol. For the first time in human history, countries agreed to stabilize carbon dioxide emissions in a globally cooperative way. The document states that the goal of the international community is the "stabilization of the carbon dioxide emissions at 5% below the 1990 level" (UNFCCC, 1998).

The Kyoto Protocol formally excludes developing countries, including China and India, from the legal responsibility of reducing emissions of carbon dioxide. The United States initially agreed to the Kyoto Protocol, but the US Congress did not ratify it because of the exclusions of developing countries, primarily China, from abatement responsibilities. The Kyoto Protocol entered into force, however, by the ratification of Russia, which put the fraction of the world emissions of carbon dioxide covered by the ratified countries to over 55% of the world total (UNFCCC, 2005).

The first phase of the Kyoto Protocol was implemented during the 5-year period from 2008 to 2012. The second phase of the Kyoto Protocol failed to be agreed upon at the Copenhagen Conference in 2009, the first year of Mr. Obama's presidency in the United States (UNFCCC, 2007, 2009). The main cause of the failure was the disagreements between developed nations and developing nations on their respective responsibilities and financial supports to the developing nations (Nordhaus, 2010, 2011).

A major conceptual flaw in the Kyoto Protocol's approach was exposed early by concerned researchers. Specifically, the limit on the 5% below the 1990 level of carbon emissions lacked rational supports and favored certain countries against other countries (Manne and Richels, 1999; MacCraken et al., 1999; Nordhaus and Boyer, 1999; Victor, 2001). Especially, the countries with stagnant economies during the 1990s greatly benefited from the agreement, whereas the countries with fast growing economies during the 1990s such as the United States and China were disadvantaged from the Protocol's limit set at the 1990 level of carbon emissions (Nordhaus, 2001).

Through the implementation of the first phase of the Kyoto Protocol, the most serious defect of the Protocol turned out to be an insufficient and declining fraction of the world emissions of carbon covered by the parties that ratified the Protocol. Exclusions of China, India, and the United States from the Protocol meant that mitigation obligation under the Kyoto Protocol is largely limited to the European Union and Japan. The percentage of the world emissions covered by the European Union and Japan declined from around 40% in 1990s to only about 13% by the end of the first phase of the Kyoto Protocol in 2012 by the Kyoto Protocol enthusiasts (Nordhaus, 2010, 2011). During this time period, the economies of the United States, China, and India grew at a high rate, but the economies of the European Union and Japan grew at a much lower rate. As such, the fraction of the world carbon emissions accounted for by the latter had declined significantly.

Another flaw in the design of the Kyoto Protocol was exposed to be emissions leakage into nonparticipants (Ellerman and Buchner, 2007; Tietenberg, 2013). Although carbon emissions from the European Union had declined as a result of the implementation of the EU Emissions Trading System (ETS), it did not mean that the emissions-causing activities were reduced because the EU countries tended to increase imports of goods from non-EU countries where there is no carbon regulation.

As a consequence, carbon emissions increased in non-EU countries because of EU consumption activities.

Negotiations for the second phase of the Kyoto Protocol failed in the widely reported Copenhagen COP15 in 2009 (UNFCCC, 2009). Since then, many countries that ratified the Kyoto Protocol withdrew from the Protocol: Australia, Canada, Japan, and Russia. The Kyoto Protocol became defunct at the end of the first phase in 2012.

However, the efforts to produce a successor treaty to the Kyoto Protocol continued in the COPs subsequent to the Copenhagen COP, culminating in the Durban Platform for Enhanced Action in 2011 in Durban, South Africa (UNFCCC, 2011a). The Durban Platform holds on to the objective newly set in the Cancun COP a year earlier that the world should contain the global temperature increase to below 2°C. The Durban Platform is an agreement among the parties of the Convention that they will launch a negotiation process for an agreeable international framework that is legally binding to all member countries of the UNFCCC and in which all members share mitigation responsibilities, which should be presented for adoption by the members at the conference scheduled in Paris, France, at the end of 2015.

In Paris in December 2015, the COP21 produced a document called the "Paris Agreement" in which all member countries participated. It has been lauded as a landmark international agreement in which all nations of the globe agreed to take responsibility in reducing GHG emissions for the first time. However, the Paris Agreement is based on voluntary emission reduction pledges and there is no legal framework that can bind the members' voluntary pledges (UNFCCC, 2015). The Paris Agreement certainly saved the faces of international negotiators, but the truth is that it does have an even weaker legal framework than the Kyoto Protocol. At the same time, it can be said that it does little to address the difficult issues that plagued the previous COPs.

In another track in climate policy negotiations, the COPs increasingly recognized the importance of adaptation efforts over mitigation efforts. The Copenhagen Accord in 2009 states the need for the GCF, which was later established formally in Cancun in 2010 with the creation of the transitional committee for the GCF (UNFCCC, 2009, 2010). In 2011, the Durban COP adopted a governing instrument of the GCF (UNFCCC, 2011b). The World Bank was chosen as the temporary trustee of the GCF. Songdo city in South Korea, one of the five competing countries, was subsequently selected as the host city of the GCF secretariat (UNFCCC, 2012). The GCF has 24 board members, which are split equally between developed countries and developing countries, and is supported by the Secretariat of the GCF.

The GCF is intended to be a primary financial instrument of the UNFCCC established by financial contributions from developed nations to support adaptation and mitigation projects in developing countries. The size of the GCF contributions by rich countries was declared to be equivalent to $100 billion per annum (GCF, 2016).

In the next two sections, the author provides a review of the major agreements and remaining issues of the UNFCCC negotiation processes: the Kyoto Protocol, the Copenhagen Accord and Durban Platform, the Paris Agreement, and the GCF. Because the Kyoto Protocol is not functioning at present, the Paris Agreement and the GCF are the existing agreements and instruments by the UNFCCC, which will be highlighted throughout this review.

3. Major Outcomes From the COPs

In this section, the author provides a review of the major outcomes from the 21 COPs held through June 2016: the Kyoto Protocol, the Copenhagen Agreements and Durban Platform, and the Paris Agreement. A review of the GCF is provided in the next section.

3.1 Kyoto Protocol

Article 3 of the Kyoto Protocol to the UNFCCC announces a major breakthrough in international negotiations and states the important agreement among the parties of the conference at the COP held in Kyoto, Japan, in 1998 (UNFCCC, 1998):

> *The Parties…shall, individually or jointly, ensure that their aggregate anthropogenic carbon dioxide equivalent emissions of the greenhouse gases listed in Annex A do not exceed their assigned amounts, calculated pursuant to their quantified emission limitation and reduction commitments inscribed in Annex B and in accordance with the provisions of this Article, <u>with a view to reducing their overall emissions of such gases by at least 5 per cent below 1990 levels in the commitment period 2008 to 2012.</u>*

The GHGs listed in Annex A of the Protocol, mentioned in the aforesaid article, are carbon dioxide (CO_2), methane (CH_4), nitrous oxide (N_2O), HFCs, perfluorocarbons (PFCs), and sulfur hexafluoride (SF_6).

The Annex B nations mentioned in Article 3, i.e., Annex 1 nations in the UNFCCC document (UNFCCC, 1992), are listed in Table 7.1. The parties who signed the Kyoto Protocol are mostly European countries. Non-European parties are, among others, the United States and Canada in North America, Australia and New Zealand in Oceania, and Japan in East Asia. The US Congress did not ratify the Kyoto Protocol citing omission of China and India, so the United States has not been a party to the Protocol.

Article 25 of the Kyoto Protocol specifies the condition with which the Protocol enters into force:

> *This Protocol shall enter into force on the ninetieth day after the date on which not less than 55 Parties to the Convention, incorporating Parties included in Annex I which accounted in total for at least 55 per cent of the total carbon dioxide emissions for 1990 of the Parties included in Annex I, have deposited their instruments of ratification, acceptance, approval or accession.*

Although the US Congress did not ratify the Kyoto Protocol, it entered into force in 2005 with Russia's ratification of the Protocol by which the total emissions reduction commitment exceeded 55% of the total CO_2 emissions of industrialized nations in 1990. The first commitment period began in 2008 and ended in 2012.

Table 7.1 Annex B Nations in the Kyoto Protocol and Reduction Commitments

Europe		Europe: Countries in Transition to a Market Economy		Non-Europe	
Party	Emission Reduction Commitment (% of Base Year)	Party	Emission Reduction Commitment (% of Base Year)	Party	Emission Reduction Commitment (% of Base Year)
Austria	92	Bulgaria	92	Australia	108
Belgium	92	Croatia	95	Canada	94
Denmark	92	Czech Republic	92	Japan	94
European Community	92	Estonia	92	New Zealand	100
Finland	92	Hungary	94	United States	93
France	92	Latvia	92		
Germany	92	Lithuania	92		
Greece	92	Poland	94		
Iceland	110	Romania	92		
Ireland	92	Russian Federation	100		
Italy	92	Slovakia	92		

Continued

Table 7.1 Annex B Nations in the Kyoto Protocol and Reduction Commitments—cont'd

Europe		Europe: Countries in Transition to a Market Economy		Non-Europe	
Party	Emission Reduction Commitment (% of Base Year)	Party	Emission Reduction Commitment (% of Base Year)	Party	Emission Reduction Commitment (% of Base Year)
Liechtenstein	92	Slovenia	92		
Luxembourg	92	Ukraine	100		
Monaco	92				
Netherlands	92				
Norway	101				
Portugal	92				
Spain	92				
Sweden	92				
Switzerland	92				
United Kingdom	92				

The Kyoto Protocol introduces the concept of Clean Development Mechanism (CDM) as one way to achieve the emission reduction targets set in the Annex B countries in Article 12 of the Protocol:

> *Under the clean development mechanism: (a) Parties not included in Annex I will benefit from project activities resulting in certified emission reductions; and (b) Parties included in Annex I may use the certified emission reductions accruing from such project activities to contribute to compliance with part of their quantified emission limitation and reduction commitments under Article 3, as determined by the Conference of the Parties serving as the meeting of the Parties to this Protocol.*

The Protocol introduces in Articles 4 and 6 of the Kyoto Protocol additional measures to achieve the emissions reduction targets such as joint implementation and transfer of emissions reduction:

> *[Article 4] Any Parties included in Annex I that have reached an agreement to fulfil their commitments under Article 3 jointly, shall be deemed to have met those commitments provided that their total combined aggregate anthropogenic carbon dioxide equivalent emissions of the greenhouse gases listed in Annex A do not exceed their assigned amounts calculated pursuant to their quantified emission limitation and reduction commitments inscribed in Annex B and in accordance with the provisions of Article 3.*

> *[Article 6] For the purpose of meeting its commitments under Article 3, any Party included in Annex I may transfer to, or acquire from, any other such Party emission reduction units resulting from projects aimed at reducing anthropogenic emissions by sources or enhancing anthropogenic removals by sinks of greenhouse gases in any sector of the economy.*

Phase 1 of the Kyoto Protocol was implemented through the ETS in the European Union. The ETS is a cornerstone of the European Union's cost-effective climate strategy and, as of 2015, covers 11,200 power plants and manufacturing installations in 28 member states (EC, 2015). The EU ETS operates on a "cap-and-trade" principle. A cap, i.e., a limit, is placed on the total amount of GHG emissions that can be released by the installations and power plants that must comply with the system. The cap is reduced over time, so that the total emissions fall. The system covers approximately half of the overall GHG emissions of the European Union. Regulated pollutants by the ETS are carbon dioxide, nitrous oxides, and PFCs.

Because only about 50% of the total GHG emissions and only some pollutants are regulated by the EU ETS, the economy-wide total emissions could increase even if the total emissions covered by the system should be made to fall over time. This can occur if emissions were to increase elsewhere in the installations not covered by the system in the European Union or in the installations relocated to the countries outside European Union to avoid the EU ETS. A carbon leakage, so is it called, has occurred (Ellerman and Buchner, 2007; Tietenberg, 2013).

In Fig. 7.1, the prices of a permit for 1 ton of carbon dioxide emissions from the ETS are drawn from 2005 to 2016. The excess volatility of the permit price is evident during the first phase of the Kyoto Protocol from 2008 to 2012, which corresponds to the second phase of the EU ETS trading period. The price fell from 28 Euro in March 2008 to 10 Euro in December 2008 and rose again to 23 Euro in April 2011. Monthly changes often amount to more than 100% down or up, which is many times greater volatility than that observed in the stock market, such as the S&P500 index (Shiller, 2005).

The high volatility of the permit price during the second trading phase (2008−2012) and the low prices in the third phase (2013−2020) reflect the impact of the global financial crisis that started in 2008. The crisis resulted in a surplus of allowances, which accumulated to 2 billion surplus allowances by 2012 (EC, 2016).

A fatal flaw of the Kyoto Protocol as a global policy to address the problem of global warming turned out to be a low rate of participation (Nordhaus, 2008). Fig. 7.2 describes the share of the total world emissions of carbon covered by the Kyoto Protocol. The share stood at 60% of the world emissions in 1990 when the United States was included. By 2010, the share fell to less than 30% without the United States. The share is below 15% if only Kyoto Protocol's enthusiasts, mainly the European Union, are considered. As the participation rate falls, the cost of the Kyoto Protocol increases nonlinearly in response to a decrease in the participation rate.

Figure 7.1 Price of a permit from the EU Emissions Trading System.
Produced from the data available at Investing.com.

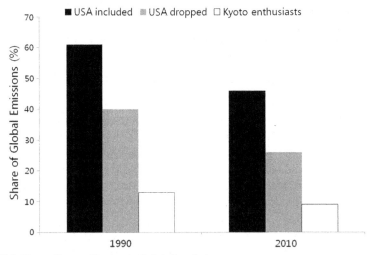

Figure 7.2 Kyoto Protocol's share of global emissions.
Adapted from Nordhaus, W., 2008. A Question of Balance: Weighing the Options on Climate Change. Yale University Press, New Haven.

3.2 Copenhagen Accord and Durban Platform

The Paris Agreement is the outcome of the COP21 held in Paris, France, at the end of 2015. It replaces the defunct Kyoto Protocol and is expected to begin its implementation period from the year 2020. Negotiators called it a major "breakthrough" at the closure of the COP21 but many also questioned the legal enforceability of the agreement and therefore effectiveness in achieving emission reductions.

The seed of the Paris Agreement was sown in 2009 at the closure of the Copenhagen Conference. Negotiators at Copenhagen COP attempted to extend the Kyoto Protocol and negotiate the second phase of the Kyoto Protocol, which would begin in 2013. They intended an extended Kyoto Protocol to all nations in the UNFCCC, with equal legal force applied to the first phase of the Kyoto Protocol.

The Copenhagen COP, amid the wide media coverage and global attention, failed to reach an agreement. The differences of opinions between developed nations and developing nations were irreconcilable, leading to a major collapse of the negotiation that had been widely reported to be in a strong position to make a breakthrough. Most world leaders came to Copenhagen in anticipation of the new Protocol, including Barak Obama in his first year of presidency.

The breakdown of the negotiation was due to the unwillingness of the developing nations who argued that global warming has been caused by the rich countries and therefore they should have the responsibility for reducing emissions of carbon dioxide. Furthermore, they asserted that rich countries are responsible for financial compensation for the damages caused by global warming on poor countries. The rich countries were not at all ready for such mitigation responsibilities and financial compensation to the poor countries (UNFCCC, 2009).

At this meeting, Mrs. Hillary Clinton, who was attending the COP as the Secretary of the State, announced that the rich countries will fund $100 billion per year to help poor countries adapt to the adverse effects of global warming. This announcement marked the beginning of the creation of the GCF, which will be explained in detail in the next section.

After the shambles at Copenhagen, negotiators convened 2 years later in 2011 in Durban, South Africa, and started a new process called the Durban Platform (UNFCCC, 2011a). The Durban Platform for Enhanced Action agrees that the parties of the conference would seek to start a process that is aimed at a global agreement in which all parties participate and is legally binding to all parties. The new agreement would be reached by the Paris COP21 in 2015 and be implemented from 2020:

> *Also decides to launch a process to develop a protocol, another legal instrument or an agreed outcome with legal force under the Convention applicable to all Parties, through a subsidiary body under the Convention hereby established and to be known as the Ad Hoc Working Group on the Durban Platform for Enhanced Action; …decides that the Ad Hoc Working Group on the Durban Platform for Enhanced Action shall complete its work as early as possible but no later than 2015.*

3.3 Paris Agreement

At COP21 in Paris at the end of 2015, climate negotiators reached an agreement called the Paris Agreement in which all parties of the conference agreed to participate. The Paris Agreement was signed by 177 nations and 15 nations ratified it as of May 2016. It entered into force on November 4, 2016.

Despite the success of reaching an agreement that was often declared as a "turning point," the downside is that it is in actuality a very weak agreement, i.e., much weaker than the Kyoto Protocol in its legal force. The nations were requested to submit a national plan to reduce GHGs on a voluntary basis. The nations agreed that each country would achieve the goal in the submitted national plan on a voluntary basis.

> *[Article 3] As nationally determined contributions to the global response to climate change, all Parties are to undertake and communicate ambitious efforts…;*

> *[Article 4] Each Party shall communicate a nationally determined contribution every five years…; Parties shall account for their nationally determined contributions.*

> *[Article 9] Developed country Parties shall provide financial resources to assist developing country Parties with respect to both mitigation and adaptation in continuation of their existing obligations under the Convention.*

Do the national plans submitted to the COP21, Paris Conference, add up to be sufficient to stop the trend of global warming? The COP21 agreement does not have a formal article on the quantitative amount of emissions reductions agreed and its significance in the fight to stop the global warming trend. Because the emission reduction targets are set in a bottom-up manner by individual nations, the total emissions reduction at the global level is arbitrarily set.

Article 2 declares the ultimate goals the Paris Agreement wishes to achieve. That is,

> *(a) Holding the increase in the global average temperature to well below 2°C above pre-industrial levels and to pursue efforts to limit the temperature increase to 1.5°C above pre-industrial levels, recognizing that this would significantly reduce the risks and impacts of climate change; (b) Increasing the ability to adapt to the adverse impacts of climate change and foster climate resilience and low greenhouse gas emissions development, in a manner that does not threaten food production; (c) Making finance flows consistent with a pathway towards low greenhouse gas emissions and climate-resilient development.*

However, as the author will provide a review of the national plans for emissions reduction, national intentions do not add up to be an effective strategy to achieve the goals stated in the Article 2. Fig. 7.3 shows INDCs submitted to the Paris Agreement of major countries. Countries adopt different baselines: 1990, 2005, or the

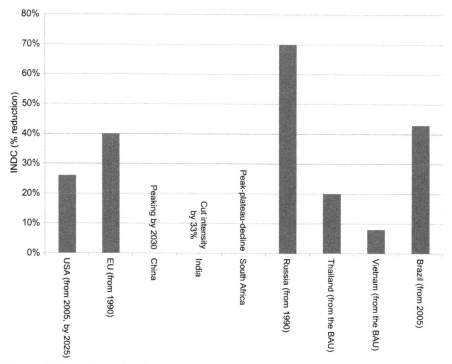

Figure 7.3 Intended Nationally Determined Contributions (INDCs) submitted to the Paris Agreement.
Note: Russian INDC is to limit GHGs to 70% of 1990 level.

business-as-usual (BAU) baseline. China, India, and South Africa do not commit to a reduction in the aggregate amount of emissions. Russia commits to GHGs to 70% level, Brazil 43% reduction of annual emissions, the European Union 40%, the United States 26%, Thailand 20%, and Vietnam 8%.

From another standpoint, the Paris Agreement does not have a legal force. There is no article in the Agreement on what shall be done in a legal nature when a certain nation fails to achieve the submitted target in emissions reduction. The agreement is entirely voluntary by the nations, so it is called "intended" reductions.

The legal enforceability is replaced by a so-called name and shame strategy. The idea is that nations look out for emissions reductions achieved by other nations and name and shame a country that fails to achieve the intended target. It is doubtful that the name and shame strategy will become a forceful strategy given many assumptions and stipulations included in the nationally intended plans.

In the final days of the Paris Conference, negotiators wrangled over who should monitor national emissions of many GHGs and whether an international body should monitor changes in emissions and provide accounting of GHGs. The Paris Agreement allows each country to take the responsibility of monitoring and accounting. The self-monitoring and accounting means that it is not possible for the international body to assess the efforts by individual nations with regards to the nationally intended plans.

What do the national plans submitted to the Paris Agreement look like? The INDCs for major players in global warming are summarized in the following discussion. Comparisons of the INDC proposals will reveal differences of ambitions and undertakings across the nations as well as major flaws in the Paris Agreement.

First, the US proposal of INDC, copied in the following text, specifies the level of abatement intended, the GHGs covered, and the sectors covered. The reference year is set at 2005 and the target year is 2025. That all sectors are included means that increased carbon sinking (absorbing) capacity from land use changes will be included. That all gases are included means that, among other things, it may be possible to achieve the target through technological changes, such as replacing HFCs in the refrigerators.

1) The United States intends to achieve an economy-wide target of reducing its greenhouse gas emissions by 26%—28% below its 2005 level in 2025 and to make best efforts to reduce its emissions by 28%.

2) The U.S. target covers all greenhouse gases included in the 2014 Inventory of United States Greenhouse Gas Emissions and Sinks: carbon dioxide (CO2), methane (CH4), nitrous oxide (N2O), perfluorocarbons (PFCs), hydrofluorocarbons (HFCs), sulfur hexafluoride (SF6), and nitrogen trifluoride (NF3).

3) The U.S. target covers all IPCC sectors.

The European Union's INDC proposal is similar to the US proposal, but differs in a number of ways. First, the target is more ambitious: 40% reduction by 2030 from the 1990 level. Second, it does not specify how land use emissions changes will be counted. Third, it does not intend to count the international credits in the accounting.

International credits are emission reduction credits it may earn internationally by, e.g., funding forest preservations in the Amazon rainforests.

1) The EU and its Member States are committed to a binding target of an <u>at least 40%</u> <u>domestic reduction in greenhouse gas emissions by 2030 compared to 1990</u>, to be fulfilled jointly;

2) Policy on <u>how to include Land Use, Land Use Change and Forestry</u> into the 2030 greenhouse gas mitigation framework will be established as soon as technical conditions allow and in any case before 2020;

3) Net Contribution of International Market Based Mechanisms: <u>No contribution from</u> <u>international credits.</u>

Notably, the EU proposal does not specify indirect emissions of GHGs. That is, even if the consumption of goods that emit carbon dioxide during production would increase in the European Union, the increase in emissions would not be counted if they are imported from elsewhere, e.g., China and India.

Also, the EU proposal does not specify how it will count the reduction in GHG emissions that is achieved through an increase in energy production from nuclear power plants. The European Union heavily relies on nuclear energy for electricity generations. For example, France and some other EU nations produce more than 80% of electricity through nuclear energy productions.

China's INDC proposal does not specify the level of abatement from the reference year. Instead, it proposes a peaking of carbon dioxide emissions around 2030. Notably, the China's INDC does not state GHGs, but only carbon dioxide. Neither does it specify the exact target year, but only "around" 2030. It also proposes a decrease of carbon intensity by 60% from the 2005 level and an increase of the share of nonfossil fuel energy consumption to 20%. Note that the China's carbon intensity is at present more than two times higher than that in the United States or the European Union. Therefore it is expected that the carbon intensity will fall to the US level even without carbon mitigation efforts.

Based on its national circumstances, development stage, sustainable development strategy and international responsibility, China has nationally determined its actions by 2030 as follows: 1) To achieve <u>the peaking of carbon dioxide emissions around</u> <u>2030</u> and making best efforts to peak early; 2) To <u>lower carbon dioxide emissions per</u> <u>unit of GDP by 60% to 65% from the 2005 level</u>; 3) To increase <u>the share of non-fossil</u> <u>fuels in primary energy consumption to around 20%</u>; 4) To increase <u>the forest stock</u> <u>volume by around 4.5 billion cubic meters</u> on the 2005 level.

India's INDC proposal is even more obscure. It does not specify an abatement target. It proposes to cut carbon intensity by 33% by 2030. As noted earlier, India and China's carbon intensity is at present more than two times larger than that of the United States. Therefore it is projected that the carbon intensity in India will fall to the US level even without carbon mitigation measures.

1) To put forward and further propagate a healthy and sustainable way of living based on traditions and values of conservation and moderation;

2) To adopt a climate friendly and a cleaner path than the one followed hitherto by others at corresponding level of economic development;

3) To reduce the <u>emissions intensity of its GDP by 33 to 35 percent by 2030 from 2005 level</u>;

4) To achieve about <u>40 percent cumulative electric power installed capacity from non-fossil fuel based energy resources</u> by 2030 with the help of <u>transfer of technology and low cost international finance including from Green Climate Fund (GCF)</u>;

5) To create an additional carbon sink of 2.5 to 3 billion tonnes of CO_2 equivalent through additional forest and tree cover by 2030.

Note that India proposes to increase the share of electricity production from nonfossil fuels to 40% by 2030, which was the primary talking point with regards to the India's INDC. However, it says the country would achieve this target only with the technology transfers and international finance received from, among other funds, the GCF.

Interestingly, Russia's INDC proposal is one of the most ambitious of all. It proposes to cut emissions to 70% of the 1990 level. The Russian INDC says much about the credibility of the Paris approach. In other words, because there is no legal liability, countries can submit anything without necessary research and considerations. From an alternative perspective, it may be that Russians are assured that global warming will increase vastly the land areas suitable for vegetation and forests, which have the capacity to absorb a large amount of carbon dioxide.

<u>Limiting anthropogenic greenhouse gases in Russia to 70-75% of 1990 levels by the year 2030</u> might be a long-term indicator, subject to the maximum possible account of <u>absorbing capacity of forests</u>.

South Africa's INDC submission is ambiguous. It proposes a PPD approach, i.e., a peak—plateau—decline approach. It does not, however, specify when it will peak at what level of carbon emissions. It only proposes a wide range of emissions: 398 and 614 Mt CO_2-eq.

South Africa's mitigation component of its INDC moves from a "deviation from business-as-usual" form of commitment and takes the form of <u>a peak, plateau and decline</u> GHG emissions trajectory range. <u>South Africa's emissions by 2025 and 2030 will be in a range between 398 and 614 Mt CO2—eq</u>, as defined in national policy. This is the benchmark against which the efficacy of mitigation actions will be measured.

Thailand is one of the fast growing developing economies in the world, so it is meaningful to look into the country's INDC submission. It proposes to cut emissions by 20% from the BAU level by 2030. Because it does not clarify what the BAU scenario is, the proposal is open to interpretations. Furthermore, it states that the abatement level can increase to 25% if there is technological and financial support from rich countries.

Thailand intends to reduce its greenhouse gas emissions by 20 percent from the projected business-as-usual (BAU) level by 2030. The level of contribution could increase up to 25 percent, subject to adequate and enhanced access to technology development and transfer, financial resources and capacity building support through a balanced and ambitious global agreement under the United Nations Framework Convention on Climate Change (UNFCCC).

The INDC proposal by Vietnam, another developing economy, is more revealing than that of Thailand. It proposes to cut emissions by 8% from the BAU scenario. However, the BAU scenario specifies that its emissions will increase from 246 to 787 Mt CO_2-eq by 2030. That is, it assumes the emissions will more than triple in the BAU scenario in 20 years.

Furthermore, it proposes to increase the emissions reduction target to 25% from the BAU scenario, but only if financial and technological support is provided by the UNFCCC through the GCF.

1) Unconditional contribution: With domestic resources, by 2030 Viet Nam will reduce GHG emissions by 8% compared to BAU, in which: - Emission intensity per unit of GDP will be reduced by 20% compared to the 2010 levels; - Forest cover will increase to the level of 45%.

2) Viet Nam's BAU scenario for GHG emissions was developed based on the assumption of economic growth in the absence of climate change policies. The BAU starts from 2010 (the latest year of the national GHG inventory) and includes the energy, agriculture, waste and LULUCF sectors. GHG emissions in 2010: 246.8 million tCO2e. Projections for 2020 and 2030 (not included industrial processes): - 2020: 474.1 million tCO2e - 2030: 787.4 million tCO2e;

3) Conditional contribution: The above-mentioned 8% contribution could be increased to 25% if international support is received through bilateral and multilateral cooperation, as well as through the implementation of new mechanisms under the Global Climate Agreement, in which emission intensity per unit of GDP will be reduced by 30% compared to 2010 levels.

Lastly, Brazil's INDC submission is more ambitious than that of other developing countries with the 37% reduction by 2025 and 43% by 2030. A number of interesting qualifications are added to the Brazil's INDC proposal. First, it emphasizes that any transfer of mitigation credits achieved in Brazil to other countries requires consent from the Federal Government. Second, implementation of the REDD+ (Reducing

Emissions from Deforestation and forest Degradation) activities, which had already been incorporated into UNFCCC activities, needs adequate payments from the UNFCCC.

What these qualifications mean is that Brazil intends to achieve the GHG emissions reduction mostly by the forest sector credits. Because the UNFCCC's COPs already committed a large amount of money for various REDD+ activities, Brazil can reduce the emissions very significantly. However, the country's commitment to the reduction target hinges on the transfer of payments as specified already in the past UNFCCC outcomes.

1) Contribution: Brazil intends to commit to reduce greenhouse gas emissions by 37% below 2005 levels in 2025;

2) Subsequent indicative contribution: reduce greenhouse gas emissions by 43% below 2005 levels in 2030;

3) Brazil emphasizes that any transfer of units resulting from mitigation outcomes achieved in the Brazilian territory will be subject to prior and formal consent by the Federal Government. Brazil will not recognize the use by other Parties of any units resulting from mitigation outcomes achieved in the Brazilian territory;

4) The implementation of Brazil's iNDC is not contingent upon international support, yet it welcomes support from developed countries with a view to generate global benefits;

5) Specifically concerning the forest sector, the implementation of REDD+ activities and the permanence of results achieved require the provision, on a continuous basis, of adequate and predictable results-based payments in accordance with the relevant COP decisions.

4. Green Climate Fund

From the debacle of the Copenhagen Conference, the GCF has emerged as a parallel track in the policy negotiations at the UNFCCC meetings (UNFCCC, 2009). Initially devised as a financial mechanism to help poor countries cope with severe climate impacts and urge them to participate in a global policy agreement, the GCF has taken shape into the primary financial instrument of the UNFCCC activities for a relatively short period of time.

The UNFCCC negotiations, from their inception, have concentrated predominantly on mitigation efforts, i.e., the efforts to reduce and cap emissions of GHGs. Adaptation was included as a part of the full set of strategies needed to cap and cut carbon emissions worldwide, but the extent and importance of adaptation efforts as a strategy for combating against global warming had not taken roots at that time (Rosenberg, 1992; Mendelsohn, 2000; Hanemann, 2000). A close examination reveals that the UNFCCC foundation document did not include a separate article on adaptation or a separate clause on adaptation (UNFCCC, 1992).

Notwithstanding, Article 4 of the UNFCCC foundation document recognizes the need for helping poor countries to adapt to climate changes. However, the article, noted underneath, perceives adaptation only as "costs of adaptation," i.e., a costly action by the victim:

The developed country Parties and other developed Parties included in Annex II shall also assist the developing country Parties that are particularly vulnerable to the adverse effects of climate change in meeting costs of adaptation to those adverse effects.

The Kyoto Protocol from the COP15 of the UNFCCC, the first major international climate agreement, was heavily drawn to the mitigation targets of the emissions of carbon dioxide, as explained in the previous section. The target of the international agreement is explicitly set on the emissions level of carbon dioxide at 5% below the 1990 level (UNFCCC, 1998). By that time, there was almost no recognition of critical importance of adaptation, as elaborated in the previous chapter, by the international community.

Article 12 of the Kyoto Protocol, which is on CDM, reiterates the principle articulated in the UNFCCC foundation document, i.e., the need to assist developing vulnerable countries adapt to adverse effects of climatic changes and help with "costs of adaptation":

The Conference of the Parties serving as the meeting of the Parties to this Protocol shall ensure that a share of the proceeds from certified project activities is used to cover administrative expenses as well as to assist developing country Parties that are particularly vulnerable to the adverse effects of climate change to meet the costs of adaptation.

In a sense, the Kyoto Protocol may have further weakened a broad interpretation and roles of adaptation in global warming policy negotiations by coupling this need of adaptation with the contexts of CDM. The aforementioned UNFCCC foundation document, by comparison, placed it as a single clause independent of the CDM (UNFCCC, 1992).

The failure to achieve the extension of the first phase of the Kyoto Protocol in the Copenhagen conference into the second phase led to the explicit expression of the GCF for the first time (UNFCCC, 2009):

In the context of meaningful mitigation actions and transparency on implementation, developed countries commit to a goal of mobilizing jointly USD 100 billion dollars a year by 2020 to address the needs of developing countries.

We decide that the Copenhagen Green Climate Fund shall be established as an operating entity of the financial mechanism of the Convention to support projects, programme, policies and other activities in developing countries related to mitigation including REDD-plus, adaptation, capacity building, technology development and transfer.

The support fund of US$100 billion annually was emphatically announced upon the arrival of the then Secretary of the State Hillary Clinton in Copenhagen. The declaration of the new funds was based on the widely held belief that low-latitude poor countries are also those who will bear the brunt of global warming damages, even though these countries did not contribute much to the buildup of GHGs in the global atmosphere (Mendelsohn et al., 2006). From Copenhagen, the efforts to make the GCF the financial instrument of the whole range of the UNFCCC activities began.

In the subsequent COP16 held in Cancun, Mexico, in 2010, the GCF became the formal operating entity of the financial mechanism of the UNFCCC. At that conference, the Transitional Committee was created for the GCF design and the trustee of the GCF was designated (UNFCCC, 2010):

> *Decides to establish a Green Climate Fund, to be designated as an operating entity of the financial mechanism of the Convention…; Also decides that the Fund shall be governed by a Board of 24 members, comprising an equal number of members from developing and developed country Parties…; Invites the World Bank to serve as the interim trustee for the Green Climate Fund…; Also decides that the Green Climate Fund shall be designed by a Transitional Committee in accordance with the terms of reference contained in appendix III to this decision….*

Six countries competed for a host city for the GCF: Germany, Namibia, Mexico, Poland, Republic of Korea, and Switzerland. Songdo city in the Republic of Korea was selected as the host city by the GCF board's consensus decision, which was endorsed at the Doha COP in 2012 (UNFCCC, 2012).

In the Paris Agreement of the COP21 in 2015, the clauses on the article of Finance clarify the current status of the GCF. The Paris Agreement proposes to set a new goal of the GCF before 2025, which should be higher than US$100 billion per year:

> *53. Decides that, in the implementation of the Agreement, financial resources provided to developing countries should enhance the implementation of their policies, strategies, regulations and action plans and their climate change actions with respect to both mitigation and adaptation to contribute to the achievement of the purpose of the Agreement…;*
>
> *54. Further decides that,…, developed countries intend to continue their existing collective mobilization goal through 2025 in the context of meaningful mitigation actions and transparency on implementation; prior to 2025 the Conference of the Parties serving as the meeting of the Parties to the Paris Agreement shall set a new collective quantified goal from a floor of USD 100 billion per year, taking into account the needs and priorities of developing countries;*

The Paris Agreement recognizes the GCF, the Least Developed Countries Fund, and the Special Climate Change Fund as financial mechanisms for the Convention.

Among these, the GCF is the only stand-alone multilateral financing entity whose sole mandate is to serve the Convention. It also recognizes the need for an Adaptation Fund.

59. Decides that the <u>*Green Climate Fund*</u> *and the* <u>*Global Environment Facility,*</u> *the entities entrusted with the operation of the Financial Mechanism of the Convention, as well as the* <u>*Least Developed Countries Fund*</u> *and the* <u>*Special Climate Change Fund,*</u> *administered by the Global Environment Facility, shall serve the Agreement;*

60. Recognizes that the <u>*Adaptation Fund*</u> *may serve the Agreement, subject to relevant decisions by the Conference of the Parties serving as the meeting of the Parties to the Kyoto Protocol and the Conference of the Parties serving as the meeting of the Parties to the Paris Agreement;*

A number of problems in the setup and implementation of the GCF have been pointed out by researchers. In the Paris Agreement, there is no clause on how the fund for the GCF with the size of US$100 billion per annum should be collected. Nor are there any assignments of individual countries' contributions to the Fund agreed by the parties of the conference.

A potentially more contentious issue in the upcoming conferences is that there is no guideline on how the fund should be allocated (Seo, 2015b). Should the fund be transferred to the poor domestically or internationally (Metcalf, 2009)? Or should the fund be transferred solely for the purpose of having a more stringent international policy (Carraro et al., 2006)? It may turn out to be a big issue in climate negotiations in the future because developing countries will compete for a larger share of the fund for various meaningful projects for the limited amount of the fund.

Given that there is no legal obligation to any country to contribute to the GCF and therefore it is entirely voluntary, it has been of interest to see how much each country would actually give. According to the Pledge Tracker provided by the GCF, by October 2016, announced and signed contributions amounted to US$9.9 billion for the initial resource mobilization period from 2015 to 2018. This amounts to US$2.4 billion per year. The signed contributions come dominantly from five countries: the United States ($3 billion), Japan ($1.5 billion), the United Kingdom ($1.2 billion), France ($1 billion), and Germany ($1 billion). Signed pledges as of October 2016 with more than US$100 million are shown in Fig. 7.4.

Several additional comments are worthy of mentioning. There is no information available on how much money the GCF has actually received out of the pledges and how the fund is allocated into different projects (GCF, 2016). Some of the above-mentioned donor countries rely on loan, instead of grant, which must be repaid in the future by a recipient. Furthermore, developing countries that are at the receiving end of the GCF funds argued that the GCF contributions are not new contributions by these rich countries to the poor countries, but rather a redirection of the already existing contributions by these countries such as development and humanitarian aids.

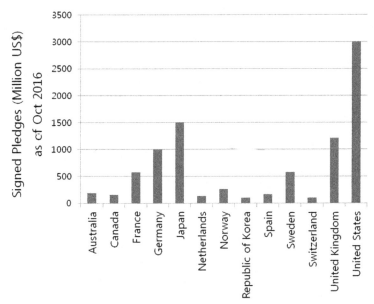

Figure 7.4 Signed pledges to the Green Climate Fund with >100 million US$.

5. Non-UNFCCC Agreements

International negotiations on climate change have been led by the UNFCCC. The outcomes of the COPs convened by the UNFCCC are explained up to this point in this chapter. Two international treaties or agreements that are not organized by the UNFCCC have gained importance in climate policy discussions. The author explains these two agreements as they are pertinent to the implementation of the Paris Agreement as well as to the adaptation paradigm of global warming policy explained in the previous chapter.

5.1 Montreal Protocol

The Montreal Protocol on Substances that Deplete the Ozone Layer is an international treaty signed in 1987 that aims to protect the ozone layer of the Earth by phasing out ozone-depleting chemicals. Countries agreed to phase out chlorofluorocarbons (CFCs), the main chemical that depletes the ozone layer, which had been used as a coolant for refrigerators and air conditioners (Molina and Rowland, 1974).

As a replacement for the CFCs, chemical companies have gradually switched in response to the Montreal Protocol to HFCs and hydrocholorofluorocarbons. Both these chemicals are, however, potent GHGs with global warming potential greater than more than 1000 times that of CO_2 (IPCC, 2005a).

Because of the practicality of the measure, bilateral climate talks between US President Barak Obama and China's Chairman Xijinping as well as between the US

President and Canadian Prime Minister focused on the phaseout of the HFCs (White House, 2013, 2016).

In Kigali, Rwanda, on October 2016, more than 170 member countries of the Montreal Protocol agreed in an amendment of the Protocol to phase out the planet-warming HFCs as a coolant. Unlike the Paris Agreement, the amendment carries the legal force of a treaty as an international Protocol.

In the amendment, the reduction of HFCs is formulated into three tracks. For group 1 countries, which are the richest countries, including the United States and European Union, the production and consumption of HFCs will be frozen by 2018, which will be reduced to about 15% of the 2012 level by 2036. For group 2 countries, which include much of the rest of the world, including China, Brazil, and all of Africa, the production of HFCs will be frozen by 2024, which will be reduced to about 20% of the 2021 level by 2045. For group 3 countries, which are the world's hottest countries, including India, Pakistan, Iran, Saudi Arabia, and Kuwait, the use of HFCs will be frozen by 2028, which will be reduced to about 15% of the 2025 level by 2047.

Resistance to the Amendment came from India, which is just beginning to afford and enjoy the benefits of air conditioning and refrigeration owing to recent economic developments. Located in a hot tropical monsoon climate zone, Indian economy and society are hampered by adverse climate conditions, which can be overcome, albeit partially, by air conditioning and refrigeration. Responding to India's requests, the Amendment gives group 3 countries 10 more years to comply with the agreement.

The success of the Montreal Protocol Amendment owes largely to technological feasibilities of replacements. As explained in Chapter 5, multiple alternative coolants to the HFCs are available and already in wide use, e.g., hydrocarbons (EC, 2016). Additional cost is expected to occur, however, to consumers by an air conditioner or a refrigerator with a replacement coolant over a conventional one with built-in HFCs.

The Montreal Protocol Amendment of 2016 is expected to play a significant role in national climate change mitigation efforts for achieving the INDCs submitted to the Paris Agreement. However, it would not affect the efforts to accomplish the INDC targets of developing countries because the commitment period of the Montreal Protocol Amendment begins around 2030 for most countries. The INDC commitments, on the other hand, are made for the period up to 2030 in most cases (UNFCCC, 2015).

A weakness of the Montreal Protocol Amendment of 2016 may lie in the foundation. To be more specific, the Montreal Protocol Amendment is not strongly tied to the purport of the initial Montreal Protocol, which is to protect the ozone layer, i.e., not the climate system (UNEP, 2016). Countries may decide to withdraw from the Protocol in the future if they were to run into high cost of complying with the Amendment.

5.2 Carbon Offsetting and Reduction Scheme for International Aviation

Carbon emissions from air travels, which accounts for approximately 2% of the world GHG emissions, have been a policy focal area of climate research as well as international negotiators (IPCC, 1999). After years of negotiations, the members of the ICAO adopted a measure to reduce emissions of GHGs in October 2016 (ICAO, 2016).

The measure, called Carbon Offsetting and Reduction Scheme for International Aviation (CORSIA), will take effect from 2021. The measure will be voluntary for the first 6 years and the countries that committed voluntarily can also opt out on short notice.

Under the CORSIA, against the baseline level of CO_2 emissions during the 2019−20 period, any increase in CO_2 emissions must be offset by airlines. This means a carbon-neutral growth of the aviation sector from 2021. Under the measure, an airline can buy credits from various programs, e.g., renewable energy credits or forest carbon sink credits to offset the emissions from the airlines (ICAO, 2016).

At least 65 countries, including the United States, China, and the European Union, have signaled that they will participate, but many small countries are exempt from the measure. This means that large airline carriers that fly into these small countries that are exempt from the CORSIA may get exemptions. Furthermore, several large countries, such as Russia and India, expressed reservations on the agreement.

The CORSIA is another example of an international agreement on carbon reduction efforts that is not coordinated by the UNFCCC. In comparison with the Montreal Protocol Amendment, several features make it a weaker commitment by the international community: many countries expressed reservation in the agreement; countries can opt out on short notice; it has a 6-year voluntary participation period.

6. Where Do International Negotiations Go From Here?

Hitherto, the author has provided a comprehensive yet compact review of international policy negotiations on climate change and global warming during the past 3 decades. Up-to-date states of the pool of key policy instruments, including emissions trading permits, emissions reduction commitments, the GCF, non-UNFCCC treaties, as well as the primary organizational foundations, are explained.

Incorporating the critical review of these past experiences, the author is inclined to make forecasts of what will happen in global warming policy negotiations internationally and nationally in the decades to follow. Future directions of the policy tracks established in the past agreements will be suggested in the context of the adaptation paradigm conceptually defined in this book.

First, a standard policy to be applied to all countries uniformly is not likely to come back to policy negotiations of the UNFCCC. For example, the Kyoto Protocol that attempted to achieve carbon dioxide emissions reduction to the level that is 5% below the 1990 level is one example of a uniform standard policy designed to be imposed across all nations (UNFCCC, 1998). This approach has given way to a multiple-target approach through the Copenhagen, Durban, and Paris Conferences.

The imposition of a globally harmonized carbon tax is another example of a uniform policy tool applied to all nations (Nordhaus, 1994). Although the approach offers an efficient solution to the problems of global warming, such a proposal may turn out to be too ambitious for nations to agree upon as the nations have strong incentives to disagree and become noncooperative (Nash, 1950, 1951; Seo, 2012a; Tietenberg, 2013).

Second, a mitigation-based approach will likely give way to an adaptation-based approach to climate policy making. As reviewed in the previous sections, the GCF, Adaptation Fund, and other funds, if these were to be established and allocated as promised, will massively encourage adaptation activities especially in low-latitude developing countries.

Past negotiations failed repeatedly to adopt an emissions-reduction oriented instrument such as the Kyoto Protocol or its extended form as a global climate protocol (UNFCCC, 2009, 2011a). An even stricter policy with more ambitious mitigation targets, whether for economic reasons or catastrophic concerns, may have little chance to be adopted as an international climate protocol (Stern, 2007; Weitzman, 2009; NRC, 2013a).

The primary reason for the possible increase in the adaptation-based policies is that adaptation research has reported large potential and observed benefits of adaptation to global warming in natural resource–intensive industries (Seo and Mendelsohn, 2008; Seo, 2010, 2012b, 2016a,b), in sea level rises (Yohe and Schlesinger, 1998; Ng and Mendelsohn, 2006), in temperature-related fatalities (Barreca et al., 2016), and in extreme events such as hurricane fatalities (Seo, 2015c; Seo and Bakkensen, 2016). Adaptation will make some changes in the climate system even beneficial to some regions. In many regions, adaptation will make the effects of global warming much less severe.

Furthermore, a large array of adaptation measures and strategies can be coupled with mitigation efforts in ways that adaptation actions also reduce the emissions of carbon dioxide and other GHGs or absorb them from the atmosphere (Seo, 2013, 2015a, 2016c). An increase in forest-based or grassland-based economic activities can increase carbon absorption (Ainsworth and Long, 2005; Crowther et al., 2015; Van Pelt et al., 2016).

Third, technological solutions will play a major role in making a global agreement on global warming as well as in implementing any agreed outcomes. Countries will invest voluntarily on technological options such as a carbon-capture-storage (Lackner et al., 2012; IEA, 2013), electric vehicles (NRC, 2013b; McConnell, 2013), solar energy (IPCC, 2011; MIT, 2015), lighting methods such as compact fluorescent lamps and light-emitting diode lamps (Akasaki et al., 2014), nuclear fusion technologies (ITER, 2015), or climate engineering (NRC, 2015) because advances in these technologies will turn out to be a critical asset to a country's competitiveness, economic and noneconomic.

Technological possibilities will also play an important role in adaptation programs. For example, heat-tolerant varieties of crops, heat- and drought-resilient animal species, animal feed additives, methane captures, and cures for animal and plant diseases are salient adaptation options to individuals that can be made available through technological innovations (Aksoy et al., 2014; US EPA, 2006; Seo and Mendelsohn, 2008; Zhang et al., 2013).

Fourth, financial transfer programs envisioned in the UNFCCC meetings in Copenhagen, Cancun, Durban, and Paris will likely wreak havoc on global negotiations. As poor countries insist on such transfer of money as a precondition for any mitigation actions, it will become a big hurdle in the negotiations between developed countries and developing countries (UNFCCC, 2009, 2015).

A more serious concern is that the reality is that low-latitude poor countries must adapt to climatic changes and global warming if they were to avoid a large damage on their economies and livelihoods (Seo, 2014). Many of these needed adaptations can be done without any international transfer of money and for the benefits of these countries. However, the international money transfer programs may turn out to be a hindrance for these countries by becoming something they wait for to act. These will likely delay actions by these countries (Seo, 2015b).

Furthermore, an international transfer of money may create a distorted incentive on the part of the receiving countries and adaptation agents. That is, it may give perverse incentives for individuals to act in a certain way in the hope of receiving the money, even though it can be a maladaptation to climatic changes (Seo, 2015b).

Having discussed the future directions of global warming negotiations and policy instruments, the author can now deliberate what a meaningful global warming policy at the international level would be like. Individuals, communities, and public sectors will do their part to adapt in response to and in anticipation of continued global warming and climatic changes. Taking that into consideration, what would be the ideal decisions that can be made at the global negotiations?

First, global meetings should be a forum for the reality of global warming and the science that underlies it. The negotiators can state the degree of global warming observed in the previous years, emissions trends, abatements achieved by member nations, and the range of future projections of global warming. This has been done by the IPCC reports, but it may turn out to be more valuable to have this process openly at the UNFCCC meetings where all parties of the convention are present. Furthermore, global conferences should discuss these scientific aspects at the national and regional scales, so that these discussions are more meaningful to participating nations.

Second, negotiators should put an emphasis on providing an international standard of a large number of measures and practices related to global warming policy discussions. For example, negotiators may provide an international standard and guideline for, inter alia, measuring emissions, sinks, soil carbon, ocean absorption, vegetation sinks, and accounting of methane emissions from ruminants and industrial processes (Martin et al., 1994; Ainsworth and Long, 2005; Van Pelt et al., 2016).

Third, international negotiations should concentrate on cooperative efforts for research among participating nations on technological breakthroughs and innovations explained at length in Chapter 5. Internationally collaborative research programs are called for—and are taking place as well—in many of areas of technological advances, which can greatly improve the capabilities of the research teams and accelerate the rates of new discoveries. International collaborations would produce a global public good, be it a technology or knowledge, pertinent to the stabilization of the climate system (Nordhaus, 2006; Seo, 2016c).

Fourth, global negotiations should become a forum for technological transfers and project exchanges between developed countries and developing countries. That is, countries should try to find mutually beneficial climate projects and technological transfers. Agreements would be made by the respective countries and need not be made by all the parties of the convention. An example of this is the agreement between the United States and China or the agreement between the United States and Canada on replacing the HFCs with alternative coolants (White House, 2013, 2016; US EPA, 2014).

A recent amendment to the Montreal Protocol attempts to phase out the HFCs with a three-tier approach in which the least developed and hot-temperature countries such as India are given more time to comply (UNEP, 2016). As explained in the previous section, the phaseout of the Earth-warming refrigerants can better be taken up by climate conferences and bilateral talks than nonclimate conferences.

Many of these mutually beneficial project exchanges are expected to be related with adaptation programs in developing countries. Furthermore, many of these adaptation projects are expected to be driven by exchanges between private sectors and nonprofit organizations of the negotiating nations. Ongoing examples include the Bill & Melinda Gates Foundation's agricultural development works in poor tropical countries such as India and the development and distribution of orange-colored sweet potato by the International Potato Center (Gates, 2015; CIP, 2016).

Finally, global negotiations can be a roundtable for designing and implementing a regulatory measure such as carbon tax or tradable carbon permits relevant to an individual nation or a set of nations (Nordhaus, 1994; Goulder, 2007; Tietenberg, 2013). Two or more countries with shared interests may cooperate jointly on introducing such a penalty measure, which is of course expected to be strongly resisted domestically by the industries that are forced to pay the penalty. Such a regulatory measure is expected to go through a legislative body in the countries that are involved (WSJ, 2017). In this way, carbon tax may be introduced to a country or a set of countries even if it may not be simultaneously adopted by all countries in the world in a harmonized fashion as was analyzed in Chapter 4.

The reasons why there would arise the need and rationale for a regulatory measure such as carbon tax was explained earlier in this chapter and in detail in Chapter 6. The rationale for collaboration among a group of countries with regard to a particular regulation can arise owing to an overall cost reduction expected from such a joint implementation.

This concludes the review and analysis of current states of climate change negotiations at the aftermath of the Paris COP, the 21st COP by the UNFCCC. The conclusion of this chapter is that international negotiations at the UNFCC level can and must play a pertinent role in the ways how societies should adapt to unfolding climatic changes for the century to ensue, as explicated in Chapter 5 and more thoroughly in Chapter 6.

References

Ainsworth, E.A., Long, S.P., 2005. What have we learned from 15 years of free-air CO_2 enrichment (FACE)? A meta-analysis of the responses of photosynthesis, canopy properties and plant production to rising CO_2. New Phytologist 165, 351−372.

Aksoy, S., Attardo, G., et al., 2014. Genome sequence of the Tsetse fly (*Glossina morsitans*): vector of African Trypanosomiasis. Science 344 (6182), 380–386.

Akasaki, I., Amano, H., Nakamura, S., 2014. Blue LEDs − Filling the World with New Light. Nobel Prize Lecture. The Nobel Foundation, Stockholm. Available at: http://www. nobelprize.org/nobel_prizes/physics/laureates/2014/popular-physicsprize2014.pdf.

Arrow, K.J., Cline, W., Maler, K.G., Munasinghe, M., Squitieri, R., Stiglitz, J., 1996. Intertemporal equity, discounting, and economic efficiency. In: Bruce, J.P., Lee, H., Haites, E.F. (Eds.), Climate Change 1995: Economic and Social Dimensions of Climate Change. Cambridge University Press, Cambridge.

Barreca, A., Clay, K., Deschenes, O., Greenstone, M., Shapiro, J.S., 2016. Adapting to climate change: the remarkable decline in the US temperature-mortality relationship over the twentieth century. Journal of Political Economy 124, 105–159.

Carraro, C., Eyckmans, J., Finus, N., 2006. Optimal transfers and participation decisions in international environmental agreements. Review of International Organizations 1, 379–396.

Centro Internacional de la Papa (CIP), 2016. World Food Prize 2016. International Potato Center (CIP), Lima, Peru.

Chan, G., Carraro, C., Edenhoffer, O., Kolstad, C., Stavins, R., 2016. Reforming the IPCC's assessment of climate change economics. Climate Change Economics 7. http://dx.doi.org/ 10.1142/S2010007816400017.

Crowther, T.W., Glick, H.B., Covey, K.R., et al., 2015. Mapping tree density at a global scale. Nature 525, 201–205.

Ellerman, A.D., Buchner, B.K., 2007. The European Union Emissions Trading Scheme: origins, allocations, and early results. Review of Environmental Economics and Policy 1, 66–87.

European Commission (EC), 2015. Carbon Market Report 2015. EC, Brussels.

European Commission (EC), 2016. Climate-Friendly Alternatives to HFCs and HCFCs. EC, Brussels, Belgium. Available at: http://ec.europa.eu/clima/policies/f-gas/alternatives/ index_en.htm.

Gates, B., 2015. Who Will Suffer Most from Climate Change? Project Syndicate. https://www. project-syndicate.org/commentary/farmers-adapt-to-climate-change-by-bill-gates-2015-09.

Green Climate Fund (GCF), 2016. Status of Pledges and Contributions Made to the Green Climate Fund. Status Date: 23 July 2015. GCF, Songdo, South Korea.

Goulder, L., 2007. California's bold new climate policy. Economist Voice 4. Article 5.

Hanemann, W.M., 2000. Adaptation and its management. Climatic Change 45, 511–581.

International Energy Agency (IEA), 2013. Technology Roadmap: Carbon Capture and Storage. IEA, France.

Intergovernmental Panel on Climate Change (IPCC), 1990. Climate Change: The IPCC Scientific Assessment. Cambridge University Press, Cambridge.

Intergovernmental Panel on Climate Change (IPCC), 1995. Climate Change 1995: The Physical Science Basis. The Second Assessment Report of the IPCC. Cambridge University Press, Cambridge.

Intergovernmental Panel on Climate Change (IPCC), 1999. Special Report on Aviation and the Global Atmosphere. Cambridge University Press, Cambridge.

Intergovernmental Panel on Climate Change (IPCC), 2000a. Special Report on Land Use, Land-Use Change, and Forestry. Cambridge University Press, Cambridge.

Intergovernmental Panel on Climate Change (IPCC), 2000b. Special Report on Emissions Scenarios. Cambridge University Press, Cambridge.

Intergovernmental Panel on Climate Change (IPCC), 2001. Climate Change 2001: The Physical Science Basis. The Fifth Assessment Report of the IPCC. Cambridge University Press, Cambridge.

Intergovernmental Panel on Climate Change (IPCC), 2005a. Special Report on Safeguarding the Ozone Layer and the Global Climate System: Issues Related to Hydrofluorocarbons and Perfluorocarbons. Cambridge University Press, Cambridge.

Intergovernmental Panel on Climate Change (IPCC), 2005b. Special Report on Carbon Dioxide Capture and Storage. Cambridge University Press, Cambridge.

Intergovernmental Panel on Climate Change (IPCC), 2007. Climate Change 2007: The Physical Science Basis. The Fifth Assessment Report of the IPCC. Cambridge University Press, Cambridge.

Intergovernmental Panel on Climate Change (IPCC), 2011. Special Report on Renewable Energy Sources and Climate Change Mitigation. Cambridge University Press, Cambridge.

Intergovernmental Panel on Climate Change (IPCC), 2012. Special Report on Managing the Risks of Extreme Events and Disasters to Advance Climate Change Adaptation. Cambridge University Press, Cambridge.

Intergovernmental Panel on Climate Change (IPCC), 2014. Climate Change 2014: The Physical Science Basis. The Fifth Assessment Report of the IPCC. Cambridge University Press, Cambridge.

Intergovernmental Panel on Climate Change (IPCC), 2016. Organization. Available at: http://www.ipcc.ch/organization/organization.shtml.

International Civil Aviation Organization (ICAO), 2016. Carbon Offsetting and Reduction Scheme for International Aviation (CORSIA). ICAO, Montreal, Canada.

International Thermonuclear Experimental Reactor (ITER), 2015. ITER: The World's Largest Tokamak. Available at: https://www.iter.org/mach.

Keeling, C.D., Piper, S.C., Bacastow, R.B., Wahlen, M., Whorf, T.P., Heimann, M., Meijer, H.A., 2005. Atmospheric CO_2 and $^{13}CO_2$ exchange with the terrestrial biosphere and oceans from 1978 to 2000: observations and carbon cycle implications. In: Ehleringer, J.R., Cerling, T.E., Dearing, M.D. (Eds.), A History of Atmospheric CO_2 and Its Effects on Plants, Animals, and Ecosystems, Pages 83–113. SpringerVerlag, New York.

Lackner, K.S., Brennana, S., Matter, J.M., Park, A.A., Wright, A., Zwaan, B.V., 2012. The urgency of the development of CO_2 capture from ambient air. Proceedings of the National Academy of Sciences of the United States of America 109, 13156–13162.

MacCracken, C.N., Edmonds, J.A., Kim, S.H., Sands, R.D., 1999. The economics of the Kyoto Protocol. The Energy Journal 20 (Special Issue), 25–71.

Manne, A.S., Richels, R.G., 1999. The Kyoto Protocol: a cost-effective strategy for meeting environmental objectives? The Energy Journal 20 (Special Issue), 1–23.

Martin, J.H., Coale, K.H., Johnson, K.S., Fitzwater, S.E., et al., 1994. Testing the iron hypothesis in ecosystems of the equatorial Pacific Ocean. Nature 371, 123–129.

Massachusetts Institute of Technology (MIT), 2015. The Future of Solar Energy: An Interdisciplinary MIT Study. MIT, Cambridge, MA.

McConnell, V., 2013. The New CAFE Standards: Are They Enough on Their Own? Resources for the Future Discussion Paper 13-14 RFF, Washington DC.

Mendelsohn, R., 2000. Efficient adaptation to climate change. Climatic Change 45, 583–600.

Mendelsohn, R., 2016. Should the IPCC assessment reports be an integrated assessment? Climate Change Economics 7. http://dx.doi.org/10.1142/S2010007816400029.

Mendelsohn, R., Dinar, A., Williams, L., 2006. The distributional impact of climate change on rich and poor countries. Environment and Development Economics 11, 1–20.

Metcalf, G., 2009. Designing a carbon tax to reduce US greenhouse gas emissions. Review of Environmental Economics and Policy 3, 63–83.

Molina, M.J., Rowland, F.S., 1974. Stratospheric sink for chlorofluoromethanes: chlorine atom-catalysed destruction of ozone. Nature 249, 810–812.

National Research Council, 2013a. Abrupt Impacts of Climate Change: Anticipating Surprises. Committee on Understanding and Monitoring Abrupt Climate Change and Its Impacts. The National Academies Press, Washington DC.

National Research Council (NRC), 2013b. Transitions to Alternative Vehicles and Fuels. The National Academies Press, Washington DC.

National Research Council (NRC), 2015. Climate Intervention: Reflecting Sunlight to Cool Earth. Committee on Geoengineering Climate: Technical Evaluation and Discussion of Impacts. The National Academies Press, Washington DC.

Nash, J., 1950. Equilibrium points in n-person games. Proceedings of the National Academy of Sciences of the United States of America 36, 48–49.

Nash, J., 1951. Non-cooperative games. The Annals of Mathematics 54, 286–295.

Ng, N.-S., Mendelsohn, R., 2006. The economic impact of sea-level rise on nonmarket lands in Singapore. Ambio 35, 289–296.

NOAA, 2016. National Centers for Environmental Information, State of the Climate: Global Analysis for Annual 2015 published online January 2016, retrieved on July 24, 2016 from: http://www.ncdc.noaa.gov/sotc/global/201513.

Nordhaus, W., 1994. Managing the Global Commons. MIT Press, Massachusetts.

Nordhaus, W., 2001. Global warming economics. Science 294, 1283–1284.

Nordhaus, W.D., 2006. Paul Samuelson and global public goods (2006). In: Szenberg, M., Ramrattan, L., Gottesman, A.A. (Eds.), Samuelsonian Economics and the Twenty-First Century. Oxford Scholarship Online.

Nordhaus, W., 2008. A Question of Balance: Weighing the Options on Climate Change. Yale University Press, New Haven.

Nordhaus, W., 2010. Economic aspects of global warming in a Post-Copenhagen environment. Proceedings of the National Academy of Sciences of the United States of America 107, 11721–11726.

Nordhaus, W., 2011. The architecture of climate economics: designing a global agreement on global warming. Bulletin of Atomic Scientists 67, 9–18.

Nordhaus, W., Boyer, J.G., 1999. Requiem for Kyoto: an economic analysis of the Kyoto Protocol. The Energy Journal 20 (Special Issue), 93–130.

Pearce, D., Cline, W.R., Achanta, A., Fankhauser, S., Pachauri, R., Tol, R., Vellinga, P., 1996. The social costs of climate change: greenhouse damage and benefits of control. In: Bruce, J., Lee, H., Haites, E. (Eds.), Climate Change 1995: Economic and Social Dimensions of Climate Change. Cambridge University Press, Cambridge.

Rosenberg, N.J., 1992. Adaptation of agriculture to climate change. Climatic Change 21, 385–405.

Seo, S.N., 2010. A microeconometric analysis of adapting portfolios to climate change: adoption of agricultural systems in Latin America. Applied Economic Perspectives and Policy 32, 489–514.

Seo, S.N., 2012a. What eludes global agreements on climate change? Economic Affairs 32, 73–79.

Seo, S.N., 2012b. Decision-making under climate risks: an analysis of sub-Saharan farmers' adaptation behaviors. Weather, Climate, and Society 4, 285–299.

Seo, S.N., 2013. Economics of global warming as a global public good: private incentives and smart adaptations. Regional Science Policy and Practice 5, 83–95.

Seo, S.N., 2014. Adapting sensibly when global warming turns the field brown or blue: a comment on the 2014 IPCC Report. Economic Affairs 34, 399–401.

Seo, S.N., 2015a. Adaptation to global warming as an optimal transition process to a greenhouse world. Economic Affairs 35, 272−284.

Seo, S.N., 2015b. Helping low-latitude poor countries with climate change. Regulation 6−8. Winter 2015−2016.

Seo, S.N., 2015c. Fatalities of neglect: adapt to more intense hurricanes? International Journal of Climatology 35, 3505−3514.

Seo, S.N., 2016a. Modeling farmer adaptations to climate change in South America: a micro-behavioral economic perspective. Environmental and Ecological Statistics 23, 1−21.

Seo, S.N., 2016b. The micro-behavioral framework for estimating total damage of global warming on natural resource enterprises with full adaptations. Journal of Agricultural, Biological, and Environmental Statistics 21, 328−347.

Seo, S.N., 2016c. A theory of global public goods and their provisions. Journal of Public Affairs 16, 394−405.

Seo, S.N., Mendelsohn, R., 2008. Measuring impacts and adaptations to climate change: a structural Ricardian model of African livestock management. Agricultural Economics 38, 151−165.

Seo, S.N., Bakkensen, L.A., 2016. Did adaptation strategies work? High fatalities from tropical cyclones in the North Indian Ocean and future vulnerability under global warming. Natural Hazards 82, 1341−1355.

Shiller, R.J., 2005. Irrational Exuberance, second ed. Princeton University Press, Princeton, NJ.

Stern, N., 2007. The Economics of Climate Change: The Stern Review. Cambridge University Press, Cambridge.

Tietenberg, T., 2013. Reflections − carbon pricing in practice. Review of Environmental Economics and Policy 7, 313−329.

Tietenberg, T., Lewis, L., 2014. Environmental & Natural Resource Economics. Prentice Hall, New York.

Tol, R.S.J., 2016. The impacts of climate change according to the IPCC. Climate Change Economics 7. http://dx.doi.org/10.1142/S2010007816400042.

United Nations Environmental Programme (UNEP), 2016. The Montreal Protocol on Substances that Deplete the Ozone Layer. UNEP, Kigali, Rwanda.

United Nations Framework Convention on Climate Change (UNFCCC), 1992. United Nations Framework Convention on Climate Change. UNFCCC, New York.

United Nations Framework Convention on Climate Change (UNFCCC), 1998. Kyoto Protocol to the United Nations Framework Convention on Climate Change. UNFCCC, New York.

United Nations Framework Convention on Climate Change (UNFCCC), 2005. Kyoto Protocol to Enter Into Force 16 February 2005. UNFCCC, New York.

United Nations Framework Convention on Climate Change (UNFCCC), 2007. Report of the Conference of the Parties on Its Thirteenth Session, Held in Bali from 3 to 15 December 2007. UNFCCC, New York.

United Nations Framework Convention on Climate Change (UNFCCC), 2009. Copenhagen Accord. UNFCCC, New York.

United Nations Framework Convention on Climate Change (UNFCCC), 2010. Cancun Agreements. UNFCCC, New York.

United Nations Framework Convention on Climate Change (UNFCCC), 2011a. The Durban Platform for Enhanced Action. UNFCCC, New York.

United Nations Framework Convention on Climate Change (UNFCCC), 2011b. Report of the Transitional Committee for the Design of Green Climate Fund. UNFCCC, New York.

United Nations Framework Convention on Climate Change (UNFCCC), 2012. Decisions Adopted by the Conference of the Parties on Its Eighteenth Session, Held in Doha from 26 November to 8 December 2012. UNFCCC, New York.

United Nations Framework Convention on Climate Change (UNFCCC), 2015. The Paris Agreement. Conference of the Parties (COP) 21. UNFCCC, New York.

United States Environmental Protection Agency (US EPA), 2006. Global Mitigation of Non-CO_2 Greenhouse Gases. US EPA, Washington DC.

United States Environmental Protection Agency (US EPA), 2014. Carbon Pollution Emission Guidelines for Existing Stationary Sources: Electric Utility Generating Units. US EPA, Washington DC.

Van Pelt, R., Sillett, S.C., Kruse, W.A., Freund, J.A., Kramer, R.D., 2016. Emergent crowns and light-use complementarity lead to global maximum biomass and leaf area in *Sequoia sempervirens* forests. Forest Ecology and Management 375, 279–308.

Victor, D., 2001. The Collapse of the Kyoto Protocol and the Struggle to Slow Global Warming. Princeton University Press, Princeton, NJ.

Wall Street Journal (WSJ), 2017. Scott Pruitt's Back-to-Basics Agenda for the EPA. By Strassel KA. On February 17, 2017. Available at: https://www.wsj.com/articles/scott-pruitts-back-to-basics-agenda-for-the-epa-1487375872.

Weitzman, M.L., 2009. On modeling and interpreting the economics of catastrophic climate change. Review of Economics and Statistics 91, 1–19.

White House, 2013. The President's Climate Action Plan. Executive Office of the President. The White House, Washington DC.

White House, 2016. U.S.–Canada Joint Statement on Climate, Energy, and Arctic Leadership. The White House, Washington DC.

Yohe, G.W., Schlesinger, M.E., 1998. Sea level change: the expected economic cost of protection or abandonment in the United States. Climatic Change 38, 337–342.

Zhang, W., Hagerman, A.D., McCarl, B.A., 2013. How climate factors influence the spatial distribution of Texas cattle breeds. Climatic Change 118, 183–195.

Further Reading

Heal, G., 2010. Reflections: the economics of renewable energy in the United States. Review of Environmental Economics and Policy 4, 139–154.

United Nations Framework Convention on Climate Change (UNFCCC), 2013. Further Advancing the Durban Platform. UNFCCC, New York.

Index

Printed in the United States
By Bookmasters